W9-CUO-707

Principles
of
Children's Services
in
Public Libraries

To my former students

Principles
of
Children's Services
in
Public Libraries

Mae Benne

AMERICAN LIBRARY ASSOCIATION
Chicago and London 1991

Cover and text designed by Charles Bozett

Composed by Alexander Typesetting, Inc. in
New Century Schoolbook and Helvetica on
a Datalogics Typesetting System

Printed on 50-pound Glatfelter, a pH-neutral
stock, and bound in Kivar 9 cover stock
by Braun-Brumfield, Inc.

The paper used in this publication meets the minimum requirements of American
National Standard for Information Sciences—Permanence of Paper for Printed
Library Materials, ANSI Z39.48-1984. ∞

Library of Congress Cataloging-in-Publication Data

Benne, Mae.
    Principles of children's services in public libraries / by Mae
Benne.
        p. cm.
    Includes index.
    ISBN 0-8389-0555-2 (alk. paper)
    1. Libraries, Children's—Administration.   2. Libraries,
Children's—Aims and objectives.   3. Libraries, Children's—
Collection development.   4. Children's librarians—Professional
ethics.   5. Public libraries—Aims and objectives.   6. Children—
Books and reading.   I. Title.
Z718.1.B46   1990
027.62'5—dc20   90-47427
                                                                            CIP

Printed in the United States of America.

95 94 93 92 91   5 4 3 2 1

Contents

Figures   vi

Preface   vii

1   Audiences to Be Served   1

2   Children's Librarian as Manager   29

3   Selection and Design of Services   66

4   Children's Collections   113

5   Planning Facilities   151

6   Children's Services in Rural Systems   193

7   The Professional Role and Responsibilities of the
Children's Librarian   239

Appendixes

   A. Budgeting Forms   266

   B. Programming Forms   273

   C. Bibliography of Collection and Service Aids   279

   D. Related Professional Associations   294

Notes   297

Bibliography   309

Index   321

Figures

1.   System with Integrated Children's Services   33
2.   Divided Authority for Children's Services   34
3.   Children's Coordinator with Line and Staff Authority   35
4.   County System with Integrated Children's Services   35
5.   Central Children's Services under Branch Services Line Authority   36
6.   Formal Education Support Center   166
7.   Popular Materials Library   167

Preface

Texts written to instruct or inform are often those the authors wished they had had whenever it was that they chose a college, bought a house, moved to California, or began a career. This one falls into the last category.

This book is intended as a resource for librarians who assume responsibility for children's services in a public library. The current and potential users serve as the focus; professional principles and managerial competencies are the major emphases. Assistance is provided the children's librarian who is given the responsibility for designing a program of service compatible with the mission of the library and the needs of the community. Ways to integrate the children's program into that of the overall library are suggested. Attention is also given to the role of the children's librarian in those activities that affect the library as a whole: planning, goal setting, policy development, budgeting, and staff training.

Two areas not often covered in texts of this kind have been included. The chapter on facilities delineates the role of the children's librarian in the building or remodeling process, and offers suggestions for the children's quarters based on children's response to the built environment. The chapter on rural libraries identifies those elements that require adaptation when encountered in this type of setting. Two issues that also affect urban libraries, school library–public library relationship and the role of the children's specialist in a system, are treated here because of their critical importance in the rural environment.

Because so much has been written elsewhere on the criteria for evaluating materials and the techniques of programming, these aspects have not been addressed, except as examples in discussions of services and collections. The reader is referred to the appendixes for titles providing a more complete coverage.

This book is intended for library school students who have chosen children's services as a career option, or are in the process of considering it, and staffs in public libraries whose professional education or experience has not prepared them for the responsibilities of children's services that are now theirs. Supervisors and administrators in the process of reconsidering the role or functions of children's services may also find it helpful. Other public library specialists—for example, young adult, reference, or outreach—can expect to find many parallels to their own situations. Experienced children's librarians will undoubtedly find opinions expressed in these pages with which to disagree or agree. Either way it is hoped that both reactions will lead to a further discussion of the roles that children's librarians should assume in the library, the community, and in the wider society as we edge closer to the twenty-first century.

I owe a very large debt to the three public library directors who served as my first mentors. The late Helen S. Gilbert, who risked hiring a former high school librarian as a children's librarian, demonstrated by attitude and deed the meaning of the word service. The late Walter H. Kaiser's interest in efficiency and innovation was never an end, but always a means to increased and improved public services. Josephine Pardee Hallauer possessed that rare quality of leadership necessary to transform a diverse group into a cohesive staff, each believing that he or she was essential in fulfilling the library's mission. I am also grateful to Ursula Meyer for sharing her experiences and refreshing insights as a colleague and later as a library director over the past three decades. Interviews with key personnel in children's services as part of a 1976–77 study, supported by a Council on Library Resources Fellowship grant, provided a valuable perspective on children's services in metropolitan library systems.

Several people offered suggestions and encouragement during the writing stages. In particular, I am grateful to my former library school director and colleague Peter Hiatt for sharing his views on adult services over the years and, more specifically, for his patient reading of first drafts and for his belief in the value of the project. I also express my gratitude to Ruth Hamilton for her comments as a former children's coordinator and library educator; Charlotte Wood and Louise Morrison for their advice on budgeting; and Kathryn Crosby and Diane Thompson for their comments on library facilities. The suggestions and challenging questions posed by Herbert Bloom, my editor, were invaluable. As he knew, they led to fuller treatments of various topics and issues.

I appreciate, too, the permission given by the Pierce County Library (Washington), the Stockton–San Joaquin County Library (California), Seattle Public Library, Queens Borough Public Library, and the King County Library (Washington) to use their programming and budgeting forms as examples.

This book was also shaped by my experiences in library education which forced a reevaluation of all aspects of children's services. I am indebted to Irving Lieberman, Director Emeritus, and Dorothy Bevis, former Associate Director of the School of Librarianship now renamed Graduate School of Library Information Science, University of Washington, for giving me the opportunity to serve as a library educator and for sharing their vision of library education as a partner in the future development of libraries. In this role, I have been privileged to work with hundreds of students, many of whom have shared their experiences as new professionals in children's services. They have validated again and again the lyrics of the late Oscar Hammerstein II in the *King and I*:

It's a very ancient saying, and a true and honest thought,
If you become a teacher, by your pupils you'll be taught.

Those librarians won't give you any trouble. I've known them to have boys shanghaied off the streets just to get them started reading. A dollar a head for captives. You know what they pray every night? "And Lord, send a nonreader into the children's room tomorrow so I can hook him on books."—Frank Bonham, *Mystery of the Fat Cat* (New York: Dutton, 1968), p.79.

Audiences to Be Served

During an interview for a pre-professional position in a public library, an applicant was asked why she wanted to work in the children's department. "Because," she said with conviction and not a little anger, "I hate adults." She did not get the position. Anyone contemplating a career as a children's librarian should be aware that although children are a major responsibility, they exist in an environment that includes a number of adults in various roles. The adult is often the intermediary through which the library serves the child. Like the young applicant who believed that children were the only users of children's services, some children's librarians operate on that assumption in their preparation for a career and in setting priorities for services.

Children's librarians not only work with adult colleagues within the library, but they also interact with adults who serve the child in various capacities: parent, teacher, day care provider, social worker, etc. Within the library the children's librarian assumes responsibilities for (1) selecting and maintaining a collection for the appropriate audiences, (2) providing information and reading guidance (advisory) services, and (3) planning and presenting programs designed to attract children to other library services or to provide experiences not possible through library materials alone, e.g. storytelling. All of these activities require the cooperation, understanding, and support of the other staff and the administration. The children's librarian serves as an advocate for children's services within the library whenever library policies are developed, in-service activities planned, or goals and objectives prioritized. Outside the library, the children's librarian promotes library services to adult groups who have responsibilities for the welfare and education of children. The librarian may also represent the library in joint efforts to solve problems experienced by the community's children and their families. In all of these roles, the ability to communicate with adults is critical.

Children's librarians serve many adults as library users and in a variety of ways. A 1979–80 study of children's services in Connecticut revealed that in several of the participating community libraries, adult users outnumbered children, even though a majority of these adults were acting, as expected, on behalf of children.[1] The percentage of adults using the circulating and special children's collections in main libraries of large urban systems has often equaled or surpassed children's use. Those who choose a career as a children's librarian must, of course, keep children as their major focus. In no other department of a public library are children's needs in the highest priority. Nevertheless, if public libraries are to be successful in reaching children in greater numbers, those adults and adult groups who also serve the child represent one of the most effective means to that goal.

The traditional approach of developing the best possible collection that children will accept and designing programs to ensure its use is an expensive process, especially if it fails to meet the needs of the community. Children's librarians should identify their audiences and community resources before ordering that first title, offering that first program, weeding the collection, or acting on an invitation to redesign the children's room.

Identifying Audiences

The preparation of children's librarians has from the beginning included the twin maxims "know your collection" and "know your community." For most children's librarians, it is probably safe to say that acquiring collection knowledge is the more attractive endeavor because this activity is often the one that draws the librarian to this specialty in the first place. Nevertheless, "know your community" has never been ignored. Anne Carroll Moore, an early pioneer in children's services, is reported to have sent new children's librarians on a walk through the community they were to serve. She believed that they should have some awareness of the environment in which the children lived.

In the present era of expanding needs and budgets that fail to keep apace, no librarian can afford to waste resources with trial-and-error methods. Although a walk through the neighborhood may be a valuable exercise, and one that could be repeated periodically, a prior exploration of the information found in printed sources would increase the understanding of what the children's librarian will see on these walks.

Knowing the community is the first step in determining the kinds of services needed and preferred by the population to be served. If user and nonuser surveys have not been done, preliminary assumptions can be made through study of various factors, such as the following:

Relative size of the various age groupings, e.g. under five years, 5 to 12, etc.

Median family income/unemployment level

Percentage of population in various types of employment, i.e manufacturing, professional, clerical, etc.

Percentage of racial/language/ethnic/religious groups

Educational level of adult population

Number of single parent households, and of those in which both parents are employed outside the home

Number of child care facilities and their services

Achievement levels of school-age population.

The workforms provided in *Planning and Role Setting for Public Libraries* for gathering information about the community and the library will suggest additional types of information use in this exercise.[2]

The process of identifying audiences for services cannot be separated from that followed in learning about the community. Discovering that the community has a cerebral palsy clinic with a preschool facility informs the librarian of a possible audience as well as a community resource. If mothers who once brought their preschoolers to a daytime story hour are in the labor force, preschool programs will require rescheduling, changes in the content, and perhaps a different location, e.g. a day care center. In the future more parents, especially those in middle-class communities, may be working flexible hours in their homes, connected to their employment facility by a computer terminal and a fax machine. When this happens, the type and scheduling of library programs for young children will again have to be adapted to a new lifestyle.

Information Gathered by the Library

Assuming the role of a user of information in one's own library is an experience that all staff should have on a regular basis. For new staff it serves as a litmus test to the consideration given users who lack an intimate knowledge of library operations.

Library Files. The library's own pamphlet and clipping files, local history collection, annual reports and studies of the library, etc. are sources that provide a background on past activities of the library and the history of the community. These are important in understanding the library, the staff, and the community.

Public Library Planning Documents. Many libraries conduct their own community surveys in preparation for planning services and establishing priorities. These may range from brief overviews to in-depth information from users or nonusers. A sizable number of single heads of households or a high unemployment rate becomes an important factor in planning. If a particular ethnic or religious group exercises a strong influence, knowledge of this group's traditions and culture is critical.

Community Information and Referral Services. Some libraries attempt to meet the information needs of their communities through an information and referral service. Individuals with special knowledge and skills, as well as organizations with their various services and resources, are included in the file or database. This information serves as a supplement to the library's printed resources. Even if this service is not identified as such, most reference librarians have probably gathered this type of information in some form. Through the process they have gained a great amount of information about the community that can be shared with the staff.

Community Resources of Information

If a planning process has not been conducted in recent years, the chapter "Looking Around Outside" in *Planning and Role Setting for Public Libraries* can be helpful in identifying sources of information useful in acquiring knowledge of a community. These include: demographics, economic conditions, social conditions, and informational and educational services.[3] Most new staff do not have the luxury of an in-depth study, but must select from the available resources those that promise to provide the best information in the shortest period of time. The following represent some of the more important resources:

1. Community surveys for a specific purpose: economic forecasting, city planning, etc.
2. Census reports
   a. population profile: age, race, sex, ethnicity, education level, etc.
   b. housing: values, types, condition, etc.

      c. occupations, incomes, unemployment patterns, welfare statistics, etc.
3. School district studies and reports
      a. enrollment and projection figures
      b. planning documents
      c. characteristics of students enrolled: academic achievement, disabilities, race and ethnicity, language spoken
4. Local and regional telephone directories
      a. private schools
      b. churches
      c. parks and recreation centers
      d. social service organizations
      e. youth organizations and centers
      f. health care facilities
      g. government offices
5. Area newspapers
      a. activities of local organizations
      b. community concerns and problems
6. Chamber of commerce
      a. reports
      b. promotional materials
7. Community councils and neighborhood groups
      a. reports, newsletters
      b. projects
8. Community bulletin boards in markets, laundromats, recreational centers, etc.
9. Community directories with activities for children, etc.

Economic and business organizations, chambers of commerce, school districts, and other governmental organizations often compile community studies for their own long-range planning cycles. The basic information needed by librarians for decision making may already exist in these documents. For example, if recent zoning changes now permit the building of moderate-to-expensive apartment complexes in an area served by a community library, the number of children is likely to decline, while single professionals and childless couples increase. If low-cost public housing in a community is anticipated, several small stations may be more effective than one large, centrally located branch. A school district study may show dramatic increases in the preschool population, a statistic that also has implications for library planning in terms of staff and material resources. These studies are usually accessible through a municipal library, the city hall, the office of the superintendent of schools, or the library itself.

Age Range for Service

Within their libraries and professional organizations, children's librarians have frequently disagreed on the age range of children who constitute their major service responsibility. There was a period in the history of children's library services when preschool children were not considered the responsibility of public libraries. During the 1930s some libraries experimented with preschool story hours, but it was not until the post-World War II period that this program became a staple in children's services, and then only after the characteristics of three- to five-year-olds determined the format and content of the program. In the 1970s programs for even younger children were developed to meet needs identified through programs such as Head Start and research in early childhood development.

At the other end of the scale, there has been a lack of consensus concerning the upper age limit that properly lies within the province of children's services. The function statement of the Association for Library Service to Children, a division of the American Library Association, identifies its primary audience as "preschool through the eighth grade or junior high school age." In preliminary discussions during the mid-1980s, the Young Adult Services Division discussed the viability of establishing ages 10 to 15 as its service group, but no recommendation was brought to the ALA Council for action at that time. Because this division continues to be pressured to recommend an age and developmental description of their client group, it is obvious that the two youth divisions will be faced with working out a compromise on the age range of their respective clienteles. The standards statement *Standards for Children's Services in Public Libraries*, 1964, used "from infancy through approximately thirteen years of age."[4] The New York Library Association issued standards for youth services in 1984 that identified "infancy through junior high school age" as the responsibility of children's services.[5] It is doubtful that children's librarians are serving the major needs of children over twelve in those libraries with young adult departments. Service divisions may be determined by librarians, but library users ignore them when they do not support their intellectual or psychological needs. Each library must resolve the age issue on its own considering the needs of its users and its institutional resources.

Preschoolers

The period from birth through age five is one of rapid development in all phases of an individual's life: social, cognitive, emotional, physical, and creative. Jean Piaget, the Swiss psychologist, divided these years into two periods: the sensorimotor stage includes children from infancy to approximately two years of age, and the preoperational stage includes the two- through five-year-olds. Children must achieve a number of developmental tasks by the time they are five and ready for formal schooling. These include achieving physical independence; the ability to form concepts; the ability to use language to describe social and physical reality; and learning the concepts of right and wrong.[6]

Several factors have contributed to the emphasis placed on preschool services in public libraries. Among these are:

1. The importance of these years to the development of the individual as supported by the voluminous research on the subject
2. The projected increase in this population group in this decade
3. Emphasis in the popular media on the importance of effective parenting in the early childhood years in avoiding costly remedial education programs.

The recent, albeit tardy, realization by governmental leaders that adequate child care is more than custodial has also given support to library programs for this age group.

Infancy to Age Two. During this stage children explore their physical world through all their senses. With experience they learn to differentiate objects in their environment and words become symbols for objects and things. Children in this stage are truly the great experimenters of the human race, and parents and caregivers need to provide a stimulating and safe environment that encourages the child to explore and to develop verbal skills. Children in this age group are ready for realistic picture books and board books with easily turned pages that focus on a single concept or theme. They also need realistic toys because they are not able to accept a substitute that looks different from the referential object.[7]

Ages Two through Three. These children have entered what Piaget considers the preconceptual phase of the pre-operational stage. They are egocentric in their behavior and outlook and are able to manipulate and use symbols and words in their discovery of the physical world. Animism characterizes their thought, and all objects, animate or inanimate, are invested with life. In what is often called the how-and-why stage, these children are eager for materials that widen their understanding of the world.[8] Programs with a strong educational base can be exciting fare for these children, eager to display their new-found knowledge.

Stories with simple plots that mirror the child's day-to-day experiences are popular with this age group. The children enjoy participating in the story through guessing, making sounds, etc., and may ask for the same story over and over again. They are beginning to understand relationships, and can enjoy materials that deal with colors, shapes, and other concepts. They learn from observing and imitating other children; later in this period, they become companions in play.[9] Children at three and a half can generally accept an object that does not resemble the real thing,[10] and they are very aware of other children and are able to adjust their behavior to accommodate the demands of the group.[11] When placed in a new environment or situation, children in this age group need the reassuring presence of a trusted adult. Without this support, they may revert to an earlier behavioral pattern.[12]

Ages Four through Five. The next phase of the pre-operational stage is the intuitive and covers the ages from approximately four to seven. Children in this phase, while still egocentric, are increasing their awareness of their environment and of human relationships. They are more proficient in handling symbols, can assume various roles in their play, and, with increasing reliance upon language as a tool in learning about the world, they are able to discuss actions to be used in problem solving. These children form friendships and are able to play cooperatively with peers who have common developmental concerns. Group membership is valued, and it is important not be be the only one excluded.[13] The children are better able to handle their emotions and to wait for their turn. Four- and five-year-olds are usually able to spend some time away from a parent or caregiver, and are less dependent upon the presence of a trusted adult when faced with new situations. Because of these competencies, activities that require more cooperative behavior can be offered to children in this group. Working on a mural, reciting in unison the last word in a story rhyme, and acting out a story are activities that can be enjoyed by this age group. Simple folktales, realistic fiction of everyday life, and single-concept nonfiction will find a receptive audience in this group. These children are ready for play materials that will let them create their own artwork or act out their own fantasies.

When planning services, children's librarians need to keep in mind the characteristics of children at various phases and stages, remembering that not all children develop at the same rate in any of these groupings. Some children may be advanced cognitively while their motor skills lag behind those of their peers. Librarians have experimented with various age divisions in preschool programs. In storytelling programs for preschoolers, some have found that a 3½- through 5-year-old group provides a compatible audience while others prefer to place the 3- and 4-year-olds together and include the five-year-olds with an older audience. Toddler programs for the younger preschooler may group the 18- to 36-month-old children together, with the parent or caregiver accompanying the child. Most would agree that the child under three has different needs in programming as well as for materials. Through a little experimentation librarians can find the most effective age grouping for their communities and their own programming style.

In long-range planning librarians should be aware of projected changes in demographic figures and school enrollments for the preschool ages. The overall population of children ages 0 to 17 is expected to increase from 45.1 million—the 1985 figure—to 47.9 million—the number projected for 1993. The increase will be felt first in the preschool ages while the number in the upper grades will continue to fall. The preschool enrollment in educational programs is projected to rise to 7.1 million in 1993 from 4.2 million in 1970, with the greatest increase expected in the enrollment of three- and four-year-olds.[14] Obviously, the attention given to services for preschool children in the past decade should be continued and strengthened if possible, with more attention given to staffs of preschool programs as a means of reaching these children and their parents.

The central location of the public library in most communities and its availability to all ages enhances its potential to serve preschoolers, their parents, caregivers, and other adult groups concerned with early childhood education. Many children's departments have also found the budget for preschool services easier to justify than those for school-age children because of a lingering perception that children's services in public libraries duplicate rather than supplement those of school libraries.

The School-Age Child

The elementary school-age child passes through several cognitive stages. Following Piaget's theory, the first- and second-grade child moves from the latter phase of the pre-operational stage into the concrete operations stage. At the end of the sixth grade many children have moved into the stage of formal operations and are able to deal with more complex ideas and materials. Havighurst characterizes this period of middle childhood from roughly age six to twelve by three outward pushes:

There is the thrust of the child out of the home and into the peer group, the physical thrust into the world of games and work requiring neuromuscular skills, and the mental thrust into the world of adult concepts.[15]

At the end of this period many basic social attitudes are set, and, although they may be changed or altered, the process is not an easy one. Through programming and vicarious experiences offered in literature, children may gain a deeper appreciation of the people who inhabit their world. This responsibility should be acknowledged through the collections and services offered to this age group.

Ages Six through Eight. These years witness great changes in the child's emotional, social, and intellectual life. Although parents are still an important source of security, these children must learn to relate to the other all-important adult in their lives— their teacher—and to their peers, whose influence becomes more important as the social world broadens. When children enter the concrete operations stage, they are able to reverse processes in thought and action. They can put groups of objects together and reverse the action by separating them again. The underlying principle on which libraries are developed—grouping like subjects together—can be understood. A child in the earlier stage will group things together, but the arrangement may be logical only to that child and at that particular time. These children have a clearer sense of time, both past and future, and are able to consider the interrelated parts of a simple story from its beginning to the end. They are highly conscious of rules and rather inflexible in their thinking about right and wrong.

Picture book stories including folktales in this format are popular with this age group, and easy nonfiction and fiction should also be promoted to children who are ready to move beyond picture books. A number of children finishing the second grade are ready to read *Little House in the Big Woods* and *Frog's Body.* Because the interests of most six- through eight-year-olds are beyond their reading ability, parents and teachers should be encouraged to continue reading to them and to select titles from a wide range of subjects.

Children of seven or eight years of age may be able to come to the public library on their own, but it is unlikely that they will venture alone into an unfamiliar place even if the community's environment permitted such independent action. Children who have first-hand knowledge of the library through visits with their parents or teachers are more apt to come on their own initiative later. In a study conducted in a Canadian city in 1976, children ages six through nine were asked how they came to the public library and with whom. Forty-one percent came with friends; boys were more likely to come alone (17.4%) than girls (9.6%); nearly 40 percent of the girls came with a parent, as compared with 26.1 percent of the boys. In the non-public library user sample, slightly over one-fourth of the respondents said that the library was too far away; nearly one-half of the girls mentioned lack of transportation or difficulty in obtaining permission from parents, while only 27.3 percent of the boys gave this as a reason for not using the library.[16]

Ages Nine through Twelve. During these years most children pass through the concrete operations stage to the period of formal operations, which covers the years from approximately eleven to fifteen. The nine-year-old is midpoint in the concrete operations stage and has probably mastered the mechanics of reading. If not, intervention is required as the child is unlikely to achieve mastery without some assistance. Children in this stage value their independence and have wide-ranging interests that may still be beyond their reading levels. If so, the use of audiovisual materials as an informational source could be popular in the library. Children in this group learn to select needed information and to ignore what isn't relevant to their immediate needs. They are able to think in terms of the future and to understand chronological order. History, fantasy, and science fiction are more easily understood by this age group. Rules that were once sacrosanct are now open to discussion and adult authority is not the final word as these children are able to consider the circumstances in which an infraction occurred. Their attitudes toward people of different races and religion are being formed, and they are aware of differences among people.

The academic program shifts at the fourth grade from a concentration on learning skills to using those skills to "acquire, understand, and use information."[17] Children become, in the adult services sense, information seekers. These are the reading years, for it is unlikely that the child will again have an opportunity to spend so much time in this pursuit. This is the time for the child to explore personal interests, and the public library has the potential to make a significant contribution. Exhibits, special programs on a myriad of subjects, booktalk programs that introduce new subjects or different aspects of old ones, materials in various formats (film, video, tape, periodical), and open access to total library resources can offer a rich environment for exploration.

In the Canadian study on children's use, nearly half of the children ages ten and older came to the library with friends, while slightly over 18 percent were accompanied by parents. Boys were twice as likely as girls to come alone (33.3% to 16.5%).[18] What is significant here is the elementary school child's reliance on friends, for either emotional or social reasons, in using the public library. This factor needs to be considered in promoting library use among children.

Ages Twelve and Up. Some eleven- and twelve-year-olds are moving into the formal operations period in which they are able to "think about thinking." Their problem-solving abilities improve, and they are able to compare various alternatives in seeking solutions. They can hypothesize and make deductions, and they are ready for instruction in dealing with the number of possible subject headings, for example, under which needed information on a topic may be found. Their ability to compare different points of view, traditions, laws, and behaviors and to judge what they read on more than one dimension opens up a whole body of literature previously inaccessible to them. Concurrent with this stage is the onset of puberty which contributes to the catalog of changes that must be accommodated. It is, indeed, a period of *sturm und drang.*

The child in this stage needs literature that is more complex in plot and characterization, but not necessarily more difficult to read. Children are idealistic at this stage, and they are more aware of social problems. They are curious about different lifestyles and values and about opportunities for the future. They seek information about their own bodies, which are suddenly strange and unfamiliar. Whether the primary needs of these young adolescents are met in the children's department or in the young adult or adult department, the children's librarian should work closely with all staff to ensure that this important age group is not ignored. The children should be encouraged to use the total resources and services of the library. Studies have shown that seventh graders' use of the library noticeably decreases at this time as academic and social pressures increase. It is important to involve the young adolescent in the planning of services and library quarters and in developing the collection.[19]

Child-Caring Adults

Child-caring adults may wear many hats: a parent may be a fifth-grade teacher, a cub scout den father, a volunteer at the children's museum, a social worker, a church-school teacher. Whatever their relationship with children, adults also have needs to which the public library should respond. It is characteristic of library users to seek information that they perceive libraries can supply. In tabulating questions asked by adults in Connecticut public library children's departments, Faith Hektoen provided the following summary:

> Adults want to find books which stress 'situational materials' for young children, and for children in school, books which reflect individual interest and special needs. Adults request realia: toys, games, 3-dimensional objects such as puppets, costumes and musical instruments. Requests for such materials for young children are accompanied by questions about how to make them, and why and how to purchase them. Queries are made about games for older children, particularly for children who are visually handicapped, retarded or emotionally disturbed. Films, filmstrips and audio recordings are sought for a variety of reasons. Adults want information on child development, such as socialization (i.e., play needs and sibling relationships) and learning to read, as well as the means and materials in many media formats to facilitate these processes. Adults seek data about community and state resources for children's special needs and for generally available entertainment, education (especially nursery schools), and cultural opportunities. Adults ask about library programs for children, and for guidance regarding children's periodicals and literature.[20]

Although many of these requests can be answered with resources in the children's department, others will require knowledge of adult collections and community agencies to which the user can be referred.

The influence of one children's librarian in a community may be fleeting without the ongoing support of adults who have daily contact with children—parents, caregivers, and teachers—and those whose encounters may be less frequent but still significant—social workers, recreational leaders, scouting personnel, church-school teachers, etc.

Parents

The emphasis on parent education is not likely to abate, based as it is on research findings and attention from both educational and governmental bodies at various levels. The Head Start program revealed that taking a child out of a deprived environment for two hours a day produced no lasting, significant change unless the home environment itself was changed. For the child, the parents are the most important influence as the source of the child's security and as his or her first and most important teacher. In planning services and developing collections, the social environment of families must be considered. With the increase in the number of working mothers, programs for preschoolers at the library may exclude those who most need this kind of stimulation. The increase in births to adolescent mothers, many unmarried, who elect to keep their babies is also a factor in planning.

The information needs of parents can be grouped in the following categories:

1. Human reproduction, including influences of heredity and environment.
2. Pregnancy and childbirth, prenatal and postnatal care.
3. Infant care, including nutrition, health, safety of children.
4. Child growth and development, including physical, perceptual and cognitive, and personal and social development.
5. Individual differences in children, and the disabled child.
6. Creative activities for children.
7. Family structure and functions.
8. Family planning and population growth.
9. Community resources to aid in parenting, including child care arrangements.[21]

Libraries have tried various ways to serve parents. The most common are parents' shelves in the children's room with selected materials on child development and child care, and programs for parents of preschoolers attending story hours. The responses to these stopgap efforts have been helpful in alerting librarians to the growing interest that exists. More could probably be done for this audience with only a modest increase in resources. When parents are invited to attend programs with their preschoolers, they have an opportunity to observe their children's responses to a stimulating activity, and to other children and adults. The librarian serves as an informal teacher, demonstrating various techniques for using literature with children and providing parents with suggestions for activities that can be done at home.

Various other approaches have been used by libraries to serve the needs of parents, including a series of workshops with community specialists who not only identify the needs to be addressed but also are program presenters. These specialists may include a kindergarten teacher, a pediatric or county health nurse, a community college instructor in early childhood education, and, of course, the children's librarian who provides the bibliographic support and presents the session on sharing literature with children. Child care is provided, sometimes with the help of volunteers. Other services have involved the circulation of toys with instructions on their use, with the intent of increasing the social interaction between child and parent. Videocassettes on

various aspects of parenting—from reading activities in the home
to the kinds of experiences that prepare children for school—can
also be purchased or produced locally.

Videocassette players are often not available in homes where
the need is greatest, but this lack is not the only barrier to library
use. In communities with families existing on public assistance,
the workshop series at the library will probably fail to reach many
who need it. Even if child care were available, a parent might
view the library as an institution requiring a certain level of erudition or attire for its use. Yet, a children's librarian in such a
community found a mother who was receptive to the idea of
hosting a group of other mothers in her home to hear an informal
discussion on children's books and reading. The success of this
program was spread by word of mouth, and more and more such
invitations followed. Discovering the librarian to be a friendly
adult who was interested in their children proved to be the
encouragement these parents needed to make that first step into
the library.

Many years ago the King County Library System (Seattle) provided a parents' program with the cooperation of the county's
Head Start program. Because parents of Head Start children are
required to meet periodically as a group, the library was given
permission to provide the program for one of the sessions. The
project coordinator and the children's librarian in the communities involved presented the program, which included the film
What's So Great About Books? produced by the Orlando (Florida)
Public Library. After viewing the film, one parent remarked, "I
always heard you were supposed to read to your children, but I
never knew why until now." Listening to comments like these will
provide clues to the types of assistance parents need.

Because of the way most public library collections are now
divided and staff responsibilities allocated, the needs of adults as
parents or caregivers cannot easily be met. Baechtold and
McKinney, in their *Library Service for Families,* propose that
public libraries serve families as a unit. They ask their readers to
recognize that "libraries do deal in more than just informational
needs, especially when they deal with children and families ...,"
and they offer a number of program ideas for a family audience.[22] If
this service opportunity is not to fall among several library departments, a team effort will be required in deciding how the needs of
parents and families can best be met in a particular community.

The position of children's librarians is pivotal because they are
often the first point of reference for parents seeking information
on child care and development. If children's librarians have a general knowledge of resources for parents available in the library as

a whole, they will be better able to assist the adult and to serve as an advocate for parents when service priorities are set. This general knowledge can be acquired only if all staff members recognize their individual and collective responsibility in sharing information about new acquisitions, services in the community, and user reactions to existing services.

Teachers

The library needs of teachers in public and private schools fall into two areas: (1) classroom instruction and (2) professional growth. In an ideal world, each school would have on its faculty a qualified librarian with an adequate support staff, and the facilities, equipment, and materials to meet the educational goals of the school. The teacher's instructional needs would then be met by the school librarian functioning in various roles as an information specialist, teacher, and instructional consultant.[23] Even if it were possible or desirable to substitute for the school librarian, most children's librarians lack the qualifications to do so. The school (media) librarian must have an understanding of the instructional objectives that extend beyond the transfer of information. Not only are children taught to find information, they must also learn to organize and use it. A teacher may request materials on housing and food of the colonial period for a social studies unit. This is a straightforward request that librarians are accustomed to dealing with in both school and public libraries, and access to this information can be gained through catalogs, bibliographies, and indexes. At the same time one of the instructional objectives in this unit may be to introduce the concept of deductive reasoning. Certainly, this skill—using information—is needed if individuals are to meet their obligations as citizens in a democratic society. Current methods of bibliographic access, however, would not serve this objective; it requires that the school librarian understand the teaching process as well as have an intimate knowledge of resources.

The instructional needs of teachers can best be met by a school media center librarian who is familiar with the instructional methodologies available and is able to provide or create, if necessary, the information in a variety of formats. The learning styles of individual students can be more easily accommodated when students have access to an array of materials and equipment, from books on several reading levels and audio and video formats, to computer software that invites the learner to engage in a variety of learning experiences. For optimum learning, these materials should be readily available at the moment they are needed.

Given the enormous problems with which many schools operate in this less-than-ideal world and the lack of resources to deal with these problems, it is clear that most public libraries will have to assume a stronger supportive role, while encouraging the schools to make progress toward the type of program envisioned in *Information Power: Guidelines for School Library Media Programs*. Many schools lack the materials support needed to demonstrate that learning can be exciting. The science and social science curricula both require a wide array of materials and the active involvement of students in learning activities. Without this support, teachers are forced to rely on the textbook as the major resource rather than to use it as a common frame of reference. As a result these subject areas may come to be viewed by children as less than interesting, an attitude that could affect the rest of their formal education.

Teachers occasionally have students whose needs fall outside the main spectrum of school library materials, such as those requiring simple concept books aimed at the two- to three-year-old; others may benefit from the challenge of adult materials. Rather than allocate funds for these little-used materials, school librarians should be invited to borrow them from the public library.

Those who teach classes on child care and family living at the high school or community college level often need materials for preschool children on a short-term basis for their instruction. Like children's librarians who are frequently invited to lecture on children's literature and its use, these teachers may be asked to serve as a resource for children's services. Community college faculty in one community wrote instructions for the use of individual toys that circulated from the public library, and a high school teacher of family living taught one of the sessions in a workshop series for parents offered by the library.

Many of the professional needs of teachers will be met by the professional collection provided by the local district. However, teachers working on advanced degrees or special certification may find the different focus of the public library collection and its interlibrary loan service of considerable value.

Child Care Providers

No other single phenomenon has affected traditional children's service more than the great numbers of mothers entering into the work force. In 1947, only 18.6 percent of women with children were in the labor force.[24] In 1970, 29 percent of mothers with children under six were working outside the home, as were 43 percent with children ages six to seventeen. As of 1986, half of all children under six and more than 60 percent of children from six to seventeen had mothers who were either working or looking for work.[25] Increases have occurred at the upper as well as the lower end of the socioeconomic scale, in two-parent families as well as in families headed by a single parent. One out of five children lived in poverty at the beginning of the 1980s; for families headed by a woman, one in three.[26] These figures remained approximately the same by the mid-1980s; however, for black and Hispanic children the odds have increased that they will live in single-parent families below the poverty level.[27] Although these changes have affected all social classes, the cost of child care is less a factor in the middle class than its availability and quality.

Whenever societal changes disrupt the patterns of family life, there is usually a period of experimentation before public policies are set in place. Libraries have been affected by parents entering the work force in several ways, but none are so dramatic or widespread as the changes in services brought about by large numbers of children in custodial care during the work day and the sizable number of school-age children who spend several hours after school without adult supervision. The care providers, children, and their families represent an important audience for children's services.

Day Care Centers and Family Day Care Homes. Not only are there more and more children being cared for outside the home, but there is a shortage of licensed day care centers and family day care homes, even though the number of both has increased. Because of the costs of day care, many children in the seven- to thirteen-age range care for themselves. The majority of younger children are cared for in their own home by a parent or another relative or in the home of a relative or neighbor.

Children may be cared for outside the home by day care personnel in a licensed or non-licensed facility. Day care centers may have a staff of 15 or 20, depending on the ages of the children and the state laws governing such facilities; cooperative day care centers have some paid staff supplemented with a prescribed number of hours of parent assistance; and day care homes generally have one adult caring for a limited number of children, usually less than five or six. The latter group is difficult and expensive for libraries to serve directly. Day care personnel in a licensed facility may be reached through the social service department overseeing the facility. The qualifications of a program supervisor of a day care center may be subject to prescribed educational requirements. In the state of Washington these include college level courses in child development, or an equivalent, and the implementation of a program designed to meet the developmental needs of individual or groups of children. Day care staff may need assistance in creating a stimulating environment that will foster growth in all aspects of a child's life. In addition to current information on child development, the staff need children's materials (books, toys, etc.) and information on how to use them with children. Their needs are not unlike those of parents, except they must meet legal standards of safety, health, and nutrition. Their preparation, however, may not have taught them the skills of introducing or sharing literature with children, and so some libraries have offered workshops and demonstrations for day care staffs on presenting preschool story programs. As follow-up support, the staff members were allowed to borrow program kits that contained books, media, and instructions for activities on various themes.

The South Bay Cooperative Library System (California), with support from the Library Services and Construction Act and the California State Library, carried on an innovative program from 1983 to 1985, demonstrating several possibilities for library services to child care centers and family day care providers.[28] Many of the services developed in this project can now be found in children's services throughout the country. As a communication link, a library newsletter featured program announcements for day care staff, children, and parents; the availability of library materials of interest; and suggestions of activities to enrich the day care center's program. Workshops were provided for children's librarians to enhance their competencies in working with this audience, and program kits were developed for their use in increasing weekend and evening programs. Workshops were also provided for day care staffs and parents' groups to promote the use of literature with children. Some targeted sites were given collections of materials and the services of a library storyteller. In addition, a working relationship was strengthened with the early childhood education faculty in the area's community colleges. This intensive effort is beyond the resources of most libraries, but it offers many suggestions that can be used in serving this special audience.

Although most of the day care children are preschoolers, older children may be part of the audience during the summer months. One library found that sacks of new paperbacks were welcomed by this captive audience.

Latchkey Children. Latchkey is a term designating those children between the ages of five and thirteen who care for themselves after the school day until their parents or guardians return home. The number of such children has ranged from .5 to 2.25 million. Accurate figures are difficult to obtain, for parents are reluctant to admit that their children have no adult supervision during part of the day. Whatever the figure, it needs to be interpreted according to the ages included, the length of time the child is alone, the type of community, and whether an older sibling supervises a younger one.

Children with no adult in the home after school may be (1) cared for by a neighbor or relative; (2) supervised by the staff of an after-school program offered by a community organization; (3) in the library or another public facility; (4) at home or elsewhere without supervision. The need for latchkey programs varies. In some communities there is a shortage of after-school programs that provide stimulating activities for the younger school-age children. The programs offered by volunteer organizations and churches have been limited in the numbers they can accommodate. One role for a community volunteer is that of a listening ear on the other end of a telephone for children who need company, assurance, or advice in handling a problem. A few school districts have experimented with latchkey programs in the schools supported by the community and a user's fee. Nevertheless, even a modest fee is often beyond the budget of many single working parents. The societal costs may be considerably higher as many of these children feel neglected, alienated, or fearful and, in some instances, act out their frustrations in delinquent behavior. Often their school performance is affected because little guidance or academic assistance is available from an exhausted parent. An early study revealed that the fears of these children are not unfounded. Their accident rate is higher, and they are convenient targets for physical and sexual abuse.[29] Some recent investigations reveal inconclusive evidence of harmful effects of self-care on the lives of latchkey children as the self-esteem and self-reliance of some children may increase through the experience.[30] Obviously, the age of the child and the type of environment are important factors in investigations of this kind.

Within its traditional role, a library has several opportunities to respond to the needs of this special audience. As an informational agency, the library can maintain a file of existing latchkey programs and after-school activities sponsored by public and private organizations, noting those that offer reduced fees for low-income families. Library resources—film, video, books, programming materials, and the expertise of the children's librarian in storytelling, booktalking, and library visits—can be offered to staffs of existing programs. Children's librarians can also provide workshops for children and parents on safety practices and on activities to do while home alone.

In their attempt to solve this community problem alone, some libraries may have inadvertently delayed the establishment of more comprehensive programs that allow parents a wider choice of programs in a safe environment that meets the needs of children for an educationally sound experience. Coleman, Rowland, and Robinson, three academics who have done considerable study and research in this area, recommend that a community task force be identified as a means of bringing together representatives from parents, community leaders, school personnel, day care providers, human service workers, child advocates, and youth leaders.[31] The children's librarian can serve as a catalyst in bringing together these representatives for discussions of this kind.

Critical to any program are funding and having staff competent enough to carry out the types of programs the task force has approved. The three themes considered essential in any program are (1) protection, (2) growth and learning, and (3) life skills.

The children need protection while engaged in appropriate age-level activities within the program, but they also need the skills to deal with situations at home and in the community when alone. The program should further develop the child's competencies through activities that are adult-directed and those that allow children to make their own discoveries at their own pace. Children need experiences that reinforce and develop social skills through an awareness of community life. With a mix of field trips and individual presentations, the occupations and roles of various community adults can serve as models.[32]

Even when community resources do not permit affordable after-school programs, there are still options to consider. Most communities have a number of child-serving organizations including schools, churches, recreational centers, Y groups, boys and girls clubs, scouting groups, and 4-H clubs. Even though their goals may differ, all have an interest in the welfare of children. Through joint efforts, a series of cooperative activities can be planned that will provide a safe and stimulating environment for children. With one or two groups assuming responsibility for one after-school day a week, the costs can be shared. When funding agencies, either governmental or corporate, see evidence of such cooperation, they are more likely to respond to requests for funds.

When affordable options for latchkey children are lacking, some parents may consider the public library the best alternative, thus placing the library staff in the role of caregiver. Children who are forced to be in the library for long stretches of time often become bored and engage in disruptive behavior or even vandalism, making it difficult for the staff to serve other users. Another issue concerns the responsibility for the safety of children who are unattended in a public institution. School-age children who come to the public library unaccompanied by a parent or another adult fall into one of the following three groups:

1. Those who choose to frequent the public library because of a natural affinity for the library environment
2. Those who live nearby and go to the library because it is preferable to being home alone after school
3. Those who are instructed to use the library as a shelter by parents or guardians who are unable to provide alternative care.[33]

Librarians cannot assume that children in any of these groups will automatically create problems for other users or staff. Nevertheless, without organized activities those in the third category are the most likely to do so, especially if they are there for extended periods of time. One library defined the "library latchkey child" as one who is instructed by a parent to be in the library three or more days a week and for two or more hours a day.[34]

There is no question that all children, whatever their circumstance, are entitled to library services. Complications arise when libraries attempt to define the nature of the library's relationship with unattended children whose numbers in some communities are increasing. Does it include child care responsibility? The voluntary nature of library use is lost when children's attendance is required. The consequences of this loss must be brought out into the open and examined. Public libraries have long been proud of their openness to all ages and conditions of users. Unfortunately, this pride was not reflected in some of the early policies developed to meet the latchkey "problem." One such policy even required that all children be accompanied by an adult when using the library.

Before taking any action, librarians would find it useful to determine the approximate number of latchkey children and the community resources currently available. The library should consider the following: (1) policies that address problems of unattended children of various ages who are in the library, (2) the library's advocacy role in meeting the needs of latchkey children and their families, and (3) the services the library is prepared to offer all children at the end of the school day. As a first course of action, librarians would find it useful to consult the position paper *Latchkey Children in the Public Library,* which represents the efforts of two divisions of the American Library Association: the Public Library Association and the Association for Library Service to Children. Guidelines are offered for developing equitable policies as well as suggestions for after-school activities.

The children's services staff cannot be expected to solve a community problem alone, and certainly not without assistance from the community and the library as a whole. The needs of these families deserve the attention of all community agencies, volunteer organizations, and the private sector, whether the need is for after-school child care or for special services to the children in homeless families. Children's librarians have not been prepared to be child care providers, nor have reference librarians been expected to look after adults who need a custodial type of care. They do have responsibilities for these publics, but these are related to library materials and their use.

Child-Serving Organizations

While parents and caregivers have responsibility for the primary needs of children, every community will have a number of organizations that serve children in other ways, directly or indirectly. Howard has defined "organization" as

> a group of persons organized to achieve specific purposes or engage in specified activities. All formally organized units of the community therefore are organizations, whether they are called agencies, institutions, associations, companies, businesses, foundations, societies, clubs, or whatever . . . .[35]

It would be a mistake to consider community organizations only as audiences to serve, although this may characterize the library's relationship at times. These organizations can become important resources for the library in fulfilling its own role in the community, and at other times they can be partners for mutual assistance in achieving respective goals.

Types of Community Organizations

Howard has divided community organizations into four sectors: (1) government (those who derive more than 50 percent of their income from taxes); (2) independent (nonprofit, tax-exempt, full-time staff and facility, supported by membership and user fees, grants, donations); (3) private (the business community); and (4) voluntary (membership supported, activities support member interests).[36]

Organizations in the government sector with responsibilities for children include the public library as well as the public schools, the county health department, juvenile detention homes, community service centers, Head Start programs, and Home Demonstration and 4-H agencies of the Cooperative Agricultural Extension Services, among others.

Those in the independent sector include the private schools, Parents Without Partners, Big Brothers and Big Sisters of America, YMCA and YWCA, and the American Red Cross, etc. Libraries have had a long working relationship with this type of organization. At the national level, children's librarians representing the Association for Library Service to Children have assisted many of these groups in compiling bibliographies for use by their leaders, as well as in exploring ways that children's librarians and the organization's staff can work together locally.

The private sector includes banks, telephone companies, department stores, manufacturing firms, legal and medical services, etc. People working in the private sector may have their occupational needs met by their firms; therefore, their use of children's services would be limited to their role as a parent or member of a child-serving organization. This sector should not be dismissed as outside the concern of the children's services department, for they can assist the library in reaching children. Doctors' offices may be pleased to make bibliographies on sex education for children available to parents, or to host a volunteer reader in their waiting room during a library-sponsored "Read to a Child Day." Banks or department stores may be asked to support a children's program as part of their philanthropic efforts; bookstores are often pleased to host a library storyteller or a librarian to advise parents during the Christmas season. One library developed a plan to blanket office buildings in their area with flyers offering to help parents select materials for children during their lunch hours.

The organizations in the voluntary sector include the American Association of University Women, the Jaycees, the Coin Club, churches, the PTA, various groups organized to help disabled children, etc. Unless the library has a file of community organizations, it may be difficult to work with several in this group. Many lack the continuity of a paid staff and a telephone listing. Yet, they represent either an audience to serve or a resource for the library in strengthening its children's services program.

Community Role of Children's Services

Organizations with programs designed to serve children or families, including the library, have several needs in common:

1. Information about other community services for children, parents, or caregivers

2. Access to basic materials on child care and development
3. Opportunities to promote their services and programs to their target populations.

The public library has the capability to serve these needs given the necessary resources. Gathering and organizing information for public use is a basic competency of librarians. A computer-produced directory of local organizations serving children which provides a description of their services, fees if any, and a contact person would further cooperation among the various organizations. Many are unaware of the range of services available in the community. This service requires a major commitment from the library staff, support from the organizations, and, in most situations, volunteer assistance.[37] Every public library should provide a general collection on child care and development. If one does not exist, these groups are likely sponsors for such a project through recommendations for purchase and donations of funds. An organization can promote its services to a wider audience by sharing its knowledge and skills with the library's public or staff training programs. The children's librarians' knowledge of materials and ways of presenting literature to children can, in return, be shared with the staff and clientele of other community organizations.

Adults Who Need Children's Literature

Adult users seeking materials for the study of children's literature fall into three groups: (1) researchers engaged in the study of children's literature or who use it as a social barometer; (2) adults enrolled in college-level classes concerned with the study and use of children's literature; and (3) other adults who find the collection appropriate for their general information needs.

Adult Students or Researchers

The audience of adult students or researchers may be small or nonexistent in some communities; in others it may represent a sizable number if the institution offering coursework on children or children's literature lacks the necessary collection support. Their needs depend on the approach used in instruction, whether theme, genre, or curricular; age levels included; and the discipline offering the course (English, early childhood education, drama, etc.). They may have unrecognized needs for standard bibliographic aids such as *Best Books for Children,* folklore and poetry indexes, or selection aids. The major responsibility for materials rests with the academic institution if the course is offered regularly, with the public library acting as a backup resource. In actual practice the academic institution may consider these materials outside their province. If the service burden affects the public library's ability to serve its other users, an equitable solution will have to be found. Overall, these adult students are an appreciative audience with many later becoming professional colleagues.

Adults who use children's literature in a research study for an advanced degree or who chart social trends through a content analysis of children's titles over a period of time can usually be served more expeditiously by special children's literature collections in large public or university libraries.[38] For this audience the children's librarian serves as a referral.

General Adult Audiences

Some adults begin their search for information in the children's department because they perceive their information needs to be more easily met by its staff or collection. Included in this category may be a commercial artist looking for a specific type of illustration, a newspaper columnist wanting the last lines of a nursery rhyme, an older person looking for a simple explanation of how computers work, or an adult seeking a poem remembered from childhood. Other adults may be referred from adult services librarians or from other community organizations. Many more requests for information could be met in the children's department if the adult services staff were informed of its resources and if children's materials were routinely included in library catalogs adults use.

Conclusion

The potential audiences for children's services are obviously greater than the public library's staff and material resources can support. Potential users are of all ages; furthermore, child caregivers, educators, and parents also have a legitimate claim on service. Once they accept this interpretation of their client group, librarians responsible for children's services have never lacked an audience to serve. The problems lie in identifying the audiences to be placed in priority over the next several years and in determining the kind of library service that is appropriate to their needs. Children's librarians should play a prominent role in making these decisions for they have the broadest concept of the benefits that can accrue to a community from a strong children's program. They also have a working knowledge of the characteristics and needs of the primary audience—the children.

Service priorities should not be set without consideration of the library's overall program of services or without the participation of community representatives whose information and views can balance those of the library staff. To be successful in this process, children's librarians need not only a broad understanding of their specialty but also effective managerial skills. As advocates they must be able to articulate a vision of the children's services program to community representatives and to help the staff devise ways to make this vision a reality.

CHAPTER 2

"Well," said Charlotte, vaguely, ". . . I'm working on a plan."

"That's wonderful," said Wilbur. "How is the plan coming, Charlotte? Have you got very far with it? . . ." Wilbur was trembling again, but Charlotte was cool and collected.

"Oh, it's coming all right," she said lightly. "The plan is still in its early stages and hasn't completely shaped up yet, but I'm working on it."

"When do you work on it?" begged Wilbur.

"When I'm hanging head-down at the top of my web. That's when I do my thinking, because then all the blood is in my head."—E. B. White, *Charlotte's Web* (New York: Harper, 1952), p.63.

Children's Librarian as Manager

The children's room or department is not a castle surrounded by a moat; rather it is one of the pillars holding up the castle. As such, it cannot operate separately, but must act in concert with other services for the benefit of current and potential users. Specialists, whether children's, young adult, or reference, have not always found it easy to view themselves in this role. Often impatient with duties that take time from their specialty (which they enjoy), some are tempted to bypass or give short shrift to the managerial tasks and the time-consuming activities of establishing working relationships outside their own area. This separateness may be a carryover from the environment in which the service developed.

When children were finally permitted to use public libraries over a century ago, a pattern was developed that has been followed by other excluded groups, e.g. disabled, disadvantaged, and institutionalized people. A population is identified that cannot be easily treated as a subgroup of another presently served and staff is appointed to find ways to meet their needs. In the process, the staff is given considerable freedom to innovate and experiment. Little accountability is required, and much attention and publicity are afforded this new service by both the administration and the community. This separateness contributes to a sense of high purpose in the staff, a close identification with the client group, and a strong commitment to the ideals of the service. Once the pioneering period is over, however, the process of integrating the service into the overall library service program begins. It can be a painful period of adjustment as the staff of the new service continues to expect special consideration while the rest of the staff, having had no prior involvement, harbor resentments because of this expectation. Charges of "you don't understand how important our work is" may be countered with "our services are just as (or more) important." The problem for the administration in these situations is how to integrate the service into the total operation and retain this strong commitment.

Because of the astounding early success of children's services, its staff generally found the integration process difficult and perhaps delayed it longer than was prudent. Ultimately, the attention given any service, in good times and especially in bad, rests on how closely integrated it is in the overall service program. Isolated services are convenient targets when budgets must be cut.

Attention to management concerns and administrative relationships is necessary if children's services are to receive the support they need. As a manager and an advocate for services to a particular segment of the community, the children's librarian assumes that a contractual relationship exists with the administration, and each party acts from a particular set of assumptions that define the responsibilities each has to the other. Together they share a responsibility for developing goals and objectives for services that meet the needs of the community, given the available resources. The implications of the contract can best be seen by discussing (1) the organizational pattern that defines administrative relationships, (2) the responsibilities of library administration for children's services, (3) the responsibilities of children's services to the administration, and (4) the development of goals and objectives for children's services.

Library's Organizational Pattern

In every library with more than one staff member, there is an organizational pattern or chart that identifies administrative relationships, showing who supervises whom and who reports to whom. Regardless of the administrative style used, this pattern shows where authority lies, and children's librarians need to know who speaks for children's services in councils where decisions are made.

Because children's librarians would prefer to have one of their own as an advocate in decision-making councils, they are quite conscious of the position that their coordinators or consultants have in the organizational pattern. If the person who represents children's services is not a highly ranked children's specialist, the children's librarians may have to exert considerable effort to keep this individual informed about the current needs for services. This is the situation in most small, unaffiliated libraries where the children's librarian reports to the head of the library and so must be his or her own advocate. In this type of library, there is no children's coordinator to assume that role. If the library is a member of a cooperative system, the consultant is too distant to substitute for the children's librarian on site, even if such participation were appropriate. In making the strongest possible case for program services, the children's librarian must recognize that the other service units also have legitimate claims on the library's resources. She or he must accept the decisions of the library's administrator and realize that tact and compromise are necessary if an effective working relationship is to be maintained among the various units.

In small libraries with professional staffs of seven or eight or less, the organizational pattern tends to be quite simple, with those representing the various service units reporting directly to the head of the library. In service areas of about 100,000 people and among members of a library system, organizational complexity occurs with the inclusion of coordinators of the various services shown in the organizational chart.

Many organizational charts indicate two kinds of relationships: line and staff. The line relationship shows supervisory authority, which usually includes the power to recommend hiring, firing, and promotion. Some staff positions like those of coordinator and consultant are generally advisory but do entail a limited supervisory authority, restricted to a specific area of an employee's activities. The position of children's coordinator is traditionally a staff position. In libraries where this position exists, a children's librarian in a branch library would have a line relationship with the branch librarian who would determine schedules and oversee the day-to-day activities. The children's librarian could also have a staff relationship with the children's coordinator, whose authority would be confined to those matters affecting the substance and quality of children's collections and services. The branch librarian as the line supervisor could decide that story hours for school-aged children would be offered; it would be the responsibility of the children's coordinator to oversee their content and quality. In some library systems the branch librarian would make the decision concerning the percentage of the materials budget to be allocated for children's services; however, the children's coordinator would have the final authority on titles to be considered for purchase. Children's coordinators with staff authority generally have responsibility for staff development programs to improve the competencies of all staff in serving children.

A staff position is a sensitive one with possibilities for conflict if there is not a clear understanding of the role. It can be a strong one, simply because of its limited authority, system-wide responsibility, and opportunities to serve as an advocate; but coordinators need a well-tuned political sense and judgment in dealing with staff confidences. Some administrators eliminate staff positions because of unfortunate past experiences. The possibility of a children's librarian having to report to two supervisors for the same task does exist if the lines are not clearly drawn. The administrative problems with this position may stem more often from the shortcomings of the staff involved or lack of administrative guidelines than from the nature of the position itself.

The pattern most prevalent in the 1950s and 1960s, and still existing in many medium- to large-size libraries today, is one in which the children's coordinator exercises staff authority in all outlets of the library where children's services are offered. This pattern, as shown in figure 1, allows for an integrated children's services program system-wide, and therefore is one given high marks by many children's librarians. (All organizational patterns shown in figures 1-5 are presented in an abbreviated form.)

The library administration does not have a responsibility to establish the position of children's coordinator, although this is an obvious way to meet its obligations to children's services. This position does offer a promotional opportunity for children's librarians who wish to continue working within their specialty, and in that sense is analogous to the head of a subject reference department. Libraries are not, however, administered for the benefit of the staff, but for the public, and only those arguments that acknowledge this fact hold much weight.

In some large systems, responsibility for children's services has been decentralized with the placement of the central library's children's room under a line relationship to the supervisor of the central library, while children's services in the branches are under a line relationship to a branch supervisor, with a branch children's consultant in a staff position. (See figure 2.)

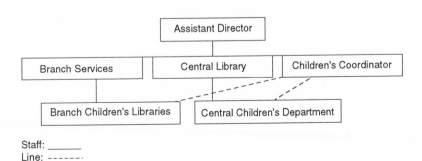

Fig. 1.   System with integrated children's services

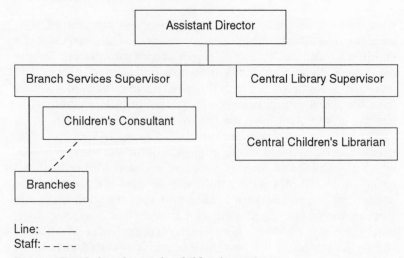

Line: ———
Staff: — — — —

Fig. 2.   Divided authority for children's services

This pattern shows the attempt to eliminate the system-wide authority of the coordinator(s). In this situation the line supervisors and the children's specialists must be willing to work together if children are to have a strong advocate within the library system, and a children's services representative (with portfolio) who speaks to the community. Other than eliminating one more person who reports to the director or assistant director, it is difficult to see the rationale behind this type of organization for most libraries, especially when it can make the integration of children's services more difficult.

In figure 3, the children's coordinator has line responsibility for the central children's library, staff responsibility for children's services in the branches, and serves on a par with other age-level specialists, the supervisors of branches, technical service, and the central library. This pattern, which is more apt to be found in medium-sized libraries, may present problems for the central children's librarian if he or she doesn't receive the information routinely given to other central library departments. For most libraries the pattern in figure 1 is preferred. When the central children's staff members have an official connection to the facility in which they work, working relationships are more easily developed. The children's coordinator can concentrate on the system's program of services without the distraction of scheduling, staffing, maintaining facilities, etc., for one of the public services outlets.

County or regional systems that offer no services from a central library will operate with a different organizational pattern.

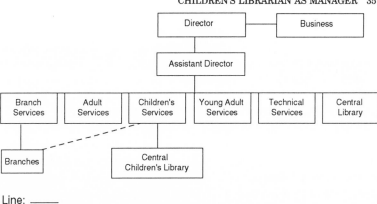

Line: ⎯⎯
Staff: _ _ _

Fig. 3.   Children's coordinator with line and staff authority

In figure 4, the special services are grouped together and the public service outlets form the other major component. From an administration's point of view this pattern has the advantage of reducing the number of staff with direct access to the director or assistant director. The specialist, however, may see this additional level as a potential problem for providing a first-hand presentation to the decision makers. The children's collection and program specialists, who have equal status, serve in a line relationship to the children's coordinator.

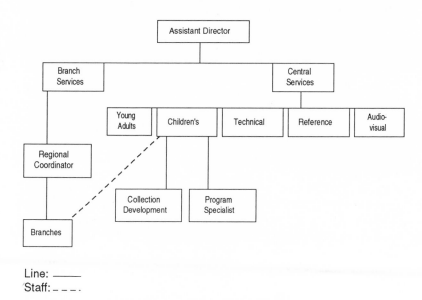

Line: ⎯⎯
Staff: _ _ _.

Fig. 4.   County system with integrated children's services

When the position of a children's coordinator does not exist, the library must find other ways of meeting its obligations to children's services. A committee of senior children's librarians could assume some of the responsibilities with either the branch department or the central children's librarians assuming others. The pattern in figure 5 assumes that the central children's library has a collection and program of services similar to that of the branches. Given the usual development of the central children's library, this would be highly unlikely. Its traditional role is to serve as the backup reference center for the branches, and to host special programs of interest to system-wide audiences. Because there is no staff relationship indicated between the central children's library and other central departments, we can assume that none is considered necessary. The juvenile materials selector in the branch department is in a position to coordinate the selection of materials in all outlets serving children. She or he may or may not see the needs of the central children's library as different from those of the branches. It is difficult to determine who, if anyone, speaks for children's services in the central library, or to the community.

The restrictions imposed by organizational patterns are not as rigid as the lines and boxes drawn on a page would appear. Staff who are represented by those boxes often act in ways that compensate for weaknesses encountered in their library's organization pattern. In figure 3, for example, the children's coordinator and the supervisor of the central library could decide on their own

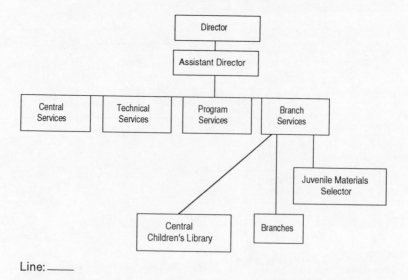

Line: ____

Fig. 5.   Central children's services under branch services line authority

that the central children's librarian should attend the central library's staff meetings and be added to its mailing list for memoranda. The children's coordinator in figure 4 may discuss with the branch supervisor the effects of a proposed policy change on children's services. There is no question, however, that the library's organizational pattern can encourage or retard the development of strong interdepartmental relationships.

Administration's Responsibilities to Children's Services

The library administration has the responsibility to provide the best possible climate for each service or department when the organizational pattern is developed. Specifically, this pattern should ensure the children's services staff:

1. Authority commensurate with responsibility
2. Representation in policy development and decisions that affect its services
3. Ease in developing close working relationships with other departments in the library
4. Participation in selection, evaluation, and in-service training of children's personnel.

Authority Commensurate with Responsibility

Whenever changes are made in the organizational pattern, attention should be given to this basic principle of administrative practice: authority commensurate with responsibility. The change may, however, inadvertently place some staff in awkward positions. Children's librarians may be pressured to increase circulation in their branch and respond by planning a coordinated series of programs. If a branch librarian does not give permission for the series, the responsibility for failure in that branch should not rest with the children's librarian. Children's librarians may be charged by the administration to promote community relationships as a means of library outreach. However, the branch librarian's scheduling may not permit a children's librarian to be out of the library. If there is a children's coordinator on the staff, he or she could mediate in situations such as these. Otherwise, the children's librarian might find it difficult to protest to the immediate line supervisor, who evaluates staff performances and recommends salary increments. Without a children's coordinator, the administration has an obligation to ensure the children's staff a recourse when untenable situations arise.

Representation in Policy and Decision-Making Councils

If administrators were asked to identify a library policy that did not affect children either directly or indirectly, they would probably be hard-pressed to name one; yet there are administrators who involve children's services staffs only when discussions concern hours of service in the children's room or the height of shelving for the children's collection. Unfortunately, there also have been children's librarians who assume that discussions dealing with policies for the overall library fall outside their purview.

Whether acknowledged or not, the administration has a responsibility to ensure that effective representation is accorded all services in decision-making councils. In most if not all situations, the most effective representative for children's services is a children's specialist. Lacking that, the line supervisor should be knowledgeable about the problems and concerns of the children's staff, know the needs of the audiences for children's services, and be willing to represent both when policies are developed. There are line supervisors of children's services who are unfamiliar not only with the department's service options, but also with the roles it could assume in the community. It is even possible to encounter a supervisor who takes a perverse pride in apparent lack of knowledge. In this situation the children's services staff (or the children's librarian) should find ways to provide information whenever a critical policy issue is under consideration, either through an ad hoc representative or a position paper.

It is to the library's advantage to involve children's librarians in planning services and in policy development. When a telephone information service was planned in one library system, no representative from children's services was included. After the service went into operation, the staff, surprised to find that children used the service, were not prepared to handle requests from children, nor were they familiar with children's materials as sources of information.

Interdepartmental Relationships

If children's services are to reach their potential in meeting community needs, they must have the cooperation of other library staff. Effective interdepartmental relationships cannot be forced, but the organizational pattern should promote their development for the benefit of all library users. There are libraries with organizational patterns drawn to control or isolate personality conflicts, often to the detriment of the services. Whatever the reasons, there have been situations in which the children's room was isolated administratively from those departments in close physical proximity and with whom a reciprocal relationship would have resulted in better service to their publics (see figure 5). It is possible, of course, to develop a working relationship with someone who has a different line supervisor, but it usually requires more time and effort. For example, a children's librarian in a central library who reports to the branch or technical services supervisor may find it difficult to justify the time in developing a joint program for parents with another central library department under the supervisor of the central library.

In any professional relationship the usual question is "how does this affect me?" In the case of interdepartmental library relationships, the effects may be increased use and improved quality of service. If budgets are determined on the basis of use, either partly or wholly, there are obvious advantages if all departments in the library promote the use of the children's collection.

Keeping abreast of new acquisitions in other departments and notifying others of new children's titles with potential value to their users does take time, but it is also an excellent means of strengthening interdepartmental relationships. A simple explanation of telecommunications for children may prove to be the perfect answer to an adult's request; while a new adult title on helping children with their homework could get much more use if the children's librarian were aware of its existence and recommended it to parents.

Interdepartmental cooperation and exchange of information should not depend solely on personal friendship; professional relationships need to be cultivated for the purpose of serving all users' needs. Becoming aware of basic reference sources in other departments is one way to improve services. If the reference librarians are unaware of poetry indexes to children's anthologies, they may never refer users to the children's room or consult them for their own requests. If adult services librarians are not aware of an increase in requests for literacy materials for adults in the children's room, this collection need may go unnoticed while an important audience for adult services remains unserved.

In one community library, the children's staff logged all requests from their users over a period of time, creating a record of the materials used to meet the requests. In sharing this log with the adult reference staff, two things happened. The children's librarians learned of adult sources that might have provided better information for their users, and the adult reference staff, amazed at the range of questions, became aware of resources in the children's collection that they might tap for their users. The quality of services was thereby improved.[1]

Staff Selection, Evaluation, and Training

Line supervisors are usually involved in the selection of staff in their department and are required to make periodic evaluations of their performance. This responsibility is defined by the organizational pattern which, from an administrator's point of view, makes for a smooth-running operation. A good staff member who doesn't rock the boat, gets along with staff, and is never late is not necessarily a good librarian. If the line supervisor admits to little knowledge about children's services, problems could arise. To be effective, the evaluation process should involve an informed opinion on the librarian's subject knowledge and competencies in children's services.

When the children's coordinator of a county library system interviewed two candidates for a children's position in a branch library, she found that only one had the necessary background. The other candidate had no knowledge of children's materials, had not taken coursework nor read widely in this or any other area. Following the procedures for hiring, she sent both candidates to be interviewed by the staff of the branch. They voted for the unqualified candidate because she "would fit into our branch so nicely" and they found her personally congenial. No one would say that a branch librarian should hire an employee who would have difficulties working with the staff, but the process should include an informed opinion on the candidate's competencies for the particular specialty.

Because of the many regulations that surround hiring practices today, the larger libraries have employed personnel directors whose professional orientation may lie in personnel rather than in library services. Some may consider the request of children's librarians to be involved in personnel decisions an intrusion on their professional turf. Either the rationale for involvement must be sensitively drawn or a working relationship carefully nurtured that allows children's staff to be evaluated in employment, tenure, and promotion processes by someone knowledgeable about their specialty. Otherwise children's services may suffer. If all librarians were generally as knowledgeable about children's services as they are about reference services, these safeguards might not be necessary. Another advantage of having a children's coordinator is to provide this kind of assessment. If both the line supervisor and the children's coordinator contribute to the annual rating, a more balanced evaluation can be provided. In libraries without a children's coordinator or a senior children's staff, the hiring process could be improved by involving a children's specialist from a neighboring library.

Administrators have a responsibility for providing opportunities for staff to learn the policies and procedures of the library, and to offer in-service training activities designed to improve their skills in the performance of their duties. They also share an obligation to encourage staff participation in continuing education activities offered by outside agencies. A staff that continues to grow professionally is more likely to provide service of a high quality and to exhibit a strong commitment to the goals of the institution.

The administration has a further responsibility to insure that when children use resources of the overall library, they encounter staff who are ready to meet their informational needs in a receptive and competent manner. If the evaluation form used in the annual rating covers the staff's effectiveness in serving users of all ages, there will be more incentive to develop skills in serving children.

Liaison with Child-Serving Groups

If the children's services department is to fulfill its role in the community, the staff members need contact with other organizations serving children and/or their caregivers. After the priorities have been established for children's services, the extent of this involvement should be clear. The administration needs to designate a representative to serve as a liaison on a sustained basis. The highest-ranking children's librarian is the obvious choice, and in those library systems with children's coordinators, this responsibility is assigned to that position. It is not enough to respond to requests for library involvement; there needs to be a liaison serving on a continuing basis. Without a children's specialist to take the initiative, the library may be overlooked when community-wide planning is done for children.

The administration and staff can also benefit from these contacts by requiring a written report on the activities of these groups. In that way community information is shared with all staff, including the system's children's librarians. Although children's librarians serve because of their specialty, they are also representing the library as an organization.

Children's Services Responsibilities to the Administration

By virtue of assuming a professional position, children's librarians accept, at the very least, responsibility for carrying out administrative policies and decisions, and for providing information on which those decisions are made. New children's librarians or those new to a library are often unsure of the authority they are expected to exercise. Their questions may include the following: How much latitude do I have if I am in charge of the children's room? What must I seek approval for and when can I make my own decisions? If there is a children's coordinator in a staff position and a branch librarian as the line supervisor, how does this affect my responsibilities to the administration? Fortunately for new children's librarians, it is the responsibility of the supervisors, both line and staff, to discuss with them the lines of authority and their own management styles and expectations. This will provide guidelines, but not answer all the questions that will arise. A children's librarian has responsibilities for (1) communication with supervisors, (2) participation in the overall library operation, and (3) staff orientation and development.

Communication with Supervisors

A professional position also carries with it the expectation that individual judgment will be exercised within general policies and guidelines. It's a toss-up whether a Nervous Nellie or a damn-the-torpedoes-full-steam-ahead type gives administrators more ulcers. The comfortable middle ground is probably the place to begin initially. There is a certain amount of risk involved in testing one's abilities and the parameters of one's authority. Mistakes are an inevitable part of the process. In my first professional public library position, I discovered two areas that made my supervisor nervous: the expenditure of money and announcements to the media. If an activity involved either, I always checked with her; otherwise, I followed the general principle that if, in my judgment, a proposed action fell within general guidelines, I would proceed with confidence. If this judgment was wrong, I also expected to be so informed.

A branch children's librarian in a system with a children's coordinator must decide which matters should first be discussed with the branch librarian as line supervisor and which with the children's coordinator. If this has not been explained in the orientation period, the children's librarian should initiate the discussion. Changes in the composition of the children's collection or in a children's service policy should first be discussed with the children's coordinator. When the topic is branch related and affects the staffing level or physical access to the collection or other facilities, for instance, discussions should be held first with the branch librarian. Because the children's coordinator is usually knowledgeable about most issues encountered in children's services, there is a tendency to take all questions and concerns to her/him. This would be a mistake. Not only is it improper procedure, but it also bypasses an opportunity to acquaint the line supervisor with the intricacies and objectives of children's services, and may create tension between the children's coordinator and the line supervisor. In writing memos or submitting reports to either supervisor, a safe practice is to send a copy to the other as a matter of routine.

Should the line supervisor's professional preparation in children's services be limited to a few lectures or a survey course in children's literature, his or her conceptions of children's services may be far from the children's librarian's views. After observing the more visible elements of the children's librarian's role, some administrators view it as that of an entertainer or the library's publicity agent. If this perception is allowed to stand, children will be cheated out of a well-rounded service program. Less management skill and responsibility may be demanded or expected from children's librarians than from other staff. Although this may be comforting in the short-term period for new librarians, it fails to recognize that children's services need the same basic management competencies as other services to achieve their potential.

Most professionals have had a colleague who served as an informal teacher or mentor. These colleagues share information and advice in palatable doses and discuss reasons for their own successes and failures. This kind of relationship is common to all professions.[2] It is less common for the person supervised to serve in this capacity to the supervisor, and some children's librarians have found themselves in that situation. The one supervised must use considerable tact, concentrate on the fundamentals so as not to overwhelm, and recognize that learning is a two-way street. The line supervisor will have much to teach the children's librarian about the library, management practice, and other aspects of the library's services. To be successful, respect for each other's special competencies must be present.

Rather than viewing the writing of monthly or annual reports to the administration or governing body as a burden, children's librarians should view this task as an opportunity to educate these influential persons about the children's service program. Reports should be done carefully and scrutinized to see that connections have been made to the library's goals, objectives, or role and mission in the community. In writing a report, one children's librarian might state:

> The children's department conducted two series of book and film discussions, six weeks each, for fifth and sixth graders at the Low Point Community Branch. Total attendance was 101, with an average of 7 at each session.

Another way to report this activity is as follows:

> To support the library's objective to increase library use and awareness of services in the Low Point Community, the children's department conducted two six-week series of book and films discussions for fifth- and sixth-grade children. Total attendance was 101, with an average of 7 at each session. Although the number reached was not as high as we would have liked (our target was 12), we believe that the major objectives of the program—(1) to work with the personnel at Elusive Heights School, (2) to demonstrate to children and their parents the range of resources available at the public library, and (3) to provide an opportunity for children to discuss books and films that have been read and viewed in common in a relaxed environment—were more than fulfilled. The titles used in each session were selected with the cooperation of the school librarian and the fifth- and sixth-grade teachers, coordinating wherever possible materials that would enrich classroom experiences. The children have served as enthusiastic promoters of the library's resources to their classmates, younger siblings, and parents. Children's circulation increased eighteen percent in March over last year, reference requests reached 100, a 230 percent gain, and the number of new users, both children and adult, was 109 as compared to 15 in the preceding year. The school librarian has offered to coordinate the scheduling of classroom visits to the public library in April and May.

Reporting allows the children's staff to describe their objectives, range of activities, current problems, and planning for the future. In so doing, a realistic picture of the service is given, correcting any preconception that may be held by the supervisory and administrative staff that children's librarians play with children, while other librarians serve information needs. In the example above, the series of book and film discussions could have been viewed as spending a relaxing interlude with children. Certainly, we would hope that the sessions were a source of enjoyment for children and librarian alike; but if that were the only objective, a more cost-effective program could have been found. Not every activity in children's services needs to be reported in such detail, but the opportunity to inform should not be overlooked.

Even if monthly or quarterly reporting is not required, consider providing it anyway, especially if the line supervisor would benefit from the information. Offer the supervisor a copy and keep one for your records. In writing the annual report this record is invaluable. Some libraries require that a form be completed for each program or activity offered to the public, and these, too, are helpful (see Appendix B). Although unsolicited reports may not be forwarded to the library director, the supervisor can use the information in decision making and in discussions with administrative staff. Children's services reports are a rich resource of human interest stories and pictures that can add zest to the director's monthly report to the trustees or city manager and provide its readers with a renewed sense of the library's mission. As every politician knows, the readers will remember the story longer than the statistics.

Participating in the Overall Library Operation

One of my library directors related an experience she had as a children's librarian in a large midwestern library in the early 1940s. She accepted an invitation to serve on a staff committee to plan the library's annual Christmas party. She was later reprimanded by the children's coordinator because "children's librarians have too much to do to indulge in this kind of activity." In recent years at least one public library system has eliminated positions for specialists in their public service staff. The former specialists are now generalists, teaching their colleagues how to serve children while assuming new responsibilities for other age groups.[3]

From emphasizing the uniqueness of children's librarians to considering all public service librarians as generalists represents a broad continuum. Most children's librarians believe that their primary value to the library lies in their special knowledge and skills; nevertheless, they also recognize their shared responsibility to all library users. It is not easy to balance these dual responsibilities, especially in a small library or branch situation with limited staff resources. Through in-service activities designed to help staff become more familiar with children's collections and programming skills, the overall service to children will be improved, but backup expertise must be available if the needs of a diverse society are to be met. A "little bit of knowledge" may indeed be a dangerous thing, if it is allowed to substitute for the competencies needed to serve the most vulnerable of library users: the children.

In some libraries children's needs may be overlooked or delegated to less qualified staff, while the children's librarian is called upon to serve adults who are more aggressive in their requests for assistance. Although children's librarians need to recognize their responsibility to users of all ages, they should also be alert to possible inequities in the assistance given to children and ready to voice their concerns to the administration.

As an advocate for their audience, children's librarians have a responsibility to become aware of the many options available in policy development, and to marshal their arguments for a position they consider the most appropriate to the goals of the overall library. Policies of use may include fines and fees, reserves and interlibrary loans, number of items borrowed at one time, and renewal privileges. Access policies bring into discussion the issues of intellectual freedom for children and their legal status in society, and the cataloging procedures that affect use of collections. Collection policies define the content in terms of format, subjects included or excluded, and the procedures used in acquiring and removing materials.

One of the most critical operations affecting children's services is the process that determines its budget. All too often the children's services budget is considered on the basis of a policy determined by others. The time to safeguard the funds is when the policy that outlines the process for setting priorities is established. If direct involvement is not possible, the line supervisor should be reminded that the children's staff is concerned and expects its interests to be represented.

Policy revision is one of those "oughts" that is conveniently postponed until an incident occurs that demands attention. Many years ago I surveyed children's librarians in Washington State, asking questions about children's access to various collections and services in their libraries. In supplying the answers, many of these librarians were obviously mentally reevaluating the need for the restrictions that existed. Once adopted, library policies may be viewed as immutable laws even though the conditions that produced them no longer exist. Every policy is established by human beings, subject to human error, and can be changed by human will.

Staff Orientation and Development

To all but the library addicts, the staff and the services they provide determine whether the library will be used and supported. Staff training is too important to leave to chance; a service orientation is basic to a successful program of services. Along with other professional staff, the children's librarian not only has responsibilities for in-service training of her or his own staff, but also for the library staff as a whole. There are a number of ways staff development can be provided: (1) manuals of procedures and policies, (2) workshops, (3) orientation for new staff, and (4) exchange of staff with other departments.

Manuals of Procedures and Policies. The children's department should contribute to the library's manual by providing, whenever necessary, interpretations of policies and procedures as they affect children. In addition, the children's department may also provide a supplement for its own staff which provides departmental goals and objectives, procedures, and services which are peculiar to the children's department. Even though this information may be given verbally to new employees, it is too important not to be written down. The public may be poorly served if the staff is not aware of all the services available.

Workshops. Some libraries plan a series of in-house workshops during the year for various levels of staff. Topics treated for the professional and pre-professional staff may range from the reference interview to bibliographies and indexes for use in various subject areas. The children's staff should assume responsibility for workshops in turn with other departments, for these opportunities to contribute to staff development can highlight the special skills and resources available in the children's department.

Orientation. Most libraries offer new employees an orientation period ranging from a few hours to several days in each of the various departments and outlets. This gives the children's department an opportunity to initiate a working relationship with the new employee, but care should be taken not to overwhelm the person with all the information ever needed about children's services. An overview of the service program and its objectives is an obvious place to begin, followed by a survey of the collection.

A mystique about children's services has developed that is reflected in various ways. One is that only the anointed can serve children; another, that the unique aspects of the service far outweigh the similarities to other services. One of my predecessors in a children's position had so convinced the staff of the mystique that they avoided the children's room, leaving me to wonder what I had done wrong. There are, of course, special needs that children have, but any librarian or experienced pre-professional should be able to respond to many requests from children, even though they may not be able to handle inquiries involving extensive subject knowledge or plan a children's services program. Some adult services librarians who are afraid of children may profess to dislike them. If fear is the root of their problem, they can be helped; if not, try to keep them away from public services.

Exchange of Staff. Some library administrators have been successful in effecting staff exchanges that permit each public service employee to work several weeks in each department. Others fail because staff resentment of the program negates the inherent gains. Some libraries encourage a voluntary exchange among departments, branches, and bookmobiles, and so on.

Unfortunately, staff in children's services often experience difficulties in finding an adult services librarian with whom to exchange. In these programs the children's staff have an obligation to help these ambassadors gain information about the services and resources in the children's department to share with their own coworkers.

Determining Goals and Objectives for Children's Services

Goals and objectives define children's services. Based on the role and mission statement and the long-range goals of the overall library, they reflect the philosophy of service; provide a direction for all children's services activities, from selection of materials to the content of programs; and serve to justify why specific services may or may not be offered. Both the administration and children's staff must work together to develop an appropriate statement of goals and objectives for children's services. In these deliberations, the children's staff is guided by the following:

1. Library standards adopted by children's divisions of national and state library associations
2. The library's role(s) and mission statement
3. Long-range goals of the library
4. Goals of other child-serving organizations in the community.

State and National Standards for Children's Services

Library standards are not the most critical factor in developing goals on which children's services are determined, but they do represent contemporary professional opinion of what constitutes good library services.

One of the functions of library associations is to develop standards for services. As part of this activity, goals are identified on which standards are based. A standard is a benchmark set up or established by an authority, as a rule, for the measure of quantity, weight, value, or quality. National and state library associations are the authorities who develop standards for library services. National standards represent a synthesis of opinion from across a wide spectrum, and as such are useful as a point of departure when considering standards at the state or regional level. State standards reflect state patterns and resources and can be extremely valuable in developing goals and objectives. For the children's librarian at the local level, standards serve as a checklist in suggesting areas that may have been overlooked.

The Public Library Association, a division of the American Library Association, is responsible for public library standards at the national level. Children's Services Division of ALA, now Association for Library Service to Children, developed standards for children's services in 1964[4] which were based on the Public Library Division's standards of 1956.[5] Public library standards for systems were developed in 1966,[6] but during discussions for standards revision in the early 1970s, the approach to standards development was changed. Instead of the best-of-practice approach, describing the resources that existed in exemplary libraries, the new process focused on the user rather than the institution. Standards that had called for two volumes per capita, for example, were institutional standards stating what the library needed to give good service. A user-oriented standard might prescribe that users have available the materials they seek 85 percent of the time.

The importance of standards in justifying funding has diminished over the years as their validity has been questioned by local budget officers and library administrators alike. A standard of two volumes per capita was impossible to defend because it could not be demonstrated that adequate service resulted from this criterion, or that all communities had identical needs. In communities with a low educational level, for example, more staff and audiovisual materials may be needed for adequate service than the standards prescribe. Until the current process of testing standards for statistical soundness has been completed, several library associations have established guidelines as an aid to planning services.

As part of the process initiated in 1970, each age-level division was asked by the Public Library Association to prepare a working paper on goals and guidelines for services to their respective audiences. From these documents—regarding children, young adults, and adults—a single statement was prepared.[7] Children's librarians would find it helpful to compare the approach used in the 1964 *Standards for Children's Services in Public Libraries* with the guidelines in the "Working Paper on Goals and Guidelines" prepared by the Task Force on Children's Services of 1973.[8] The former is primarily institution-oriented, stating what the library needs to provide good library services, while the latter focuses on the users' needs and the responsibilities of the community as a whole for meeting them. The 1964 standards prescribe the education and experience for a children's coordinator, while the guidelines stress the general responsibilities of management to children's services in the library and the community. How management is to meet these obligations is not dictated.

The book *A Planning Process for Public Libraries* was the next step in the process toward a more rational base for standards, and one that encouraged the local library to follow the guidelines in developing services relevant to its own community needs.[9] This title was superseded in 1987 by *Planning and Role Setting for Public Libraries.*[10]

A few states have developed guidelines for children's services in recent years. The statement *Foundations of Quality: Guidelines for Public Library Service to Children* was prepared by the Children's Librarian's Section of the Illinois Library Association.[11] It was preceded by a survey of children's services in the state which offered a realistic base on which to work.[12] The guidelines delineate responsibilities for each level concerned with children's services: (1) local library, (2) library system, (3) state library, and (4) state library association, and cover such areas as goals and evaluation, budget and finance, personnel, services, programs, materials and equipment, and facilities.

For the children's librarian at the local level, user-oriented standards or guidelines require that documentation for funding requests be couched in output rather than input terms. The focus is on the benefits and services to the users, rather than the needs of the institution. A request for $15,000 for materials because the collection is in poor condition may be a valid request, but it probably will not be as effective as stating that services to preschool children and their parents (services identified) require the addition of 150 picture book replacement copies, the latchkey program for school-aged children requires five computer programs and 10 short videocassette films, the booktalk programs for fourth to sixth graders need 100 duplicate copies of titles used, or improved access to the collection requires the purchase of subject bibliographies and indexes. This output way of thinking commits expenditures to the benefit of the users through connections to services, discourages impulse buying, and simplifies the process of accountability. Staffing needs can be treated in the same way: to support a particular program for users, X number of staff of specified levels will be required. The message to the administration is clear: if this service is to be offered, the support will have to be provided.

The next step in the search for standards was the development of a common method of measurement based on benefits to the users. The publication in 1982 of *Output Measures for Public Libraries: A Manual of Standardized Procedures* represented the Public Library Association's effort to provide this type of measurement.[13] A second edition was issued in 1987.[14] The manual provides detailed instruction on gathering data, definitions of the data elements, and how to interpret the results and make improvements if the library decides the results require this response. Although the approach assumes a total library effort with one figure for each measure, it would be possible to adapt the process to a particular service, such as children's or reference, and this is under consideration. Caution should be exercised, however, in using the measures in isolation from the service goals and objectives. Large attendance at preschool programs may be incompatible with a goal of establishing a relationship with each child; therefore, program attendance per capita would not be a critical measure to use. Separate data for children's services for some measures may be too difficult to isolate from the total figure. Nevertheless, several of the measures can serve as effective indicators of the services and resources offered. Basic to most measures is the designated age-level population for the area served, e.g. ages 0–13, 1–12, etc.

The Wisconsin Department of Public Instruction, Division of Library Services has done a pilot study with several libraries in the state to test the appropriateness of output measures to children's services.[15] Seven of the twelve measures were selected by the children's librarians participating in the pilot study. In considering the goals of most children's services, these appeared to be the most critical:

1. Juvenile circulation per juvenile capita
2. In-library use of juvenile materials per juvenile capita
3. Juvenile library visits per juvenile capita
4. Annual juvenile program attendance per juvenile capita
5. Library registration of juveniles as a percentage of juvenile population
6. Juvenile collection turnover rate
7. Juvenile reference completion rate.

In collecting data for the last measure, the question arose of how to treat inquiries asked by adults on behalf of or for use with children. The recommendation was made to treat this measure as "questions answered by juvenile services staff or the juvenile collection."

If one of the objectives is to increase the percentage of registered borrowers among the children in the community, it would be necessary to know the number of children in the community eligible for cards and the number of children registered. It is possible that a library's high juvenile circulation is attributable to a relatively small percentage of the community's children and that attention should be given to broadening the base of users. On the other hand, it may suggest that a large number of adults are taking out materials for children.

The appropriateness of the children's collection for a community can be indicated in the juvenile collection turnover rate. If the number of items in all formats is 50,000 and the annual juvenile circulation is 125,000, the juvenile collection turnover rate would be 2.5. Unless the collection serves an archival function or has a moderate-to-heavy reference use, this figure may indicate that the collection needs evaluation for content and condition, or that more promotion of materials is needed. A high in-library use figure (those materials consulted but not checked out) may reveal that the collection is used for reference and study or that parents forbid their children to check out materials for fear of fines or fees for lost or damaged materials. A low reference-completion rate may suggest that the collection is inadequate for this use or that the staff's reference competencies need improving.

Measures not used in the study for whatever reason were:

1. Juvenile reference transactions per juvenile capita
2. Title fill rate
3. Subject and author fill rate
4. Browsers fill rate
5. Document delivery rate.

It is possible that the participants considered these measures not compatible with their service goals, or too difficult to gather because of the large number of adults using the services on behalf of children, or that the time allotted permitted only the most pertinent measures to be tested.

Most children's librarians would not care to have their collections evaluated on whether all titles of a mass market series or the title featured in a recent television special were available for every inquiry during the sampling period, unless that was one of the library's stated objectives. Although children's demands may be one determinant of the collection, it is not the only one. Children's browsing experiences often involve the intervention of staff who take an active role in promoting titles. Because children's interests are usually brief in duration, document delivery within a 7-, 14-, or 30-day period is of questionable value. Before using any of these measures, the manual should be thoroughly studied and questions about data collection resolved.

Role and Mission Statement of the Library

With so many opportunities to serve, a public library must weigh each alternative carefully, and consider its effect on the community as a whole and the staff and material resources needed for its implementation. In deciding which audiences should be given priority in allocating its limited resources, the public library must define its roles and mission as an institution within its community. Each role selected describes (1) what the library is trying to do, (2) whom the library is trying to serve, and (3) what resources the library needs to achieve these ends. The mission statement is:

> a concise expression of the library's purpose. It specifies the fundamental reasons for the library's existence. In this sense, it builds on, but is not limited to, the roles chosen by the library . . . In one sense, the mission is like a job description: it gives direction to the library's daily activities.[16]

This purpose, expressed in a mission statement, has been called the "why" statement—why the library exists in the community.[17] It is relevant to the community environment and the population served, and states who is to be served and by which services. Although stated in broad terms, it can be used to judge the appropriateness of services under consideration.

The children's department cannot ignore the stated role and mission of the library if it hopes to make a lasting and substantial contribution to the community. In the 1960s a children's librarian observed that "before any specialty can exert itself, the framework into which it fits must first be determined in absolute."[18] This may explain why children's services enter a crisis period whenever public libraries (the framework) falter in defining their role in society. Programs and services that support or strengthen the library's role will receive a more favorable response to funding requests than those that do not.

Developing a role and mission statement is not an easy task because it brings to the surface the divergent philosophies and concepts held by individual staff, trustees, and community representatives. It is for this reason, however, that it should be undertaken, because it will provide a basis for goal-setting, allocating resources, and measuring the impact of library services. In developing the role and mission statement, children's services should be represented by staff and user groups that can bring a broad understanding of community resources and needs and act as effective advocates. What is needed in such discussions are more documentation and analysis, and perhaps less missionary zeal.

It would be difficult but not impossible to develop a role and mission statement in which children's concerns were not addressed, either directly or indirectly; nevertheless, it is much easier to plan children's services if their unique needs have been recognized in the final statement. Consider a children's services program in the context of each of the following sets of role and mission statements.

Roles selected. Primary: formal education support center and reference library; secondary: preschoolers' door to learning and independent learning center.

Mission statement. The Morningside Public Library provides materials and services to help community residents obtain information meeting their personal, educational, and professional needs. Special emphasis is placed on supporting students at all academic levels and on stimulating young children's interests in and appreciation for reading and learning. The library serves as a learning and educational center for all residents of the community.[19]

Roles selected. Primary: community information and activities center; secondary: independent learning center for all ages.

Mission statement. The Night Falls Public Library provides current information on community organizations, issues, and services, and works with other community agencies and organizations to provide a coordinated program of social, cultural, and recreational services. Library resources are provided to individuals of all ages who are pursuing a sustained program of learning independent of any educational provider.

Children's services operating under the first role and mission statement would be limited only by the available resources, both staff and materials, in setting goals and objectives. All possible audiences for children's services are mentioned directly or indirectly.

The second statement would be more appropriate for a community with retired citizens as the largest population group. Children's services are rather narrowly defined. The secondary role would curtail services to children seeking materials for class assignments, unless they could demonstrate a sustained interest in the topic. Because children's individual interests are often stimulated through classroom experiences, the staff would find this role difficult to implement. Programs for preschoolers and parents which have traditionally had a strong educational basis might not be appropriate, or at least not in their present form. Even though this statement would present obstacles for traditional children's services, it would be possible, with effort, to develop a limited program of services for them.

The role and mission statement as a working document is important, but the process by which it is developed is equally valuable because it lays the foundation for its acceptance and implementation. If the library as a whole shows no interest in developing such a statement, the children's department cannot provide one on its own. Efforts should be made to convince the director and staff of the benefits accruing from such a statement. The manual *Planning and Role Setting for Public Libraries* describes several possible roles and benefits of each and also identifies the necessary resources and output measures to consider for each.

Library's Long-Range Goals

Along with a mission statement, goals are a product of the planning process and are subject to revision whenever the cycle is repeated, normally every three to five years. Objectives are often set to coincide with the annual budget cycle, although some may carry over several years with progress reported yearly. Because one person's goal may be defined as another's objective, these terms should be given a working definition. Goals may be grouped into two categories: service goals and management goals. They are stated in nonspecific terms and represent ends toward which the library intends to move in the future (time period undefined). Objectives, on the other hand, are specific targets or ends to be achieved, and are measurable and time limited. They begin with *to* and an action verb and advance the library's efforts toward its goals. Activities or strategies are the means employed to accomplish the objectives.[20] The following examples may be helpful in understanding the relationships of goals to objectives and activities.

Service Goal

Goal	Preschool children and their parents have access to a wide array of services and materials.
Objective	To increase the attendance at toddler and parent programs by 25 percent in the next calendar year.
Activity	Offer a workshop on preschool and parent services for public services staff.
Activity	Conduct three series of toddler-parent programs, eight weeks each, for each branch library.

Management Goal

Goal	The library provides collections of materials appropriate to its mission and the community served.

Objective   To evaluate for content and condition the nonfiction collection by ———
Activity   Conduct a workshop for all concerned staff on weeding children's collections.
Activity   Assign various sections of the nonfiction collection to each children's librarian for recommendations of retrospective titles to replace or withdraw, and new titles to consider.

When the library as a whole develops goals, children's services staff should be involved. Goals that affect children's audiences should be part of the goal statement of the overall library and the objectives set by each department should relate to these broadly based library goals, as demonstrated in the examples above.

Unlike the role or mission statement, the children's department can and should state its own goals even if the library as a whole fails to do so. It would be prudent, however, for the statement to be submitted to the library's administration and other department heads for their recommendations and suggestions for effective ways of implementing the goals.

Goals of Other Child-Serving Organizations

A chronic condition of all tax-supported organizations is one of limited resources. For this reason libraries cannot afford to be viewed as duplicating other community services; some needs may be better served by other organizations. Because of the emphasis in the past decades on planning and accountability, most institutions have developed a set of goals on which their services are based. The children's department of the public library is not the only agency in the community that would benefit from knowing the goals of other child-serving organizations. In particular, children's librarians should be aware of the goals of the public schools and of the children's programs offered by the department of parks and recreation because of their effect on the community. Not only can unnecessary duplication be avoided, but library services can also be more easily justified to budgeting authorities.

There have been situations in which other service institutions have preempted the role of the public library to the detriment of both institutions. For example, when a public school offers preschool programs or develops a collection that serves the recreational needs of children, but fails to acquire materials needed for the school's instructional program, this role reversal can only shortchange users. When a city recreational program offers storytelling but slights those activities that enhance motor skills or demonstrate the value and enjoyment of team participation, questions need to be asked. Just as academic libraries should not use their resources to meet the needs of high school students before they have satisfied their primary user groups, child-serving organizations have an obligation to place in top priority those activities that represent their unique contribution to the life of the community.

The Children's Services Budget

Budgets define the priorities of the institution. A children's services budget that represents five percent of the total speaks more eloquently to the perceived value of that service than any glowing rhetoric. Children's librarians are generally knowledgeable about their own departmental budget, but tend to ignore the overall library budget. They know if their budget for materials is more or less than the year before, but they may not be aware of the percentage of the total materials budget that is allocated for the children's collection. If children's librarians are pleased whenever they are excused by their director or line supervisor from what some may perceive as the onerous task of developing a budget for their department, they should not be surprised if monies for their programs and collections are reduced or eliminated when the total requests exceed existing revenues.

Children's librarians need a working knowledge of the budgeting model used, as well as the process, in order to include the necessary information when presenting requests for funding. The library administrator who asks only for a simple "want" list has a right to expect that proposals for new services and programs be presented in an organized manner. This is also true of any requests made during the year to meet an unanticipated but critical need. In addition to a brief description of the program or service, these proposals should state

1. The objectives of the program or service
2. The goals and objectives of the overall library they support
3. The costs for materials, staff, promotion, etc.
4. The method of evaluation (or output measures) to be used.

If not obvious, the proposal should also describe any additional demands on the non-children's staff. Brevity is a virtue when dealing with busy supervisors; if the essentials can be presented in an uncrowded outline form on a page or a page and a half, the request will probably receive greater consideration. A brief explanatory memo may accompany the outline. For an example of both, see Appendix A.

There are advantages in presenting requests in this manner. Although the request may ultimately be denied, the careful documentation is more likely to be rewarded with stated reasons for denial. A revised request the following year may be successful. Should the program be approved as a library's priority, the background information provided in the children's services' proposal can be edited and adapted in preparing the preliminary budget to outside officials who need only an abbreviated version. See Appendix A (Programmatic Change Description) for an example of an edited request that appeared in a library's proposed budget. The more detailed proposal should be retained as a working document.

Budgeting Process

Budgeting is an ongoing process, with notations made throughout the year of equipment to be replaced or acquired, additional staff hours needed, changes in materials requests, etc. The children's librarian should not only rely on her or his perception of needs, but also solicit those of the children's services staff. The responsibility of each service department is to state as accurately as possible its needs in fulfilling its goals and objectives; the administration's role is to make the final decision on what can be afforded given the available funds.

During the formal budgeting preparation period, the library's funding agent, whether city or county, will issue a set of guidelines to use in preparing the preliminary budget. These guidelines will define terms and codes for various categories, provide forms, and describe the format to be used. The library administration may in turn provide each department with an edited version of the guidelines in which the terminology and examples have been adapted to the library's operation. These usually include

1. A timetable for preparation
2. Definition of terms
3. Sample forms for personnel, supplies, equipment, etc.
4. Instructions for estimating expenses, including the inflation rate, for the various categories
5. Information that will be provided by the administration
6. Information that should be supplied by the department.

As can be seen in the following introductory passage from such a document, attempts are made to guide the staff through the budgeting cycle in as painless a way as possible:

1. Review your 1988 budget form and retain narrative which is still relevant. In many cases, the General Program Description and Long Term Goals may change little for 1989. Where appropriate, relate narrative and long term goals to the Board of Trustees Long Range Plan.
2. The Short Term Program Objectives will be specific to those objectives you wish to accomplish during 1989. Include reference to the Board of Trustees Long Range Plan where appropriate. Include all major objectives you would accomplish if your Preliminary Budget Request were approved. It may be necessary to modify those objectives once your final 1989 Budget Authorization is determined.
3. On the Input and Output Sections, complete data through the *Preliminary FY '89* column. *Final FY '89* data will be added once your final 1989 Budget Authorization is determined.[21]

Materials and personnel are the major categories of library budgets. Personnel costs may range from 65 to 85 percent of the total, depending on the size of the operation. In computing employees' costs, various benefits such as insurance and pensions must be added. Libraries are reluctant to add staff unless it can be shown that the need is critical to the library's operation. When additional staff hours are required, the children's librarians' role is to state the need in terms of a permanent or temporary position, whether full- or part-time. The administration may respond to a request for five additional page hours, for example, by making adjustments within the library or by adding these hours to those requested by another department to create a new position. Determining the best way to meet this need is not part of the children's librarian's role; his or her responsibility is to provide a written justification to accompany the request.

In estimating costs of materials, the library may provide figures to use for the various categories; if not, the library's jobber can usually supply them. It is important to know whether these figures reflect the library's discount and include the costs of shipping and taxes. To arrive at the number of volumes needed in the coming year, it is necessary to consider the adequacy of the various categories and formats in meeting the needs of the public, as well as the physical condition of the materials. Another factor that must be kept in mind is the staff hours required to use funds to the best advantage. Many collections need a complete overhaul, but if other responsibilities are to be met, these efforts may have to be spread over a two- to four-year period. The cost of equipment can also be estimated by checking vendors' prices. Staff may be given an overall inflation rate to use in computing costs for expenditures in the programming area, e.g. outside talent, paper, printing, photocopying, and film rentals.

Even though the children's librarian may be given the opportunity to present the budget in person to the administration, the written budget should carry explanations for noticeable changes from the previous year. (See explanations for the starred items on Program Budget Form in Appendix A for examples.) As a former budget officer of a state library once remarked about the hazards of not explaining declining figures in governmental budgets, "It is imperative to escape the automatic downward revision by bean counters and CPAs." Budget justifications need to focus not only on numbers, but also on the potential for benefiting the community at large, i.e. the public good.

Public sector budgets leave little or no room for a credit card mentality. The only area where expenditures should exceed allocations is in the materials budget. Orders placed near the end of a fiscal year may not be received or paid for before the final cutoff date. To assure the expenditure of all budgeted funds for materials, libraries often submit orders that encumber a certain percentage of the next year's materials budget. A new children's librarian should discuss with her or his supervisor the library's practice in this area. Beyond this exception, however, the children's librarian should guard her or his reputation as a prudent manager of funds. Monies not spent revert to the general fund and may not be reallocated to the department the following year, while budget allocations that are overspent create unnecessary problems for the administration. In the former instance, the administration may conclude that the department was over-budgeted; in the latter, that the children's librarian is incapable of managing money. In either case, the children's services department should not be surprised when its budget is reduced the following year.

Budgeting Models

Through the years, most libraries have had experiences with several variations of a budgeting model, if not with more than one model. The major budgeting types are (1) line-item budget, (2) planning-programming-budgeting system, and (3) zero-base budgeting. Zero-base budgeting is not widely used because it is time-consuming to prepare and its advantages for most libraries do not offset the preparation costs involved. Because adaptations of the first two are more common, these will be described in more detail.

Line-Item Budget. This model has been widely used for many years. It is divided into operating expenses and capital outlay and may include categories for (1) personnel services, (2) employee benefits, (3) materials and supplies, (4) contractual services, (5) lease/

purchase equipment, (6) capital outlay, and (7) categorical funds.[22] Each category is normally assigned a code number used in all units and departments of the governing body. An example of a line-item budget format can be found in Appendix A. Although it is intended to be used by the library as a whole, children's librarians could be expected to select the appropriate categories and codes when preparing their departmental budgets. Whenever an increase in a category is requested beyond the usual inflation rate or a discernible decrease occurs, a justification is normally required.

An advantage of this model is that it can be used to monitor expenses over a three- to four-year period. The expenditures for the previous two years plus the current year are shown, making it relatively easy to project the figure for the coming year. A major disadvantage of this model is that cuts can be made without making a conscious connection to a specific service. Reducing the materials budget ten percent is less traumatic than eliminating a preschool program in a program/planning budget. Because goals and objectives are not integrated with the various categories, this budget model is not useful in planning.

Planning-Programming-Budgeting System. Many local governments have adapted a form of PPBS with the resources needed for each program arranged in line-item budget order. A program budget is developed around the goals and objectives of the institution with emphasis on the outputs of services, that is, the services actually delivered to the client group. Program budgeting often requires a statement regarding the consequences of not funding a particular request, or a suggestion of an alternative program that could fulfill the same objectives. (See the Program Budget Form in Appendix A as an example.) Another important element found in many variations of this model is evaluation, which adds to its value as a planning tool.

The proposed program outline in the Request for Program Approval found in Appendix B could be adapted to a program budget by adding the library's code numbers for the budget categories and by indicating whether or not alternative program(s) would be possible. The children's librarian could conclude that no alternative was possible if the program objectives were to be met, or he or she might decide that the overall effectiveness would not be seriously compromised by reducing the number of sessions or using volunteer staff for various tasks. Whenever two programs are of equal value in meeting the objectives of a children's service, the decision should favor the one making the most effective use of existing staff and material resources. Governmental units that use a variation of this model may require justifications only for new programs or for those targeted for elimination.

Libraries usually select their own program components from a range of possibilities:

Programs are usually defined by the functions the library staff perform: administration, acquisitions, technical processing, circulation, and reference. They can also be defined by the clientele served: adult, young adult, and children's service, outreach to community groups, and service to business. Still another way to define programs is by service centers, that is, branches, bookmobiles and deposit collections, and main-library services.[23]

In Appendix A, Program Budget Form, excerpts from a proposed children's budget are provided. Children's services is one of the program components receiving separate attention in the budget of this county library that serves many urban communities and some rural areas surrounding a medium-sized city. Other program categories include general services (administrative), outreach services, audiovisual services, public information offices/reprographics, circulation services, automated systems, and branch services, with subcategories for regional area branches.

The goals and objectives of each program component provide the foundation on which governing and/or funding bodies make their decisions. The information requested under "Output" for materials, programs, and services correlates quite well with output measures. When increased services are projected, additional staff resources are often needed. The Personnel Budget Request Form in Appendix A is an example used to justify this kind of request.

For those accustomed to line-item budgeting used in household accounting, a new way of thinking will be necessary. The focus must change from the resources the library acquires—materials, staff, equipment, etc.—to the services delivered to the public. Attention is given to how each expenditure contributes to the service offered the users. Depending on the variation of the model used, there may be categories that deal with (1) the provision of services to the public, (2) access to materials, (3) maintenance of facilities where materials are housed and services provided, and (4) management to oversee the coordination of all of these aspects into an efficient operation.

Provision of services to the public. Activities included in this category are those given inside or outside the building to individuals or to groups, or indirectly through liaison with community groups. Promotional efforts such as booklists or newspaper columns also fall into this category. The levels of staff needed and the time involved would need to be estimated as closely as possible. If a program for parents of children with reading problems is offered, the cost of a librarian's time conferring with school personnel outside the library, as well as the clerical time spent in typing a bibliography of library materials for parents, would be part of the cost.

Access to materials. Budget allocations to provide access to collections include not only the expense of the materials, but also the staff hours estimated in selection and acquisition, cataloging and processing, binding and repair, and other related tasks. Another facet of access to materials is the cost of circulating the materials from borrowers' cards to overdue notices. These costs are difficult to predict depending as they do on public response. In assessing the costs for a parents' program, an estimation for materials, their selection, acquisition, cataloging, and processing may be all that is required in the budget request.

Costs for facilities. This expense includes building repair and maintenance, utilities, and equipment. A department may be assessed a certain percentage annually for several of these items, unless special equipment is needed. For example, an annual charge may be levied based on the square footage used by the program or service. Equipment costs could also be treated in this way or assigned to the service making the greatest use of an item. If, for example, filmstrips were among the materials for use in our parents' program, it would be necessary to provide projectors for circulation. Depending on the anticipated use of the projectors, this program might have to absorb the major cost of this equipment.

Management and administration. This category covers the costs of supervision, staff training, preparing budgets and reports, conducting surveys, and planning with departmental staff and with other library personnel in coordinating services. In the program for parents of children with reading problems, it would be essential that other library staff know the objectives of the program, have an awareness of the materials available, and be able to respond to questions from the public. The time involved in preparing the presentation falls under services to the public, while orienting or training staff is entered under management and administration.[24]

Zero-Base Budgeting. This model "requires that the cost of all programs, both current and new, be justified at the beginning of each budgetary cycle."[25] Existing programs must undergo the same rigorous examination as new ones in this model. In the process, it may be determined that a new program will achieve an objective better. The manager must begin with zero dollars and provide a justification for each unit included in the budget proposal. The units are called "decision packages," which include the principal activities performed by the unit, e.g. circulation, children's services, reference, etc.[26] The costs of the activities are computed and prioritized, making it possible to select a pattern of service at a level that can be supported with available funding. Because this process is very time-consuming and intricate, it is not widely used. Librarians might engage in some of the thought processes demanded by this model when prioritizing their services; this exercise could provide the incentive needed to forsake a tried-and-not-too-true program for a new one with greater promise in achieving objectives.

Conclusion

To a greater or lesser degree, all children's librarians are managers of resources, both personnel and materials, in their own area. Once children's librarians focus on managerial responsibilities as an integral part of their work, they will find that the competencies they have developed through other aspects of their job are transferable to this role. The kind of planning, organization, and attention to detail that ensures a successful program for a children's audience is also needed in outlining duties for an assistant or in presenting and justifying a budget. Management skills are used not only in setting the framework for services and collections, they are also necessary in executing each of these functions. The necessity to "keep it simple" for children is also useful in successful communication with busy administrators and the public.

The promise of children's services in a community cannot be met without the support of the library as a whole. This support is more easily achieved through the involvement of the library's staff with the children's program of services and through the involvement of the children's staff in the total library program, from the development of policies to the setting of priorities. Both require a competent level of managerial skills in building a team approach. Whenever the children's librarian is involved in setting service priorities for the library as a whole, for example, she or he gains a more complete awareness of the financial resources of the library as well as needs of other service units. This knowledge is important in all aspects of planning of services and programs. Knowing the financial health of the overall library and the needs and concerns of other library units will enable the children's librarian to be more considerate of colleagues and to support whenever possible their service programs. If a team approach is to be achieved, a cooperative environment must be present.

Promoting a team approach will, of course, be easier if the organizational pattern establishes the role of children's services as a key component of the library's services. Lacking that, children's librarians will have to forge strong professional relationships with their peers, as well as with their supervisors, and to take advantage of opportunities to strengthen their role as a team player. They must accept their primary obligations to children's services, while acknowledging their responsibilities to the overall library. As professionals they are expected to step into the breach whenever they see the public floundering in another part of the library without staff to assist or whenever another staff member is in danger of being abused by a member of the public. The "it didn't happen on my watch" attitude may be the correct response for those who intend to race up the corporate ladder. As part of a publicly supported institution, however, and in the long tradition of the profession, librarians share responsibility for the quality of services given in their library.

A successful manager of children's services keeps current with developments in public library management. The planning techniques and measurements developed in the past decade under the auspices of the Public Library Association are examples that now permeate all activities in a vast number of public libraries. Mission statements, goals and objectives, activities and output measures have been widely accepted as a part of good management practice. They will continue to be used and refined in the years ahead. Children's librarians can expect to operate in an environment that requires flexibility in adapting to changes that result from technological advances, budgeting practices, and social turmoil. The proposed solutions to these changes should be evaluated in conjunction with the principles on which children's services are based. The proposals may not always be compatible in every particular and may require some adaptation, as was discovered in working with output measures.

CHAPTER 3

[Francie] was reading a book a day in alphabetical order and not skipping the dry ones. . . . Saturdays were different. She treated herself by reading a book not in the alphabetical sequence. On that day she asked the librarian to recommend a book.—Betty Smith, *A Tree Grows in Brooklyn* (Philadelphia: The Blakiston Co., 1943), p. 14.

Selection and Design of Services

For the purposes of design and evaluation, librarians have constructed various models of services based on the qualifications of staff or the types of requests. For the purpose of this discussion, however, children's services will be divided into two categories. One is basic services, which are ongoing and available in some form on an individual basis whenever the library is staffed. Information or reference services fall into this category. The other, often referred to as programming, involves those activities and strategies selected to support specific objectives and are offered to groups, either occasionally or regularly as a series. Programming may serve as an invitation to use library resources or may offer educational or cultural experiences that are valuable in themselves. This use of terms does not represent a hierarchy of effort that should operate in all instances, with basic services always having priority. In communities where use is low, for example, programming may be the stimulation needed to encourage use of basic services. Librarians who serve children and young adults generally allocate more of their resources to programming activities than do their adult counterparts. Both categories should be carefully planned in order to achieve maximum benefits.

When children's librarians refer to a program of services, they usually mean the entire pattern of planned activities (programming) and services that promote the users' interaction with resources in ways that support library objectives. Children's librarians also assert their roles as community educators and caregivers through the program of services they offer. School librarians have adopted a broader interpretation of program by also including the "information, personnel, equipment, and space resources needed to support activities and services."[1] Because the term program is also used to describe a single planned activity, the context in which it is used must be considered.

Fundamentals in Planning the Program of Services

Goals and objectives of the library provide the basis for both services and programming; if the library has completed a planning process, these will be in place and planning may proceed. Without them the children's staff will need to develop their own with the approval and cooperation of the library administration. The process may include the appointment of a community-based committee or another approach may be necessary in which the children's staff gathers as much information about the community as possible in the time allowed, and, together with the administration, drafts a working set of goals and objectives.

Information about the community is a critical factor in planning. The discovery of a large number of home-school children in the community, for example, would raise a number of questions regarding the services needed, as well as the service level the library could support. If most parents of young children are found to be in the work force, more preschool programming at day care facilities would be a logical response. Without knowledge of the community, service priorities may be made solely on the basis of staff preferences rather than community needs. Most librarians have a favorite activity or an acknowledged competency, whether it is storytelling for preschoolers, providing subject access to the historical collection, or working with a special community group. If the library administration's experience with children's services has been limited, these activities may be accepted without question as a necessary part of the program of services. Worthy as these activities are in themselves, unless they reflect priorities for services as determined by community needs, the children's department will lack a coherent and defensible program of services. Staff competencies are best considered when deciding which of several desirable programs to offer to meet a particular objective.

Too often the objectives emanating from or assigned to the children's department are considered the exclusive responsibility of the children's department, while those originating in adult services are accepted as library activities. As a corrective measure, children's activities might be be referred to as library programs or services *for* children. No children's activity can reach its potential unless all staff are involved and assume responsibility for its success. When one examines the percentage of circulation or program attendance represented by children's services, it cannot be denied that service to children is a vital part of the overall library services. Indeed, it would be a rare public library mission statement that excluded children by word or inference or assigned the total responsibility for serving them to the children's staff. When responsibility is shared, it is important to remember that its corollary, involvement, should also follow. Suggestions from adult services staffs should be invited and considered.

Although much discussion and planning precede the statement of goals and objectives, both continue during the next phase—translating objectives into programs and services. Consider the following goal and supporting objective in the context of a mission statement from the Morningside Public Library discussed in Chapter 2.

> *Goal* The library actively promotes its services and resources to all county residents.
>
> *Objective* To work with the school system(s) to establish regular annual visits to the library by all elementary students over the next three years.

The objective is obviously one for which the children's librarian takes the leadership in fulfilling. Before designing or planning the program, she or he should:

1. Review the library's mission statement for direction
2. Determine the priority level assigned this objective, if that has not already been done
3. Have procedures in place for enlisting suggestions from staff and outside personnel as needed
4. Determine what actions, if any, should be taken by others before and during planning
5. Devise a timetable for action.

The children's librarian assumes the dual role of planner and educator, one who understands the library's mission and is aware of the characteristics and needs of children at various ages, as well as the educational goals of the school.

The Morningside Public Library mission which emphasizes the "personal, educational, and professional needs . . . [of] community residents . . . and supporting students at all academic levels . . ." places the library in a strong educational role that should be apparent in the content of the program. Knowing that the priority ranking of an objective is high, for example, informs the librarian that programs with a lesser priority may need to be dropped or modified should the final cost exceed available resources. This particular objective has far-reaching importance for a smooth-working relationship with an important constituency. Because of this, the library director may prefer to make the initial contact with the school's superintendent(s), if they have not had previous discussions concerning mutual goals. The program also needs the endorsement of the school administration and the full cooperation of the school library media staff, if the resources committed to meeting this objective are not to be wasted. In addition, the program should be an enjoyable activity for the children, compatible with learning objectives of the teachers, flexible in its scheduling, and visible to parents.

A timetable will allow the planner to proceed in an organized manner and to report progress on the objective at various stages. A timetable for this program might resemble the following:

1. Contact school administration for an appointment to discuss the feasibility of this program (by February 1)
2. In consultation with representative staff and school librarians, develop a draft of orientation activities for each grade that are also compatible with learning objectives. Enlist suggestions for scheduling (by April 1)
3. Develop a detailed draft with more exact estimates of staff time, facilities, materials, and equipment the library must commit for this activity. Prepare a tentative schedule for the next school year (by April 15)
4. Present draft to supervising librarian for suggestions and approval (by April 15)
5. Send school superintendent or designate the draft for suggestions and approval (by May 1)
6. Send final draft and promotional materials to schools (by August 1 or date requested).

Planning Steps

Each of the following elements should be addressed before presenting the program, but these steps are not necessarily to be completed in turn.

Content. The goal—to increase general awareness of resources and services available to county residents—should determine the content of the program, while the age of the children should determine its range and complexity. The program may support other objectives recommended by the library staff, the teacher, or school librarian provided these do not detract from the major goal. A more complete discussion of the goals and objectives of orientation tours and classes or groups to the library appears later in this chapter.

Awareness of services is best conveyed to children through examples. If story hours are regularly offered, a sample should be part of the program. Titles from a variety of genre may be promoted through booktalks and displays. A discussion on how to use the library should be limited to instructions that children need in order to browse effectively and to check out materials, if that's part of the program. Time should always be allowed for children to explore on their own, for this freedom is also a library resource.

If the library is to be promoted as an interesting place, its special attractions to children of various ages should be considered. For first-graders this could be the depressible book bin into which library materials land once they are pushed through that mysterious slot, and for second-graders, the contents of the display case. Fourth-graders are generally impressed with the out-of-town telephone directories and with a microprint image of the first page of the local newspaper issued during the year (or the day) of their birth.

In planning the content of the program, the responsibilities of staff who are indirectly as well as directly involved should be identified. If the program impinges upon the work of staff other than children's, this should be cleared with the supervisors involved. For example, the circulation staff must be prepared for the possible confusion a group of active children can create through lost library cards or unpaid fines. They must be able to respond intelligently to telephone calls about the program from school personnel and to children who ask for "the red book about dinosaurs the lady talked about yesterday." If staff understand that the objective of the program is to encourage new users, they are more apt to be sympathetic to behaviors otherwise considered inappropriate. This may be the first library visit for many children, and the tone that is set will determine whether or not they wish to return. As part of the planning, staff suggestions should be encouraged and acted upon whenever possible. Consequently, they should share in the credit for the program's success.

Measurement and Evaluation. One of the essential parts of any program or service is its evaluation. The objectives should provide the basis for measurement as well as the focus of the report. Some possible measures for this program are:

1. Number of participants, both children and adults
2. Number of new borrowers
3. Circulation of materials by type or class, compared to previous month or year
4. Reference transactions compared to previous period.

If output measures are used, statistics from this program would contribute to annual visits per capita, circulation per capita, in-library materials use per capita, program attendance per capita, reference transactions per capita, and registrations as percentage of population. Valuable as this "hard" evidence is, it is only an indication of success. "What was the impact of the program on the audience?" is at the heart of evaluation even though it is impossible to measure. At best, such evaluation is only fragmentary. Nevertheless, the report of individual programs should not ignore the evaluative comments made by the audience and the library staff. The following sources of such evidence for this program might include the following:

1. Comments of children and teachers attending the program
2. Follow-up contact with teachers four to six weeks after the visit
3. Staff observations
4. Description of a typical incident revealing that progress toward the goal has been made (or not made).

The evaluation by the library staff can be extremely valuable, as they have a more informed basis for comparison and less obligation to be polite than the audience. In addition to recording the name of the school, teacher, grade, and titles promoted, a brief narrative description of what was or was not effective can provide the basis for improvement. No matter how satisfied the users were, it is a rare program that cannot be improved, either in content or presentation.

Promotion. Programs for children must be promoted to the children or to their caregivers or both. If this program is to succeed, all levels of school personnel, from the administration to the school secretary, need information. Classroom teachers have a critical role and, at the very least, need printed information on what the library is prepared to offer their students. This may be conveyed through a letter or brochure describing the program and reinforced, if possible, by an in-person appearance at a faculty meeting.

In any program where information is given to children, libraries should provide the same information in written form to an influential adult—teacher, school librarian, or parent. In keeping with the goal of this program, something concrete should go home with the child, e.g., a brochure or bookmark that lists some of the services available and the location and hours of the library and its various outlets.

Costs. In estimating costs for an activity, overhead charges for space, utilities, etc., are not usually required. Staff time and materials are estimated when the decision is made to offer one desirable program and not the other. The costs of this orientation program would involve the staff time spent in planning and consulting with school and library personnel as well as the time of all levels of staff in preparation and presentation of the program itself. In addition, the costs of promotional materials and any additional library resources acquired solely for this program must also be included. Costs are usually considered in relationship to the number of participants; if the cost per user of this program is two dollars, it would probably be considered a cost-effective activity when the benefits are assessed.

Redesign. This step may occur at any time during the program, as the staff becomes aware of those elements that are not effective. Some of the desirable changes may not be possible with an ongoing program, but these should be identified for those who undertake this or a similar program in the future.

Functions of Basic Services

The provision of information is a common goal of all libraries and one that has received much attention in public libraries over the last two decades. Considerable effort has been made to improve the quality of services and to attract a wider audience. However, the studies conducted on the information-seeking behavior of adults reveal that most people fail to see the library as a place for information; a 1979 study revealed that only five percent of those sampled identified the library as a source of information, although in a survey conducted in 1984, this figure had risen to 29 percent.[2]

The term reference service is often used interchangeably with information service. Rothstein identified its three functions as (1) the provision of information, (2) reading guidance, and (3) library instruction.[3] Using these functions as a point of reference, Aceto found that when librarians who worked with children were asked to define reference service, school librarians emphasized library skills, while public children's librarians gave reading guidance the highest priority; for neither group was the provision of information of first importance.[4] An examination of school and children's courses in library schools also reflects these emphases.

Adult services educators and others have been exploring a fourth function, stimulation, and its place in the continuum of library service. Based on the work of Margaret E. Monroe, stimulation encompasses public relations and those strategies and activities that build a climate for use. The librarian's task is not only to create an awareness of library services, but also to provide an environment in which users feel secure.[5] On the surface it would appear that children's librarians may have incorporated many aspects of this function into their operations without identifying them as such. It should be emphasized that stimulation as it is used in adult services requires a fuller explanation than can be given here. Children's librarians could profit from monitoring developments in adult services for models and theories that can be applied to their own services.

Provision of Information

In designing information services for children, several factors should be considered: (1) policies, (2) collections, (3) facilities, (4) staff competencies, (5) promotion, and (6) measurement and evaluation.

Policies. For the school-aged child, class assignments are a major reason for seeking information. This fact presents both an opportunity and a potential problem for the public library. When children are successful in their search, the perception of the library as a provider of information is strengthened; if unsuccessful, they may view the library as inadequate or as a source of frustration. Some libraries have developed defensive policies covering school assignments that discriminate against children. When the answer to the question, "Is this for a school assignment?" is "Yes," the child is routinely referred to her or his school library. In attempting to use general reference services, some children have been sent automatically to the children's room before being able to voice their requests. Both of these situations are library versions of "shooting oneself in the foot." If we expect children to become adults with favorable attitudes toward libraries or to view the library as a source of information, we have to do better than that. The role of the children's librarian in these situations is that of an advocate.

The business of school-aged children is education, and libraries should approach their school-related needs as seriously as those of a professional or businessperson. Businesspeople are not expected to exhaust their company's resources before turning to the public library, nor are their requests routinely judged for compatibility with the library's goals. Admittedly, taxpayers are supporting both the public school and the public library, and they expect the resources of each to be appropriate to their respective institutional goals. But, because of their differences in goals, school librarians seek out information that has curricular value, whereas public librarians take a community view in developing a collection that can serve a broader array of needs. Children cannot be expected to understand that each library selected *Black Indians: A Hidden Heritage* (Katz) for different reasons, that the public library doesn't have the fourth-grade arithmetic textbook, or the school library collection doesn't include a specialized and expensive title on ballet. Care must be taken that the staff not convey the impression that some requests made by children are not legitimate. Children are quick to learn that a request for *Wind in the Willows* puts a happy glow on the children's librarian's face, while one for the skeleton of a cat evokes a different reaction. Serving the educational needs of children benefits the community certainly not less, and perhaps even more in the long run, than those of the business community. Even though the library's materials may be exhausted by the early seekers, staff interest and concern should not be. Policies for handling school assignments need to be stated and made known to library staff and school personnel alike.

Should children be required to learn how to use the library in order to retrieve the piece of information they need for a school assignment or for a personal interest? Posing this question to a group of librarians usually initiates a lively discussion. Should there be a double standard—one for adults who call the library for information that is located and held for them, and one for children who need information to complete an assignment? One group argues that the quest for information should not be considered an opportunity to teach library skills, unless the major objective of the assignment has been so designated. Others observe that reading guidance is freely given without the intrusion of library skills; therefore, the provision of information should be provided on the same basis. If it is not, librarians may be sending the message that acquiring information is difficult and time-consuming. A counter argument states that equipping children with the skills to find information on their own is freeing them from dependence upon the librarian who, even if available, may not always interpret their needs correctly. All would probably concur that when children show interest in learning to use the library, they should be assisted.

Because the ability to access information will become more, not less, important in the coming years, public librarians cannot avoid responsibility in this endeavor, nor can they sacrifice the traditional service goals of the public library in providing assistance when requested. One compromise might be to support the school's instructional objectives when they are part of a library skills exercise (and the librarian is so informed), but to treat all other requests as standard informational questions.

Another area where policy and role need a clear definition is in open access for children. Should children have access to adult materials and services in order to satisfy their information needs? The policy recommended by the American Library Association after years of wrestling with this question is that access to services and collections should not be based on the age of the user. Justification stems from the following: (1) librarians are not *in loco parentis* in their role,* (2) chronological age as an indicator of maturity is not always valid, and (3) the wide range of family backgrounds and child-rearing practices preclude consensus on what is appropriate for children. Consequently, parents should assume responsibility for restricting (or not) their child's access. The following statements provide an interpretation of the Library Bill of Rights as it pertains to children's access in libraries:

1. Free Access to Libraries for Minors, adopted June 30, 1972, amended July 1, 1981[6]
2. Restricted Access to Library Materials, adopted February 2, 1973, amended July 1, 1981[7]
3. Library-Initiated Programs As a Resource, adopted January 27, 1982[8]
4. Access for Children and Young People to Videotapes and Other Nonprint Formats, adopted June 28, 1989.[9]

These should be consulted in determining access policies for public libraries.

Intellectual freedom policies deal primarily with physical access rather than the quality of service. The library staff still has the responsibility to create a hospitable environment for young information seekers, and to help them find information and materials that match their developmental needs and intellectual levels. A favorite kind of question asked in interviews for children's services positions is one that tests the candidates' understanding of children's information services as well as their attitudes toward an open-access policy. "What would you do if a nine-year-old wanted to check out *The Joy of Sex*?" is such a question. In responding, the candidate should consider whether the child's interest stems from the subject or the particular book, whether the child can read the text, or whether materials on her or his own level would be preferable. Is the child, in fact, seeking answers to an information need? In short, the discussion ensuing should be the same as if the title had been *The Rise and Fall of the Third Reich*. If, after examining titles offered by the librarian, the child insists on the original choice, the librarian follows the library's access policy.

Libraries also find it difficult to develop policies governing how much time should be spent on a user's information need, and how

---

*This statement is more applicable to public libraries, where attendance is voluntary; the role of school librarians is not as clear-cut.

much users should be expected to do on their own. The complexity of the request and the ability of the user also enter into the discussion and preclude setting an absolute rule. These questions lie more securely at the heart of information services than do debates about the proper response to seldom-encountered queries from twelve-year-olds for instructions on how to construct a letter bomb or the various methods of committing suicide.

Collection. The collection and its arrangement transmit a message in themselves, informing children that information exists in various formats and on several levels of difficulty. The practice of integrating juvenile and adult nonfiction into a single collection has been adopted in many libraries. In some combined collections, children's folklore, poetry, biographies, or nonfiction for those below the fourth grade have been removed from this arrangement. Children's librarians are divided on the efficacy of this practice for the good of most children. It has, without question, benefited adults and young adults who profit from easier materials as well as the bright, self-possessed children who are in need of more challenging fare. In addition, it saves space and avoids unnecessary duplication. Staffs prefer it because it means looking in only one location for materials. Investigation of Canadian public libraries adopting this arrangement identified two prerequisites to success:

1. Staff must be committed to the idea; careful planning should precede its implementation, and ... needs of the community [carefully] considered
2. The total collection of books should not exceed 40,000 volumes and ... these should be housed on one floor.[10]

In those libraries where it was considered unsuccessful, the following was noted:

1. Too many titles in one subject area are confusing and overwhelming, especially for children
2. Children do not browse as much; if they come in for project material, they may ignore, or may not be aware of, the fiction books situated in another part of the library
3. During class visits, and sometimes individually, adults resent children at the shelves and noise is often a problem
4. Books shelved on stacks geared to adult borrowers are not easily accessible to children
5. Young people and adults may take the bulk of the children's books, leaving little for younger borrowers.[11]

Children may find the transition from picture books to the juvenile fiction collection much easier than to an integrated nonfiction collection. Some librarians have observed that children use the integrated nonfiction collection for information, but seldom for browsing. This practice may in fact discriminate against children who prefer nonfiction for leisure reading because they may be intimidated by the size of many integrated collections and the difficulty in locating materials on their level. Once collections are combined, it is difficult to separate them again. Children tend to accept the status quo not realizing that another arrangement could be offered. In working with integrated collections, librarians should assess whether these disadvantages exist and, if so, find ways of overcoming their detrimental effects.

Bibliographic access to library collections has usually been a compromise between what is desirable and affordable within existing technologies. Access to children's collections has been improved with the Library of Congress Annotated Card Service, but many libraries have opted not to add subject entries for adult or juvenile fiction titles as an economy measure. Children's needs for a book about divorce or going to the hospital are often best served with a fiction title; consequently, the lack of subject access is not a policy that treats all ages equally. Where funds have permitted, children's librarians have added subject bibliographies, or where time has allowed, they have created their own files for frequently requested subjects. These half measures are both costly and inefficient, especially if they are available only to the staff. As computer-based bibliographic systems develop at the library or system level, children's needs must be stated forcefully during the discussion phase. Even though it may be true that most children's librarians know their collections intimately, few libraries can insure that this knowledge is ever-present or evenly distributed among all staff who serve children.

Many school-related requests are predictable and may be handled by duplicating packets of materials, developing up-to-date vertical file resources, and preparing short bibliographies for staff and children's use. In the past two decades the number of bibliographic aids that improve access to children's collections has noticeably increased. Unfortunately, these are seldom treated in courses on subject bibliography and may not be part of a librarian's preparation. Although frequently expensive, they can increase the efficiency of the staff who use them when a children's specialist is not available, and they can help the children's staff make more effective use of the collection. If they are also available to the public, their cost can usually be justified. A selected list can be found under "Reference/Information" in Appendix C.

Facilities. With the exception of those in central children's departments in large library systems, children's librarians have been reluctant to devote space for a large reference collection. This stems from the nature of children's use and their information needs. Because children's librarians strive to say "yes" as often as possible, they tend to place "in reference only" those materials that provide access to collections or cover a wide range of topics, such as encyclopedias and almanacs. Even here, circulating sets of encyclopedias are considered necessary. The need is usually for something to take home, whether the request is made by the child or a parent. Contemporary lifestyles are not conducive to long, uninterrupted periods at the library. As a practical solution, many small or branch libraries have provided a joint adult-children's reference collection, located for easy access to both audiences. Children should be made aware that this resource has also been planned for them. Larger libraries have also established information and referral services, but, without an orientation, children may not understand their functions or realize that the services are available to them; or conversely, they may attempt to use them, then be inadequately served by a staff unprepared to meet their needs.

Staff Competencies. With the promise of information available through computers, as well as the growing use of online catalogs, children's librarians have now an even more important role. They must help children become efficient users of this technology while continuing to be the great motivators that have characterized children's services from the beginning. Regardless of the formats information and bibliographic access take, the reference interview will continue to be the key to effective service.

Although there are similarities between children's and unsophisticated adults' searches for information, there are several differences. First of all, children have probably had less experience with seeking or using information than have most adults; past library experiences may have been limited to recreational reading, giving them only a vague notion that libraries also deal with information of all kinds. Second, children below the fourth grade, unlike adults, tend to state their needs in rather specific terms which are generally more compatible with library subject entries. In the primary grades, children complete exercises that ask them to color the one that is different. By about the fourth grade, the child has learned these lessons well, and no longer asks forthrightly for something about pigeons, but for something about birds. Third, the parent who accompanies the child often assumes the role of the spokesperson. If a lasting relationship with the child is to develop, the staff must consider her or him as an individual, not as an appendage of the parent. Even if a parent initiates the inquiry, the child should be questioned and encouraged to respond. The parent's perception of the information need may be accurate, but concentrating on the child conveys the message that her or his questions will be considered seriously, even without the intervention of an adult.

With these factors in mind, any standard reference interview model can be adapted to children of various ages. One role-playing technique used in sensitizing staff is to stand the "librarian" on a chair, with the "child" looking up, asking for help. Taylor identified five filters through which a question passes and from which librarians select significant data to aid them in their search. Although these emerged from a study involving special librarians, they are also useful to children's librarians:

1. Determination of subject
2. Objective and motivation
3. Personal characteristics of inquirer
4. Relationship of inquiry description to file organization
5. Anticipated or acceptable answers.[12]

Adapting this process to children, we might enumerate the steps in this way:

1. What is the subject of the request?
2. Why does the child want the information?
3. What is the age, grade, or reading ability of the child?
4. Explore ramifications of the request by suggesting available library resources
5. What will the child accept?

Much of the frustration experienced by both librarian and the nine-year-old boy in the following example could have been averted had the librarian followed such a process.

Librarian	Are you finding what you're looking for?
Child	Yeah, . . . you got any books on art?
Librarian	Yes, we do . . . we have many books on art. Is there a particular period of art you're interested in?
Child	Huh?
Librarian	Are you studying early American art, or the art of the Eskimo, or something like that?
Child	No, we studied Eskimos *last* year.
Librarian	Is this a project for school or are you interested in learning more about art for yourself?
Child	Oh, it's for *school.* I'm not very good in art.
Librarian	What grade are you in school?
Child	Fourth.

Librarian	Are you studying any particular country now at school?
Child	Yes! Japan.
Librarian	Are you looking for Japanese art?
Child	No, we haven't had that yet. We're doing haiku.
Librarian	Have you done any watercolor in the way or style of the Japanese painters?
Child	Teacher says we can't do watercolor until after Christmas.
Librarian	Would you like art books on how to learn how to draw or maybe books on famous paintings like the Mona Lisa, or George Washington?
Child	Oh, art books on winter.
Librarian	Maybe you'd like some pictures of winter scenes— skating, skiing, or snow falling?
Child	Well, if they tell how to make snowflakes.
Librarian	You want a book that shows how to make snow-flakes? How to cut them out of paper, perhaps?
Child	Yeah. My group has to decorate the bulletin board next month and teacher said you have art books that can help.

Step 1: What is the subject? Our librarian's first response indi-cated a positive attitude toward probable success which is essen-tial in dealing with children. Had she considered that art in a child's experience usually involves a product, she might have asked: "Do you want to make something [handicrafts] or do you want pictures of famous paintings or statues?" The child would have probably stated that he wanted to make something, and may even have volunteered what it was.

Step 2: Why is it needed? Librarians don't agree on whether the user should be asked directly the purpose of the information, or, in the case of children, their age or grade in school, but chil-dren are usually more than willing to share both types of informa-tion about themselves. When the librarian asked the child if the information was for a project at school, she had not yet identified the subject. Even so, had she asked the following question, much time could have been saved: "What, exactly, is your assignment (or project)?"

Step 3: What is the child's age or grade and reading ability? Knowing the grade is probably more informative than the age; determining ability is a sensitive matter. In some instances this is better delayed until Step 5 when materials of varying difficulty can be given to the child for his inspection. Information about the child's level of expertise might be learned by asking the following questions: "Do you like to work with paper?" and "Have you had much experience with decorating bulletin boards?" Even though some excellent materials may be too difficult for the child to use independently, his access to assistance from a parent, teacher, or older sibling could be determined.

Step 4: Explore ramifications of the request. The librarian in our example did engage in this step, but unfortunately did so before completing the first three steps. Although the child may be satisfied that the request has been properly identified, the information need may actually be somewhat broader. The librarian who knows the organizational system can suggest possible ramifications of the subject based on her perception of the child's need. Is how to cut paper snowflakes all he needs to know to create a bulletin board? The librarian is aware of magazines with suggestions for decorating snowflakes, books that tell how to design displays or create letters, and films that demonstrate paper art. In this step, the child could have been led to redefine or broaden his stated information need to include suggestions for winter bulletin boards, a subject closer to his actual information need.

Step 5: What will the child accept? The librarian should be aware that the child probably has a vision of the answer when he first asks the question, and that there may be limitations surrounding the use of the information. The vision may have changed during the interview process, but the limitations of time will still be operating. If the information is needed for tomorrow, materials in circulation cannot be suggested. If a slide projector is not available, that format cannot be considered. After several resources have been identified, the librarian can assist the child in making the best selection by characterizing each briefly as they relate to his information need.

Promotion. Asking children who seek answers "Is this for school?" is legitimate, but unless children realize that requests emanating from personal interests are also welcomed, they may consider the library an extension of school to be dismissed once the educational experience is over. Another preconception which may be all too correct is that libraries deal only with information found in books. In promoting information service to children, care should be taken to correct or avoid giving either of these impressions.

Selected questions with answers can be posted on the library's bulletin board, included in a children's or school newspaper, or used as the subject of a bookmark. In one community, sixth-graders were asked to identify a non-school-related question they wanted answered before their class visited the public library. The visit was scheduled when the library was closed to the general public, and the staff assisted the children in finding answers to their questions. Displaying reference or nonfiction aids with samples of intriguing questions answered by them will help children make the connection between information and libraries.

Measurement and Evaluation. Any request that requires use of library resources or staff competencies is considered a reference question. Requests that fall into this component of reference service are more easily correlated with adult reference services that are measured by reference transactions per capita and reference completion rate. Children's staff may wish to record requests for information separately for a period of time in order to evaluate the adequacy of the collection and competencies of the staff in providing quality information services.

Reading Guidance

The early leaders in children's work considered reading guidance to be at the heart of their services; "the right book for the right child at the right time" was part of the credo handed down to new children's librarians. Reading guidance involves the process of connecting readers (and viewers) to materials they want or need, whether the need has been expressed or not, and whether it exists now or will exist in the future. It requires a broad collection selected with children's interests in mind and a library staff that knows it intimately, is eager to know the child, and has a working schedule that allows the necessary time. Few libraries can ensure that these ideal conditions are present at all times; nevertheless, they serve as a goal toward which progress can be made.

The term guidance came to have a negative connotation during the 1960s, as some librarians viewed it as a form of manipulation. Awareness that it can be used to such ends underlines the librarian's professional relationship to the child. If librarians avoid this activity for whatever reason, they leave it up to mass-market advertising and to parents, teachers, and peers whose experiences with literature may be dated or limited.

Overall, there are few activities or programs offered in libraries for children that are not preliminary to or part of the guidance services, whether they are booktalks in classrooms, displays on a particular topic, or programs for parents. All encourage the users to avail themselves of this service. Reading guidance is more than responding to the request, "I want a good book to read," although this may initiate the process. In an ongoing relationship, the librarian is aware of what the child has read and enjoyed or rejected, and so has knowledge of the child's preferences in library materials. The task is not merely to provide more of the same materials, but to help the child gain experience with literature he or she may enjoy once introduced to it. Progressing from known preferences, the librarian can help the child to the next level of complexity or to widen her or his interests. In an ideal situation there are opportunities for the child to talk about the titles he or she has read and enjoyed.

There are no standard patterns for reading that every nine-year-old should follow, although librarians are concerned that children have the opportunity to sample a wide range of materials. Serendipity is an element in reading guidance, for no matter how skilled the librarian or how well-known the child, there will be responses that are totally unpredictable. The uniqueness of each child is to be respected, whether in choosing materials or in refusing assistance.

A considerable amount of reading guidance is done through parents and other adults in a child's life. In the Connecticut Documentation Study, the overall percentage of reading guidance requests from adults for children was surprisingly low: approximately one-fourth to one-fifth of the total. Even so, this type of request ranked second only to the school-related question.[13] Many requests for specific fiction titles not on the shelves do evolve, of course, into this category as librarians suggest related titles.

In planning for reading guidance, several factors need to be considered: (1) the collection and its access, (2) staff competencies, (3) promotion, and (4) measurement and evaluation.

Collection Access. If reading guidance is a process that encourages readers to broaden their interests and to move from their tried-and-true level to the highest level they will accept, the collection, both fiction and nonfiction, must provide for a wide range of tastes and abilities. Librarians sometimes categorize titles as (1) bait books (easy to read, with wide appeal, some may be of marginal quality), (2) popular reading (those with both child and librarian approval), and (3) special titles (those of unusual quality and appealing to a smaller number of children and to discerning adults). In collection building, librarians need to consider their own biases and responsibilities to the community. There is a tendency for librarians to find children who like to read what the librarians themselves enjoy, calling it "reading guidance." At the other end of the scale, librarians must assume the responsibility for selection delegated to them and decide what materials demanded by a vocal few are not appropriate for the collection. The proportion of each category of book should be a conscious decision in accordance with the overall goals of the library. A collection with a majority of bait titles may win an easy first acceptance and temporarily boost circulation, but unless there are a sizable number of titles in the next level and encouragement to read them, children may go back to television. Not all children will be able or willing to try large numbers of special titles, but they should be made aware of them. If children leave childhood without having read *The Hobbit*, it should not be because their librarians did not introduce it. In those libraries with inadequate staffing, the collection itself may provide the only reading guidance available.

When the service emphasizes reading guidance, libraries may be tempted to arrange the fiction collection in reader interest groupings: animal stories, mysteries, family stories, etc. In addition to the difficulties of categorizing some titles, librarians have identified the following disadvantages of these groupings:

1. Discourage use of catalog
2. Further children's tendencies to read only in one genre, thus impairing efforts to widen interests
3. Require more space
4. Make finding specific titles more difficult unless location is marked in catalog and materials.

The following are among the advantages:

1. Provide some assistance to users when libraries are poorly staffed or subject access for fiction titles lacking
2. Satisfy the casual browser.

Adding tapes with symbols that designate genre—mystery, science fiction, etc.—to the books' spines, and shelving in alphabetical order, offer a compromise to a subject arrangement.

Some librarians have experimented with taped booktalks. A cassette and recorder are offered to the child who asks, "Do you have a good book to read?" and the librarian can not assist at that moment. The computer can also be programmed to call up a selected number of annotated titles by subject for the child's consideration. Neither is a substitute for a librarian.

The current demands made on collections go beyond requests for titles in specific genre, or those about a particular ethnic group. There may be a need to identify materials that include characters with a disability, deal with a contemporary problem, or are written on a low reading level. In an effort to supplement the catalog's subject access, libraries have provided in-house lists for popular topics. In considering these stopgap measures used in lieu of full subject access, a school specialist suggests that libraries catalog for reading guidance.[14] Not only should new taxonomies for reading guidance be developed, but also systems should be devised to permit searching on several characteristics at once: number of pages, level of difficulty, character types, situations, etc. In lieu of this kind of access, the reader is referred to

"Reading Guidance" in Appendix C for a list of published bibliographies compiled for this purpose.

Staff Competencies. Reading guidance involves a more intimate knowledge of the collection than any other library service. Knowing the focus of a videotape, several nonfiction titles that actively promote the scientific method, a periodical's range of topics, or the effectiveness of a reading guidance aid for a particular request can be acquired only with diligence and effort. "Knowing the collection" is the accolade given children's librarians who achieve this level of competency. Having an awareness of children's probable reading levels and interests by age or grade is a good start in getting to know individual children, and this information can usually be found in a standard children's literature textbook.[15] The approximate reading ability of an individual child may be discovered by asking the title of the last book she or he read and enjoyed.

Some publishers and reviewing aids now provide a readability score for trade books, which is determined by applying a formula to a number of sample pages, but librarians should treat these scores only as indicators. One formula that is commonly used is the Fry Readability Graph. What is measured are the number of syllables or letters and the sentence length; not measured are reader interest, complexity of the vocabulary, the sophistication of the literary elements, or the appeal of the format. By considering all of these factors, including word and sentence length, experienced children's librarians become surprisingly adept at estimating readability. They may have a tendency, however, to overestimate the abilities of children because they interact more often with the better readers.

Knowledge of children's interests and the collection does not ensure that librarians will be successful in reading guidance; they must also be approachable. Although children should be granted freedom to browse without being smothered by the staff, assistance should be offered when it is obviously needed. By observing body language or making eye contact, librarians can usually spot the children who need assistance. Children are more likely to approach the librarian who gets up from behind a desk and wanders to the shelves, for they have been conditioned not to bother adults when they are reading. When making recommendations, titles of varying difficulty should be presented for the child's acceptance or rejection. If children find it awkward to refuse the librarian's recommendations, they may not ask for assistance again. This situation can be eased by telling children where to leave the materials they don't want, and to ask for further help if none of the suggested titles are suitable.

At the center of one-on-one reading guidance is the 30-second booktalk which is best delivered at the stacks with volume in hand. Enthusiasm is more important than polish, for it is necessary to hook the reader in as short a time as possible. Many elements can catch a child's attention: conflict (with parents, siblings, peers), running away, fear, need for affection, magic, or a character one can cheerfully dislike. The delivery should be given in a conversational tone and with spontaneity. Compare the following two examples using the same popular title:[16]

When her mother told her that they were leaving the city and buying a house in the suburbs, Anastasia threatened to kill herself by jumping out the window . . . as soon as she finished her chocolate pudding, of course. They lived on the first floor so it was unlikely she would have been successful. Her parents said they were doing it for Sam, her baby brother, who needed more space—but Anastasia considered it a disaster for it meant changing schools, leaving her friends, and living in a house identical to all the others, and with small rooms that had no bookcases. It was then that her parents said *she* could help choose the house. Even though Anastasia sometimes lost arguments with her parents (who doesn't?), she always managed to gain at least *one* advantage in the process—and you can be sure she always made the most of it.

Anastasia's father was a professor at the University; her mother was an artist; and she had a two-and-half-year-old brother, Sam. She lived in a city apartment which she loved. When her mother told her they were going to move to the suburbs, Anastasia was very upset . . . but she learned that even the suburbs could be interesting. She had a wonderful room in a tower. And she made friends with senior citizens in a retirement home whom she invited to a party at her house . . . without telling her parents. She discovered that some of the kids she met were quite interesting, so gradually, she stopped seeing so much of her best friend in the city.

In the first example, conflict with parents and Anastasia's personality are the hook. The second example tells too much plot, mentions too many characters, gives unnecessary detail, and manages to make this intensely interesting title sound somewhat ordinary.

Librarians can hone their skills and broaden their repertoire of suitable titles by comparing their usual response to a particular reading guidance request with the responses given by other librarians and the suggestions in the reader's advisory aids. One such exercise revealed that children's librarians tend to suggest the same titles repeatedly to the exclusion of others equally or more appropriate, and, at times, to recommend unsuitable titles.[17]

Promotion. In addition to on-the-floor booktalks, users should expect regular displays that feature a range of materials on a topic, and promotional materials such as reading lists (If you liked *Pippi Longstocking*, try these) and theme-oriented book-marks that bring together titles from a variety of genres. Even though reading guidance is accepted as an integral part of library services to children and parents, it should be enhanced by printed materials and talks to groups of all ages. Adults who have had little experience in libraries may not be aware that they can receive this service on behalf of their children.

Measurement and Evaluation. Libraries using output measures will have to decide how this service should be measured, whether as reference transactions per capita, browsers fill rate, subject/author fill rate, or title fill rate. Reading guidance activities may occur whenever children seek staff assistance while browsing, or the librarian initiates the process. Because staff assistance is involved, reference transaction per capita may be the most appropriate measure to use. Should the children's staff wish to evaluate their competence as well as the adequacy of the collection for this service, they could record reading guidance transactions separately. The requests and the titles recommended would both need to be logged during the sampling period.

Library Instruction

The third component of reference service, library instruction, is aimed at helping users acquire those skills necessary to identify, locate, and use library materials effectively. There are several advantages to users acquiring basic library skills. Those competencies that enable children to find what they want at least part of the time bolster their self-esteem. This feeling of power may be a factor in their continuing use of the library. When users are able to cope with their more routine information needs, librarians can devote their attention to those requiring a higher level of assistance. Children's librarians need to use opportunities available to them to help children gain competence in using libraries, but without insisting that they do. As online catalogs replace card and microform catalogs, librarians will find children to be the most enthusiastic learners of new technology and generous in sharing their knowledge with wary adults.

Factors to Consider. Library media skills are a primary concern for librarians in the elementary schools, a fact that doesn't free the public library from all responsibility for this component; at the very least they must help children make the transition from the arrangement used by their school library to that followed by the public library. Whether the school's program is an informal outline of lessons to be completed or a detailed plan with competency-based learning objectives for each grade, the public library's staff would find it useful to examine this program before determining its own use policies regarding school assignments. Individual tutoring has proven to be a most effective method in teaching library skills. Given only when the child shows interest, this instruction can build solidly on what the child already knows. While neither appropriate each time a child seeks assistance, nor possible given the normal staffing of public libraries, one-on-one attention given by the children's staff can make a valuable contribution to the child over the course of several years.

Should elementary schools not be staffed with librarians, principals or teachers may ask children's librarians to assume responsibility for library skills. In determining a workable policy regarding the public library's involvement with this request, the children's librarian should understand that schools may have a different concept of the term "library media skills." The children's librarian usually considers the ability to locate information through the library's catalog or periodical indexes as the major, if not only, objective. The school librarian, on the other hand, also considers the child's ability to make effective use of information found through standard reference aids from dictionaries to atlases, various audiovisual materials, and computers and their software. More emphasis is placed on the skills necessary to locate, select, use, and understand media.[18] The only aspect of this program that the public library should attempt to teach, if it proves necessary, is the use of the catalog and, for older children, the *Readers' Guide*. Other skills are better learned within the regular classroom or school library under the direction of the teacher who can integrate the activities into the instructional program.

Whenever the public library attempts to teach catalog skills, the children's librarian should insist that the children be able to alphabetize or the exercise will end in frustration. When children are brought to the public library for this activity (1) the visit should not be their only one during the year, (2) the instruction should not overwhelm the children by its length or complexity, and (3) children should be given time to browse. The advantages of having a school librarian on the faculty should be stressed whenever possible. Several of the aids listed under "Library Instructional Activities/Resources" in Appendix C include activities that could, with adaptation, be used by children's librarians in library instruction.

Staff Competencies. Young children are frequently awed by the ability of the librarian to pick out the wanted title from thousands. Flattering as this may be, the librarian must be ready and willing to share this expertise with children whenever it seems appropriate. In all instruction, librarians should have their objectives clearly in mind. A few concepts common to all libraries could be regularly emphasized in assisting children:

1. "Like" things are arranged together
2. Numbers or some combination of letters and numbers are used to insure that "like" subjects are shelved together
3. The catalog is the directory that gives the call number (or address) of the item
4. Subject catalogs are similar to the yellow pages of the telephone directory.

The role of the librarian is more like that of a tour guide than a teacher. Children, like adults, are sometimes in a hurry, nonreceptive to extraneous information, or impatient with the librarian's questions. Their moods should be respected. Whenever informal instruction is attempted, the librarian should verbalize the steps taken to answer the request and invite the child to ask questions about the process. If tutoring is attempted, the instruction should be given in very small doses, with the child aware that the librarian is there to assist at any step along the way.

Promotion. Many library activities offer opportunities to develop or reinforce library skills. Displays involving nonfiction materials can spotlight the fact that classification numbers are equated with subjects. In helping children locate titles on a given topic, comment on the fact that materials are grouped together by the use of numbers. In designing bookmarks by subject, include the various classification numbers and subject headings under which similar titles can be found. Whenever signs and labels for the children's area are planned, the potential for learning should be kept in mind.

A few libraries have taken a more systematic but informal approach to teaching library skills. In the 1960s, one library system developed a series of flyers for the public to use or take home. Among the topics explained were the information from the title page, how to use an index, the elements on the catalog card, and a selected Dewey Classification outline keyed to subjects of general interest to children and adults. A self-shelving program was also developed for children; when checking in their books, children were invited to reshelve them if they wished. After demonstrating three times that they had mastered the task, they were given a button to wear and permitted to reshelve their books whenever they chose to do so. The assumption was that children who know how to reshelve can also find titles they want.[19] Another possibility is to use the Cataloging in Publication data to explain to children that similar titles can be found under subject headings preceded by Arabic numerals.

Measurement and Evaluation. Whether library instruction is considered reference transactions per capita or program attendance per capita will probably depend on the situation in which instruction is given. Unless the library isolates this component for promotion by inviting users to avail themselves of instruction, either by the librarian or through a programmed exercise, measuring this component separately will be difficult. Further evaluation may not be useful because mastery of the library's catalog may be due to the school library's instruction rather than to any program or assistance given by the public library. Librarians should also be aware that when children's library skills improve, their requests for information and reading guidance may decrease.

Traditional Programs for Children

While basic services reach patrons on a one-to-one basis, library programming attempts to reach individuals through group activities. A group situation, like storytelling, may be used because the presence of other participants increases the enjoyment of the individual, or it simply may be more efficient in terms of service delivery.

Several traditional programs are associated with children's services: story hours for all ages, film programs, booktalks—whether at school or in the library—reading clubs, orientation tours, and class or group visits to the library. These activities may be offered occasionally, on request, or as series throughout the year. In the past several decades children's librarians have increased both the range and number of programs offered. The programming aids listed in Appendix C are designed to help librarians and other adults improve their effectiveness in this area.

The major objectives of programming are to introduce literature and to promote the use of library materials. In addition, a program may provide an experience or information for children or adults unavailable in any other format. The program becomes a library resource, worthy of support on the same basis as the purchase of a recording, film, or book. A presentation by a children's illustrator offers a child an opportunity to interact with a creative mind, an experience that other library resources cannot provide.

Selecting Programs

Several factors must be considered in selecting those programs that are the most appropriate for a particular community. Again, the goals and objectives of the library in general and the children's department in particular should guide the selection of programs offered. If a program designed to attract new borrowers reaches only the library regulars week after week, it could be considered a failure, even though the attendance is high and the comments favorable. There may be several reasons why this program does not attract its target audience. The two areas that should be reevaluated first are the promotion given and the time the program is scheduled. Discontinuing popular programs for the library regulars in favor of ones intended for a harder-to-reach and smaller audience—e.g. children with hearing disabilities— entails some risk for the library in terms of public relations. To continue the first is to respond to demand, while opting for the second is to consider need. It is here that goals and objectives, especially if developed through a community-based procedure, can be used to select and justify programs that will make a lasting contribution to the community.

If one of the objectives of the children's department is "to increase the use of the nonfiction resources by ten percent during the coming year," the following activities might be considered in fulfilling this objective:

1. Offer a series of eight science programs twice a year for grades four to six
2. In booktalks to elementary school classes, use nonfiction titles for half of the titles presented
3. Offer a four-part film series on nature subjects, correlated with booktalks and exhibits
4. Provide displays of easy nonfiction for preschool parents' meetings and conferences.

In deciding which activities should be undertaken, both community and library resources should be considered.

Community Resources. If the YMCA plans to host a program series for children to view and discuss nature films, the library could drop this activity and offer to contribute to the YMCA's program. The library's limited resources could then be allocated to the other activities.

Library Resources. Assuming that all of the possible activities are equally desirable, the children's staff must consider the collection, staff, space, and equipment required for each. For some alternatives, the collection would need strengthening; others might require space or equipment not currently available. If the staff lacks the expertise to undertake a desirable program, the use of non-children's staff or paid or volunteer talent would have to be considered. Libraries with ongoing program activities usually keep a file of program plans that outline materials, staff, and preparation needed for each. This file is invaluable in reducing planning time. See Program Resource Form-Program Outline in Appendix B for an example. Other forms useful in programming can also be found in Appendix B, Program Resource File (King County Library System), which evaluates performances of volunteers or paid performers, as well as Program Monitor Report for Central Library (Queens Borough Public Library) and Program Evaluation Form (Seattle Public Library), both of which provide a statistical record and allow for a critical evaluation.

Program Design

Basic to the design of all programming in children's services is the necessity to consider the needs and characteristics of the intended audience, whether toddlers, children with special disabilities, or parents. The materials and activities selected for the individual program, the space and equipment requirements, the techniques used to promote the program or series, and the frequency and time of day it is offered are all considered in terms of the audience and its needs.

It is easy to overlook the needs of children who fall outside the mainstream. Many children who are visually or physically disabled are able to benefit from programs designed for the regular audience and should be encouraged to do so. Some children's librarians have even learned to sign stories for deaf children. There are children, however, who are better served with a special program designed to their needs. Stories and films paced for regular audiences may be too fast for children who are mentally retarded. These children would profit from slower-paced programs with fewer activities, and with more opportunities to talk to an attentive librarian. Their caregivers should be asked to suggest the types of activities that would be appreciated. Some of these children have artistic talent and would be pleased to have their work exhibited in the library.

Children under six and school-age children new to the library require shorter sessions and more variety. As a result, puppetry and crafts are often integrated into story hours (which may be more appropriately called "storytimes"). The complexity of the stories, as well as their length, must be matched to the developmental level of the average listener in the group. The sophistication of "The Swineherd" makes it an inappropriate choice for the average audience of elementary school children, even though there may be a few listeners in the group who would appreciate its satire. Titles for booktalking to a group of reluctant readers need a preponderance of proven favorites. *The Phantom Tollbooth* may delight sixth-graders in a gifted class, but *The Celery Stalks at Midnight* would be more suitable for a class of slower learners.

If interaction with the programmer is an objective, the physical space should make this possible. Young children are more comfortable in a cozy environment that can be created by the use of screens in an auditorium or a quiet corner in the children's area. Older children need space in group activities or behavior problems are likely to result, thus diverting attention from the programmer.

The length of the individual program is dependent on the attention span of the audience, as well as their experience with library programming. Toddlers accompanied by an adult are usually content in a group situation for 15 to 20 minutes. The four- and five-year-olds can enjoy programs that last a half-hour, longer if a physical activity concludes the session. Programs for school-age children who have been conditioned by the school routine can run from 35 to 45 minutes or more depending on the audience's age and the type of activity. Film programs are generally longer than storytelling sessions, unless the latter is interspersed with interactive games, music, or puppetry.

The duration of the program series depends to a large extent on the staff resources at the library. Few libraries can support storyhours or film programs for any age group all year around and maintain the quality that attracts and holds an audience accustomed to the sophisticated fare of the mass media. In addition, there are periods during the year when efforts expended in a program series simply do not produce an adequate return, e.g., the first three weeks of the school year and the period between Thanksgiving and Christmas Day.

The family situations in which children live must also be kept in mind. Parents in the work force, unsafe streets, and lack of transportation are only a few of the factors that affect children's attendance at programs. Programs for latchkey children need options that reflect a range of needs. Children accustomed to libraries and their services and programs may be able to interact with library resources with only a minimum of assistance; others of the same age without this experience may need a structured situation, with activities initiated and led by an adult. Preschoolers in families where parenting skills are poorly developed would benefit from programs in which the parents were also involved. The stories and activities chosen for these children should initially be quite simple, because these children lack experience with literature.

When staff and materials are limited, librarians feel a special obligation to design the programs they do offer to make the greatest possible impact on the audience. One common device is using a program theme in booktalks, story hours, film programs, and reading clubs. Not only is this aesthetically satisfying but it also makes a more lasting impression on the participants because each program element, from promotion to activity, reinforces the theme. Perhaps it should be said that a theme is not obligatory for each and every program element. In a booktalk program, children would benefit more from hearing about a fascinating title not on the theme, than a dull one that is. Using a similar routine from week to week in a program series is another device, one that is especially important with preschool audiences. Knowing that "this is when we sing a song" is not only comforting, but also increases the child's anticipation and enjoyment.

Promotion of Library Programs

Promotion and public relations are terms used to describe the advertisement of library services and programming to target audiences and the general public. Simpson has offered the following distinction between these terms:

> Promotion involves getting the word out that the library is offering this program or is making that resource available to its patrons. It includes advertising, publicity, in-house displays, regular features in the print and electronic media, and even "word of mouth" campaigns. ... Public relations is more truly communication in that it is a two-way process dependent on feedback in both directions. PR is dialogue with the community, while promotion is more of a monologue where the library simply articulates what it is and what it is doing.[20]

When excellent programs are paired with effective promotion, the effort invested in both reaps benefits. There is no benefit, of course, in promoting programs of poor quality. It is also a waste of resources to develop the perfect program series if no one attends. With so many voices in society clamoring for attention, the wise librarian plans promotion as an integral part of programming.

Many larger libraries have a staff member who assumes responsibility for public relations. That person has developed contacts with the local media and is knowledgeable about their preferences for format and content of news releases as well as their deadlines. The basic facts about the program are given to this specialist who prepares appropriate releases for the various media. He or she may also be adept at designing posters, bookmarks, or flyers that advertise various library events or may oversee their production.

In smaller libraries, each department is usually responsible for its own media releases and contacts. Children's librarians may have an advantage here because their audience is an endless source of human interest stories and photographic subjects. Many local radio and TV stations still carry public service messages and should be routinely notified of upcoming events. One question that usually arises when children's librarians write their own copy is, "Who is this addressed to, the child or the adult?" In a study of children's public library use and nonuse the following recommendations were made:

> Publicity about collections and programs for children under ten should be aimed at the parents as much as at the children through newspapers, community organizations, local radio and television . . . for children ten and over [it] should, for the most part, be aimed directly at the child through flyers distributed in schools as well as the methods mentioned above.[21]

Because libraries cannot afford to give every offering extensive publicity, they need to select contacts most likely to be effective with the target audience. Summer reading clubs should be promoted to the children at school and to the parents and teachers through PTA meetings and school newsletters. Promotion through the media is good public relations for the library, but is of secondary importance in reaching the audience for this program.

In writing a news release, the who, what, when, where, and how information is still a good rule to follow, articles with incomplete information are not likely to be used. The most difficult type of program to promote is probably the single event, such as a performance by an author or illustrator. One expert has recommended the following procedure:

> [Have] at least three press releases: one to inform the public that the library is planning a particular program, the second to remind the public that the program will be presented one week hence, and the third to show what a marvelous time was had at the program. This last should have black and white pictures or glossies to accompany it. Newspaper deadlines are often seven to thirteen days prior to publication . . . Your press releases are more apt to be accepted if they are couched in simple clear English and are to the point. If the editor has less work to do with your work he will accept it more readily. Let your first sentence be provocative. The second should contain the library's name and the name of the program. The third and fourth can tell something about the . . . subject matter. The rest tells the time, place, date, whether tickets are needed, age limitations. Don't get flowery, but try to transmit your enthusiasm in the article.[22]

There are a number of texts available to guide the novice in becoming more proficient in library promotion. Several are listed in the bibliography.

Reevaluation of Traditional Programs

In some quarters the word "traditional," when followed by program or service, has become a pejorative term; in others, the availability and success of traditional programs are standards by which children's services are measured. Even though they have proven successful with previous generations, that doesn't ensure that they will be received favorably by contemporary audiences in every community. They must be periodically evaluated on how well they support the goals of the library.

When library administrators press for innovative programming, the children's staff should reevaluate its schedule of programs before striking out in a new direction. The reasons for this request need to be pinpointed; some of the following may underlie the complaint:

1. The need for a public relations program that captures the public's imagination and gains favorable publicity for the library as whole
2. Traditional programs need to be adapted to address contemporary societal concerns more effectively
3. A particular program is no longer appropriate for the changing community
4. Technology should be considered to reduce staff time in the delivery of programs
5. The programs need to be more cost-effective.

Whether or not criticism has been expressed, these factors, with the exception of the first, should be considered when reevaluating traditional programs. In addition, the children's staff should be alert to the need to protect basic services and to avoid assuming a disproportionate burden for the library's public relations. Some libraries are so over-programmed that children attracted to the library through programming do not receive the basic services implied in the invitation to become library users. Because traditional programs are so widespread and in many libraries so firmly entrenched, the children's staff needs to be aware not only of the planning steps outlined at the beginning of this chapter, but also of the persistent issues surrounding each. These programs will be discussed in terms of their (1) goals, (2) objectives, (3) range and types, (4) issues and concerns, (5) cost-effectiveness, and (6) measurement and evaluation.

Story Hours

Goals and Objectives. In addition to the more general goals for programming, storytelling may (1) introduce audience members to their literary or ethnic heritage, (2) provide a valuable aesthetic experience, (3) improve listening skills and increase vocabulary, and (4) provide an opportunity to exercise imagination. Measurable objectives based on one or more of these goals can be developed during the planning phase. Objectives will also include target figures for attendance, circulation, and the number of library registrations even though success is not necessarily equated with numbers.

Range and Types. When story hours were introduced in the New York Public Library in the early part of the century, the intended audience was school-aged children. In an era that included no radio or television, this popular program quickly achieved a central place in children's library services and children's librarians were carefully trained in the storyteller's art. They also learned to manage groups of children without appearing authoritarian and to design an effective program of stories. The Saturday morning story hour at the local library became a traditional offering.

The decline in popularity of this program as traditionally designed has been attributed to various factors ranging from competition from the mass media to the failure of children's librarians to achieve the degree of mastery needed to attract the contemporary child. In addition, few libraries can allocate the necessary staff resources to offer the program on a year-round basis. Storytelling demands a level of listening skills and involvement from the audience, skills that today's children may not develop as early or as well as previous generations.

Librarians who consider this traditional program worthy of support have made adaptations to fit the needs of their community and the resources of the library. A holiday program as a single event or a four- to six-week series in the late winter months has proven more successful, although it is usually the younger children who attend in greatest numbers. Instead of a Saturday morning, a weekday afternoon has worked well in some communities, while others have broadened their audience with family story hours in the evening. Today's ideal audience for the traditional program may be the residents in retirement homes.

Some librarians have experimented with changing the content of the school-age story hour to appeal to a broader range of interests. For older children who experience a great deal of passive viewing, the opportunity to engage in an activity may be an added attraction in the library program. Learning how to tell stories or present a puppet show, or participating in readers' theatre or creative dramatics are added activities that may increase the story hour's appeal for older children.

To increase children's exposure to this art, storytelling has also been included in other programs given at schools, recreation centers, or during a scheduled visit to the library. One children's librarian responded to a plea from a fourth-grade teacher who found her class unable to attend to a classroom lesson for any length of time. Beginning with short picture book stories, the librarian presented a twenty-minute story session each week for several months, gradually increasing the length and complexity of the stories as she moved from picture books to traditional storytelling. The increase in the children's attention spans carried over to their lessons. This program has been used in several classrooms and with comparable success.[23]

The preschool story hour has been a staple in public library programming since the post-World War II era. Building on a solid educational foundation, this activity meets the needs of three- to five-year-olds for stimulation and builds on their great potential for learning. Adapted to the needs and abilities of this group, the content usually includes two to four picture book stories supplemented with other activities such as fingerplays and exercise games, creative dramatics, a filmstrip story, or a simple craft. An opening and closing routine is also important. When parent education became a recognized need, some libraries designed this program to include parents who learn by the librarian's example how to introduce literature to children.

The difficulty of accommodating very young children at preschool story hours, and the awareness that younger children could benefit from a group activity, encouraged libraries to design toddler programs for eighteen- to thirty-six-month-old children and their parents.[24] Activities are planned that introduce concepts such as colors, sizes, and shapes, or involve repetitive and rhythmic language (songs, nursery rhymes, poems). Flannel board and puppet stories supplement simple picture books. Watching the storyteller try on different kinds of hats or dressing and undressing a doll or teddy bear can be a fascinating experience for toddlers. In some communities programs are scheduled on Saturdays to allow working fathers or mothers to attend with their children.

Issues and Concerns. The most common problem in the library's storytelling programs involves the age range for a particular program. As a standard practice, all promotion for library programs should clearly state the intended age range of the audience. Almost every parent seems convinced that her or his child is precocious and would enjoy a story hour planned for an older age group. In dealing with such a parent, the librarian may agree to let the child attend, provided the parent remains. Should these requests come from a sizable number of parents, however, the librarian should reconsider the range and scheduling of story-telling offerings.

The size of a storytelling audience is impossible to predict in a public library situation unless a control is built into its plan. In story hours for preschoolers where the objectives preclude great numbers, libraries have required that parents preregister their children. For popular activities for the school-age child, tickets given out ahead of time have proven to be a workable solution. In many communities these controls act as barriers to attendance and should be used only as a last resort.

Cost-Effectivenss. To improve the cost-effectiveness of a program the children's staff has three options: (1) increase attendance, (2) reduce staff costs, or (3) reduce the cost of materials. Increasing attendance is not always an option where the benefits of the program depend on a limited number. This is frequently the situation in programs for preschoolers that are designed with child-storyteller interaction as one of the major objectives, or when techniques for introducing literature to children are demonstrated to the parents attending with their children.

Many excellent storytelling programs fail to attract an audience because of the time they are offered. Experimenting with various times or surveying a sampling of parents may be necessary. Some working parents may simply lack the motivation or energy to take children to the library. In order to reach their potential audience, story hours may have to be moved to day care or recreational centers. These programs can also provide the foundation for a workshop designed to train day care staffs to conduct their own literature programs for young children. Day care personnel are also in an excellent position to promote public library resources to parents.

One obvious way to reach a wider audience is to have the program taped for cable television or to videotape a live performance for individual viewing in the library. Librarians have discovered, however, that successful programs using these media demand more than simply taping a live story hour. A different approach and expertise are needed for a successful program when the medium changes. Research findings raise doubt about the effectiveness of televised storytelling, at least for younger children; the ability of preschool children to use and comprehend language showed greater improvement from attending live story hours than from viewing live programs that were televised. Because of the sophistication of the media, film programs were also more effective than the televised story hours.[25]

By their nature, story hours are labor-intensive activities, whether stories are told from memory or presented with a picture book. Every aspect must be planned ahead of time to allow the storyteller freedom to interact with the audience. Preparation for an audience of five is as time-consuming as for twenty-five, but the cost-effectiveness is measured by comparing the cost of the program with the number of attendees. To reduce staff costs, libraries have considered using volunteer or paid talent. In those libraries where programming has been established in the budget as a resource, less resistance is encountered in paying a professional storyteller or puppeteer to present a program. The quality is easier to judge than with volunteer talent, but with both, staff time must be budgeted for planning, promotion, audience control, etc.

Another alternative is to train nonprofessional staff to conduct story hours. Many libraries find this solution a workable one for preschool programs, but less satisfactory when parents or school-age children are part of the audience. If one of the objectives is to promote the use of library resources, it is important that the story-teller be able to capitalize on the rapport established with the audience. Unless she or he is knowledgeable about children's literature or the materials that parents need, an opportunity may be lost.

When the story hour was a standard offering, libraries devoted funds and space for a storytelling collection not only for staff use, but also for patrons who wished to learn this art. Collections that support other contemporary programs should also be considered. Flannel board figures, puppets, and filmstrips are materials to be acquired and reused as program offerings dictate. Several libraries have developed program kits on special themes—such as families, seasons, colors, etc.—for loan to day care centers and other preschool groups. For those materials made in-house, costs may be reduced by using volunteers. In some instances, commercially produced materials may actually be less expensive when staff time is measured. One administrator was overheard to remark that he would be happy to buy the puppets, if only the children's staff would spend more time helping parents.

Measurement and Evaluation. The number of people in attendance contributes to the output measure, program attendance per capita; materials checked out the period before and after the program contribute to circulation per capita; and the number of new borrowers contributes to registrations as a percentage of the population. These figures can be supplemented with comments from staff, children, parents, or caregivers. Many libraries use a standard reporting form that serves multiple uses: information for monthly and annual reports, record of program activities and materials, types of audiences reached, and assessment of effectiveness. An example is provided in Appendix B. Measuring the value of a story hour as an aesthestic experience is difficult, if not impossible, even though staff who observe may have useful comments to offer. Librarians who stay in one community for an extended period of time may someday have the pleasure of being introduced to an adult who remarks, "Oh, yes, I remember the story you told when you visited my third-grade class." Unfortunately, this type of comment is usually a generation late for the purposes of evaluation.

Reading Clubs

Goals and Objectives. Libraries have had considerable experience with the traditional summer reading club designed for school-age children. In addition to objectives of increased circulation and library registrations, the goals of the program may be identified as follows:

1. To provide an opportunity for children to maintain and increase their reading skills
2. To introduce children to a wide range of library materials
3. To promote reading as an enjoyable leisure activity
4. To develop a relationship with the child that will continue after the program ends.

If the child gives reports on the books read or has an opportunity to discuss them with other children, a fifth goal could be:

5. To offer opportunities for the child to discuss books in a nonthreatening environment.

In addition to these goals, which may be featured in the program's promotion, librarians may also have some in-house goals such as:

6. To gain favorable public relations for the library among parents and teachers.

The implications of club membership should be exploited to the level of the library's resources. If staff or volunteer resources do not allow time for children to gather regularly on a voluntary basis to discuss books or hear the librarian and club members booktalk interesting titles, a number of related activities should be offered that involve some interaction of club members: craft activities, previewing films or videos considered for library acquisition, etc.

Range and Types. The summer reading club usually begins the moment school is out, and is limited to those children who either know how to read or those who have completed the first grade. It may run for six to ten weeks or continue on until school resumes. A shorter period allows the staff to offer other types of programs and avoids the interest lag that occurs with a nine-or twelve-week program.

This program can be adapted to a wide range of children: those who are disabled, use bookmobiles, or order their reading materials through the library's mail order service. Developed around a theme, either locally inspired or based on a topical interest, materials and programs can include a talk by a zoo attendant for an animal theme or a series of nature films for an environmental theme.

Children are usually given a log to record the titles they read. Libraries may set a low arbitrary number of titles to read or contract with the child for an agreed-upon number reasonable for the time period. The only competition children should experience is with themselves. The good reader who polishes off 106 books during the summer has probably not exerted as much effort as another child who struggles to finish six that are on his or her own level. The attention given the first child may make an interesting news article, but if it discourages those children who need the incentive to read, the program will be a failure. (That good reader needs to spend more time at the swimming pool!) Proof of completion of a title may be verified by a brief oral or written report of some type, or a parent's signature. Some libraries simply accept the child's word. A tangible incentive—a stamp or small token—is sometimes given to the child for each title read, with a certificate presented for completion of the requirements. The child may be encouraged to include a certain number of titles from a recommended list, or from more than one genre, or not to include titles previously read. Most libraries keep the rules to a minimum and enforce them gently.

Variations of this program include read-to-me clubs in which an older child or parent reads to a preschool child; a more sophisticated version for middle or junior high school readers; an adaptation for children with disabilities; book discussion programs for a limited number of participants conducted during the school year; and a program scheduled at any time for children experiencing reading difficulties.

Issues and Concerns. Some librarians consider the disadvantages inherent in reading clubs to outweigh the advantages and adopt, instead, other types of programming to achieve their objectives. In spite of efforts to eliminate or reduce competition, parents and teachers may inadvertently introduce it when they encourage the child to enroll and complete the requirements. When this occurs, the child may view the library as an extension of school rather than a nonjudgmental agency upholding the freedom of choice. Children may also think that they must participate in the program in order to use the library.

Another issue is the use of incentives. When reading clubs are explained to children in the primary grades, an inevitable question is "What do I get if I win?" We are conditioned in this culture to expect rewards for effort. Nevertheless, most librarians strive to keep the reward as modest as possible in order to help children experience reading as an activity that brings its own rewards. The age at which this realization occurs, if it does, varies with each child and is dependent on a number of social and psychological factors.

Research conducted a few decades ago on achievement motivation revealed that children differed in their ability to reward themselves without a concrete incentive to measure progress. This developmental process was shown to be affected by class differences and child-rearing practices. Children in families with lower class values usually performed better with a tangible reward while those in families with more middle class values were better able to reward themselves. Children in the latter group responded positively when they knew how well they were performing. Librarians need to consider their objectives and the characteristics of their target audience when considering the use of incentives. If given, they should support the library's objectives and not overshadow the intrinsic values of the reading experience. Many commercial establishments are eager to donate the tangible incentive in order to improve their own public image and to promote their product to a wider audience. If children are not to be exploited, these offers should be weighed carefully and critically. There are also nonprofit organizations that sometimes seek the library's endorsement of their reading programs. These, too, should be examined for their effect on children, regardless of their worthwhile goals.

The most sensitive question involves the reading level of titles acceptable on an individual participant's record. Children are usually asked to select titles that are neither too difficult nor too easy. The approximate reading level of library regulars is often above the average and is probably known by the staff. Among the nonusers librarians hope to attract are undoubtedly children who are reading well below grade level. Challenging their selections may result in their discontinuing library use. On the other hand, titles that fall several levels below the participants' abilities will not benefit them intellectually or ethically. If the role of the librarian is not to change from helpful guide to enforcer of rules, a great deal of tact, sensitivity, and leeway must be used.

Many of these disadvantages can be mitigated by a more careful program design. Children are more apt to select titles on their own level when the contract method is used, reading experiences are shared, and promotional materials to parents emphasize both the maintenance of skills and reading enjoyment.

Cost-Effectiveness. Increasing attendance or participation in reading clubs serves to improve the cost-effectiveness. Better promotion may benefit not only this program, but also other library services. Some librarians favor a high quality presentation in a school assembly, while others prefer promoting the program classroom by classroom, where the children's attention is easier to hold, questions can be encouraged, and teachers can add their endorsement. Additional efforts include informational sheets for teachers explaining the objectives of the program, posters where children and their parents are likely to see them, talks to parents' groups, and news releases to the local media.

Reducing staff time or using less expensive staff will also improve the cost-effectiveness, provided it can be done without impairing the potential values inherent in the program. Judicious use of pre-professional staff and volunteers in designing and producing the materials for the program is one possibility. If the program is to achieve its objectives, however, children should be assisted by staff who are competent to provide encouragement and guidance in selection. The children's staff should be trained to the highest level of its ability and provided with lists of suggested titles for various ages and abilities. In making staff assignments, the more routine tasks should be delegated, if possible, to those who are less able to assist children and their parents.

The cost per participant can be lowered by reducing the cost of materials. Some states sponsor a statewide reading club, with materials produced and distributed at cost to libraries. Materials on a limited number of themes are also available commercially. These should be compared with those that can be produced in-house. Community organizations—such as the Lions Club, AAUW, or Friends of the Library—may be willing to underwrite the costs of this highly visible program. If a local theme is used, promotional materials from the Chamber of Commerce or a similar organization can often be adapted. In addition, there may be volunteer groups with talented members willing to assist with designing and producing materials for a children's program.

Measurement and Evaluation. The numbers game should be suspect when it comes to reading clubs, but this is difficult because librarians have been conditioned to count anything that moves. There are important values that admittedly can't be measured, such as the benefit to an individual child from the social interaction with peers and library staff, or the increase in self-esteem gained from personal accomplishment. The single output measure, program attendance per capita, can provide only a rough idea of the program's success. The goals of the program provide a better basis for evaluation and these should be emphasized whenever possible in reports to the administration. Sampling second- and third-grade teachers in the fall for their reactions will provide insight into how effective the program has been in maintaining or improving reading skills. There is some research that shows a strong correlation between summer reading and improved reading scores. In one study the children who read six or more books during the summer consistently gained more than children who did not read during the summer.[26] In libraries with automated circulation systems, it may be possible to analyze the juvenile circulation by class to provide information on how successful the program was in broadening children's reading choices. One of the external benefits of the program is the favorable attitude that teachers and parents gain of public library service through successful programs of this type.

Booktalks and Class Visits

Goals and Objectives. In addition to achieving the basic objectives of programming, booktalking in schools (1) demonstrates the educational aspects of the children's librarian's role in the community, (2) strengthens professional relationships with school librarians, teachers, and administrators, and (3) encourages class visits to the library. Librarians often ask teachers what topics or activities the class is engaged in before developing their booktalk programs. If Africa is a topic for a fifth- or sixth-grade class, the children's librarian can focus a presentation on appropriate fiction, folklore, poetry, and music, as well as nonfiction written in a popular style. The film and video resources could be suggested to the teacher as well as any human or institutional resource (a recent traveler, exchange student, or museum collection) in the community. Through this approach, children's librarians reinforce their educational role by supporting the teacher and school librarian in stimulating interest and developing an appreciation of another culture. Even the booktalk programs that promote recent library acquisitions stimulate interest and develop appreciation of literature, an educational goal shared with the school's faculty.

"School is where the children are" is true for those between the ages of five and fourteen for at least nine months of the year. The classroom becomes an obvious place to promote reading and library services to children and teachers. Because teachers meet with many parents during the year, they are also in a position to promote library use as a family activity.

Range and Types. Many librarians have a regular schedule of school visits and attempt to visit each classroom in their area at least once a year; more frequent visits would be desirable if they were possible. Activities in the classroom include presenting booktalks or, in the case of the primary grades, telling stories. Children below the fourth grade are less able to deal with booktalks that fail to reveal how the stories end. The format developed for the primary grades should run about twenty minutes. A twenty-five-minute classroom visit can spotlight five or six titles for children above the third grade; two or three titles can be given three- to five-minute booktalks, with the others discussed more briefly. The titles should be selected with the interests and abilities of the children in mind, and include representative titles from more than one genre. Poetry is often included in booktalks, and magazines and recordings brought along as examples of library resources. Following a booktalk, the librarian should verify that children know the location of the public library, discuss the process of getting a library card, and correct misconceptions that children may have of libraries. There is usually one child at least who believes that a fee is involved in getting a library card or in using the library.

A booktalk program can be initiated by the librarian or requested by a teacher or school librarian who wants children to be aware of public library materials. A booktalk may be given in the library when children come as a group, or adapted for adult audiences interested in children's literature or concerned with children's reading.

Issues and Concerns. School officials have generally been hospitable to public librarians who request time to visit classrooms to present booktalk programs. This welcome is one envied by dozens of other organizations that would also like access to this captive audience. The children's librarian is obligated to provide a program that supports the goals of the host institution while serving the objectives of the public library.

The principal, school librarian, and teachers have concerns that should be recognized in the children's librarian's planning for school visits. The resources of the school library should also be promoted to the children and their importance recognized in conversations with teachers and administrators. The best schedule developed for individual classroom visits is one that offers the least disruption for the teachers, and should be adhered to as closely as possible. The choices an individual child makes are not to be restricted, with the formal selection policy governing only the librarians' choices. In the school, however, the children's librarian is a guest. She or he is governed by the policies of the school without necessarily approving them. If possible, the teachers and the school librarian should be given lists of the titles used. If applications for library cards are to be distributed, the teacher or school librarian should be asked to recommend a workable procedure.

One issue to be resolved is whether the books should be checked out to the children or teachers in the classroom, left with the school librarian for several weeks, or returned to the library to serve as an incentive for initiating public library use. This is a special concern in dealing with isolated schools or with children who encounter barriers to public library use. If the primary objective is to encourage the reading of the books, leaving them in the school building may be the only way to accomplish it.

When library staff and administration are unaware of the objectives of this program, it may fail to reach its potential. Staff may resent the added responsibilities they must assume when the children's librarian is away from the library. In one region of a system, the children's librarians presented their booktalk programs at a staff meeting. For the first time, the staff became aware of the preparation involved and of its role in achieving the objectives of the program; for the children's librarians, it served as a dress rehearsal. Administrators may fail to understand the potential of this activity in promoting library use among teachers and parents. Teachers are reminded of another community resource available to them, and parents are lobbied by their children to take them to the public library.

After titles are presented in booktalks, demand for them usually increases. If possible, librarians should use different titles for each classroom or a number of titles by authors who have several books to their credit. Staff should be given a list of the titles covered in booktalks, together with alternate titles to suggest.

Cost-Effectiveness. There are few, if any, practical ways to reduce the costs of this program if the objectives are to be realized. Yet, children's librarians should be ready to respond to the following suggestions made by cost-conscious administrators or supervisors.

Combining two or more classrooms in the school library is one alternative, but the children's librarian should be aware that the dynamics of the group will be changed. The children's attention will be more difficult to claim, and discussions about public library use more easily confused with school library use.

Another suggestion sometimes offered is to videotape booktalk programs and make them available for viewing in the school library. With this, too, the librarian lacks the opportunity to answer questions or for librarian-class interaction. Although such a videotape could serve in a number of ways, there are limitations on its substitution for the librarian in the classroom. Further, it is doubtful that teachers would take class time to view it in the school library.

The use of volunteers or nonprofessional staff loses the value of the program in initiating and strengthening a professional relationship with teachers, school librarians, and administrators. The success of this program requires knowledge not only of the library materials presented, but also of related library resources and their potential use in instruction.

Measurement and Evaluation. The output measure for this type of offering is program attendance per capita. Other possible measures are the number of new borrowers, including parents, and requests for titles promoted. Even though these may serve as indicators, they do not measure the values of a closer working relationship with the schools. Children's increased use of the school library is a benefit that could also be noted, for experience has shown that booktalks and class visits frequently result in increased school library use and subsequently increased public library use. The school librarian is in the position to provide the most effective evaluation of the program because of direct contact with both teachers and children. With encouragement, she or he might be willing to provide this information and to make suggestions for improvement.

Tours and Class Visits to the Library

The public library belongs on the list of possible field trips for every school and organization in the community. No matter how diligent the library staff is in appearing before adult and children's groups, the physical act of going to the library and seeing first-hand what it can offer makes a more lasting impression on children.

Goals and Objectives. Group visits to the library provide the library an opportunity to acquaint children with (1) the various types of materials and services available for their use, (2) procedures and regulations governing library use and behavior, (3) arrangement of materials and ways of accessing various collections, and (4) the library staff's responsibilities to assist users.

Range and Types. An orientation tour may range from a simple walk through the library, sometimes called the "sheep-dip" approach, to a full-fledged library skills lesson. Neither of these extremes match the more common use of the term, which is to provide an enjoyable and educational introduction to the library. The most important message to give out is that the staff is eager to establish or continue a lifetime relationship of library use with each child. Some systems have developed manuals to guide staff in its programming for orientation tours, while recognizing that a group may also have a special reason for the visit that should be considered in the planning. As discussed at the beginning of this chapter under "Planning Steps," the children's interests and needs should determine the activities that are planned for the library visit. The following are things to keep in mind when developing manuals for orientation tours or group visits to the library:

1. Goals and objectives for each grade or age group
2. An appropriate explanation of the concept of the library, and as a community-supported institution
3. The role of staff and its relationship to users
4. Justification for care of materials and behavior expected
5. Circulation processes: getting a card, checking out and returning materials, determining due date; and, for older children, how to renew and reserve titles
6. How to find appropriate materials: reading signs and labels, using a bookmark with classification numbers, or noting differences between the school and public library catalogs, etc.
7. The program for the visit: story to be told, booktalks, film presentation, or tour of various areas of the library
8. Browsing period.

Issues and Concerns. The children's librarian's public service time should not be so tightly scheduled with school classes that he or she is seldom available to individual users or other community groups. A balance must be achieved that is fair to the rest of the community. When a school is within walking distance of the library, for instance, a teacher may assume that class use of the public library can be incorporated into the weekly lesson plans. Although the librarian may be in sympathy with this effort to secure materials, especially if the school library is inadequate, he or she will find it necessary to establish a policy concerning the number of class visits per year that can be accommodated, in order to meet the library's other obligations. Another problem that often arises is the unscheduled class visit. Even though information on scheduling tours and class or group visits to the library may have been highlighted on all promotional materials, there will be groups who suddenly decide to include the library at the end of a field trip to another community institution. If possible, libraries should have a contingency plan for these emergencies, as they usually occur at the most awkward times. It is important not to mar the children's enjoyment, while conveying to the teacher or leader that a more productive experience could have been provided had the visit been scheduled.

Cost-Effectiveness. Some administrators may consider orientation tours by classrooms as a cost-effective means of increasing program statistics, especially if they are conducted by library friends or volunteers. Although this kind of tour may satisfy adult users, it fails to meet the needs of children who lack understanding of the basic concept of a public library as well as the services offered. Because these initial contacts are so important, orientation tours should be planned and conducted by professional staff or by the highest level of staff in a community library. The expense of transporting children to the library and the time away from other educational experiences represent a sizable contribution from the school or organization. This should be matched by the library with the most effective and well-planned program the library can offer. Nevertheless, the efficiency can probably be improved through manuals of procedures, careful planning of handouts that can be used in other programming, and the development of program formats requested many times. One library videotaped a program on Martin Luther King, Jr. that was asked for by many teachers. It was incorporated into the librarian's presentation, but it did not substitute for her presence.

Measurement and Evaluation. The output measure, program attendance per capita, is enhanced through programs such as these. Depending on the program's scope, juvenile circulation, reference completion rate, and number of new library registrations may also be used. The value of well-planned orientation and class or group visits is difficult to pinpoint. Library use by the whole family may result. In addition, the child's relationship with the staff can have a positive beginning. Younger children often assume that the children's librarian remembers them from their recent class visit. If that is not the case, the librarian may not only be permitted a "white lie," but be encouraged to tell one.

Conclusion

The possibilities for programming and innovative services are limited only by librarians' creativity and energy and the library's resources. Children's librarians develop programming abilities to a high level, an art that is also transferable to other age groups. I once asked a young children's librarian what she had learned in her two years in a large eastern urban library system. Without hesitation, she said, "programming." Looking around a university's faculty dining room where we were having lunch, she continued, "I could even program this room." (No mean accomplishment, that.)

It is easy to become caught up in the excitement and stimulation of programming and overlook the fact that for many children, the program may assume less importance than finding a book to read or information for a homework assignment.

A program of services is larger than programming. When children's librarians design a program of services for their libraries, they are guided by the library's mission, goals and objectives, and priorities. They take responsibility for evaluating their services and programs, using appropriate output measures and comments from users and staff. They also consider the long-term goals of their service when options are offered or choices proposed, and accept the responsibility to plan cost-effective programs that are compatible with these goals. These are also responsibilities that children's librarians share with other specialists.

In the past several decades more emphasis has been placed on programming that serves a public relations function for the library and provides a role for the children's librarian that may take less effort to justify to funding authorities. The programming aspect of the service may represent the essence of children's services to the profession at large through the attention given it in library literature. Beginning children's librarians (and some library administrators) need to be cautioned that descriptions of the fascinating programs they read in their journals are only part of a larger responsibility. Programming offers a license for experimentation and innovation, as well as interesting topics for professional journals. Because the basic services—the provision of information, reading guidance, and informal instruction of library skills—are so widely understood by librarians, they are featured less often in the articles they write or in discussion at conferences.[27] Children, however, are not aware that these services lie at the core of library service. Basic services need the same attention and staff support as that routinely given programming. Their importance should be apparent in the resources allocated, the staff training provided, and the services promoted to the public.

Without question, the group experience provided through programming is valuable and offers many benefits, including the opportunity to develop a one-to-one relationship with children, if this has been identified as one of the objectives. However, the basic services offer a greater opportunity for the library staff to establish a life-long relationship with the child. As our society becomes increasingly impersonal, children, like adults, value those occasions when their individual needs have the undivided attention of a competent and friendly librarian. Children who experience this kind of interaction are also apt to be more favorably disposed toward libraries and learning.

The library is full of dust. Mrs. Simmons sits in the middle and George Washington hangs in the hall. In the library are three kinds of books. Books people like to read. Books people do not like to read, and books people never will read. Mrs. Simmons says people like books with spice. Spice comes from India. . . .—Virginia Cary Hudson, *O Ye Jigs and Juleps* (New York: Macmillan, 1962), p.30.

Children's Collections

The principal difference between children's and adult collections is that adult services librarians generally spend a larger portion of their budget on new titles, while children's librarians spend more of theirs for replacement and duplicate copies. This fact, and the inclination of the book-buying public to select older titles when purchasing gifts for children, is also reflected in the number of new titles published annually. In the decade from 1977 to 1987, new juvenile titles—including hardcover, new editions, and trade paperbacks—ranged from approximately 2,400 to 4,600, while the total for all titles ranged from 41,000 to 56,000 titles.[1]

Most children's librarians believe that there are too many juvenile titles published each year, as they have been ever since the number reached 900. This complaint persists because many children's staffs still expect to read or examine most of the year's output in making their selections. As children grow and change, they progress from *Goodnight Moon* to *Jacob Have I Loved*. The number of titles at any one reading level is not overwhelming, nor should it be. Children read through the collection vertically, making preliminary explorations into the next level and nostalgic journeys back to previous ones while enjoying the offerings most compatible with their present interests and abilities. In comparison, we could describe the reading pattern of many adults as horizontal, but even here, many adults could probably be helped to expand their reading choices. If we believe that *Where the Wild Things Are* offers something special to the child during those magic years from three to five, then a sufficient number of copies must be acquired. Single copies of a large number of titles for this age group may prevent most children from ever encountering titles best experienced at a particular age.

The content of the adult and children's collections also reveals a somewhat different service emphasis. If children's librarians were asked to define the major purpose of their specialty, most if not all would emphasize the reading experience and the obligation to help children become readers of literature that can make a difference in their lives. They actively seek out those materials they believe will support these goals. Through programming and promotion, children's librarians attempt to create demand among users and nonusers for materials; they are not content just to respond to requests for popular items or to leave alone those less aware of the choices available. Materials not selected initially by users are thereby given their day in court.

If adult services librarians were asked to respond to a similar question, many would probably rank the provision of information as their major purpose. Adult reading preferences are considered to be less susceptible to change, and librarians respond more to demands than they influence choices. The number of adult titles published annually may preclude any other response. Nevertheless, there has been a renewed emphasis on the reader's advisory function in adult services in recent years.

Children's librarians have also exerted considerable influence on what has been published for their audience. Modern children's book publishing began in the 1920s, when editors were appointed to head juvenile departments. These editors worked closely with children's librarians who were then the major market, responding to their needs, heeding their criticism, and extending to them some of the courtesies afforded a major client group. Whatever the disadvantages, this relationship resulted in children's books of exceptional quality that editors were proud to publish and librarians were proud to offer. Overall, librarians have not exerted the same influence on adult book publishing, or on audiovisual materials, because adults hold a power of the purse that invites producers to target them directly and bypass librarians. The leveraged buyouts of the 1980s have driven publishers of adult books to aim for mass markets.

Trade Book vs. Mass-Market Book Publishing

The children's book collection consists primarily of trade books, although a sampling of mass-market titles may be acquired to support a library objective. Mass-market titles are recognizable by a series name and are marketed through many commercial outlets, e.g. supermarkets, discount stores, bookstores. In comparison to trade books, few mass-market titles are published, but the number of copies may be 15 to 20 times greater. The emphasis of publishers for this market is not on expanding the boundaries of children's literature but in finding titles similar to those with a successful sales record. The evaluator of mass-market titles will seldom, if ever, encounter a topic or a treatment of a subject that evokes controversy. The art work is usually representational and conforms to the expectations that the majority of the public have for children's book illustrations. These titles can be promoted to a small number of buyers who select for national bookstore chains. The price of a mass-market title is therefore much less than that for a trade book which must be promoted individually, the exception being those with a devoted following, like Beverly Cleary, Judy Blume, or Maurice Sendak. Trade books are sold primarily to libraries, schools, and quality bookstores. Because of their professional goals, librarians are constantly seeking titles for the wide range of needs and abilities they hope to serve, an effort trade book publishing has supported.

A tension sometimes develops between children's librarians who work directly with children and their coordinators over popular materials of poor or marginal quality. Some children's librarians have favored the acquisition of more popular titles, including mass-market titles, as a means of leading children to the reading experience. The coordinators who carry the responsibility for the overall quality of the collection often place more emphasis on first-hand knowledge of books and promotional efforts in getting children to read. Even though the influence of the library market on trade books has lessened in the past few decades, children's coordinators recognize that their expenditures continue to affect what is published for children. They maintain close relationships with children's editors and are interested in supporting publishers who strive to offer a broad range of titles chosen not only for their literary and aesthetic qualities, but also for their depiction of the diversity of experience found in our society.[2]

Each children's librarian must develop her or his own philosophy concerning the use of mass-market series, from the ever-with-us Nancy Drew and Hardy Boys to those of more recent origin, Choose Your Own Adventure and the Baby Sitter's Club. These appeal primarily to middle-class children, the targeted market. As these series have proliferated in the last decade, many children's librarians have expressed concern that the better-written, non-series title may have fewer chances of being published today. Whenever this issue is raised in professional discussions, charges of elitism or censorship and of irresponsibility are exchanged by those who would and would not include these series in their collections.

More basic to the decision about inclusion is the question of whether the series provide the best support for the goals and objectives of children's services in a particular community. Those who see their role as promoting good children's literature will probably exclude them or keep their numbers low, while devoting more funds for duplicate copies of higher quality titles that have proved popular with children and placing more effort on promotion. Those who believe that their role is to make available materials in the popular culture and to be responsive to demand will probably allocate a considerable part of their resources for them. Regardless of the policy adopted, the children's librarian should be able to provide a valid justification for their inclusion or exclusion. If these materials were added without evaluation, it may be difficult to explain why time for careful selection of trade books is necessary.

Approaches to Collection Development

A children's collection may be viewed in two ways: as support for the library's goals and objectives, and as an entity in itself, to be evaluated on its internal strengths and relationships. With the emphasis on planning and the use of some aspect of program budgeting, the first view has received more attention in recent years.

Support for Goals and Objectives

A collection in an inner-city branch should be different from one found in a large urban library with a major research and archival responsibility. Each year the Library of Congress adds to its Rare Book Collection a small number of children's titles which the selectors have judged to be of value for future scholars and researchers.[3] Even though some or all of these might also be found in an inner-city library, their place in the collection would be justified by a different set of objectives.

The library's goals and objectives, as well as the objectives of the children's department, provide direction in developing collections. Consider the implications of each of the following service goals which has been paired with a supporting objective:

Goal   Services to population subgroups now underserved will be developed to a level comparable to that provided the general population.

Objective   To increase the proportion of the Hispanic population using the library from 10 to 25 percent by (date).

Goal   Services to those unable to use traditional library services will be increased.

Objective   To increase the number of homebound served from 15 to 30 percent by (date).

Goal   A concerted promotional effort will be made to increase use by adult county residents.

Objective   To alter the ratio of materials circulated to county residents from 50 percent adult and 50 percent juvenile to 70 percent adult and 30 percent juvenile by the end of the next five years.[4]

In the first pair of goal and objective, attention must be given to the collection to determine if there are materials that would meet the interests and needs of the targeted minority groups. If expectations raised through programming and promotion cannot be met, the group may become cynical about libraries, thus defeating the purpose of the library's efforts.

In responding to the second pair, the staff may need in-service education in order to select materials for specific disabilities and to identify suitable titles already in the collection. For instance, deaf children may respond to some wordless picture books and films with no narration as readily as children without hearing impairments.

The third pair of library's goals and objectives is open to more than one interpretation. One way to achieve this objective is to reduce children's circulation by cutting the materials budget or services; the other is to concentrate on those activities that will increase adult use. We can only assume that the latter course is the one intended. Nevertheless, children's staff need to be alert to actions that would strengthen other services at the expense of their own, especially if their success has resulted from careful planning and hard work.

Even when children's librarians develop collections that support their goals and objectives, there is another overarching goal in children's services: helping children become perceptive readers. This goal may or may not be stated, but it adds a nonutilitarian dimension to children's collections. It requires materials that will lead children from one reading level to another, from *Bunnicula* to *Cricket in Times Square* to *Wind in the Willows*. Most children's collections will, as a matter of course, contain a small number of titles that represent the literary heritage of children, such as *Babar* or *Pinocchio*. These traditional titles may appear to fall outside a library's stated objectives, but they are an essential component in providing a common reading background in this society. These are titles that many adults expect to find in a children's library. In fact, for some parents and their children these titles serve as the doorway to the world of modern children's literature. As such, they serve a community need that should be recognized as a legitimate goal, whether or not they can be tied to a specific objective.

By their nature, objectives are short-term, while collections are developed over time. Although a community may experience rapid population growth that results in subsequent changes in library service objectives, most libraries hesitate to rid their collections of all the children's titles not being used. They usually retain some materials as a hedge against further changes, even though the amount of duplication may be reduced, and the more ephemeral materials removed during the first collection reevaluation.

Librarians who develop collections using this approach do not ignore quality; they select the best available materials the targeted group will accept, whether they are comic books, periodicals, videos, or foreign-language books. The needs of the audience take precedence over traditional standards. Materials written for sixth-grade children reading on a second-grade level, for example, will probably never be considered for a literary award, but they are necessary if this audience is to be served.

Collection as an Entity

Viewing the children's collection as an entity can be a valuable exercise. The collection acquires a shape and focus resulting from myriad additions and deletions, decisions to duplicate titles or not, and additions of new formats: videocassettes, software programs, etc. Social and technological changes affect the content of collections, but these changes are usually incorporated at a pace that allows the staff to evaluate its service possibilities.

Many years ago Elizabeth Nesbitt described the dimensions of a children's collection as a core of classics that should be in every children's library and a small but important segment representing the best of current titles. The bulk of the collection is composed of those standard or basic titles read by a generation or more of children and regularly replaced, such as *Henry and Beezus* and *My Side of the Mountain*. Some of the current titles will eventually join the standard titles, but the majority will, in time, be discarded or replaced by newer materials.[5] In many ways, this approach served children well. Less addicted to the bestseller syndrome than adults, children tend to value those titles that give them pleasure regardless of copyright date. In collection development, it is well to remember that while the new titles keep a collection vital and up to date, they should compete for a more secure place with older titles still approved by readers.

Societal changes will prompt a reassessment of standard titles and even some classics. In the past three decades a number of standard titles have been found dated because of the changing attitudes toward women and racial and ethnic groups. Difficult situations have arisen over popular titles challenged by an adult or group concerned with a social issue. For guidance in developing a policy to deal with issues of this kind, librarians should consider the statement "Diversity in Collection Development," adopted 1982 and amended 1990 by the American Library Association.[6]

Other titles read by two or more previous generations may appear to lack interest for today's audiences. A rural setting is common in many of the titles considered standards at the end of World War II, even though the country was becoming increasingly urban. In selecting titles for booktalking, for instance, librarians may have favored stories with an urban or suburban setting because of its easy recognition for today's children. The setting is, however, only one element among several to consider. *Understood Betsy*, the Moffats series, and several of Lois Lenski's regional stories reveal human situations that are universal and may need only an introduction to find an audience. Although classics are more enduring, there may be some that no longer serve the audiences of the children's department as they once did before young adult services became more common (e.g., *Ivanhoe, David Copperfield*).

Changes in tax laws, reductions in federal funds for school library materials, and changes within the publishing industry itself have caused publishers to trim their backlists, and many standard titles still sought by libraries have not been available except in a paperback edition. New titles (frontlist) may have had an advantage over the backlist in the last two decades, as orders for older titles have often been returned marked "out-of-stock" or "out-of-print." Recently, there are signs that the trend may be reversing. The demand for backlisted titles has not abated from either the public or the librarians, and some reprint publishers have begun to add standard children's titles to their lists. Many publishers appear to be reluctant to drop their production rights to a title, however, preferring to retain the option of a reissue or a paperback edition.[7] Nevertheless, librarians who intend to provide a basic hardcover collection for their audiences should be aware that the period of time a new title is kept in print ranges from two and a half to three years for many publishers and five years for those independently owned.[8] Because this period is usually long enough to judge the usefulness of a title, librarians could routinely check orders placed two years previously for titles to reorder before finding them unavailable.

Access to Community and Network Resources

The children's collection cannot be considered only as a resource housed within the library's four walls. An important component of any collection is access to resources in other libraries that is provided through informal agreements or through membership in a system or a state, regional, or national network. If the concept of community responsibility for children's services is accepted, the public library must plan with "all library agencies in the community and other agencies concerned with the needs of children."[9]

A community may support a number of libraries including those in public and private schools, churches, art museums, family planning centers, etc. They are analogous to special and academic libraries with which adult services librarians develop a professional relationship for the mutual benefit of their respective users. Their resources for children—both the collection and staff expertise—can be tapped for those occasional needs that the public library is not prepared to meet. The public library does attempt to meet the general needs of children in house, because children are less able or willing than adults to wait two weeks for materials they request today. Nevertheless, there are occasions when their requests, or those made by caregivers on their behalf, would be better served elsewhere. A need for sex education materials for a parent of a blind child is not a request that most children's librarians are prepared to meet. An institution serving blind children or a planned parenthood group would probably be able to provide more expert assistance to the parent. These referrals are not just one way; community institutions also refer their clients to the public library for materials or programs.

Other Community Libraries or Information Centers

Children's librarians need to be informed about the resources in the community's school libraries and to consider ways to supplement their resources when developing their own collections. Even though the school libraries' first responsibility is to the instructional program, their collections and faculty expertise represent a community resource that should not be overlooked in serving the general public. School librarians' experience with educational nonprint materials is such an example.

The public often considers school and public library services to children a duplication of tax monies. A study to determine the amount of actual overlap between elementary schools and public library children's collections was conducted in four communities in Illinois. It revealed that the average overlap of school library titles with public library children's collections was close to 50 percent.[10] Although the public may view this a high percentage, most librarians would have expected a greater overlap, considering that both types of libraries use many of the same reviewing aids in selecting from a relatively small number of titles. What is not often understood by the public is that titles can serve different objectives. *Sarah, Plain and Tall* can be used in a study of pioneer life in a school; the same title in a public library can be offered to a user wanting a story about step-mothers. Because of these multiple uses of materials, school and public libraries could consider the viability of short-term loans, especially in smaller communities. During the school year, the public library could supplement the school resources on energy for classroom study, while during the summer months, the school library's collection could be tapped for easy reading materials for second-graders. In this way, cooperation is demonstrated and community needs are handled more effectively. Public libraries are occasionally asked for a textbook used in the public schools. The parent making this request may not recognize that she or he also needs additional information on the use of the text, which is best provided by the teacher or school librarian. Because of this and of financial constraints, public libraries do not acquire textbooks unless they are the best source of information on a subject. The school and the public library together should develop a policy for handling this need that recognizes their joint responsibility to the community.

Many religious institutions (churches, synagogues, etc.) have developed libraries as part of their educational program. Not only do they include materials of a doctrinal nature, but they may also provide general trade titles that support their instructional goals. Most public libraries have not acquired materials in the former category, unless they provide information about the beliefs on the faith in a nonproselytizing manner. Because of the intense interest in religion in some communities, librarians will need to consider carefully their collection policies in this area. Staff need to be aware of the types of materials in the various religious libraries in order to provide appropriate supplementary materials and user referral.

Accessing the online catalog of another community library via a terminal in a user's own library or home is a dramatic way to demonstrate that community resources are being used effectively. If the public library has developed a computer-produced catalog in a microform format, a copy of the new or a previous edition could be offered to the school librarian, for instance. School systems that have catalogs of audiovisual materials or computer software may be willing to provide a complimentary copy for the public library.

The public library, as the most broadly based informational agency, can act as the link between agencies as well as between user and agency. The adult who wishes information on establishing family day care may find the information in the library to be helpful, but referral to the community licensing office will provide more practical assistance through contacts with others providing such a service. The educational staff of one church with a successful library program for children may be a better source of help for staff of another denomination than the children's librarian. Maintaining contact with these community agencies will enable the children's librarian to make more valid referrals.

Network Libraries

State, regional, and national networks have provided bibliographic access and encouraged the sharing of resources. Cooperative systems (often called networks) have produced catalogs and bibliographies of local and specialized materials that expand collection resources. A cooperative system may also maintain a collection of items that are too expensive or specialized for a member library to buy, considering their projected use and the library's limited space. Even so, there are users who would benefit from having such materials available even for a short time. Children's librarians are often asked for titles that adults enjoyed as children. Network membership offers a much higher success rate with this type of request.

As full-text transmission becomes more economically viable for networks serving public libraries, the concept of collection will need to undergo further transformation. Books will undoubtedly remain; their convenience and appeal are undeniable. It is possible, however, that information on rapidly changing topics, such as developing countries and some areas of science, may in the near future be accessed by the child at a terminal in her or his home, classroom, or library. Up-to-date titles on these subjects are difficult and expensive to produce. Publishers and librarians recognize that as soon as the title is available in a library, much of the information may be out of date. If this kind of information is constantly updated and is accessed through an electronic publication, charges for its use should be budgeted as an essential part of the collection. Considering the frustration that our present system inflicts on children seeking information, we should welcome this innovation for the quality and convenience it offers.

Policies for Children's Collections

Some libraries develop a collection policy that sets down guidelines and then permit each department to prepare a more detailed document for its own use. Other libraries give attention to the various format and age-level services and treat each separately within a single document. Whatever approach is used, the children's staff needs to be represented in drafting the overall guidelines as these will affect the children's collection. Community representatives should also be invited to participate in this process. They bring a different perspective and can subsequently serve as unofficial liaisons to the community when library materials are challenged. A member of the library's governing body, which will be asked to adopt the document as official policy, should also be included.

Having a policy in place offers several advantages: (1) community needs are kept in focus, (2) delegated authority and responsibility for collections are identified, and (3) selections as well as omissions are more easily justified. Nevertheless, a policy cannot solve all problems that may arise. Interpreting policy guidelines expressed in general terms is not the same as following instructions in a cookbook or a procedures manual. If it were, this responsibility could easily be delegated to less qualified staff. The philosophy on which these policies rest must be understood by those who interpret and defend them. Collection policies may be changed as the need arises, but a written document is a safeguard against hasty decisions. An official policy gives weight to the statement that selection is a professional activity and ensures that intellectual freedom principles will be supported through a procedure that allows challenged titles due process. It also provides a measure of continuity when staff changes occur. In spite of all advice to the contrary, some librarians have resisted putting their policy in writing. When one children's librarian was asked why his library had not, he replied, "We don't want to be prevented from buying what we want." Inadvertently, he had demonstrated the need for a policy.

Responsibility for Collection Development

In most libraries the collection responsibility rests with the children's librarian or the children's coordinator. Because the collection development process is so closely tied to the service function, children's librarians resist relinquishing it to a central acquisitions department. "Knowing the collection" is necessary for good children's services, but it does not mean reading every title in the collection, although children's librarians do read or skim a large portion of their collection. Reading a review or hearing the title discussed by a reviewer is another way that children's librarians gain knowledge of their materials. Several of the large systems have a position in children's services for a children's collection specialist. In a few instances, this specialist may be part of the acquisition or branch staff and, as such, may be responsible for centralized selection and ordering, thereby removing a large part of this function from the children's staff. When the specialist is in the children's department, her or his responsibilities may include coordinating the reviews of the children's librarians, identifying and locating titles for review, selecting materials for new libraries, and chairing committees that develop new acquisition or replacement lists or re-evaluate collections.

Collection vs. Selection Policy

Public libraries have used the term "selection policy" until recently when it was replaced by "collection development policy." The latter encompasses a broad range of activities basic to the provision and maintenance of a collection designed to meet community needs. It may include:

1. A brief description of the community to be served
2. The mission or purpose of the library
3. Intellectual Freedom Statements of the American Library Association adopted by the governing board
4. Overall goals and objectives of the library
5. Selection policy, including authority and responsibility, criteria, sensitive or problem areas, selection aids, gifts, etc.
6. Collection maintenance, covering duplication, replacements, weeding, and methods of evaluation
7. Audiences to be served
8. Special materials, such as serials, microforms, realia, maps
9. Procedures to be followed in handling complaints.

The policy may also address the levels of acquisition for types of outlets in a system. For instance, a central children's department is usually expected to acquire reference materials about children's literature in greater depth than that maintained in a branch; a branch collection normally carries more duplication of titles.

The processes involved in collection development extend beyond making title-by-title decisions of materials found in the library reviewing aids. Librarians are expected to take a more active role in studying the community, re-evaluating the collection, and seeking out needed materials not reviewed in the traditional channels.

Policy Issues and Concerns

In discussions that precede a final collection development draft, a number of issues will probably be raised that require some measure of resolution. One such question is whether selectors should strive for a balanced or well-rounded collection or one that serves the needs of its present users. Another persistent issue involves using demand as the basis of selection rather than other criteria, such as quality or future use. Even if unacknowledged, these issues are present when selectors disagree on titles considered for purchase. Although these issues will never be completely resolved, they do merit discussion and attention in developing the collection policy.

Balanced Collection. In an earlier era the concept of a well-rounded or balanced collection was thought to be a worthy goal. Attention was given to the composition of a collection which considered all subjects or genre known to be of interest to the traditional users of public libraries. Children's interests and needs were considered to be similar across the country because of their common developmental needs, similar school curricula, and exposure to the popular media. Therefore, a basic aid that provided a balanced collection of retrospective materials selected by experienced librarians could be used, supplemented by a few titles that addressed local or regional needs. This interpretation of a balanced collection is at odds with the goals-and-objectives approach to collection development, which gives considerable attention to the unique characteristics of a community and to the needs of its potential users. Nevertheless, basic aids are still useful for identifying materials to be considered, but they should be used judiciously. They also have value in providing a workable collection in a new library or in a rapidly changing community where patterns of use are difficult to determine, as well as in libraries where qualified staff is lacking and funds must be spent quickly.

Most metropolitan systems have dropped the policy that required the central children's department to add a title before any of the branches could do so. As a result, branches are able to develop collections that better meet their community needs, even though they may be unbalanced when compared with those in other libraries or with a basic selection aid.

Some library administrators have been concerned with title count, which may restrict duplication of titles until the collection reaches an arbitrary number of titles. This approach, too, fails to consider the needs of individual communities as well as the goals of children's services.

A collection today is more likely to be balanced according to the population to be served, including both users and nonusers, because it is the normal consequence of the goals-and-objective approach to collection development. An equitable division of resources among the various groups—age, ethnicity, socio-economic status, or occupation—guides librarians in their selections. If the African-American community represents 10 percent of the population and children under five represent 15 percent, comparable percentages of the collection may be allocated to their needs. Because we expect collections to reflect the communities they serve, those that do not are considered anomalies. I once visited a children's library in a predominantly Hispanic community that contained one shelf of Spanish-language books (and these were on such a high shelf that probably few children discovered them). Even though the majority of school-age children may have been able to read the English-language titles, the importance of their culture was not recognized in the collection. Those parents who wished to read to their children in Spanish would have been poorly served as well.

Through their collections, librarians are expected to represent several viewpoints on current and historical issues as expressed in the policy statement "Diversity in Collection Development" referred to earlier in this chapter. While recognizing this ideal in balancing a collection, children's librarians also realize that children are in the process of learning that issues are surrounded by more than one view. In providing materials for elementary school children on such issues as gun control, for example, children's librarians should assume that the author or producer has a personal viewpoint which would be obvious to a perceptive reader. But because children are the audience, librarians should select those works with a discussion of conflicting views for the reader's consideration. By the time children reach junior high school age, they are more aware that what they read or view is not necessarily the only possible or correct viewpoint on the subject.

Demand. Demand is a legitimate basis on which to develop collections, but the argument usually centers on the weight it should have. When a library has completed a study of its community and determined its role or mission (activities in which the children's librarian participated), the children's librarian is in a stronger position to consider demand in the context of overall community needs. Some demands may in fact represent a sizable portion of the community. Others may never be met to the complete satisfaction of the users, for instance, those who continually want more horse or mystery stories. Weighing these demands against the needs for more materials for children with learning disabilities or for materials to attract a growing number of African American children is the responsibility of the children's librarian who must represent those who do not voice demands.

Children's librarians generally encounter two types of requests: one from the user who asks for a title but is more than willing to take a substitute, and one from a child who is actively seeking a specific title or more titles in a genre. The former represents a need for assistance in finding something of interest; the latter represents a demand the library meets either by purchase or interlibrary loan or by employing the strategies of a reader's advisor in persuading the child to try something else. Most librarians find it difficult to refuse a request to add materials (or to remove them); however, refusal may be necessary if the library is to have the funds and the space for a collection that recognizes the needs of the community and its potential users. There is always a temptation to use the materials budget to serve current users, especially if circulation is the primary measurement.

Few would contend that librarians develop perfect collections for audiences that do not now exist and possibly never will. The collection should not serve as a monument to the librarian's personal taste, an attitude shown in "I wouldn't have that title in *my* library." In avoiding the pitfalls of this situation—more common in an earlier period—some present-day librarians may have fallen into another trap: developing collections through popular demand that offer little to sustain the more curious and thoughtful readers who wish to explore a subject beyond a superficial level.

Sensitive Areas. Among the areas usually treated in a children's collection policy are abridged children's classics, textbooks, long runs of series, and popular series of poor or marginal quality. Criteria for evaluating titles in such sensitive areas as religion, sexuality and sex education, race and ethnicity, drugs, abortion, and evolution may be given in some detail. In general, libraries strive to provide materials on these and other subjects that are informative, accurate, free of misconceptions and a proselytizing tone, and appropriate for the age of the intended audience. It is difficult if not impossible to think of a subject that would not be suitable for a children's library, provided the readers' level of understanding and their developmental needs were considered by the author's presentation of the topic.

Request to Reconsider or Remove Materials. Children's, school, and young adult librarians deal continually with complaints on library materials as well as on the users' free access to collections. The complaints usually come from adults acting on behalf of children whom they wish to protect. A collection policy will outline the steps to be followed when complaints are officially lodged, but the materials should not be removed until the process has been completed and the decision to do so made. The library staff must not assume that the complainant is always wrong and the librarians always right, or that every question raised is a demand to remove materials. Listening is an art to perfect, as is reading body language, for understanding the complainant's point of view is necessary if genuine communication is to occur. Because these concerns have the potential of igniting a public debate, some administrators ask for a brief report of all such complaints and how or if they were resolved.

The desire to protect children is not one that most of us would like to see eliminated from our society. The complainant's concern is worthy of respect, especially if the person is a parent who takes seriously her or his parental responsibilities. The children's librarian must recognize a parent's right to guide a child but not the right to impose standards on the community's children without following a procedure required by official policy. If the library lacks such a policy, assistance can be obtained from the Office of Intellectual Freedom of the American Library Association. Of particular importance to children's librarians in collection development are the following policy and procedural statements:

1. Evaluating Library Collections, 1981[11]
2. Dealing with Concerns about Library Resources (a procedural statement), revised 1983[12]
3. Statement on Labeling, 1981[13]
4. Expurgation of Library Materials, 1981 and amended 1990.[14]

Samples of policies, letters to complainants, and program formats intended for library audiences are also available from the Association for Library Service to Children, a division of the American Library Association. In addition, many state library associations provide assistance to librarians in their defense of intellectual freedom.

Librarians who remember angry adults accusing them of personally endorsing every idea expressed in the collection must guard against becoming defensive during the selection process. The choice facing the librarian may be expressed something like this: If I don't select this title, is it because it falls outside our goals and objectives and the collection policy; or am I subconsciously avoiding a possible controversy or an unpleasant scene? For other librarians the question may be even more uncomfortable. Am I buying this title only to prove to myself and my colleagues that I am not a censor; or can this purchase be justified on the basis of its potential contribution to our service goals and to meeting the needs of our users? In reality, there is no practical way to avoid controversy, even if avoidance were a professional option. The most innocent-appearing titles have been the object of complaints, leading librarians to conclude that nothing lies outside the purview of the would-be censor. Selection must be a positive action—acquiring materials for a service program and for users—rather than a negative one—keeping out titles that might become controversial in the community.[15]

Budget for Children's Materials

The fair share of the library's materials budget that should be assigned to children's materials is determined by the service goals and objectives placed in priority by the library. The budget cycle normally covers a twelve-month period which correlates well with the annual objectives required of the library's departments. In fact, the objectives may serve as the major justification of the requests for materials and staff hours. The library's goals are determined at the end of a planning process, which is usually conducted on a three- to five-year cycle. The goals are important in explaining major shifts in the overall budget, but they lack the specificity needed in most annual budget justifications.

In submitting requests for materials, the average costs of the various categories should be included, and, if required, the cost of selection and processing. The budget proposed by the children's librarian may pass through several offices, perhaps even twice, before the final figure is determined; the supervisor, the library administration, and the library's governing body (board of trustees or city manager) may all look at the proposal. At any point along the way, it may be revised downward for a number of reasons, from lack of funds to a weak justification. Should the final budget be a lesser figure, the objectives placed in the lowest priority will be dropped or postponed, along with the funds budgeted for materials needed for their support.

Children's librarians who would like a set percentage of the materials budget fail to understand the way most budgets are justified today in the public sector; they must compete with other worthy services for support within the library. There are risks in this process as well as opportunities to increase awareness of the needs of children's services. As a check on their own effectiveness, children's librarians can monitor changes in the percentage of the materials budget allocated to children's services from year to year. Unless demands for children's services have dropped noticeably or the library has made a strong commitment to other services, this percentage will not fluctuate greatly. If it has, a stronger justification or improved communication with the administration may be necessary.

Factors Affecting the Children's Materials Budget

In evaluating the adequacy of the budget for children's materials, there are a number of factors to be considered; most lie outside the control of the children's services staff.

Range of Materials. Children's librarians should familiarize themselves with the range of materials that must be covered by their budget allocation. These may include some or all of the following:

Picture and board books	Reference materials
Fiction and nonfiction	Videos and films
Recordings	Computer software
Periodicals	Pictures and slides
Realia, toys, games	Pamphlets and ephemera
Access to materials: rentals,	Parenting materials in the
interlibrary loans, etc.	children's department

Some libraries set aside a certain percentage of the materials budget for all reference materials and periodicals. A schedule for replacing reference books, such as encyclopedias, dictionaries, and atlases, with new titles or revised editions is often followed and may not be charged to any of the departmental budgets. Audiovisual and parenting materials located in the children's department are often items in the children's budget, while those in the general collection are charged respectively to the audiovisual and adult materials budgets. The children's materials budget also covers the cost of nonbook items used in programming, such as films, puppets, recordings, and craft materials. Many children's librarians have difficulty viewing nonbook materials with the same enthusiasm they have for books. One approach to giving these materials more consideration is to search first among nonbook materials—videos, realia, filmstrips, recordings—when acquiring materials on a particular subject.

Demographics. During the baby-boom years of the 1950s and early 1960s, children's department circulation made up 50 percent of the total in many libraries. Children's departments were often allocated a third of the materials budget, with the justification that children's titles usually cost less than adult titles. With the ratio of children to adults now at a more normal figure, and with the population aging, children's librarians may have to present strong justification for funds to support their programs and services. A valid case can be made for programs that prevent illiteracy, e.g. prereading activities for preschoolers; for programs that emphasize the parent's role in the reading process; and for those that contribute to the community's efforts to deal with the needs of latchkey children and those that are most at risk in contemporary society. The potential audience, either nonusers or a population group new to the community, also requires special consideration during the budget process.

Status of the Library. To a large extent the library's status defines its collection responsibilities. A neighborhood branch with easy access to materials in other outlets would not need to maintain the collection required of a central children's department or even that of an independent library serving a comparable population.

Use of the Library. Basing budgets on circulation figures places those libraries with a large proportion of children from nonreading homes or with poor learning skills at a disadvantage. Out-of-library circulation may never be high in these communities, but lack of funds for materials will only aggravate the situation. Circulation cannot be ignored entirely; a heavily used collection can disintegrate quickly unless funds are available for a systematic replacement of worn-out copies.

When service objectives are set, the collection should be assessed for its potential in providing the necessary support. If the collection is to be used by a non-English-speaking target group, its content should be evaluated with the help of representatives aware of the group's needs and interests. It is possible that a different schedule of services and programs should be offered, but the collection should not be overlooked as the cause. If it is the cause, asking for a larger portion of the materials budget would be a legitimate request.

Adequacy of Elementary School Libraries. When federal funds stimulated the growth of school libraries during the 1960s and early 1970s, some hard-pressed public library administrators used this development to justify cutting budgets for children's materials. Unfortunately, the funds available for most school libraries were still inadequate to support the instructional program, and children were ill-served by both libraries. Nevertheless, in those communities fortunate enough to have strong elementary school libraries, the public library should give increased priority to the many other audiences for services. This change in priorities may or may not result in a smaller materials budget; the range and level of service needed will be the determining factor.

Budgeting as an Administrative Tool. During austere periods administrators may have little choice other than to cut the materials budget. The priorities set during planning will determine the cuts, but without such a plan, a decision may be made to eliminate a category of materials (films, recordings, etc.), as the least disruptive or more dramatic course of action. Should the targets for reduction or elimination be framed art prints for adults and toys for children, the children's librarian should assess the results of these cuts to see if they are comparable. As Diane G. Farrell once observed:

> Play materials are part of the information needs of children. Sand and clay and other manipulative materials—puzzles, toys, games—are "media" through which the young child derives certain kinds of information in the same sense in which books and films are media through which older children and adults derive other kinds of information.[16]

This kind of background information is essential in policy discussions and is more likely to be supplied by a children's librarian.

Budgeting may also be used to change the composition of a collection. If 20 percent of the materials budget for each department is designated for audiovisual materials, the collection would be greatly changed at the end of ten years. Should a collection be perceived as stagnant, reducing the funds for duplicates and replacement copies offers one form of corrective action, even though that may not be the most desirable alternative for children's services.

Managing the Children's Materials Budget

One of the most common mistakes new children's librarians make is to spend most of their book budget for new titles, overlooking the fact that the strength of the collection lies in retrospective titles. The division of expenditures between new and retrospective copies should be planned. If a library is part of a system in which replacement lists for the various categories are issued on a regular schedule, an estimated figure should be assigned for each category. In a given year duplicates and replacements may account for 25 to 55 percent of the children's book budget, depending on the condition of the collection and the service objectives. The allocation for new titles can be divided roughly among each of the selection sessions with adjustments made for the heavy fall and spring publishing periods. As in any household budget, this practice demonstrates quite clearly how selective one must be.

If some form of program budgeting is used, then expenditures must be expressed in a format required by the funding agency. Care should be taken that materials acquired to support the various services and programs include both new and retrospective book titles, as well as appropriate nonbook materials.

Children's services should be prepared to take advantage of those nonallocated funds that often become available at the end of a fiscal year. Those who are able to demonstrate need and ability to use the funds wisely within a short period of time may reap the windfall. Replacement lists for this contingency and a want list of titles to be bought with gift monies should be kept.

Collection Development Aids

Librarians with the responsibility for children's collections can choose from among the growing list of printed aids those that best serve their needs and fall within their budgets. (See Appendix C for these titles.) Children's librarians are usually diligent in their attention to the reviewing aids for current titles and announcements of annual lists and awards. Areas that receive less consistent attention are alternative press titles, foreign language titles, high interest, low vocabulary titles, and nonbook materials.

Sources for New Materials

The reviewing aids for new current materials generally fall into the following categories:

1. Inclusive and nonselective: those that list what is available but make no judgment on the value or quality
2. Selective with stated criteria for inclusion: titles are recommended based on quality or value to their audience
3. Titles promoted to libraries: reviewed and rated on a scale of not recommended for most collections to highly recommended for all collections.

Those who use these and other announcement lists should be knowledgeable about the purpose(s) of these aids.

Publishers' Catalogs and Announcements. Publishing houses provide spring and fall catalogs to promote their new titles, along with a list of titles published several seasons ago but still in print (the backlist). The annotations are written for promotion and therefore should not be used as a selection guide; nevertheless, the information provided about the title, illustrations, format, binding, and honors received is useful.

Forthcoming Books. This service provides a prepublication listing of titles for all ages. In 1987, *Forthcoming Children's Books* began publication on a bimonthly basis. *Publishers Weekly* also devotes two issues a year, spring and fall, to forthcoming children's books with brief, descriptive annotations supplied by the publisher. New titles, as well as those scheduled to be reissued in new or paperback editions, are also included. Should these aids be available, most children's librarians would find them useful but not essential to collection development.

Reviewing Aids for Current Titles. Some librarians with a sizable children's staff read or examine every title before purchasing as a a matter of policy, using selection aids primarily as screening devises; others rely almost entirely on selection aids for their purchases. In choosing selection aids it would be well to include both those that review only recommended titles and those that aim for a broader coverage. The selector should become familiar with the features and policies of the reviewing aids in order to use them effectively. Regardless of the method of selection used, printed reviews serve as a standard librarians can use to measure and hone their own evaluation skills.

Annual Lists. Children's literature is a field replete with "good," "best," "notable," and "outstanding" lists of titles issued by various associations, library systems, and professional journals. Not only books, but also films, filmstrips, recordings, and computer software are treated in this way. Because the selection is based on quality, these titles are certainly worthy of serious consideration. However, the decision to purchase must still be made on a title's value in meeting the goals and service objectives of the individual library. Use of annual lists as the only measure of collection adequacy is highly questionable.

Awards. It is almost a truism that every organization that has any connection with children or their literature eventually establishes a book award. The criteria for the award may range from literary quality to the state residency of the author. The sponsor's objectives as well as the criteria used should be known. A title receiving a graphic arts award for illustration or book design may be marred by an uninspired text or one not suitable for the library's public. On the other hand, titles that have won popularity awards may be an excellent source for bait or popular titles: those that have won Coretta Scott King Awards provide suggestions for ethnic materials; and well-written mystery stories can be found among the Edgar Allan Poe Award winners.

Problem Areas. If a library encounters difficulties in finding materials on a particular topic or genre, other library and professional groups probably have had similiar experiences. When trade bibliographies prove to be inadequate, consider (1) publication catalogs from professional associations concerned with children or children's literature, (2) regular columns in book reviewing journals which identify ephemera and useful materials not widely promoted, (3) alternative press titles, and (4) browsing through special interest bookstores.

The catalogs of publications of the American Library Association, the International Reading Association, and the National Council of Teachers of English may be excellent sources for bibliographies of materials for poor or reluctant readers, children with disabilities, and ethnic groups. An association's catalog of publications is usually available free of charge, regardless of membership. (See Appendix D and the Association Catalogs and Publications List in Appendix C.)

Many professional journals spotlight useful items through a regular column. Examples of these are shown below:

Horn Book: The Hunt Breakfast

School Library Journal: Checklist

Wilson Library Bulletin: Marketplace

American Libraries: The Source

Reading Teacher: Classroom Reading Teacher

Bulletin of the Center for Children's Books: Bibliography for Librarians, Teachers, and Parents.

The Children's Book Council's *Features* offers this kind of information from time to time, and ALA's *Booklist* carries annotated lists of foreign-language materials with U.S. addresses for ordering, as well as selective bibliographies on timely topics.

Reviews for alternative press titles have been difficult to find, primarily because reviewers often are not sent copies or the materials may not meet the journal's criteria for review. Recently, however, *Booklist* has added recommended alternative press titles to its reviewing columns. The overall quality of these materials varies considerably and for that reason they should be evaluated before being added to the collection. Many of these publishers operate on the proverbial shoestring and cannot offer return privileges. Because their formats are often not suitable for normal library circulation, some titles may be better candidates for the vertical file. In spite of all these potential problems, alternative press titles may offer the best material available for some subjects.[17]

Libraries have been criticized for collections that ignore sizable groups in the community. One example is the growing number of conservative religious congregations whose views on several social issues are not represented in the collection. The children's librarians in one library system routinely visit the various religious bookstores in their region of the city and purchase review copies of titles to consider for the library's collections.

Sources for Retrospective Titles

No matter how diligent librarians are in using the sources for new materials, useful titles may be overlooked. Because several of these may be preferable to current titles, it is important to consult references that identify recommended retrospective titles.

Subject Guide to Children's Books in Printing. This aid can be a valuable resource in identifying titles on a particular subject, but selectors must keep in mind that the titles *have not been evaluated*. If the need is for current materials on evolution, for example, this aid will supply titles, but the selector must either search for reviews or request review copies before adding them to the collection.

Basic Collection Aids. There are several basic aids that list retrospective and recent titles recommended for children's libraries. The three most widely used are the *Children's Catalog, Best Books for Children*, and *Elementary School Library Collection*. Each is regularly updated, but judgment must still be exercised for not every title is the best choice for all libraries.

Subject Bibliographies and Indexes. Although the primary purpose of these aids is not selection but use, new editions of these works can provide a collection check for the subject or genre covered, provided their coverage is selective rather than inclusive. For example, reading guidance aids such as *Popular Reading for Children* could be used by a selector to increase the number of readable titles that many children have enjoyed. The *Subject Index to Poetry for Children and Young People* provides a listing of poetry collections analyzed. If the choice lies between two comparable poetry titles, one that is indexed and one that is not, obviously the former has an advantage. (See Reference and Information and

Reading Guidance Lists in Appendix C for aids that may also be used for selection.)

Jobbers

Jobbers supply titles from many publishers, thereby reducing the paperwork involved in the ordering process. Libraries usually have an account with one or more jobbers who supply materials for all ages, plus one or more who deal with children's prebound editions. Local or nationally based paperback jobbers may be used for materials in this format. Discounts are dependent on the volume of orders placed annually.

The catalogs issued by some jobbers are extremely useful because they list the cost of children's titles in different types of binding, and indicate the ratings given each retrospective title by the major reviewing aids. Jobbers may also offer other services, such as cataloging and processing services and examination collections of new children's titles.

Acquiring audiovisual materials is much more complicated, for there are no jobbers comparable to those found in the book world. In many instances, libraries have to deal separately with the various distributors for films, filmstrips, toys, and realia, although local or nationally based jobbers may be available for videocassettes, compact discs, and recordings.

Selection Process

Because selection of new titles is a task enjoyed by most children's librarians, it is tempting to spend a disproportionate amount of time on this activity at the expense of public services. Children's librarians are often asked to justify the time spent in review and discussion of titles with other librarians. The observation is made that adult services staffs select almost entirely from reviews or from examination without full staff discussion. Why can't children's librarians do the same? Introducing children to literature requires that their librarians be knowledgeable about the content and range of materials. Discussions during selection meetings inform librarians of titles that should be read or examined and of gaps in the collection that require attention. Librarians who spend long uninterrupted periods with children experience unusual demands on their energies. An opportunity to interact with others in like situations may provide the stimulation and renewal necessary to prevent burnout. These reviewing sessions are not only the means to more effective selection; they also serve as in-service education.

Selecting Current Materials

Children's librarians usually maintain a consideration file of titles wth pertinent comments and overall ratings from various reviews, including those done in-house. It is important that there be a process by which the public and staff can make recommendations for specific titles or subject-oriented materials. Requests from the public are often generated from promotion in the mass media or from such journals as *Psychology Today* or *Parent's Magazine*. These can add a needed dimension to the collection if they fall within the collection guidelines. It is the librarian, however, who has the broadest picture of the needs of the community as well as knowledge of the range of materials from which to choose. Requests for materials the library has decided not to acquire should be examined to see if there is a need that can be met more effectively in another way. I once had a request from a staff member for more children's fiction by authors with a last name beginning in "N" because of constant gaps in that section of her bookmobile. We found another solution to this problem. In some instances, audiovisual materials may be a better alternative than books of marginal use or value. There are times when a policy exception may be necessary. Adding a local author's vanity press title for an indeterminate period may be the better part of valor.

In-house Reviewing. An in-house review offers several advantages to the library. Even though it may also include pertinent comments from printed reviews, the major focus is usually on the title's value to the particular library and how it compares with other similar titles in the collection. Only those systems with many children's librarians can hope to review the major output of a publishing year. In lieu of a children's collection specialist, the children's coordinator assumes responsibility for coordinating staff reviews and developing order lists for new and replacement titles. In medium-sized systems, the decision may be made to review picture books and fiction in-house, and to rely upon printed reviews for evaluating the content of nonfiction, supplemented with a staff examination of format.

Cooperative Reviewing and Examination Centers. School and children's librarians in a community or area may devise a procedure for sharing reviews of a selected number of books and audiovisual materials. Should several school districts and public library systems be involved, publishers may be able to provide review copies. Monthly reviewing meetings can be supported by a modest membership fee assessed to cover the costs of compiling and printing the reviews. The Association of Children's Libraries of the Bay Area (Oakland, California) and the Puget Sound Council for Reviewing Children's Books (Seattle) are examples of this kind of organization. The reviews are often available at cost to those outside the region as well.

Examination centers are provided by some state libraries (Missouri is one) or through the cooperation of several public and/or private organizations like the Cooperative Children's Book Center at the University of Wisconsin, Madison. Because the centers have some staff resources, they can often provide a certain level of services to their client groups.

Use of Published Reviews. It would be difficult to prove that in-house reviewers are more competent than those who contribute to professional reviewing journals. On the contrary, the latter may include subject specialists or those with an expertise not found in the library's staff. For many libraries, there is no option; opportunities to examine the titles themselves do not exist.

It is quite possible to develop an excellent collection using printed reviews. Consulting four or five reviewing aids on a regular basis will allow a selector to gain a fairly adequate evaluation of most titles. Some purchase as their base file the *School Library Journal* Reviews-on-Cards and add comments from other reviews. If a promising title receives mixed reviews or is difficult to assess, a copy can be ordered for evaluation. In using this approach selectors need to develop a tolerant attitude about the inevitable mistakes. There will be an occasional title whose content has been accurately evaluated, but the reviewer has neglected to state, for instance, that the format is inappropriate for the intended age of the reader. Its potential use may not equal the expense of adding it to the collection. These lapses should be treated as overhead expenses to be written off before they cost the library more in processing charges, or send the wrong message to children. I once overheard a twelve-year-old girl explain to a friend that Madame Curie was dull. Unfortunately, her opinion was based on the library's biography probably purchased because there was nothing else available at the time.

Opinions vary concerning the characteristics of a good review.[18] In addition to a brief description of the content of the book, an assessment of its quality, and a comparison with other titles, reviews should have comments on the book's potential use and a notation of those elements that might detract from its use, such as format, vocabulary, or the treatment of sensitive issues. In requesting that elements likely to evoke controversy be identified, librarians should not use this information to avoid purchase but as an opportunity to evaluate the title more carefully. English teachers in the secondary schools are advised to write justifications or rationales for the titles they intend to teach.[19] Children's librarians might find this a useful exercise in dealing with titles identified as controversial, for it places those elements in perspective, and gives the library a ready-made brief for defense. Even though this process will not deflect challenges, it could offer a degree of security to those who tend to avoid controversy.

Selecting Retrospective Titles

In developing collections that support service objectives, librarians should, as a matter of practice, consult retrospective aids for appropriate titles. If one of the service objectives is to increase the use of science and technology materials among school-age children by 15 percent over a three-year period, the collection would have to support this objective. The out-of-date materials would be removed and the number of copies of current and useful retrospective titles increased. Larger systems may assign the responsibility to a committee that uses the shelflist for a title-by-title evaluation, recommending that specific titles be withdrawn and others placed on replacement or current buying lists.

Replacement titles may be added to order lists for new titles, or accumulated and placed during less busy periods. Many library systems operate on a schedule of replacement orders that includes not only replacement titles requested by individual libraries, but also a number of retrospective titles within the genre or category recommended by the coordinator or a reevaluation committee.

The Binding Maze

Those who select children's books are faced with a range of choices concerning the type of binding most appropriate for a particular title. The task is to select a binding suitable for the book's projected use and value. Librarians would like the binding and the pages of a book, after a suitably long life, to give away all at once like the "Deacon's One-Hoss Shay." We've all looked ruefully at titles in "eternal" buckram that circulate twice in three years and have been dismayed that a trade edition hasn't survived one circulation to a healthy American child.

Types of Binding

For many titles, several binding options exist: (1) a trade edition, (2) publisher's library edition (reinforced), (3) prebound, class A binding in buckram, or (4) a paperbound edition.

Trade Editions. Because there are no standards for trade editions, each publisher sets its own. Within a publishing house, the quality of bindings may vary depending on the subject, the age range of the intended users, or the format. Music books, for instance, need a binding that permits them to lie flat; nonfiction with little projected use will be accepted in a less sturdy binding. When publishers find it necessary to reduce costs in order for a title to be marketable, reducing binding costs may be considered the best available option. Experience is the most reliable method in judging the overall durability of the publisher's trade editions. A perusal of the copies removed because of condition can be very revealing in noting which publishers' trade editions have not survived normal use, and therefore should be ordered in a reinforced edition. For librarians who must order from reviews only, there is no longer any reviewing aid that describes the bindings of trade editions. The code formerly used by the *School Library Journal* indicated whether the title was smythe or side sewn, had a cloth cover, etc. Therefore, buyers who can't examine the trade editions will have to assume that they are all alike when making decisions on which to buy. The publisher's announcement catalogs may describe the type of binding used, but retrieving it for each title is probably not cost-effective.

Publisher's Library Editions. After years of complaints from children's librarians who wanted something between the trade edition and the class A buckram binding, the publisher's reinforced library edition was introduced in the 1950s. Some publishers have dropped the trade edition for several or all of their titles and carry only the library editions, which are fully discounted. Like the trade editions, there are no standards for these bindings, and the materials invested in their reinforcement vary from publisher to publisher. Covers are usually treated to resist soil, water, and vermin, but the durability of the binding cannot be predicted. Again, past experience is the best indicator. Children's librarians should examine the contract negotiated with the library's jobber(s) for the discount rate given these editions.

Class A Bindings. Standards have been set for the class A binding by the Library Binding Institute and apply to titles ordered in a prebound edition and to titles rebound by a certified binder.[20] The contents are encased in a heavy buckram cloth treated to resist the usual hazards. Although practically indestructible with normal use, a class A binding will not survive a dip in the wading pool or a puppy's teething. To avoid the institutional appearance that a collection in buckram bindings presents, libraries may add plastic covers. The cost of these editions is computed on a set discount rate plus a charge for the binding. Most libraries pay this net price, although a further discount may be offered for large volume buying. Because children's librarians who buy the bulk of their titles prebound make few demands on the bindery budget, adjustments should be made in their materials budget. Charges for rebinding are based on the height of the book.

Paperbound Editions. Most of the juvenile titles originally published in paperback are still aimed at the young adult audience. For some retrospective titles the only option may be a paperbound edition. When additional copies are needed, they also serve as acceptable budget stretchers. If the title's projected use is high, a paperbound edition can be ordered from a jobber specializing in reinforced bindings, guaranteed for a specified number of years or circulations.

Guidelines for Binding Choices

Each type of binding offers its own advantages in terms of durability, cost, attractiveness, and maintenance. Selectors who order from reviews only must decide whether to make decisions title-by-title, or to establish guidelines to be followed by an order clerk, acquisitions department, or jobber. Librarians should periodically compare costs for a selected number of titles in the various available editions as a check on the soundness of their guidelines. The following are suggestions only, for each library varies in the time available for collection development, size of the budget, and level of staff support.

Trade Editions: Fiction titles by less known authors; nonfiction when recency is important or use is projected as average or less; board books and music or craft titles that need to lie flat; and most titles for older children.

Publisher's Library Editions: New picture books, fiction, and nonfiction with above average projected use.

Prebound Editions: Replacements and most added copies; new picture books and fiction by popular authors or illustrators; heavily used nonfiction when recency is not a factor.

Providing Access to Collections

As advocates for children, children's librarians must be alert to cataloging practices and procedures that may create barriers to materials. These may be less dramatic than the censor's efforts, but they are often more effective.

A good working relationship with the technical services staff is of utmost importance in developing guidelines for handling the various access questions that arise. Will the classification and subject entries identified in the Cataloging in Publication data be followed without exception? What differentiates a picture book from a juvenile fiction title? How much information should be present before a title is considered nonfiction rather than fiction? These and other questions should be discussed and a common understanding reached. Borderline cases can be set aside for discussion. Raising objections after the title is cataloged creates an awkward situation with an implied criticism of a colleague's professional competency, in addition to the need to invest more time in making the changes. If all of the recommendations requested by children's librarians cannot be followed, they should be prioritized.

Catalog Access

An issue that once engendered a great deal of discussion was whether the children's room needed a separate catalog with entries only for children's materials. Several factors entered into the decision, including the size of the combined catalog, its location, and the expense involved. The sheer bulk of the combined catalog acted as a deterrent to children's use in some libraries and made a separate catalog advisable. Because of the expense involved, entries for children's titles were frequently omitted from the main catalog. As a result, the adult public was often unaware of the resources in the children's collection. With the computer-produced catalog in a microfiche or microfilm format, the combined catalog became less of an issue, for the computer can produce combined and separate catalogs quite easily if preliminary planning has allowed for such versatility. If separate microform catalogs are used, a copy of the adult catalog can be made available for those children who need or want advanced materials. With the advent of an online catalog, children's collections should be an integral part of the database.

Another issue involved the respective advantages of the dictionary catalog and the divided catalog, with one for subjects and the other for authors and titles. Although the concept of the divided catalog is easier for children to grasp, there are advantages in following the arrangement used in the library's main public catalog. The transition is easier for both children and adults.

Physical Arrangement

The status quo in the physical arrangement of the collection needs to be challenged from time to time to see if it is working to the advantage of the users. The various categories—picture books, juvenile fiction and nonfiction, reference—account for the book resources, while other materials are often separated by format: recordings, periodicals, filmstrips, realia, etc. It is possible that this arrangement, fostered by tradition, may not serve the greatest number of users. Should audiovisual materials be shelved by subject with books? Should specialized periodicals, such as *Pack-o-Fun* and *Ranger Rick*, be found with their book counterparts—handicrafts and science—or with other periodicals? Should nonfiction materials for primary-age children be segregated if adult and juvenile nonfiction are interfiled? Within existing patterns, collections should be shifted occasionally, for children, like their elders, tend to use more heavily those materials at eye level.

Collection Maintenance

In addition to the collection evaluation that follows the reassessment of community needs and the determination of new service objectives, collections benefit from periodic and systematic reevaluation for content and condition. It is fairly easy to set up a procedure that will remove copies from circulation for condition; but only a volume-by-volume examination will uncover wallflowers in poor condition or unattractive formats, or out-of-date titles unsuitable for present-day users.

One of the reasons this task is often delegated to a mythical future with limitless time is that some librarians find it difficult to discard materials. Others approach the task with alacrity. In between is a *noblesse oblige* group that will weed if discards can be given to a poor but deserving organization or donated to a library book sale.

Advantages of Weeding

Whether it is called reevaluation, weeding, or deselection, the process of removing materials no longer needed is as important as adding new titles. Public library standards in the past recommended that five percent of the collection be withdrawn annually. Although this figure would not serve the needs of every library, it is a reminder that reevaluation is an activity requiring constant attention.

After I had weeded the children's collection of a library joining the system in which I worked, and before a single volume had been added, a parent remarked, "Well, I see we have some new children's books." Removing the deadwood allowed the gems that were there to shine, and made me a firm believer in giving weeding a higher priority than it usually attained.

In addition to removing materials no longer needed, the librarian who undertakes the weeding task increases her or his knowledge of the collection, its content, and history of past use, and uncovers titles that should be promoted. The first time I weeded a collection, I found it necessary to read or skim many of the titles for which a decision was difficult because of my meager reading background. One title had a nondescript cover, no dust jacket, and was not (then) listed in any of the basic aids. Nevertheless, something about it indicated that it should be read or examined further. That book was *The Lion, the Witch, and the Wardrobe*. The other titles selected for reading or skimming offered no such reward, and the decision to remove them was not difficult.

Evaluation Process

Weeding for content requires judgment in decision-making and a deliberate allocation of time. New librarians in charge of children's collections should allow a settling-in period before attempting to weed a collection on a volume-by-volume basis. A library policy may require that a children's librarian work with a collection for six months or so before rearranging or removing materials. This requirement permits the librarian to become better acquainted with community needs and patterns of use. Librarians whose knowledge of children's materials is still in the embryonic stage will find their first effort time-consuming, for they will need to rely on some of the basic aids for assistance or on one of the prebound jobber's general catalogs that carry ratings given by the various reviewing aids. Titles not listed should not be automatically removed, for they may be out-of-print but still useful, or be of local interest. On the other hand, inclusion should not ensure that a title always remain. Because of the judgment that must be exercised, final decisions on withdrawal of titles are a professional task.

Systematic weeding involves a series of choices as outlined below. The first choice to be made is whether to keep or remove a title. An item must earn its space on a shelf or have qualities that justify its inclusion in a collection. The decision must be made on the basis of its actual or potential contribution to the library's objectives.

Keep a Title. Among the factors to consider are the title's circulation record for the past year, if available; its inclusion in a recent edition of a basic aid; the appropriateness of its content for the community; and its physical condition.

Remove. Materials that are removed from the shelves are those (1) in poor condition, (2) with out-of-date information, and (3) with little interest to current users because of subject, level of difficulty, quality, or format. In addition, there will be titles that require reading or further examination. In considering their final dispensation, the librarian has three choices: to (1) replace, (2) repair, or (3) withdraw from the collection.

Replace. If the material is useful, has not been superseded by a revised edition or by newer titles, and the condition of the pages or its inside margins does not allow rebinding, it should be a candidate for replacement. The number of copies ordered will depend on the condition of the library's other copies, if any, and its projected use. For those titles out-of-print, the basic aids provide suggestions for alternative titles. If, however, the subject is one that dates quickly, the *Subject Guide to Children's Books in Print* (or a comparable source for nonprint materials) should be consulted, and reviews located for the most recent titles.

Repair. Library materials in poor condition do not encourage children to care for them. If the physical condition of the book allows for rebinding, the next decision is whether to replace it with a new copy or to rebind the old one. This will depend on the relative costs of each. Before the decision to mend is made, staff time, as opposed to rebinding costs, should be considered. Rebinding results in an attractive copy, while a collection with a large number of mended books is seldom inviting. Most libraries limit mending of books to those that require less than 15 minutes or those that cannot be rebound or replaced. Splicing damaged films without seriously affecting the presentation is less expensive than replacing. Unless it is a classic, a film is usually replaced with a newer title.

Withdraw. Materials that are no longer useful in the collection should be withdrawn. Because children are not copyright readers, it is extremely important that the information provided children be as up-to-date as possible. Titles that refer to the president as Gerald Ford will not have much credibility with children who consider ten years a lifetime. The circulation record of a non-fiction title cannot be used in assessing its value. A school assignment on Mexico may put everything on this subject in circulation, including a volume with a 1940 copyright date.

Fiction titles that are dated in their approach to contemporary social issues should be withdrawn unless they serve a particular library objective or have achieved the status of a classic. These books may be useful in an academic library for research purposes, but they should not be offered to a poor relation. The children in developing countries, a new public library, or a migrant workers' camp need better fare. Having some materials, however poor their quality, may encourage those with the responsibility to relax their efforts in acquiring what is needed. Librarians should put their energies into securing more suitable materials for these audiences.

Other candidates for withdrawal may be best described as librarians' mistakes. Assuming that the worst of these were never added to the collection, most of this group would be candidates for library book sales. Also included in this category are classics in editions that will never be read given the choice of other editions. A 1920 edition of *Little Women* in small, crowded print may be in perfect condition, and will probably remain so well into the next century. Unlike some wines, librarians' mistakes do not improve with age.

Titles of acceptable quality that are not appropriate for a particular library may be useful in another. Those in good condition should be offered to another library on an indefinite loan or as a gift, whichever is more compatible with the state's library laws. Unwanted duplicates of older, standard titles may be needed in a local college offering courses in children's literature or in a new school developing a collection. A title on the history of children's films may be more useful in a system's main library than in a branch. If excellent titles are little read even after promotional efforts, consider their value for another age group. Through transfer to an adult or young adult collection, a title may find its audience.

Children's librarians cannot assume that copies of titles are being saved for the use of future scholars. A curator of a public library's special collection once remarked that children's literature is the last literary field that has not been thoroughly explored. A few large public and university libraries are making a conscious effort to save last copies from their own collection and to accept unique titles from other libraries, e.g. Chicago Public Library, Providence, R.I. The collection policy may be quite selective, or it may be aimed for inclusive coverage. An example of the latter is one adopted by the University of Washington Libraries several years ago. Libraries in the states that make up the Pacific Northwest Library Association have been invited to send a list of their last copies for possible inclusion in the Children's Literature Collection. This last copy collection is restricted to titles published up to 1941 or through 1945 if the subject treated is World War II. With few exceptions, the books are available on interlibrary loan. Children's librarians through their state or regional associations should investigate what is being done in their area to save this important body of literature. There may be a university or a large public library in the state interested in serving as a depository.

The evaluation process used for books can also be followed when weeding the nonbook materials. Periodicals not indexed in the *Subject Guide to Children's Magazines* or *Readers' Guide* can be considered for clipping or discarded after a year or two. If the accessioning date is added to the materials in the vertical file, weeding will be a more simple task. Reevaluation of filmstrips, slides, and tapes for content requires professional judgment, while examination for condition can be made by nonprofessional staff.

Conclusion

Children's librarians cannot escape the fact that the collection is an integral part of their program of service. Collections for which no actual or potential audience exist are as indefensible as the efforts to implement a quality service program without the support of an equally appropriate collection. The term "collection development" encompasses a number of activities of which selection is only a part. Community needs provide the foundation on which the library's mission and role statement is formulated and the library's service goals and objectives determined. These are considered along with the long-standing goals of helping children become perceptive readers and consumers of information whenever children's librarians make selection choices, develop systems for collections maintenance, and recommend ways to improve their user's access to the library's collections. In an information age the concept of collection must also be broad enough to include information delivered on a computer screen or by a telefacsimile printer, as well as materials in other libraries and institutions. The attendant costs represent a legitimate item in the materials budget.

Librarians operate within the boundaries of collection policies that are stated either as broad principles or in rather specific terms. In general the policies provide the rationale for the materials added and those not selected, as well as procedures for enlisting public involvement. In assuming responsibility for their collections, children's librarians must assimilate the principles of intellectual freedom into a working philosophy that governs not only the content of the collection, but also the policies of access to it. Complaints may come from individuals who wish to protect children from materials they consider harmful or from organized groups attempting to further their cause through the removal or addition of materials thought to influence children. The staff must insist that board-approved policies and procedures be in place when responding to such requests.

The staff resources invested in the planning and promotion of services and programs are considerable, and libraries expect increased use of library materials to be one of the major dividends of these efforts. Obviously it is easier to promote an attractive product that potential buyers need than one that is shabby, lacks current information, or is unsuitable for its intended use. For this reason, collection maintenance deserves a high priority.

Librarians who enjoy the public service aspect of their positions may have to make a conscious effort to schedule the time necessary to develop and maintain a collection worthy of their program of service. There are, of course, librarians who appear to prefer collection development to public services if the time spent on each is an indication. Those who have a consuming fascination with the collection must guard against considering the public's requests for assistance an interruption of their work. The collection derives its importance from its use. It is a means to library services, not the service, itself.

Architects and children are related. Appreciation of space is the most obvious connection: give a child a vertical and she will climb, give her a horizontal and she will run, give her a step and she will jump, give her a slope and she will slide. In short, she will do physically what the architect does conceptually. . . . Nearly every building and public space or lack of it has some impact on the quality of childhood and, it follows, on the quality of children.—Christine Benglea Bevington, in a review of *Children's Spaces* . . . in *Architectural Record*, October 1980, pp.41, 45.

Planning Facilities

Most beginning children's librarians assume that they will never have the opportunity to plan new quarters for children's services. And while this may be true, every librarian must at one time or another evaluate existing space as it advances or impedes efforts to meet the service objectives. Many children's librarians are frustrated in their attempts to provide services for today's audience in space that reflects the needs of children and families in a previous era. For example, the architectural isolation of the children's library with a separate entrance does not further today's goal of integrated services to families. The decision to locate the children's area away from the mainstream may have been a carry-over from an earlier period when children were not served in public libraries.

For the children's librarian faced with the task—or opportunity—of participating in the design of a new or remodeled library, the paucity of useful information on children's library space may be an unexpected complication. Many of the earlier texts on library buildings either ignore children or provide only a few pages of practical dos and don'ts derived from experiences in designing several libraries. We lack a text with knowledge grounded in research comparable to one that deals with learning theory, for instance. Research in how children respond to their built environment is scattered across several disciplines—developmental psychology, education, sociology, and environmental psychology. Only in recent years have attempts been made to integrate what findings exist for those professionals who design spaces for children.[1]

As part of a public library staff, children's librarians need to be aware of some of the processes and steps that go into building a new or remodeled library, as well as the information they should provide, whether explicitly requested or not. The ease or difficulty of fulfilling this charge will depend on the relationships children's librarians have previously established, their knowledge of the process, and the background experience they have to contribute.

Library Building Program

A written building program is an essential step in creating a successful building. Rohlf described it as

> (1) a written statement of the objectives, policies, and goals of the library, and (2) a description of the physical areas and space needs for the achievement of these goals and objectives, the relationships of these spaces to each other, the nature and amount of furniture and equipment required for these spaces, and whatever limitations must be considered.[2]

Mason observed that "it is also a checklist, like one used to assemble equipment for a camping trip, to make sure that nothing is left behind at the last moment, when all looks complete."[3]

Even though a well-developed building program represents a consensus of the client group about the needs to be addressed, it should not impose a specific design on the architect, or plan an exact arrangement of furniture. The architect should be given an opportunity to respond to the needs and problems that have been identified, using her/his own professional abilities in creating a plan for the client group to critique.

With the advent of a new building, use will inevitably increase and demands for new services and materials usually follow. Unless the governing body has dealt with this eventuality, staffing will probably remain at the same level, as one of those ever-present realities. Nevertheless, an overemphasis on this point at the beginning stage should be avoided. In the view of one public library consultant, this stage is the time

> to dream impossible dreams, accept no restrictions, and plan the perfect library for that community before testing those imaginings against reality, for reality is expanding, and its limits are an unknown.[4]

Roles of the Specialists

The cast of characters in creating new or remodeled libraries may range from professional to amateur, with no guarantee that each will adhere strictly to the role assigned. Like the blind men describing an elephant, each specialist considers the building and its interior from her or his own perspective. Elements of the proposed facility assume a different importance for each specialist. There is the client group—librarians, trustees, and perhaps citizen representatives (usually not children!)—and the specialist group which, depending on the resources available, may include the building consultant, the architect, interior designer and/or decorator, and representatives of manufacturers and vendors. Their contribution to the building will vary from extensive to minimal depending on their contract, the chemistry among the various client and consultant groups, and the size of the operation. Even though many communities will not be able to afford the services of some of these specialists, their contribution must be assumed by someone or a group.

Building Consultant. The building consultant's role is to explain effectively the needs of the community and the service program to another group of professionals: architect, designer, engineer, etc. The duties of this consultant may include the following:

1. preparing the building program or advising the library on its preparation;
2. assisting in site selection or conducting the actual site selection study itself;
3. interpreting the service relationships within a building;
4. analyzing each floor plan or plans;
5. reviewing architectural drawings, specifications, sections, elevations, etc., as they are prepared;
6. assisting the interior specialist in the specification and even the design of the furniture or, as is often the case, being the interior specialist and actually specifying the furniture and equipment; and
7. assisting the librarian in developing improved operating techniques within the building itself.[5]

Building consultants are often librarians who have had extensive experience in building libraries. Some small communities may use a consultant from their state library or hire one to guide the director and staff in developing the building program. Even when the staff appears certain of what it wants or needs in a new building, it may not have considered the effect of its proposals on the building as a whole, or on the future should population growth require a different arrangement. Built-in features, access points, and traffic patterns need an impartial eye. A building consultant's experience, which is not confined to a single building or community, enables her or him to deal with this type of situation.

Architect. The architect provides schematic drawings based on the library's building program, and, in general, acts to guard the library's interests during the building construction. The role of this professional has undergone changes in recent decades, with many architecture schools preparing their graduates to take responsibility for the total building: the site work, interior design, furnishings, and equipment. Large architectural firms may have on their staff designers, engineers, and other specialists.[6]

Interior Designer. This professional's task is to incorporate all the elements within the library into a harmonious whole, considering the traffic patterns, needs of the public and staff, and the various functions and activities to be carried out in the building. In addition to recommending colors and textures for walls, ceilings, floors, and decorative features, the designer may review the furniture arrangement as to its suitability; locate dealers and compare quality and prices of furnishings; recommend colors, textures, styles, and shapes of furniture and equipment; and write specifications for each. The architect may hire a designer or the library may engage a professional designer at the beginning or some step of the process.

Manufacturers and Vendors. Representatives of these groups may perform some of the functions of the interior designer in writing specifications for library furnishings and equipment. They offer knowledge of library requirements, but it must be remembered that they have a vested interest in selling their own product whether it be shelving, tables and chairs, or equipment.[7]

Role of the Children's Librarian

Each department has a vital concern in how its services are defined and described in the building program and in the architectural plans subsequently developed. With the promise of new quarters, the staff has an opportunity to view services in a physical environment that supports services rather than working around space limitations imposed by an earlier design. Instead of simply moving the current operations into new quarters, librarians need to distinguish between those procedures and policies developed because of space limitations and those that support the service program, regardless of the building space. Because children's librarians are in the best position to interpret the needs of children in relation to the service program, they should be involved not only in preparing the building program, but also throughout the project as critical changes are often made during the construction process. Unfortunately, this involvement is not always considered necessary. Among children's librarians, complaints about their facilities encountered by Bush in 1977 were: a lack of space, a feeling they had had no say in planning new or recently expanded buildings, and unhappiness with the inconvenient structural features that could not be changed.[8] Several years ago I visited a new library in an affluent community in which the city officials had refused assistance from library representatives. The children's room on the mezzanine could only be reached by a closed stairway, and there was no elevator in the building. Library materials and children in wheelchairs or strollers were obviously expected to rise like dew on a midsummer day. Because such oversights adversely affect services, children's librarians must be aware of tactful ways to offer information in developing the building program.

Planning Space for Children

Even though the outline or format required by each director or building planning committee will vary, there are several general elements that should be considered for inclusion. One children's librarian, as a result of her involvement in a building program, identified the following:

1. Type of space—be as specific as possible as to the size of the room or rooms needed, such as program space, storage and workroom needs, and space for offices, seating, circulation, display, and shelving.
2. Function to be included—mention all services and tasks for which space must be provided such as circulation, cleaning and repairing of materials, reference, and readers guidance, and audiovisual services. During an average week, keep a diary of all the activities that go on and the tasks that are performed in the children's room.
3. Location of areas within the department and the relationship of children's services to other departments. This will allow the architect to plan for efficient work flow patterns within the building.
4. Special requirements or provisions such as floor wiring, accommodations for the handicapped, visual control of the department; "built-ins" features such as puppet stages or play equipment, restroom facilities, coat racks, and boot storage
5. Shelving and storage needs. [Consider] not only the present and future print and nonprint collections, but all materials used in the department. Include information on extra-width shelving needs, oversized storage units, storage for audiovisual equipment, and number of feet of shelves needed with specified heights
6. Furniture and equipment needed. Be as specific as possible about the different types and sizes. Indicate the quantity of each and include manufacturer, description, and illustration of types you have seen or are interested in. . . . [9]

In addition to this basic advice, it is also important to include what Mason calls "the feeling" that each area should evoke.[10] One library system engaged in building several new branch libraries found it necessary to divide the specifications for children into two distinct age groups—preschool to age 7, and 8 to 13—because the various building specialists tended to concentrate on the younger group at the expense of the older.[11] The area used for reading and study by the older group needs few distractions, both aurally and visually, while younger children need more stimulation to encourage interaction with materials. Safety must also have a high priority in any planning of children's quarters.

Children with disabilities have special needs which should also be considered in planning facilities. Federal and state building specifications require that public buildings be barrier-free, and architects and builders will undoubtedly be aware of these specifications. The 1986 standards for buildings and facilities serving physically disabled people issued by the American National Standards Institute were intended to serve as a model for states to adopt or adapt as part of their own building code.[12] However, these specifications were developed to meet the needs of disabled adults and, other than a recommendation that adjustments be made for children, no further direction is given. In making adjustments for children, differences beyond that of size should be recognized. For example, a ramp that can be negotiated by adults in wheelchairs may not be "barrier-free" for children whose physical strength is less developed.[13] They also have less coordination and dexterity in using bookdrops or in opening doors.

In planning the children's space there are several problem areas that need attention. Changes in floor level of even six inches and carpeting with deep pile become barriers for those in wheelchairs or on crutches. If the program area is a sunken well or a room with carpeted tiers, children in wheelchairs or on crutches will have difficulties becoming part of the group unless accommodations are made. Choices in the types of seating should be available. Beanbag chairs may be comfortable for children with severely deformed bodies, but impossible for others who need a sturdy chair.[14] Some of the tables should be high enough to allow children in wheelchairs easy access to a working surface; sinks and drinking fountains fastened to walls are easier to use than ones positioned on pedestals. The needs of children in wheelchairs should also be considered when designing listening stations, computer terminals, and library catalogs. The width of aisles, placement of furniture, and availability and height of directional signs are also factors in designing a barrier-free environment.

Children with disabilities have the same needs for social interaction as other children. Insofar as possible, library facilities should provide opportunities for them to operate with a measure of independence and to become an integral part of a group. To this end, every access point, from shelving to information desks, should be evaluated with the needs of these special children in mind.

Other Areas Used by Children

The plans for the areas children use in common with adults need to be viewed from the standpoint of their probable affect on children. It is difficult to argue that children are welcomed as users when the building has entrances with heavy doors that require adult strength to open, checkout counters too high to permit easy communication, and bookdrops that require adult height and dexterity to use. Other barriers include elevators with control panels beyond reach, drinking fountains and restroom fixtures too difficult or high for children to use comfortably, and glass doors and partitions with cautionary symbols too high for children to notice.

Some adult services staff naturally assume that a crying tot trailing after a parent using the adult collections is the responsibility of the children's staff! Actually, the needs of users with infants should be a library responsibility. If efforts are made to encourage library use of adults (and this includes parents), then a better argument could be made for a playpen in the adult area than in the children's room. A changing table belongs in both the men's and women's restrooms instead of those used by children.

Gathering Information for the Building Program

Children's librarians should look to their own staff for suggestions, because it is in a position to identify potential problems in such areas as work spaces, shelving sequences, and traffic patterns. Children, too, have ideas about the kind of library facility they would like to use. Huntoon asked forty children in the Chicago area for their ideas on topics ranging from seating arrangements to preferred floor level and found that if the reason for the library visit was to study, the majority of children opted for an individual study carrel; twenty-six children chose the first floor (ground level) as the most desirable location (which coincided with its location in four of the five libraries surveyed.)[15] Other methods of soliciting ideas from children include making bulletin board space available for suggestions; comment sheets attached to popular books that circulate; and time scheduled in programs for dialogues with children or parents, or both.[16] Tapping into users' ideas may prevent the facility from having an all-too-familiar institutional look, but should not be the only consideration in designing space. The goals of the service and safety aspects must be weighed against children's or staff members' personal preferences.

Children's librarians may discover that priorities of the various building specialists are counter to their own. For example, many designers and architects place a higher value on aesthetics than function, durability, and service. On the other hand, librarians may lean too heavily on the side of function by "setting up lines of stacks in uninspired rows."[17] The specialists are often more knowledgeable about the needs of adults than of children. If their experience has been limited to institutions with custodial responsibilities, such as schools or hospitals, the role of the children's librarian is to remind them that the public library's relationship with children is characterized by voluntary use.

Background Factors Affecting Library Buildings

Children's space as an integral part of the library building is affected by several factors outside the staff's control. These include (1) population growth and demographic changes, (2) limitations imposed by building codes and the site, and (3) changes resulting from the use of new technology in library operations.

Community and Demographic Changes

A growing or changing population can render a building out-of-date within a decade. The building program must describe the present and project the future needs of the community, and these projections should be translated into concrete terms of space and collection needs. The burgeoning birthrate among young homeowners in the community may translate into a present need for services to preschoolers, but in the next decade, young adults will require more space for resources and services. Low educational levels in a community may suggest that space should accommodate an integrated adult and children's nonfiction collection. Projected changes in zoning may result in a new or increased clientele for the library. When an area of the community that was once industrial becomes an urban renewal site with low-cost family dwellings, this change could produce a new user group and one with different spatial needs. Should literacy programs, homework assistance, and latchkey programs be identified as needs, small study rooms and a children's activity area for group and individual pursuits should be considered along with space for a larger collection.

Conventional wisdom seems to support the notion that twenty to twenty-five years is a reasonable limit in the life of a building before extensive remodeling becomes necessary. The present needs, however, should not be sacrificed for a projected future, but flexibility needs to be considered whenever possible. Permanent walls and built-in furniture reduce the options and lessen flexibility.

Demands of Site or Building Codes

The site exacts its own demands on the planning of libraries. Many sites lend themselves to a variety of architectural designs, while others may create problems, such as oddly shaped space, limited or no natural lighting, and traffic noise. Although a triangular or sloping site will exact limitations, it may also stimulate the architect's creativity in rather exciting ways. In one community the architect of a branch library to be built on a triangular site designed the building as a triangle; a small loft was built in the children's area at the smallest angle which offered a cozy out-of-the-way reading nook. A sloping site may require a split level arrangement with public services offered from both floors, thus creating long-term problems with which to deal.

Some local safety regulations may not be stringent enough to ensure a safe physical environment for children. Long flights of stairs to reach a room for programs or restrooms are common hazards in many public buildings. Planners should be aware that the National Building Code requires that facilities for children in the first grade or younger be placed at the ground floor, because young children do not have the maturity or the physical development to cope with stairs or windows in either a normal or emergency situation. Some of the architectural features that should be avoided are:

1. Doors too heavy for even eight- or nine-year-olds to open
2. Banisters too high for children to reach
3. Story areas with steps too steep for children to maneuver safely
4. Safety designs on glass doors or room dividers placed too high for children
5. Floor-level windows that open out with space large enough for small children to fall through.[18]

Librarians involved with architects soon discover that building features such as weight-bearing pillars and heating ducts have priority over their own ideas for furniture and shelving arrangements. Electrical and communication outlets may complicate the placement of furniture and the space for individual and group activities. Pillars painted in low-visibility colors may be a hazard to active children. Some architects have dealt imaginatively with pillars by building table or seating space around them, or by transforming them into display areas.

Technological Changes

Because technological advances are made at a dizzying rate, it is difficult to predict how soon their adaption to library services will be available or affordable. Those of us whose careers have witnessed the change from the ink pad and dater to the mechanical charger, and from photographic charging to the light wand of automatic circulation systems have also observed the accompanying changes in space and staff requirements. The evolution from the card catalog to the computer-produced book catalog, followed by the microfiche and online catalog has exacted its own unique requirements for space. Public and staff use of microcomputers must also be planned for, as well as listening and viewing areas with their present and projected hardware and access points. If audiovisual services for children have consisted of a pair of earphones and a cassette player, both the level of service and its location need to be addressed. Perhaps a listening-viewing room serving all ages would be a better alternative, or, if funds permit, a central unit providing remote access and dial-up service to stations in the children's area.

Library Factors Affecting Children's Space

The space provided for children is determined not only by the size of the community and the spatial needs of the various age groups to be served, but also by the type of library outlet, the organizational relationships within the library, and the role, mission, goals, and objectives established for services.

Type of Library

The role of children's services in a suburban community branch of a metropolitan system is somewhat different from that in an independent city library. Even though they may both serve a population of 75,000, the space designed for children's services will reflect the status of each library. For example, a suburban library branch will not have responsibility for collecting little-used materials; this will be done elsewhere in the system. Each will also make different demands for space in collection development. The children's librarian in an independent city library may need a different type of office space in working with city-wide agencies. The children's room in the main library of a metropolitan system will require space to match its unique services and clientele, which may include a large number of adults—students, parents, or personnel of agencies involved with children or their materials.

Relationship of Children's Services to Overall Library

The location of children's services often reflects its status within the library. It may be a valued member, well integrated into all library operations, or it may be physically isolated, existing in many aspects as a separate entity. The isolation of some children's rooms is due to the architectural design of a previous era; in others it is the result of administrative decisions.

Although children's libraries housed in separate buildings have been common in some countries (the Soviet Union and Latin American countries), there are few such facilities in the United States. They are expensive to maintain because of the necessary duplication of adult materials and the level of staffing required. A separate facility for children would complicate attempts to serve families, a stated goal of most, if not all, public libraries in this country. Few communities can ensure that children can go to the library on their own in relative safety, and public transportation is not always available or affordable for all families. Still, the impulse to isolate children's services within the library lingers and is rationalized on the premise that children's spontaneity and exuberance disturb adults. Because the tolerance level of the children's staff is not inexhaustible, the children's noise, which is usually purposeful, seldom rises beyond that created by gregarious adults or young adults. Nevertheless, when a new facility is planned to replace a crowded, noisy one, older users tend to favor isolating the children to solve a problem that may no longer exist in a larger building. Some librarians provide quiet rooms for those adults who long for a silent environment remembered from their past. In determining the location of the children's area within a building, the needs of users should be considered, the staffing level projected, and the reciprocal use made of collections.

Responsibility to Children as Users

User Needs. Not only should children be heard in libraries, but they should also be seen as a legitimate part of the audience to be served. More adults are probably pleased to see children using the library than are disturbed by their presence. It is for that reason that the children's area is often located near a busy street as a public relations tactic. (One hopes this is also done to provide windows with natural lighting for children.) When children observe adults reading and using library materials, the concept of lifelong learning is more easily acquired. Young children are less apprehensive if they can see into the area used by their parents, but a location near the browsing section is obviously preferable to the reference and study areas. One of the unfortunate facts of contemporary life is that children in all kinds of communities cannot be entirely safe from those who might wish to harm them. If the children's space is located in a basement, on a second floor, or in an isolated wing, the staffing must be at a level that guarantees an adequate measure of safety for both children and staff.

Staffing Levels. The most efficient use of staff is to centralize as many processes as possible. If the children's area is located too far from the circulation and registration desks, a separate operation will need to be staffed in the children's area. If these activities have been the responsibility of the children's staff, a new building offers an opportunity to combine the functions into one operation. Some children's librarians believe that separate service desks offer more opportunity to provide guidance, elicit reader response, and ensure that children encounter a staff sympathetic to and knowledgeable of their needs. Strong as these arguments are, however, those who support an integrated operation point to a better use of children's staff who are able to assist children in all areas of the library, freed from a charging desk with its clutter and confusion. One should question whether a circulation staff inhospitable to children is really effective serving other age groups. Children have more opportunity to interact with adult users at checkout counters and to become acquainted with other staff who can ease the transition from the children's collection to other library resources. When these functions are carried on in a central area, more space becomes available for services and programs in the children's room. An integrated operation is also less likely to result in a closure of the children's library when budget cuts are made.

Reciprocal Use of Collections. If users of one collection make frequent and heavy use of another, or if the library hopes to encourage this type of behavior, the advisability of placing them in close proximity should be considered. Whereas older children in particular need access to adult collections, many adults would profit from using children's nonfiction titles. In addition, adult students or professionals concerned with children or their materials would be well served if adult materials on education, child psychology, and child care were in close proximity. On the other hand, some arrangements may not offer reciprocal advantages. Older children would find it convenient if the young adult collection were nearby; however, the needs of young adults would proscribe a location as far removed as possible from the children's area.

Role, Mission, Goals, and Objectives

The library that has determined its role(s) and operates within the context of a written mission statement and set of goals and objectives has a firm foundation on which to plan facilities. If the library's mission statement stresses service to families, discussions of its space requirements can be included in the overall planning. A combined children's and family department or a location near frequently used adult collections can now be explored. If the library's mission is to serve as a center for community activities, the needs of children should be considered in planning and designing auditoria, meeting rooms, and program areas.

The role selected for the library also proscribes the type of space and its allocation within the children's area, and should be kept firmly in mind throughout all planning. If the library's role is to serve as a community activities center, activity and program space within the children's area would need to be considered. It might include an activity area for crafts or puppet productions to accommodate children singly or as part of a small group. A glassed-in mini-theater for storytelling, for film and video showings, and for other programs might be attached to the children's room. Display space, community bulletin boards, an audiovisual production lab, and cable TV studios are also suggested when this role is selected as the most appropriate for a community.[19]

In comparing the space allocations for two libraries with different roles and mission statements as proposed below, the impact on facilities becomes readily apparent.

Formal Education Support Center. Libraries adopting this role may target particular age groups in a mission statement as follows:

The Night Falls Community Library assists students in elementary and secondary schools in meeting educational objectives established during their formal courses of study. The library offers tours for classes, instructs students on using library tools, and provides homework assistance and supplementary print and audiovisual materials for classroom use.

This mission does not ignore the other uses that may be made of the facility, such as recreational reading, community information, or programs for preschoolers, but the statement embodies the major focus.

In planning space for activities, furnishings, and equipment needed for this particular mission, the children's staff might include the following items in a list submitted to the building consultant:

1. Carrels, with some wired for audiotape listening and video viewing
2. Table space and chairs for children ages 9 to 12, and for tutors
3. Shelving for small reference and reserve collections
4. Microcomputers, printers, and study skills software
5. Copy and telefax machines in close proximity
6. Conference room(s) for small groups of children or tutors
7. Accommodations in auditorium for library instruction
8. Small study rooms for all purposes: tutors and students, adults seeking quiet space, two-student conferences, etc.
9. Office space for the children's librarian for conferences with children, tutors, teachers, etc.

Communities adopting this role and mission would probably be those with low educational skills. Unless the combined collection of adult and juvenile nonfiction is small, the latter should be located in the children's area, easily accessible for assignments and for leisure reading. The spatial requirements needed to support this role and mission could result in a children's area similar to the one in figure 6.

Popular Materials Library. When this role is identified as the major one for older children, young adult, and adult users, it is sometimes accompanied by another for young children: the Preschoolers Door to Learning. For purposes of contrast, however, our example will ignore the secondary role in the mission statement.

The library seeks to provide a collection of materials in a variety of formats that are current and selected with the interests and needs of the Morningside community in mind. The library also provides promo-

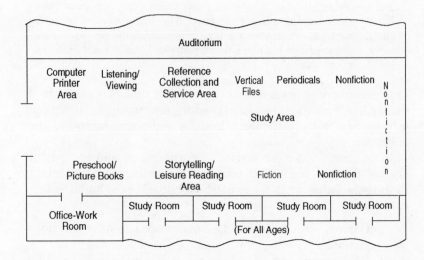

Fig. 6.   Formal education support center

tional programs designed to support the leisure and cultural interests of its citizens.

The spatial requirements of libraries adopting a Popular Materials Library role are somewhat different from those serving as a Formal Education Support Center. Libraries with this mission stress the merchandising of materials that are made easily accessible and heavily promoted through displays, booklists, and programming. Because the major focus is the use of materials, attention is given to display areas, comfortable seating, and effective signage.[20] The needs of the children's area in libraries with this mission might include the following:

1. Casual seating: cushions, beanbags, a loveseat for parents and preschoolers near picture books, lounge furniture
2. Tables and chairs for each age group: 3–6, 7–10, 11–13
3. Low benches and stools near combined nonfiction stacks
4. Space for easy nonfiction, 3–8; folklore, poetry, and biography for ages 8–13
5. Display area for library promotion and for children's artwork
6. Video viewing/book discussion room in close proximity
7. Computer and listening area
8. Close proximity to auditorium that can be partitioned off for a variety of children's programs.

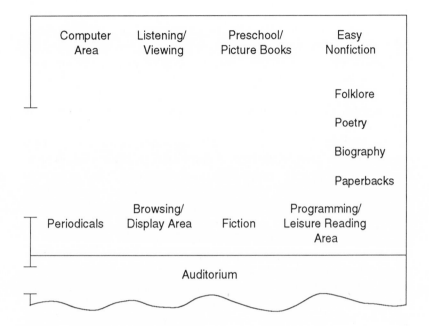

Fig. 7.   Popular materials library

The spatial requirements necessary to support a Popular Materials Library role could resemble the diagram depicted in figure 7.

Goals and objectives are also important to consider in allocating space within the children's area. If past experience has shown that these have had to be prioritized according to space requirements, it becomes obvious that the area should be planned with flexibility as an important factor. Rapidly changing social conditions and uncertain levels of staffing often dictate a different spatial arrangement, and insofar as it is possible, such arrangements should be considered in planning.

Children's Space: A Humane Environment for Users

In a humane environment, children can recognize that a special area has been planned for them by the size and type of furnishings, by the signage, and the decor. In addition, the psychological needs of children to be as independent as possible, including those with disabilities, have received special attention beyond

those specifications required by law. Space for users in wheelchairs has been considered when shelving, width of aisles, furniture placement, and access to program areas were planned. This
planning is also evident in the design of those areas used in
common—checkout and information desks—and in the accessibility of such amenities as restrooms, telephones, and drinking
fountains.

Because each individual has a specific reason for using a
library at any one time, and that reason varies depending on
mood or motivation, the spatial arrangements have been
designed to acknowledge that. A child, like an adult user, cannot
be classified strictly as an information-seeking type, a recreational reader, or a faithful participant at library programs even
though he or she may fit more comfortably within one group or
the other.

Architects and designers have recognized that their efforts to
please one age group may offend another, that what is attractive
to toddlers may alienate twelve-year-olds who are protective of
their emerging adult status. (Even the name of the area can
become an issue: Children's Room; Young People; Youth Services,
etc.) Within the children's space, each child is able to recognize
the area that fits her or his age, size, and particular library need.

All who have engaged in the planning have recognized that a
humane environment for children is one that provides choices
and offers opportunities to interact with others or to withdraw to
a private space to read or listen, concentrate, or daydream. This
environment, however, also supports the major purpose of a
library—the invitation to interact with materials.

Spatial Preferences and Needs of Children

Most of what is known about children's responses to a built environment (as opposed to the natural environment) in library settings is based on observation; the social environment has received
more attention. Much of the research in this area has centered on
children's response to spatial elements in schools and classrooms,
institutions for children with disabilities and, to a lesser degree,
in the home. One approach used in the field of education has been
to study the impact of the environment by comparing academic
scores or performances on educational tasks in different settings.
Other methods involve observing behavioral responses to a specific environment or environmental element such as color, or to
ask children directly for their reactions to situations imposed by
their environment. Nevertheless, the studies that do exist can

provide helpful insights to those responsible for designing children's libraries.

Response to Structural Features. Studies have confirmed what librarians have long observed: children's conception of the built environment is qualitatively different from that of the adolescent or adult. Children are much more concerned with "paths and boundaries, with hiding places and other special places for particular things."[21] When children were asked to make recommendations for play spaces in their homes, they described "neat places" that were geometrically irregular and multileveled. Small spaces such as cubbyholes, closets, or areas behind furniture, also had high value. "Really neat" was an accolade reserved for unexpected, secret, or hidden space such as a trapdoor, or furniture in a wall.[22]

Children's responses are developmental in that their reactions are dependent on their psychological growth. Young children make no distinction between the accidental features in their environment, such as the climbing properties of the trunk of a tree, and those planned by humans; nor do they recognize the historical significance of such features as a schoolhouse clock or the replica of Laura Ingalls' log cabin home. These will be appreciated (or not) on another level.[23] In one early study children were interviewed concerning their responses to their city environment, including a department store. For the six-year-olds, the stairs, escalators, and elevators became the focus of interest as the children contemplated how these could be used in play. Items for sale did not hold much interest for the six-year-olds. For the nine-year-olds, the store represented an enormous fair from which to collect mementos, such as advertising giveaways. The twelve-year-olds saw the store as a "microcosm of the world of adults," a place to try on adult roles and behavior.[24] Applying these findings to libraries, we could predict that an area of uninterrupted space would invite small children to run; children at tables for four or more could be expected to engage in social conversation; displays at eye level would be examined; and children would inevitably touch realia placed within easy reach. Children of various ages would respond differently to a treehouse in the children's area; it would represent possibilities for imaginative play for the young child, the nine-year-old would test the various uses it could be made to serve, and the twelve-year-old would, publicly at least, consider it too juvenile for attention.

Control of Space. Children, like adults faced with a perfectly designed and furnished room, may hesitate to mar its perfection. The message conveyed is "look but don't touch . . . everything is perfect . . . don't change anything."[25] In contrast, the somewhat underdesigned room invites interaction and conveys the message that change is not only permitted, but encouraged.

The need of children to control their environment has long been observed by librarians. Given the opportunity, children rearrange pillows or mats by color or size, place stools in a row to form an imaginary vehicle, and use furniture in ways for which it was not intended; a child will lie on benches or sit under a table. The staff must decide how much direct supervision is actually necessary. By their overt actions in controlling use of space and furnishings, staff may convey the impression that the library is theirs. An overemphasis on the staff's need for surveillance may defeat the goal of creating a child-centered facility. A balance should be strived for in responding to children's needs for autonomy and the staff's goals to maximize the effective use of resources for all users and to provide a safe environment for children. There are ways to share control of space with children. Instead of "orderly arrangements of wall decorations and placement at adult level sight lines,"[26] why not designate a display area for children's use?

Considerable research exists on the personal space of adults, that "area immediately surrounding an individual which has invisible boundaries."[27] Although culture, age, sex, degree of acquaintance, and personality affect the amount of space used, children at five years of age have acquired a certain level of interpersonal distance behaviors. The amount of space used increases until about age eight when it appears to remain fairly stable.[28] In one study, kindergartners were less attentive to a story when crowded around the teacher than when more dispersed.[29] In another study, four-year-olds were more involved with the planned activity when space conditions were "moderately crowded" rather than "most crowded" or "least crowded."[30] In crowded conditions, young children's social contacts decreased and aggressive behavior increased. Older children in similar conditions behaved in less socially acceptable ways or removed themselves from the situation.[31] Librarians who have requested screens or movable walls to shrink or expand space in meeting rooms for story hours have been on firm ground. Individual seating mats for children also offer opportunities to exercise some control over personal space.

Need for Privacy. A young child's need for security as represented by the presence of a trusted adult or friend is more important than a place to be alone. For school-age children, the definition of privacy has been found to vary as they select the most important aspect at a particular time. In a study involving 900 children ages 5 to 17, children in urban high-density areas often equated privacy with no noise; for some, it was being with others without being interrupted or bothered. Some described privacy as being alone, or being able to control access to space. A private place for still others was a place to be alone to read or to think without others knowing one's thoughts.[32]

Children's responses to two different types of classrooms—open and closed—have also been evaluated. In both types, children expressed a need for withdrawing periodically during the school day. When asked what they did at those times, the children identified a number of private places: the bathroom, a relatively secluded reading area, space under a table. Others resorted to daydreaming. A rather extreme solution was to misbehave in order to be banished to a desk outside the classroom door. The children often took their work with them to these retreats, away from the classroom noise and the watchful eye of the teacher. One observation made by the researchers that has particular implications for librarians is that children made very little use of the quiet, secluded places available in both types of classrooms, possibly because they did not have free access to them. Teachers regarded their use as part of the reward system, and many of them were uncomfortable with the absence of control inherent in such areas. It is not surprising that in the minds of the children, the classroom belonged to the teacher who controlled space.[33] When one adds the adults' control of time, it is not surprising that children feel powerless.

Need for Social Interaction. A child's desire for companionship and social contacts not only meets a psychological human need, but also a developmental one in learning to get along with peers. It may be debated how much responsibility libraries bear in providing opportunities for the latter. Nevertheless, the library environment must support its service goals and be attractive to children whose attendance is, for the most part, voluntary. One of the goals of children's programming is social interaction—between programmer and child, and among individual children. There is no hard evidence that one type of environment is the most successful in encouraging children to engage in recreational reading or to seek information for personal needs, although there are indications that the environment may be a factor in encouraging recreational reading in school libraries. These findings may not be applicable to public libraries because voluntary use changes the psychological environment. Also, the social environment that encompasses such factors as staff attitudes cannot be entirely isolated from the physical environment.

One elementary school librarian attempted to increase children's reading by adding paperback books full of violence and suspense, but this worked with only a few. When someone donated a large red shag rug and some colorful pillows, the librarian removed most of the tables and chairs and allowed the children to sprawl on the rug. This altered environment allowing interaction brought so many children into the library that space on the rug had to be rationed. (Children were required to have a book in their hands to gain access to the rug.) Children in such close proximity naturally conversed, but, after some initial horseplay, they usually became engrossed in reading while lying on their backs, sitting up, or stretching out on their stomachs.[34] Even if their reading had not increased, these children would have gained a more favorable attitude toward libraries and their resources.

A more recent study conducted in a school library in Israel used a video camera to record children's responses to a nontraditional environment. Instead of the usual tables with seating for six or eight people, the carpeted library contained very little furniture except pillows, several chairs, and a few three-sided cubes that could be fashioned into benches, tunnels, or carrels. Social interaction was allowed—also outside the normal pattern of permissible library behavior. Children tended to group themselves in dyads. When there were fewer pillows than children, the partner would guard the space and the pillows while the other browsed. Some dyads joined others to form a circle. Although reading in groups or dyads was preferred by a large number of children, many sought space in which to be alone for a period of time, often in corners or against walls.* The authors concluded that choices were important in the beginning phases of library use and reading for pleasure.[35]

The child's need for interaction with peers often conflicts with the librarian's need to be in control. Assuming that children will misbehave when given the opportunity often becomes a self-fulfilling prophecy. Some studies suggest that unruly children may be reacting to unstimulating surroundings. The adult responsible for overseeing a group of active children may opt for an environment that has a calming effect and one that lessens interaction. In so doing, however, the children may feel

> confined and bored, and end up trying to generate arousal and pleasure by interacting amongst themselves. In the ensuing battle,

---

*Another observation from this study was that children moved their bodies almost constantly while they were immersed in reading. They read in practically every position possible—standing, seated cross-legged, on cushions, lying face down or face up on the carpet, or kneeling beside a friend.

the more dominant members of the ... community [adults] extend restrictive regulations which even makes it tough for kids to communicate with each other, to share laughter or hurt, or to spend relaxed or thoughtful time together.[36]

In the interest of service that is good from a child's point of view, spatial arrangements should allow easy access to staff assistance and opportunities to be alone or to interact with a friend or parent.

Furnishings and Equipment

When selecting furnishings for adult areas, comfort, attractiveness, and durability—usually in that order—enter into the decision. When children are the audience, the ranking is often reversed, with safety placed before comfort. Furnishings that are impervious to all known substances are also uncomfortable for humans. In one study on children's responses to the built environment, the authors observed that

an impervious environment seemed to elicit a more destructive response than environments built with traditional, more easily marked materials.[37]

The rise in the number of incidents of vandalism in libraries has elicited a response that deals with the effect, not the cause. More attention should be placed on creating an environment that evokes a favorable personal identification from its users. Many years ago, when a community in Washington State built a new elementary school, considerable effort was made to create a humane learning environment. Movable walls and carpeting were then new in the children's experience. The first time it rained, the children, on their own initiative, removed their shoes before entering the classroom. They felt a shared sense of community and a personal responsibility for their environment.

When adults place durability above all else in selecting furnishings for children, the resulting environment may be one of hard surfaces: tiled floors, table tops of formica, noncushioned plastic, or wrought-iron chairs. In such an environment, one might envision the principal cleaning tool to be a water hose. Although it would be sensible to avoid upholstery materials with tempting threads to pull or a design to decorate, the materials used should not be so indestructible that a child feels challenged to try. Table tops able to withstand day-to-day hazards are preferable choices for all ages, but chair styles for children should be chosen as much for comfort as durability. Furnishings that respond to touch and soften the environment can also be provided in smaller items such as pillows and cushions placed on lounge furniture. Mats of plush carpeting and a few soft beanbag chairs, for example, do much to relieve the institutional feeling that formica, plastic, and hardwood evoke.

With few exceptions, children are not destructive of their environment if they understand the value and purpose of the items in it. An elementary school principal once exhibited his antique furniture pieces on a rotating basis in a central hall for the children to enjoy. He explained the history and value of each piece, and the children responded to his trust by treating each with care.

Furnishings for Recreational Use. A carpeted floor is today considered an integral part of the furnishings. Not only does carpeting offer acoustical advantages, but it also serves as alternative seating, especially if pillows, cushions, beanbags, or polliwogs (cushions with molded backrests) are provided for children to create their own reading spaces. These need to be in materials that can be easily cleaned, but pleasing to the touch. Many seating choices should be available. One common mistake is to select seating that is much too high for young children. After observing teenagers and adults choose low stools or benches in the children's room even when other choices were available, I began to look at the height of the seating from the standpoint of the children. The benches for the sloping picture-book table were fifteen inches, and the stools intended for casual seating were twelve. Young children using the picture-book section could not sit for any length of time at the sloping table in comfort without sitting on their feet. A comfortable low stool for young children was closer to eight inches than the customary twelve. The favorite piece of furniture in one branch library was a locally designed padded bench, approximately four feet long and six inches high. The children lay on it while they read, and moved it to various parts of the library as their needs dictated.

Safety is a major concern, especially in selection for small children. Children's furniture designed expressly for institutions will probably be free of sharp corners and edges, but those items that are built-in or custom-made should be examined for potential hazards. Some lightweight chairs of plastic or wrought-iron wire are attractive and add a noninstitutional note to the room, but they should be checked for stability because when children stand on them, which they do, they should not tip over. In the search for a properly designed institutional chair for children, some libraries have chosen smaller versions of sturdy adult chairs which are difficult for the children to move, thereby adding another frustration to their environment.

Furnishings for Study and Contemplation. When children use the library for homework assignments or for their own information needs, space is needed for writing, as well as for library materials. These activities are best supported in the most quiet parts of the children's area. Because comfort is rated highly by children, furnishings should be examined with this criterion in mind. Children working together require table space, with chairs at a height that allows them to sit comfortably with their feet on the floor. Some children may prefer an appropriate size study carrel when alone.

In many libraries, seating for the intermediate-size child, age eight to ten, is often lacking. The expectation is that this child can select between the picture-book seating and seating provided for the older child. A rule of thumb suggests that there should be ten inches between table and chair heights (probably less for very young children). Intermediate-size children need tables 25 inches in height, with chairs at 15 inches. For older children, tables of 27–29 inches, with chairs at 17–19 inches are recommended.[38]

Square or rectangular tables are often interspersed with round ones to avoid an institutional appearance. Round tables offer the advantages of no sharp edges and easier communication among children who work together. If juvenile and adult nonfiction collection are integrated, appropriate seating and table space for children should be available in that area. Too often the accommodations in this area indicate that it is an adult-only province.

Accommodations for parent and child to sit together invite interaction with materials. Loveseats or cushioned benches adjoining the picture-book sections, and away from heavy traffic patterns, invite such use. Adults who use the children's collections for educational purposes would probably find the study carrels or tables intended for older children quite appropriate for their needs.

Service Areas and Equipment. The service areas, such as circulation counters or registration desks, need to be adjusted to allow for children's use. These service points should be visible to children learning library procedures. Children develop favorable attitudes toward institutions where they can demonstrate a measure of self-sufficiency. Part of the circulation desk can be adjusted to the height of children and those in wheelchairs. Children should also be able to use the bookdrops unassisted. If a card catalog is used, the choice must be made between a separate one for children limited to children's entries, or a combined one at a location and height easily accessible to children. (Technology may have rendered this question moot for a growing number of libraries, though.) But whatever the format of the file—3-by-5-

inch cards, microfiche or microfilm, or online—children's needs require attention, either by locating equipment or terminals in the children's area, perferably near the children's staff desk, or by designating specific stations for children through the provision of child-size furniture. A service desk within the children's area should be easily accessible to users, with directions for obtaining assistance whenever the desk is not staffed.

Amenities. Adults sometimes forget the feeling of security that easy access to restrooms provides for children, especially for the younger ones. If restrooms must be shared with adults, not only should the height of the fixtures be considered, but staff surveillance is also necessary in the interest of safety. Restrooms planned as part of the children's area are a more desirable alternative, if not a mandatory one. For the legion of children who must operate by adult time schedules, a clock (with numbers rather than dots!) should be positioned at a height easily visible to children. Drinking fountains can be an attractive nuisance if highly visible, yet one adjusted to children's height should be located in or convenient to the children's area. In colder climates especially, coat, boot, and schoolbook storage designed for children's heights are other amenities to consider; in other localities, wet bathing suits and towels may need to be accommodated. Given the pattern of library use in most communities, easy access to a copy machine would be appreciated by both the child and parent when homework requires the use of reference materials and time doesn't permit long periods of in-library study time. In placing public telephones within the library, children's use should be planned for, even though the children's staff may allow emergency calls to be made on the library's phones.

Space for Collection and Equipment

Whatever the format, the collection is basic to children's library services and makes its own demand for space. Although it is the nature of collections to grow as knowledge increases and new user groups are added, the size of the collection serving children is determined primarily by the amount of duplication needed and the functions it must serve. Small independent libraries and branch libraries control growth through careful weeding, relying on other libraries to serve the archival function or research needs of adult students. Nevertheless, before building plans are developed, the collection should be thoroughly reevaluated for discarding and replacement. Growth predictions for children's collections may be more reliable based on population and service responsibility projections than the measure obtained by averaging the net growth of various categories of materials—such as picture books, fiction, etc.—over the past several years.[39] Even though this latter measure may be useful, it would be more significant to translate service objectives—increased services for older children—and population projections—a growing ethnic population—into shelving needs.

Windows that provide lots of natural light and space uncluttered with rows of shelving often lose out to the reality of housing a collection. Low windows mean less wall space for materials, and space free of shelving tiers may mean higher units elsewhere.

Shelving Requirements

The present collection and projected future growth should be translated into linear-foot shelving, recognizing the requirements for each format. The formula used in transferring adult books to linear feet must be adjusted for the variety of sizes found in children's collections. Shelves are considered crowded when their capacity surpasses three-fourths full.[40] The number of picture books per standard shelf is approximately 60; juvenile fiction, 30; and juvenile nonfiction, 28 or 30. The height of the shelving is dictated by the size of the children rather than the tempting storage capacity offered. Seven-foot shelves are more economical than five, but for short adults and most children, they discourage browsing, which accounts for a large portion of public library use. The "let 'em stand on stools" attitude overlooks the fact that children may make this effort only if they know the title they want is on the top shelf of a seven-foot section. Although no research has been reported on the effect of the height of shelving on children's use, common sense and the observation of their librarians strongly indicates that shelving over five feet tall restricts the use of materials.

The variety of sizes of children's books may range from 3½ to 14 inches high, with widths from 2 to 13 inches in the picture-book categories. The nonfiction collections will also include a number of large, irregularly shaped volumes. Segregating the latter into an oversized section will save shelving space and give a more attractive appearance to the shelves, but they may be overlooked by those using books shelved in the regular sequence. A rule of thumb for shelving is as follows:

Picture books	Height: under 42 inches high, 12 inches wide, with dividers every 6 or 8 inches. Consider alternating slanting display

	shelves and regular shelving. Low free-standing bins may be used.
Fiction	5-foot wall shelving, 9 or 10 inches wide, or 42-inch freestanding units.
Nonfiction	5-foot wall shelving, 12 inches wide, if collection is shelved in regular sequence; 9 or 10 inches, if 12-inch shelving is provided for an oversize section. 42-inch free-standing, double-faced units may also be used.
Storage	Space in workroom or storage area for books little used, used seasonally, or removed for reevaluation. Alternative space may be provided in top two shelves (covered) if 7-foot shelving is used for fiction or nonfiction collection.
Reference	42-inch shelving or counter height, 12 inches deep, whether located in children's area or combined with adult reference.
Paperbacks	Shelving that allows users to view spines and some covers, or circular rotating racks.
Periodicals	Shelving that allows users to view covers, with heights to accommodate young children, 12 inches deep, with space for limited number of back issues.
Pamphlets	Separate vertical file with hanging files, stored in princeton files shelved with subject area, or combined with adult materials in vertical files, two or three drawers high.
Recordings, Tapes, and Compact Discs	Bins, approximately 25 inches high, or picture book shelving for recordings. For audiocassettes or CDs, circular rotating racks, which allow covers to be viewed, or integrate with book collection by using specially constructed "book-size cover." (Consult catalogs of library supply houses for latest display possibilities.)
Videos	Slanting shelves (place videos with spines up), whether videos are for circulating or programming or for individual or group viewing; regular shelving as well.
Realia and Toys	Space to accommodate a variety of sizes; to examine and display some items.

Pictures	Two-drawer vertical or horizontal files.
Posters	Drawers or special vertical shelving, with display options.

When collections of nonprint materials are very small, children's titles are often shelved in a combined adult-juvenile collection located in a central area. If the collection is expected to increase, space in the children's area should be planned.

The arrangement of the collection should be logical to users. Both fiction and nonfiction should flow without confusing detours or breaks in the sequence. If the fiction collection, for example, begins on wall shelving and ends in freestanding, counter-high shelving, users may not be able to make the transition.

Space for Equipment

If accommodations are made available upon request for listening or viewing in the library, space for users engaged in these activities must be planned. The larger, and often more affluent, libraries will be able to provide listening and viewing stations in various parts of the library, controlled from a central unit, with earphones that can be used in various parts of the library. Some are only able to offer access to earphones and a cassette recorder operated by the listener. Video equipment may be located in a separate area available to users of all ages, or stacked on a portable cart for use in the children's or activity room, available upon request or programmed by the children's staff. A counter near a children's staff desk could be designed to accommodate all equipment used by the public. Space for the various pieces of equipment, storage space for earphones and other paraphernalia, and the appropriate electrical outlets could be somewhat centralized in this area. Seating arrangements for one or more children, depending on projected use, could also be designed for each equipment station.

Sound filmstrip players with earphones require a stationary location if extensive use by individual children is projected. If used in programming in a storytelling or meeting room, a portable AV cart is desirable.

Microcomputers may be located in an area for use by all ages, or one or more may be located in the children's room as an integral part of the service program. Because instruction in use of the computer is often needed, put the computer near the children's desk. Audiovisual equipment assigned to the children's room and used by the staff or circulated to the public requires space in a work area or storage closet.

Space Requirements for Services

One of the requirements of a building program is to identify the activities that will be carried on within the various areas of the library. The space planned for these activities should not be limited to that presently offered, but should also include what is projected by the mission statement and the goals and objectives of the library.

Basic Services

The following represent a sampling of activities performed as part of children's services:

1. Readers advisory services for children and adults concerned with children
2. Reference services for children and adults, using circulating and reference collections, vertical files, etc.
3. Catalog use and instruction
4. Browsing and studying as independent activities
5. Listening to recordings, viewing filmstrips, and watching videos as an individual activity
6. Art and craft activities as individual pursuits
7. Microcomputer use and instruction
8. Discussions with a friend, the library staff, a parent about reactions to materials
9. Children assisting other children in using materials, the catalog, or equipment
10. Requesting information on materials not in the collection, or filling out a reserve.[41]

Program Services

Group activities make demands for space that may overtax existing areas. Nevertheless, as the twenty-first century approaches, we need to assess the role of community libraries that purport to be vital forces in the lives of their users. Depending on the role the library assumes, the facility may serve as a center for social interaction, for cultural enrichment, and for independent learning for all ages. Space for these functions should not be considered frills, but, rather, as necessary adjuncts to the quest for information.

Among the traditional programming activities carried on by libraries are:

1. Preschool and toddler programs
2. Educational programs for parents, teachers, day care personnel, etc.
3. Story hours and puppet programs for school-age children
4. Class visits to the library for an orientation to resources or instruction in its use
5. Dramatic activities performed by children: skits, puppetry, reader's theatre, etc.
6. Craft-making: puppets, musical instruments, painting, paperfolding, etc.
7. Clubs: book discussion, special interest (science, stamp, chess, etc.)
8. Film and video programs
9. Reading clubs.

Obviously, a separate space for each age group or for each type of activity is not possible and trade-offs are inevitable. After considering the space needs of the service priorities, select the best combination of activities that can be carried on in the same type of space. In most small- to medium-size libraries, program space is often shared, and so the children's staff cannot design the space expressly for children. An auditorium that is shared with the adult and YA departments as well as the community could have adjustable walls and display areas that can also be decorated at a child's-eye level. Storage for children's chairs or storytime cushions needs to be included. An area in a quiet section of the children's room may be designated as a program space, with seating mats for young children at storytimes or group visits, and chairs with 15-inch-high seats stacked in an adjacent storage area for visits of fourth- to seventh-graders. When not in use for programming, this space, with the addition of cushions, could serve as a recreational reading area. A carpeted, tiered room as part of the children's area may also serve many uses from traditional storytelling to film or demonstration programs, as well as space for a small group of children to view videos from the library's collection. Space that accommodates craft activities should include a sink, storage for materials, an easily cleaned floor, and a display area for children's work. This type of space may also be used for club meetings, although a carpeted floor would be preferable for this purpose.

Display Space

Most children's librarians would agree that it is possible to have too much or not enough display space, or to have it in the wrong location. Display areas are viewed in a variety of ways by librarians—as a potential educational or informational medium, an opportunity for artistic expression, or an empty space demanding to be filled. Displays serve three important functions: (1) to convey information about services, collections, and community, (2) to elicit suggestions from the public on services and resources, and (3) to recognize the achievements of children in the community by providing an opportunity to display their work.

Bulletin board space in the entrance can be used to promote programs and services. Slotwall boards within the children's area or at the charging desk may hold promotional materials, or serve as a background for three-dimensional displays. Unlike peg or cork boards, slotwall boards are attractive even when not in use. Display space may be planned as part of the shelving to promote various topics or as part of the catalog facility to provide instruction on its use. Portable display boards should be considered for the flexibility they offer.

Some display items need the protection of a locked case, such as a child's model car collection, the favorite childhood books of the community's leading citizens, or the library's Beatrix Potter figurines. These may be freestanding cases that can be moved to other areas as needed, or built into the shelving at a child's eye level. The ceiling should not be overlooked as a base from which lightweight banners or paper objects can be hung.

Storage for Program Materials

Because many materials created for a particular children's program can be recycled, storage for these items needs to be planned. A wooden clown used in a summer reading club may serve two years hence to announce children's programs for the coming season. Posters of children's book illustrations or award-winning titles can also be used in creating new displays or may become valuable in their own right as have Children's Book Week posters that serve as a history of children's illustration in this country. Some libraries integrate all programming and display items that are classified and made available for use by all departments. A pictorial record of successful displays using these items invites replication or adaptation.[42]

Space Needs for Staff and Equipment

Space should be estimated for the size of the current staff, and for any increase envisioned in the next decade. The work space of a staff member has been estimated to be 100 to 150 square feet, depending on the equipment or activity involved.[43] If circulation processes and technical services are done elsewhere, the space allotment for the children's workroom can be greatly reduced. In small libraries, office space for the children's librarian may be incorporated within the workroom. In either configuration, a glass-paneled wall permitting visibility into the public service area is desirable for both the workroom and the children's librarian's office. The addition of drapes or blinds allows for privacy when necessary.

The activities to be carried on in the staff areas should be enumerated as part of the building plan. These include (but are not limited to):

1. Selection: reading reviews, ordering review copies, preparing orders for replacement and duplicate copies, etc.
2. Directing and supervising staff
3. Reference interviews with public
4. Planning and preparing programs for the public and in-service activities for staff
5. Planning joint activities with staff and other community agency personnel
6. Writing reviews, letters, and program announcements, and compiling and designing bibliographies
7. Preparing displays, designing promotional materials
8. Sorting materials for shelving
9. Evaluating materials for condition preliminary to discarding, mending, or bindery shipments.

This space must also accommodate equipment and materials, such as:

1. Desk for children's librarian and assistant(s)
2. Filing cabinets
3. Typewriter(s) or word processor and printer, with stands
4. Online catalog terminal or microfiche reader
5. Telephone or extension
6. Book trucks
7. Audiovisual equipment for circulation or programming
8. Audiovisual software for programming; computer software
9. Sink
10. Office and programming supplies
11. The working reference and professional collection of the children's librarian
12. Bulletin board for staff communication
13. Staff coats, boots, and handbags (if locker space is not available elsewhere).

Aesthetic and Functional Considerations

Individuals from the interior designer to the president of the board of trustees may view the children's room as the "jewel in the crown," the area where human fancies override the more prosaic ones. The children's room risks being considered a community status symbol in much the same way as an indoor olympic-size swimming pool serves at the local high school. The decision-makers may need to be reminded that the children's space must, first of all, meet the library needs of children and others who use its services. Children of various ages should be able to establish a feeling of personal identification with the area. It is possible to create an environment that is overstimulating or distracting, a situation that may produce restlessness, tension, and fatigue. If the goal is to encourage interaction with library materials, this kind of environment would not be supportive. On the other hand, it is possible to err on the other side by creating such a calm environment that children fail to interact with materials.

Function vs. Fancy

Although the public should be able to identify the children's area by its functional design—smaller-scaled furnishings, shelving heights, and general arrangement—a touch of fancy should not be totally banished as a sacrifice in the name of function or flexibility. For some children, the library may be the most beautiful building in their lives. Those aesthetic "hyacinths to feed thy soul,* which some might consider a frivolous waste of taxpayers' funds, may be more important to children in their development than maintaining a room at a temperature recommended for perfect health.

I once took a group of third-graders from a depressed neighborhood and their teacher through a new library. As we passed the director's office, she came out to greet the children. While the adults chatted, the children wandered into the opulently furnished boardroom. As we looked around for the missing children, we found them sitting three to an upholstered chair, with their not-too-clean elbows resting on the polished walnut conference table, beaming. Whatever the room had cost was at that moment worth it. It is more important to consider aesthetics in economi-

---

*If thou of fortune be bereft
 And in thy store there be but left
 Two loaves, sell one and with the dole
 Buy hyacinths to feed thy soul.
 —James Terry White, *Not by Bread Alone*, after Hippocrates.

cally depressed communities than in middle-class ones. Function and aesthetics are not always at odds, of course; it is possible to have both. But when aesthetics and safety are in opposition, safety must win.

Color

Perhaps no other topic of discussion in the interior design of children's libraries evokes such a passionate response as color selection. While personal taste is desirable in selecting colors for walls of individual offices, choices for public institutions need to be based on more expert opinion. A distinction should be made between individual children's bedrooms and institutions serving many children, who are not, of course, fashion-conscious. They need to be surrounded by colors that enhance their activities and create an attractive environment. One color expert states the requirements of schools as follows:

> School buildings are for the populace at large, one where democratic rather than sophisticated values should dominate. Colors such as green, blue, yellow, coral and red have well-known appeal, as revealed by psychological research in color preference. They have impulsive and spontaneous charm recognized by most persons. To venture afield from these known qualities of pleasure in color is to contradict the direct and unprejudiced purposes of education.[44]

As a background to color decisions, children's librarians may find it useful to consider the information derived from research on children's responses to color. Although little research can be found on this topic as it pertains to libraries, that done in school classrooms may be applicable, for the school is another institution that serves a broad spectrum.

Studies have shown that human responses to color are both biological and psychological. Response to color and color preference is dependent on such factors as age, activity, mental health, personality, and, according to some studies, complexion types. Young children are more responsive to color than to form and, in matching figures, will sort first by color rather than by shape. As children grow older and more disciplined, color may lose some of its appeal.[45]

A three-year study conducted with German children showed clearly that environmental color affected their learning capacity. Classrooms with low ceilings were painted different colors. In rooms with light blue, yellow, yellow-green and orange ceilings, IQ was raised as much as twelve points; while white, black, and brown ceilings caused a drop in IQ scores. The former colors stimulated creativity and the children appeared more alert, while the dull or neutral colors had the opposite effect.[46] From various studies on infants, adults, and hospital patients, experts accept the fact that people need variety in their environment. If monotony is forced upon them, they may experience sensory deprivation.[47]

Most studies reveal that small children are likely to favor warm and luminous colors such as red, orange, pink, and yellow. The warm colors provide visual and emotional interest, appropriate for places of diversion and relaxation frequented by preschoolers and primary-age children. Birren, a well-noted color expert, believes that it is a fallacy to think that small children will be calmed in an environment of cool colors. Rather, the reverse may be true—that "bright colors may relieve nervousness by creating an outward stimulus to balance an inner and wholly natural fervor."[48] In areas used by older children who are engaged in thought, contemplation, or concentration, the cool colors are considered more appropriate.[49]

Because children in a classroom generally face the front of the room, that wall is often painted a color as intense as the chalkboard it surrounds in order to lessen visual fatigue. Contrasting colors on the other walls can provide the needed visual variety.[50] Librarians may apply this finding in recommending colors for activity or story hour rooms that house puppet theaters or provide a backdrop for the storyteller.

Color harmony throughout the library can be accomplished by using different hues of the same color family. For instance, paler hues of the colors used in the children's area can be effective in other areas of the library. Colors of walls and furnishings can also be used to designate areas in a library.

Lighting

Because lighting is so important in libraries, expert assistance should be available during discussions of color selection and shelving and seating arrangements. The benefits of an exemplary signage system may not be realized because of incorrect lighting. Children may not be aware that their feelings of discomfort in the library stem from inadequate lighting. Recommendations by the Illuminating Engineers Society for library illumination do exist and library planners would find them helpful.

What distinguishes natural lighting from artificial is the variability of the former.[51] Natural lighting, which changes in intensity during the various times of day and the seasons of the year, affects not only colors but also the level of illumination needed. Climate and geography must also be considered when determining lighting requirements. Even with these complications, the psychological benefits and decorative possibilities of at least some natural lighting compensate for such potential problems as glare, heat, and deterioration of materials.

Signage

The term signage refers to that part of library graphics related to the internal environment of the building. It involves those signs, labels, and symbols that assist the users and staff in using library resources.[52] The signage used outside the building should be easily seen at the child's level, as well. Signs may be placed on walls, freestanding surfaces or easels, floors, or hang from ceilings. Types of signs include:

1. Directional: needed whenever an area is not visible or obvious to the user
2. Identification: helps user locate materials, services, and facilities such as checkout counters, nonfiction sections, and classification numbers on the shelves
3. Informational: assists users on how to operate equipment, use the catalog, etc.
4. Regulation: describes special conditions such as library hours or fire and safety information.

Another type of library graphic is promotional—bibliographies, bags, and bulletin board decorations—and is not generally considered a part of signage.[53]

A well-designed and effectively signed library sets a welcoming tone and conveys the impression that users are important. Handwritten scraps of paper tacked at the end of stacks or letters missing from major identification or directional signs give an opposite message. Signage anticipates the users' directional questions and attempts to answer them, insofar as possible. It may be the determining factor in a patron's success in using the library because some users, regardless of the willingness and availability of staff, will not ask for assistance. Careful labeling of shelves and sections is also essential in assisting users to become more independent in using their library. I once attempted to find the children's room in a large metropolitan library. Children's services was omitted from the display board that listed the various departments, and I had to ask for instructions to find its location. When I later explained my dilemma (tactfully, I hoped) to the children's coordinator, she explained that children's services was not a department, but a complete library in itself—a concept that was obviously important to the staff making the decisions. Unfortunately, the public is not aware of such distinctions, nor do they care. Just as highway engineers should not be in charge of directional signs for motorists, the library planning team should solicit the suggestions of user representatives when a signage system is developed.

Signage for children may also serve an educational function in much the same way that labeling objects of furniture helps deaf children learn words and terms. "Information" or "Ask Here" signs on or above a desk suggest that such a practice is expected; instructions on how to use the catalog not only provide assistance, but also recommend its use.

Ideally, signage should be planned as part of the building design; this will provide a check on the effectiveness of space arrangements and traffic patterns. If difficulties arise in signing the library, the arrangement may not be logical or easy for the public or staff to use. If made part of the initial planning, signage becomes an aesthetic component rather than an element that competes with the decor. Some libraries engage a specialist to coordinate the graphics throughout the building; others may work with a local firm that provides signs for individual buildings, or they may design their own sign system. If signage must be done in-house, plastic or vinyl letters may be purchased for the larger directional and identification signs, and instructional signs and labels can be made on a sign machine or with a computer graphics program.

Several criteria should be kept in mind when planning for signage regardless of when it is discussed:

1. Information should be provided only at the point it is needed.
2. The terminology should be simple and understandable.
3. The signage system should be coordinated throughout the library.
4. The type font needs to be simple and unadorned (helvetica medium is often recommended) with both upper- and lower-case letters used.
5. With few exceptions, signs should be placed horizontally, rather than vertically or diagonally.
6. Signs should be easily replaced or moved when they become worn, new wording is required, or collections or services are changed.

A basic rule for all signage is that the letters should be large enough to be read at the point where the sign is needed.

Special consideration should be given to areas that children use. The Central Children's Room in the Buffalo and Erie County Library uses laminated cubes of shelf height with a combination of picture symbols and words to designate areas of the nonfiction collection. These can be moved as the collection shifts. The word "Science" on a brightly colored cube, with a silhouette of an insect not only identifies the materials, but also informs and promotes. The terminology should be scrutinized for its effectiveness with children. "Reference" and "Circulation" are library terms that may mean little to children (and to some adults, as well). "Checkout" and "Information" or "Ask Here" communicate more directly to children. In labeling sections of shelving, "dinosaurs" is more appropriate than "paleontology." The terms used, however, should be correct. Nonfiction is a term within the comprehension of children and one they need to learn when using all libraries; "fact books" is not only incorrect, it is also unnecessary. Signs should pass a rigid test of need. Some behaviors are so obviously inappropriate that featuring them in a sign may result in a situation not unlike the familiar "don't stick beans up your nose." Within the children's area, the signs should be at a height easily read by children, even though adults also use the children's collection.

> Signs mounted flush on walls, doors, and book stack ends ... should be 5' 3" from floor to top of sign, except in picture book areas, where the recommended height is 3' 3" to the top of the sign.[54]

Signs designating broad areas such as nonfiction or magazines, especially if suspended from the ceiling, can be placed high enough to be out of reach, approximately seven to eight feet.

The shape and color of signs should be as uniform as possible throughout the library, with attention given to their visibility. If color coding is used for each area, the signs will need to harmonize with the decor. Choice of color and color combinations are particularly important in areas that are dimly or brightly lit.[55]

Decorations

Decorations are frequently considered an integral part of the children's area. Those that cannot be changed may ultimately present problems for the staff. Murals of storybook characters on permanent walls, especially if done by a local artist, may reduce the flexibility of the space should the children's area move to another location. If the art is too contemporary, it may look dated in a few years, especially if it is not of high quality. When figures such as Winnie-the-Pooh and Peter Rabbit dominate the walls, older children may avoid the area. Figures well known to a current generation of children may fall out of favor or be ignored with the next. Paintings from *Ivanhoe* executed in the 1920s grace the walls of a children's room in a large central library, but few, if any, children read *Ivanhoe* today. Both painted and ceramic murals should be done on surfaces that can be moved or removed, if necessary.

Decorations with which children can interact add to the interest of the room. One of the most popular decorations is a tape measure at the end of a book stack with traditional and/or metric measures. Pieces of sculpture that children are invited to touch can serve as a focal point or a symbol for the area. Touching the sculpture may become a ritual for some children during each of their library visits. Such figures as a child reading or children listening, and artistic renditions of favorite animals or storybook characters can evoke contemplation. They must be firmly anchored, however, and incapable of being overturned. Plants soften the environment and offer opportunities to observe growth. Most should be chosen for their hardiness and overall attractiveness, but some may provide educational experiences for children. Among the plants that children can grow at home are sweet potatoes, carrots, beans, avocados, and citrus seeds.

Realia, such as dollhouses or building models, may need to be positioned on table space somewhat inaccessible to very small children. Although these may be interesting to children, they can become problems if they cannot be retired to storage from time to time. If the library is not to become the attic for the community, gifts of this kind should be carefully considered, and the terms of acceptance understood by all parties. Treehouses and other built-in objects add interest and opportunities for play, but must be weighed against their space requirements and loss of space flexibility.

Some children's librarians have assumed responsibility for live animals, ranging from tropical fish to gerbils. Although there may be advantages to having these charming creatures, especially to communities where pets are a luxury, the problems involved make them a dubious choice for a library. The cost of protecting and maintaining the health of the animals must be considered. Librarians may find it difficult to justify a job description that includes animal care. They must also be prepared to handle the trauma caused when an animal bites someone, gets sick, or dies.

Remodeling Present Quarters

Remodeling requires many of the same processes involved in planning children's space in a new building. If the children's area is the only space to be remodeled, there is the complication of coordinating the changes with the existing building.

Remodeling and rearrangement of space should be considered when it becomes difficult or impossible to meet service goals and objectives. The most common complaints about inadequate quarters are lack of space and an uninviting environment. The area should be examined to see if space can be gained with a different arrangement of furniture. Rearranging shelving is a more difficult task. If the room is carpeted, there will be light and dark patterns which may be unsightly. Removing little-used furniture can also be considered. An uninviting environment can be improved with a fresh coat of paint, new carpeting, or a ceiling treatment. Adding furniture or providing readers' seating in oddly shaped space, for example, may also be means of improving the appearance of the area. These relatively simple changes could be financed by a local organization interested in children or community betterment. New display items or pieces of furniture could be added to a wish list made available to individuals and groups willing to contribute funds or labor to benefit children.

If extensive remodeling is necessary, a well-reasoned justification should accompany the request, identifying the difficulties with the present quarters and the advantages, in terms of use, to be gained with remodeling.

Conclusion

The planning of a new building demands that every aspect of children's service and its relationship within the library be re-evaluated. At no other time are children's librarians forced to take such a global view of their service program while projecting future needs. Each aspect is to be questioned with the realization that "what is, doesn't have to be" in a different physical settting.

The role of children's librarians is that of advocate for their major client group. They should be aware of the space requirements necessary for their program of services and of the users' preferences and needs. A considerable amount of tact may be necessary in negotiating with others who operate from a different orientation. The task of the children's librarian is particularly sensitive as many people consider themselves experts on what is appropriate for children, having once been a child.

The opportunity to participate in a building program seldom comes at the right time in a librarian's career. Children's librarians who are new to the profession may find assistance in dealing with issues peculiar to their services from the state library's children's consultant, if there is one, or from children's librarians in the state who have had experience with new buildings. Gaining knowledge of children's responses to the building environment requires a literature search among the various disciplines involved. Not all of these findings will have relevance to a library setting, and judgment should be used in applying them to a public library whose service program is determined in part by its own traditions and in part by community needs. Nevertheless, as this field of research expands, librarians may be able to gain valuable insights that will help them in planning facilities for children. At present the most helpful information is probably found within the accumulated wisdom of children's librarians who have had experience planning a new or remodeled building. They can identify those features to which children have responded positively or negatively. As a group, librarians are remarkably frank in sharing this type of information as well as comments on architectural design and furnishings that impede or advance the program of service. However, judgment will have to be exercised as programs of service and community needs make their own unique demands.

Like many children's librarians with perfect hindsight, I have regretted not keeping a file or notebook with ideas for library furnishings and decoration. Suggestions for new or remodeled children's libraries can be gathered from visits to new libraries or other institutions serving children, exhibit areas at library conferences, stores that sell children's furnishings and educational equipment, home shows, and design and marketing journals.

... the Bookmobile arrived at Three Corners. . . . Here were fresh books again. What excitement would its shelves offer her this week? What far places would beckon her interest? What new lives would she be invited to explore? . . . People were converging upon the Bookmobile from several roads away. Some were in cars and many were afoot, but all came eagerly, with books in their arms.—Doris Gates, *The Cat and Mrs. Cary* (New York: Viking, 1962), pp. 126–127.

Children's Services in Rural Systems

The previous chapters have discussed services as performed by children's librarians in municipalities in moderate to heavily populated counties in the United States. Most of the literature that exists on children's services is about libraries in this type of community. The previous discussion, especially in chapter 2, applies equally to systems. Nevertheless, there is a sizable geographic area of our country still served by very small (and often staunchly independent) libraries and county and regional library systems that encompass sparsely populated rural areas. In number, these libraries exceed those serving urban areas. Although the preceding and following chapters are intended to be of general assistance to staff serving in these situations, there are differences that require adaptations or unique responses. It is hoped that this chapter may identify some of the differences and offer assistance to staff assuming responsibilities for children's services.

The Center for the Study of Rural Librarianship defines rural as an area of 25,000 or less population outside a metropolitan region. The U.S. Bureau of the Census considers a rural area as one having a population base of less than 2,500 outside an urban area. Some definitions consider factors other than population size. For instance, the Library Research Center at the University of Illinois defines a rural public library as one which serves a population center under 15,000, with 80 percent of its land devoted to farming.[1] Another group defines rural as being a half- or full-day's drive from an urban area. Providing quality library services to an area using any of these definitions is hampered by limitations on the financial base, recruitment of staff (many of whom prefer the amenities offered in urban centers), and the lack of awareness on the part of many rural people of what modern library services can contribute to their lives. These have been long-standing problems. Nevertheless, the gulf between the urban and rural citizen is less pronounced than it once was because of advances in communication and transportation.

Rural Library Development

Public library development was an urban phenomenon. As cities grew, branch libraries were built whenever the population growth and the distance from an existing library met the library's plan for cost-effective services. With one political jurisdiction and tax base, growth was relatively stable and orderly.

Library development in rural areas could not follow the urban pattern given the difference in population density and growth, distances from an existing library, and the multiplicity of taxing jurisdictions. A town of 2,500, thirty miles from an existing library, and in another political jurisdiction, simply could not be measured by the urban standard if the residents in the town or surrounding unincorporated area were ever to experience adequate library service.

State Involvement in Rural Libraries

The state library agency movement began at the turn of the century with responsibility for promoting library development throughout the state. In some states it was separate from the existing state library which provided service to state government and developed collections to support studies of the state's history and government. In others, it became an integral part of the state library's service program. Many state library agencies attempted to meet their obligations to rural areas by supplementing the local library's meager resources with boxes of books loaned on a regular basis. Although this short-gap measure partially met the needs of the adults and children for reading materials, there remained the problem of too many small, inefficient libraries with tax bases inadequate to support modern library services.

An important component of library development throughout the state was the field consultant who advised trustees on a multitude of problems, and provided training and counseling for staffs which, for the most part, lacked formal higher education or library training. The consultant was usually a generalist, although some did have experience in children's services. Because many of the libraries had been established by women's clubs and supported by voluntary contributions, the consultant's work during this period was concentrated on helping these groups secure tax support from the local government, and helping the staffs develop policies and procedures compatible with recognized library practices. In the next phase, the field consultant's task was to encourage small and ineffective libraries to join a county or regional system, or, if none existed, to join with their neighboring libraries in creating one. If successful, the field counsultant in effect changed the nature of her/his job. With the establishment of this larger unit, a professional staff could be hired to provide the assistance previously offered by the state library consultant. Those states that still have a number of small unaffiliated libraries continue to need a field consultant to assist local trustees and staffs.

The problem of inadequate tax revenue was addressed by library agencies and library associations that lobbied their state legislators to enact laws enabling local jurisdictions to establish a county, multi-county, or regional library district. Another response to this problem was state aid. Again working through their library associations, librarians in many states were successful in persuading their legislatures that this was a necessary function of state government. Because states were responsible for education, libraries as educational institutions were entitled to this support. At present, only a handful of states do not provide some form of financial aid to public libraries, either on a per capita basis or through support of systems.

When county and regional libraries were first established in rural areas, their pattern of services to children tended to concentrate on the schools, just as the urban libraries had done in their early years. School service was considered the most cost-effective method of reaching children, especially in rural areas.[2] Children's librarians who were part of this era discovered that what was standard practice in urban libraries often had to be adapted to fit their situations. Improvisation was needed to deal with problems resulting from widely scattered populations, vast distances, and the lack of professionally trained staff. These problems were seldom acknowledged in conference programming or library literature.

Federal Involvement in Rural Libraries

The federal role in public libraries has taken many forms, in addition to the gathering of statistics. In the 1930s, library service was extended to over two million people when several states established county libraries with funds made available through the

Works Progress Administration (WPA). The National Youth Administration of that period financed young adults who worked in libraries and other community agencies, freeing the staffs from some of the routine tasks. These experiences not only provided the foundation for subsequent federal legislation in the post-war era, but also demonstrated that in many regions of the country, the county was too small a unit in which to establish an economically sound library system.[3]

In the post-World War II era, library associations at all levels and state library agencies focused considerable attention on enacting federal legislation to improve existing rural libraries and to extend services to unserved areas. It was reasoned that the tax base in these areas would never be large enough to finance the cost of establishing a library system, but, with federal seed money, local and state funding would be sufficient to maintain adequate services, provided the unit was large enough to generate the necessary tax revenue. When the Library Services Act (LSA) was passed and signed into law in 1956, it provided funds on a state matching basis with the responsibility for administration assigned to the state library agency. Some states had plans in place for library development, and also had a core of consultants ready to take advantage of this new opportunity. Others used the first monies to strengthen their state library agency or, in one instance, to establish one, before submitting for approval a plan for extending services to their rural areas.

In 1964, the Library Services Act was amended to include grants for urban areas as well and for the construction of library buildings (Library Services and Construction Act). In subsequent years LSCA has undergone several revisions as the focus on rural areas was broadened to include inner cities, services to the institutionalized, and support for cooperative efforts among libraries of all types. The underlying goal of this legislation was to make library services more accessible to

> persons who, by reason of distance, residence, or physical handicap, or other disadvantage, are unable to receive the benefits of public library services regularly made available to the public. . . .[4]

In 1984, this goal was restated by the Congress along with a second one, "to assist libraries in coping with the revolution in information technology."[5]

Rural libraries obviously qualify in both instances. Funding for federal library programs has decreased over the years, and attempts have been made to eliminate libraries from the federal budget. Nevertheless, the precedent of federal and state aid in

local library development has been established, and it serves as a
legacy to today's librarians as they devise new patterns to serve
the library needs of their publics, wherever they live.

State Children's Services Consultant

The need for state children's consultants had been acknowledged
in the pre-World War II era, even though their role was perceived
differently within the various states. In her 1943 text *Work with
Children in Public Libraries*, Power lamented that too few state
libraries had trained children's librarians,

> they are ... needed to buy books, make up book collections, compile
> lists and to give advisory services to small libraries.[6]

She also quoted one state librarian who saw the need to hire a
state school specialist as a way to meet the state's obligation to
children's services. Several states had adopted this model in the
1930s with the school specialist as part of the state education
department or, less often, the state library. In 1956, before the
passage of the LSA, children's consultants were employed by
eight state library agencies.[7]

In addition to strengthening the state library agency, the LSA
enabled the agency's staff to give more attention to the services
and programs in local libraries. Depending on the philosophy governing the state library agency or the resources available, a children's services specialist was added to the consultant staff. The
number of states with a children's consultant having a full-time
commitment to children or to children's and young adult services
probably never exceeded twenty-two. In 1989, slightly less than a
third have a youth services consultant on their staff. It is possible,
of course, that some of the general consultants may have had children's experience. The role of the state children's consultant and
her or his relationship to the children's consultants of state-supported regional systems was not always clear. This is not surprising considering that the model for public library consultants
had been generalists, not specialists.[8] In the late 1960s, a role
statement prepared by the Discussion Group of State Library
Consultants on Public Library Service to Children attempted to
delineate the responsibilities of this position. The statement was
approved in 1970 by the Board of the Association of State
Libraries. The primary goal of this consultant was to

stimulate excellent library service to children by working to equalize the opportunity in all parts of the state and to promote, primarily on the state level, awareness and an informed concern for the quality of public library service to children.[9]

The children's consultant, in improving and creating children's programs, performed some or all of the following:

1. Assisted in planning the agency's development plan for systems and in the development and implementation of standards.
2. Stimulated intersystem cooperation among system-level or regional children's consultants.
3. Identified continuing education needs and assisted in planning ways of meeting them.
4. Provided a channel for professional exchange of trends, information and materials.
5. Assisted in collection development by establishing examination centers, traveling collections, etc.
6. Represented libraries in cooperative activities with other state agencies concerned with children.
7. Advised and assisted in programs of services for children in state institutions.
8. Explored opportunities for cooperation with school officials at the state level. . . .[10]

As county and regional systems developed and children's specialists were hired at that level, the need for a state children's consultant was considered less acute, especially when declining funds forced more rigid priorities. It is interesting to note, however, that the state children's consultants who have enjoyed long tenure are those whose activities adhere quite closely to the role statement of 1970.

In assessing the current need for a state children's consultant, each state should make the decision based on its plan of development. Children's librarians who lobby their state library to add a children's consultant cannot assume that a common understanding of this position exists. The resources of the state, as represented by the state library agency, state library association, and library school (if one is located in the state) should be measured against the existing needs in identifying the role this consultant is expected to assume. In general, the responsibilities of this consultant will fall into the following categories: advisory, advocate or representative, and research.

Need for an Advisor. States differ in the progress made toward extending modern library service to every citizen and in the methods used to reach that goal. Those with sizable rural areas dotted with small, independent libraries without children's librarians need a consultant who can offer advice on a wide range of topics: collection development, services, planning or improving library facilities for children, programming, and other services normally provided at the system level. This consultant should, however, avoid filling the role of a "super" children's librarian who serves as the programmer for local libraries.

Need for an Advocate or Representative. In addition to serving as an advocate for children's library needs in state library agency planning, the consultant also represents libraries and children's services when serving on state-level committees that cut across various disciplines. She or he may also act as a liaison to state organizations that have a counterpart at the local level—state PTA, state educational association, cooperative extension, etc.—thus making it easier for children's librarians to develop a working relationship with their local units. Information gained from these state-level contacts should be shared with the librarians in the state. These are time-consuming activities and the emphasis given to them depends in part on how much time must be devoted to the advisory role.

Need for Research and Information. Research needs have traditionally been addressed by library school faculties and, if state supported, often in cooperation with librarians through their state association or the state library agency. Some state libraries have had on their staff a consultant who conducts surveys and formal evaluations of services. State library associations are obviously not prepared to undertake this responsibility, except as contractors. Many library schools in the last two decades have dropped positions that were once held by faculty with expertise and experience in children's public library services. When no faculty member considers this field to be a major interest, there is little likelihood that research topics will be chosen by other faculty, given the low prestige afforded it by many universities and outside funders. State-supported universities, however, are not immune to consistent pressure from constituent groups. The primary role of the library association and state library agency is to identify areas that need to be researched and to provide whatever consultation and data are necessary to support the project.

In those states without children's consultants, a general consultant who may or may not have had experience in children's services serves in the advisory role when needed. In some states, this alternative may have been dictated by a lack of funds; in others, resources may have been used for specialists whose expertise is judged to benefit all ages, such as automation or special populations. Children's librarians have a right to expect that these consultants "for all ages" have some awareness of children's needs, and are able to apply their expertise to problems in children's services. If the number of children's librarians in the state library association has made a youth services division or chapter a viable option, this group can assume a number of statewide responsibilities through its newsletters and publications, conference programming, and other continuing education activities offered in cooperation with the state library agency and the library school or another educational unit. It is the advocate or representative function that is the most difficult to fill without a children's consultant. As a stopgap measure, state library agencies could consider appointing a children's librarian from the field to represent libraries on a statewide committee concerned with children's issues, or hiring a children's specialist for the advisory function on a short-term basis.

One of my children's coordinator friends was once asked by a small rural county system in her state to give an all-staff workshop on the philosophy and goals of children's services because the state library could not provide this kind of assistance. Her own library system was generous in allowing her the time to be away, but she would not accept unless the state library agency had been informed of the request. Only in this way could the demand for children's expertise in the state be documented.

Librarians are somewhat unique in their willingness to share expertise and publications whenever possible. Many of those states with children's consultants have made publications developed for their own librarians available at a nominal charge or through ERIC. Examples of these include planning for facilities (Connecticut); summer reading club manuals (North Carolina); and activities for latchkey children (Missouri).

The System Concept

System is a term that has been used to denote a variety of diverse organizations, with its meaning often dependent on the context in which it is used. At its most basic level, a system refers to two or more libraries that have entered into a contractual relationship in order to improve service to their respective user groups. Network has often been used interchangeably with system, but the former usually involves telecommunications and computer technology. The sharing of materials and professional expertise is generally assumed in most library systems. They offer the advantage of economy of scale—larger discounts for materials, more efficient processing, employment of professionally educated staff, etc. A library serving a population of 2,500 probably cannot support one professional staff member, let alone a children's specialist; however, ten to fifteen such communities may be able to share a children's librarian to work with local staffs in improving collections and providing in-service training in such competencies as reading guidance, reference work with children, and programming.

Although state library agencies have made progress in system development, many small public libraries in the rural areas remain outside, either because there are no systems with which to affiliate or because they perceive their current level of service to be satisfactory. They are dependent upon the state library agency or their own resources for professional advice and assistance.

The future of systems is debated within the profession. As current technologies improve and become more affordable, urban libraries may be able to provide services for their users through informal agreements without system support. Nevertheless, for rural libraries the system offers a realistic hope for improvement of its services.

Because of the growth of systems in rural areas during the last three decades, children's librarians may find themselves working in a member library of a system, as a consultant in a cooperative system, or as a coordinator in a consolidated system. The legal and administrative structures of the system, as well as its rural environment, should be understood by children's librarians who assume the responsibilities of one of these positions.

Administrative and Legal Structure

Laws defining systems may vary from state to state; each operates within a legal structure considered appropriate to its geography, resources, and political traditions. Defining types of systems is not unlike deflating a rubber raft; whenever it appears to be under control, it breaks out in an unexpected direction.

Consolidated Library System. A library district that includes several governmental units, such as one county with several contracting towns; two or more counties; or a city-county combination, may make up a consolidated library system. A multi-county or city-county merger often uses the term "regional" to denote its legal status. A consolidated system is governed by one administrative board, agency, or manager with one budget and one director. Upon its establishment, a system board is appointed in accordance with the state law and replaces the governing boards of the local libraries as the administrative or governing body. The local boards may retain some authority, such as provision of facilities, for example, but in general they assume an advisory role. Depending on state library laws, this type of system usually requires a vote of the citizens to establish it or action by the governing bodies of the respective jurisdictions. Asking people to vote for an abstract concept such as better library service, without really understanding what this entails, requires a herculean effort that may fail at the polls. In the 1950s and 1960s, some states used federal and state monies to fund a two- or three-year demonstration period of quality library service before voters in a designated area were asked to decide the issue. Although expensive, and dependent on a knowledge of local politics, these efforts improved the rate of success at the polls.

Once established, the internal staff relationships in a consolidated system are not unlike those in a municipal library. Staff in all library outlets are responsible to the director of the system. A children's specialist may be given the title of coordinator or consultant, the former more appropriately because of the type of authority exercised. Although a staff position, the children's coordinator in a consolidated system will carry delegated authority that usually implies control over selection of materials, maintenance of standards for children's services and programming, and responsibilities for working with city and/or county agencies concerned with children.

Cooperative Library Systems. The difficulties faced by state library agencies in promoting the establishment of consolidated systems probably led to the cooperative system. This innovation, often financed by federal-state funds, attempts to bring the benefits of a consolidated system to small, independent community libraries without a direct vote of citizens, and without changing the legal basis or the internal structure of the participating libraries.

> In a cooperative system each member library remains autonomous, retains its own governing board, hires its own staff, and usually receives most of its funding from local government. Generally the system is governed by a board, representative of the member libraries.[11]

The services of cooperative systems vary; they may include centralized acquisition and cataloging/processing, reciprocal borrowing by users, reference services, short-term loans of materials, in-service training, consultant services to staff and trustees. Sharing of computerized data services may also be one of the services, but unlike a network, it is not the primary focus of the organization. A local library board or city council may agree to become a member by following the procedures and policies commonly agreed upon by the member libraries. A small system staff, typically housed in the largest or most central library, is usually supported by state funds, with the expectation that should these funds disappear, the member libraries would assess themselves to continue the system's activities. The status of cooperative systems in some states has been mandated and financed by the state as a form of state library aid.

The director and governing board of the system may add to the staff various specialists, such as reference, technical services, or children's. Some cooperative systems may be restricted to one or two functions, such as reference and interlibrary loan, and the delivery of materials. The system staff serves only in an advisory capacity to staffs of member libraries. When funds permit, cooperative systems in rural areas may add a children's consultant, especially if many of the system members lack children's librarians. The consultant accepts the role of teacher-advisor, realizing that all advice may be ignored and all instruction disregarded.

Federated Systems. Members of a federated system also retain their autonomy as an independent library while contracting with the system for various services, such as technical processes, staff, reference, children's, audiovisual, etc. The definition of a federated system may vary among the several states where this type exists. In general, the members select one or more services on a fee basis, and, in so doing, accept the system's policies and guidelines for that service. The fee may also include a charge for administrative costs of the system. The sponsoring governmental unit of the library—e.g. a county—appoints the system's governing board.[12] This appointed board assumes responsibility for policy development and coordinated services.[13] If a member library, for example, contracts for selection and acquisition of materials and for technical processes, various staff of that library may participate in the selection of titles to be placed on the new material and replacement lists, and in the development of policies and procedures governing cataloging and processing. The role of the consultant for each service is that of a mediator who serves to move the members toward consensus whenever possible, and reports the various positions to the administration for a decision when consensus is not possible. Attempts may be made to accommodate a minority member's wishes, but if a customized service or process is necessary, it will be reflected in the charges levied. Because the role of the children's consultant in this type of system is similar to that in a cooperative system, the role of the children's consultant need not be considered separately.

The System in a Rural Environment

Almost every region of rural America consistently experiences ongoing changes brought about by depressed conditions in agriculture, lumbering, or fishing, for instance, or by the influx of well-educated people bringing with them expectations of certain amenities previously taken for granted.[14] Levels of sophistication cannot be predicted by where people choose to live, and most rural librarians have at least one story to tell about a time they underestimated a particular user or group. Still, rural populations as a whole tend to be less hospitable to change and more pragmatic in outlook. Although they are affected by television and other media in the wider society, one sociologist believes that, in general, rural populations tend to be

> more traditional in moral orientation, less accepting of minority rights, more ideologically religious and conservative, more likely to oppose the intervention of federal or state governments, and are genuinely more satisfied with their present lifestyle.[15]

These characteristics do not fit every rural community, of course, as age, income, education, sex, race, and geography all exert an influence on attitudes and behavior.

There are as many variations among rural library systems as there are among the more urbanized ones, even though they may share the same type of system definition. Some of the differences can be attributable to the size of the professional staff and its background and experience. Rural systems are frequently understaffed as well as unsuccessful in recruiting experienced staff. Not only is the relative isolation a problem, but also salaries are often not competitive. The geographic area to be covered in a rural system may be several times that of an urban system, but with a much smaller and more widely dispersed population. Many rural systems must negotiate with several jurisdictions in various types of contractual arrangements which are both time-consuming and politically sensitive. Funds are often limited because of tax restrictions imposed on unincorporated areas.

My first professional position in public libraries was as the children's coordinator in a recently formed consolidated system resulting from the merger of a city and a county library. The position involved serving as the children's librarian for the city library and as advisor to the branch and bookmobile departments on children's collections and services. I was ill-prepared for these responsibilities, but experienced children's librarians were then, as now, difficult to find for rural areas. A few years later, I took a position as the only children's librarian in a newly established, five-county rural consolidated system, serving a population of approximately 140,000 and covering 15,000 square miles, a geographic area as large as Connecticut and Vermont. Only one county had previously been served by a library system; in the others, service, where it had existed, had been given in libraries serving small towns. The establishment of the system had followed a three-year demonstration period after which the citizens had voted for its continuance.

The professional environment experienced by a children's coordinator in this type of situation cannot be fully comprehended nor appreciated by one's urban colleagues. The simple act of discussing professional issues in one's field usually involves leaving home. The compromise between standard practice (as performed in urban libraries) and what is possible is confronted daily. For new children's librarians there is the occasional remorse of not serving children directly but through others, who may fall short of one's professional ideals.

On the plus side, there is enormous satisfaction in seeing a nonprofessional staff eagerly accept new challenges and discover the rewards of introducing children to books and reading. For some children and their parents in rural areas, library services are not yet taken for granted, but are new and extraordinary, producing a quiet excitement that can be felt. The appreciation expressed may not be eloquently delivered, but it is warm and forthcoming. Working with previously unserved or underserved populations and observing subtle changes happens often enough to keep children's librarians pushing back the barriers to quality services. The child who asks the librarian to renew a biography in the Landmark Series "because my dad is now reading it," or hearing that the high interest-low vocabulary titles you sent were just the encouragement needed to persuade a third-grader that reading was worth the effort are major triumphs in our profession. There are also unexpected non-library benefits that may be equally important in the lives of children. After I had told stories and given booktalks to children in a remote two-room school in a cattle ranching area, one of the teachers said, "Thank you for coming—the children see so few people."

The system staff of which the children's coordinator is a team member can be a source of professional in-service education. Most rural library directors involve all professional staff members in policy decisions as a matter of course, and there is usually a recognition that the children's coordinator represents an important constituency in these discussions. One of my former directors once remarked that "this library cannot afford to waste *any* professional expertise," and observed that the two largest systems (urban) in the state probably wasted more professional staff hours than our rural library had to run its system! Both of my rural library directors naturally assumed that children's librarians had an interest in general library issues equal to those of other librarians and acted accordingly. As a result, it was less difficult to break out of the boundaries that others afford the specialist's role. For example, as a children's coordinator in one rural system, I read adult reviews and attended the selection meetings where I contributed a point of view as a former community librarian and identified needs of adults concerned with children. Adult services librarians were also welcome to participate in children's selection meetings.

There are, of course, areas where a specialist's knowledge and experience must take precedence. A reference librarian's daily use of online databases or reference titles provides a more solid basis for deciding which service or title to add, just as a children's librarian's familiarity with children's needs enables her/him to make a more considered judgment in designing children's services. Nevertheless, the opinions of other staff can broaden one's own vision and improve the quality of decisions made. Sharing information and professional views is a two-way street. Observing how these colleagues react to issues affecting children's services may force one to rethink many tenaciously held positions and to learn effective ways of defending others. Rather than thinking of oneself as the poor relation of urban colleagues, the more positive aspects should be stressed, such as the opportunity to develop competencies not possible in a more structured and traditional setting.

Role of the Children's Coordinator or Consultant in a Rural System

The title "children's coordinator," when used in an urban system, not only denotes delegated authority for children's services but also the coordination of professionally educated children's librarians, who in turn provide a program of services carried on throughout the system. If this is a correct interpretation, then the title, as used for the rural counterpart, is primarily a courtesy, for there may be no children's librarians, professional or otherwise, to coordinate. If it refers to the coordination of children's services regardless of who delivers them, then the term is properly used.

One of the principal differences between a children's coordinator in a consolidated library system and a consultant in a cooperative system, whether located in a rural area or not, is that the latter has no legal authority over the internal affairs of member libraries. Her or his involvement with services and collections is by invitation only, and, as such, serves in a role analogous to that of a state children's consultant.

Children's services in rural areas were usually developed in a pattern opposite to that found in urban libraries. The first children's librarian employed in an urban library was responsible for services given from a single library within the jurisdiction of a city or town. As branches were established, this children's librarian normally served in an advisory role in addition to current duties, until branch children's librarians were added. Coordination of services and selection of materials were often done informally as a committee under the leadership of the senior children's librarian. When this became unworkable, a coordinator was added who not only assumed the managerial responsibilities for children's services but also represented children's services in system-wide planning and policy discussions and to the community at large.

The first children's specialist hired in most rural systems was assigned responsibility for developing collections and services throughout the system. In scope, these responsibilities were comparable to those of an urban children's coordinator, even though the resources for meeting them were quite different. When another professional children's librarian was added, he or she was usually assigned to assist the coordinator, either by assuming responsibility for some aspect of the service, such as collection development, or for the services in a specified region of the system. In the next developmental stage, children's librarians were added to the larger branches while the smaller ones continued to be served by a regional children's coordinator. Rural library systems seldom reached this latter stage, or if they did, they were probably no longer rural.

Systems, like individual libraries and other institutions, are growing, changing organisms. Rural systems are affected by the same outside forces experienced by all institutions—technology, changing family life, population growth or decline—as well as those affecting the internal environment, such as the staff's accumulated experiences, levels of competency, and trust in the system. For these reasons, a job description written for a children's coordinator several years ago may be inappropriate when compared to the system's present level of development.

The Teaching Role

Rural children's coordinators, as well as consultants, have had to operate between two different aspects of their role. Like the urban children's coordinator, they are perceived as teachers or trainers of staff who in turn provide the day-to-day public service. If the competency level of local staff is such that few, if any, children's services are offered, the children's coordinator may be tempted to assume a more visible role. This hands-on role needs to be considered carefully because the urge to be actively involved is particularly strong in children's librarians and only somewhat dormant in coordinators.

Dorothy Broderick has made a convincing case for the teacher relationship in describing the role of a consultant in a cooperative system.[16] It is impossible to disagree with her position as it relates to cooperative or federated systems, or to consolidated systems in urban areas. Teaching a hungry man to fish is preferable to giving him a fish, even though this alternative requires more time and patience, and even then the effort may fail. The principal role of the children's coordinator or consultant is to teach the local staff "how to fish." If only a modicum of success is achieved, the improvement will be more long-lasting.

Whenever the local librarian or an able trustee can be persuaded to assume some responsibility for children's programming, school visiting, or talks to groups on library services, this option should be taken. A young mother's group in one community took responsibility for school visiting to promote summer activities, which not only accomplished the objective, but also heightened the group's interest in the children's activities throughout the summer. If the political climate permits, the teacher role should not be abandoned before every effort is made to assist and encourage the local librarian to assume at least part of the programming responsibilities, or to locate an individual or group in the community to assist in that role.

Over time a children's specialist can help local staffs develop and improve several basic competencies. If the staffs have had little training, focusing on those services presently offered may be the best approach. Most libraries welcome classrooms of children for visits at various times during the school year. In a workshop with an actual class, the specialist can demonstrate simple activities within the competency level of the group that can improve this service. A follow-up discussion period offers an opportunity to address the problems the group may have encountered with this audience. Should booktalking or storytelling skills be developed through subsequent training sessions, the staff may be encouraged to add these activities to its class visits.

Other areas of training include the demonstration of steps necessary to maintain the collection in good condition or ways to improve a vacation reading program. Information skills can be improved through workshops on various reference and reading guidance aids, with practice questions provided through newsletters. Preschool programs should have a high priority because of the need for them in most rural communities, and because these skills are more easily acquired than storytelling for older groups. The specialist can also assist these staffs in setting objectives for enjoyable but worthwhile film programs that integrate other library materials and activities into a unifying theme, or that help children develop a general appreciation for film as an art form.

Care must be taken not to inundate an already burdened staff if additional staff hours cannot also be provided. Every training session need not result in an added program responsibility for a local library staff. The information itself may be valuable in other ways. For example, the background gained from workshop sessions on book discussion groups or booktalking may be helpful to the librarian in talking about books with individual children.

When a staff member with designated responsibility for children's services is added to a local library, more specialized training can be offered. In a rural system with limited resources, this staff member is not likely to be professionally educated. At best, the person may possess an undergraduate degree, some experience in libraries, and a desire to work with children. With training and experience, staff at this level can assume most of the responsibilities for day-to-day services. They can also provide information critical to discussions on selection of materials, policy revision, and other service aspects.

The Participating Role

Even though the teaching role should be given preference by children's specialists in both types of systems, the role of the coordinator in a consolidated system is complicated by an inescapable fact: the coordinator is the *de facto* children's librarian for all communities, and not every local librarian has adequate programming skills, or the aptitude, time, or willingness to learn them. If children are not to be shortchanged, the children's coordinator may have to assume a more visible role, at least in the short run. The refusal of the local librarian cannot be used as ground for reprimand or dismissal. In many situations this staff person is already performing beyond her or his job classification level. The system staff must recognize that the local librarian's knowledge of the community is valuable. Then the staff must attempt, as far as possible, to compensate for skills and competencies the local librarians lack.

When the children's coordinator assumes the active role, she or he should, whenever it's feasible, use the occasion as an in-service demonstration. The coordinator must resist, at all costs, becoming the celebrity who swoops into town, bringing a reputation as a storyteller, puppeteer, or booktalker, and leaving the local librarian with no incentive to offer any program for fear of unflattering comparisons. The local librarian should be involved and visible in the activity and deferred to whenever possible. The local librarian must understand the objectives of the activity if success is to be realized. This understanding is more easily gained through involvement.

Professional Competencies Needed

The children's specialist, whether coordinator or consultant, needs the competencies of a good children's librarian, the problem-solving abilities and tact of a consultant, and the knowledge and instincts of an effective manager. The rural system, in particular, needs specialists who can share with all levels of staff and lay groups a vision of excellent children's services as a goal toward which to strive. This specialist also acts as a communications link to regional and national library associations and child-related organizations, and identifies research and legislation that have implications for children's library services. As the only children's specialist, the coordinator must be willing and able to acquire competencies that will be needed as the system evolves and matures.

In the staff advisory role, the children's specialist provides information about children's services to the administration and key personnel in the system. She or he respects confidences of staff and judges when and what kind of response to problems should be proposed. A collegial attitude based on mutual respect for the other's competencies is the basis of a good working relationship with local librarians. In addition to their native (and often latent) abilities, the local librarian's knowledge of the community may include who is related to whom, whose father lost his job, and the assignments of most of the teachers. No matter how impressive this is, it would be prudent not to assume that all local librarians are equally knowledgeable about all segments of the community. I once persuaded a community librarian who seemed to know everyone in town to offer the summer reading club as a means of reaching new users in her community. She was reluctant because she believed all the children were currently library users, and she was not willing to visit classrooms to promote the program. She agreed, after I offered to do the school visiting. At the end of the first week of the program, she ran out of supplies, exclaiming, "I don't know *where* these children are coming from—I've never seen some of them before."

In the managerial role, the children's coordinator in a consolidated system should have the ability to:

1. Identify and prioritize needs in a variety of situations
2. Plan, implement, and evaluate services and programs on a system-wide basis
3. Teach and evaluate various levels of staff who serve children
4. Work cooperatively with library administration, staff, and trustees to formulate goals and prioritize objectives for the system and for individual communities
5. Represent the system in working with schools, social agencies, and volunteer groups concerned with children and their welfare.

Tolerance for individual initiative is also essential, for procedures, policies, and standards set by the system cannot be imposed in a uniform manner on outlets or services operating at various levels of development. A local librarian, for example, may persist in shelving certain titles at eye level regardless of their correct sequence. If the turnover rate is the highest in the system, it would be difficult to argue that this deviation shouldn't be allowed. In another situation with a larger collection and staff, this practice could be counterproductive. Only on those critical matters, such as freedom of access or reserve privileges for children, should uniformity become an issue.

The competencies of the children's consultant should also include those enumerated above, even though the person may not exercise them in her or his role except by invitation or demonstration. In performing other duties as a consultant, the consultant should heed Gregory and Stoffel's general guidelines for cooperative system consultants:

1. The use of an advisory service and the acceptance of its results must be recognized as a voluntary on the part of the member library;
2. Such service must be available on an equitable basis to all member libraries;
3. The participation of the consultant in the affairs of the local library must be temporary;
4. The consultant's contribution must be fact-finding, counseling, or training and not actual performance (except when performance serves as a demonstration in training situations or as explicitly determined by contract arrangements); and

5. The consultant should encourage the feedback of results from the local level and the building up of system case files to be used for referral.[17]

Within this role, the children's consultant may conduct in-service workshops designed to improve staff service and programming competencies or to strengthen collections. Children's consultants assume a more active role when dealing with system resources. Under their direction, the system may maintain backup collections and programming materials available on short-term loan to member libraries or their users, and from which requests are filled that cannot be handled locally.

System Demands

The position of two children's coordinators in a state may be quite different even though their rural systems cover comparable geographic areas and are at a similar stage of development. Among the factors that shape this position are responses made to (1) the political climate surrounding the establishment of the system, (2) the principle of equitable services, and (3) in the consolidated system especially, the occasional demands for the skills of a generalist. Obviously, these are not positions for those who need concrete guidelines and comfortable boundaries.

Political Climate. This factor is more evident in a consolidated system where voters have had to overcome a natural antipathy toward state or federal funds often seen as intervention, and a reluctance to give up total control over existing libraries for the promise of better service. The loss of local control is more feared than realized, but system staffs need to be sensitive to what the library in a small community may symbolize. Often begun through the efforts of volunteers, financed by money-raising efforts, donations from organizations and individuals, and perhaps by modest tax funds, the library may be wholly inadequate as measured by any professional yardstick. Nevertheless, it has been a source of community pride and achievement, and the system staff must strive to maintain and build on this pride while involving local people in the needed changes.

The children's coordinator may be further affected by expectations developed when the system concept was first promoted. Local boards, as well as voters in favor of the system's establishment, were often persuaded that their children would substantially benefit as a result. In the early years of a system, both the "ayes" and the "nays" may watch the development of library services to see if these expectations are met. Children's librarians may have to put aside the logical process of developing services and concentrate on a few system-wide programs that do benefit children, but, more important, demonstrate the advantages of a system. Any tendency of the coordinator to spend the bulk of the time in the largest library, even though it may house the working collection, must be avoided. Staffs of the member libraries are also apprehensive about the changes facing them as part of a system. It is crucial that these local staffs identify with the system as quickly as possible and experience the satisfaction of a common effort. A system-wide reading club for children, for example, can be the means of establishing a common bond with counterparts in other member libraries. These first activities may set a pattern for the services offered and the responsibilities assumed and, in so doing, partly define the role of the children's coordinator, for better or worse.

The establishment of a cooperative system is less politically sensitive because administrative control is retained by the local trustees. The public's access to larger collections and improved services are benefits that involved no local tax increase. The local library's governing body still retains control over those internal operations that affect the users.

Equitable Service. For consolidated systems, this principle is manifested in two ways: in the service offered to the public and in the assistance given member libraries. It is not possible to ensure that every citizen, regardless of residence, will enjoy exactly the same service from the community library or bookmobile stop as he or she would in using the library with the largest collection or the most experienced staff. In planning services and programs, the children's coordinator must keep the goal of equitable services in mind and consider ways that this might be accomplished. If children in the larger libraries are offered summer vacation loans, this privilege should be available to children in the smaller libraries, even if the request must be filled from the headquarters pool collection. Program kits for day care services developed in response to requests in one community should be made available system-wide. If a traveling puppet troupe performs in the largest community, either their services should be offered to other communities, or performances should be widely publicized to children and their families throughout the system area.

Ensuring equitable service to users in a cooperative system is beyond the capability of a consultant staff whose involvement in internal operations is limited. The resources of each member library will determine to a large extent the service available to users. Nevertheless, equitable service to member libraries and staffs should be the governing principle. This does not require that members be treated alike—they have different needs—but that they should be treated equitably.[18] This principle is sometimes difficult to follow, for inevitably some member staffs will be more eager to learn whatever the consultant teaches, while others remain satisfied with the status quo. Libraries experiencing a censorship problem or designing new children's quarters will require more assistance as well.

System-wide Demands. Even though a children's coordinator in a rural system seldom, if ever, has a spare moment, there will be demands requiring time and professional judgment beyond the children's area. Because of the distances involved in some rural systems, the system staff may not be able to visit every community library or station as often as desirable. Therefore, whoever visits the local library is not only a specialist, but also someone from headquarters who can assist with problems. If the question involves an aspect of children's services, such as a demand for more service from a school or the shelving of children's materials for toddlers, obviously the children's coordinator is the best person to counsel the local librarian. Should the problem center on the system's legal relationship with local authorities or on adult services, the children's coordinator may have to act, using her or his own best judgment or by phoning the appropriate headquarters staff for assistance. If, during a branch visit, the reference consultant is presented with a problem in the children's area, she or he may have to respond immediately and then inform the children's coordinator of the action taken and of any follow-up that may be needed.

Initially, the children's consultant may be the only children's specialist in the cooperative system but, by working with staffs in member libraries, a full-time children's librarian may become a priority for a member library should funds become available. If a number of member libraries add children's librarians, the position of children's consultant could be eliminated in favor of another specialty, or the position revised to include some responsibilities outside the children's area. When this position is supported by state or federal funds, its tenure from year to year is often in doubt. Even with this uncertainty the position offers a unique opportunity for gaining valuable experience in children's services.

Development and Maintenance of Collections

In developing children's collections in a rural library, the librarian must take into account several factors that often characterize the social or cultural environment. In general, knowledge of children's literature among adults is even more limited than in urban centers. Reading as a leisure activity may not enjoy a high status in some communities. Quality bookstores are rare if not nonexistent in most of rural America. The retail outlets selling books usually have a number of mass-market series for the middle grades and the picture book age, a few classic editions, titles by several popular authors, and children's titles written by well-known adult authors. If children are to experience quality literature or even see it, the library may offer the only opportunity.

Children in this environment need the concerted effort of all child-caring adults if they are to become print literate. Librarians hope, of course, that they also acquire the reading habit. The librarian's responsibility is to provide the best collection possible for these purposes, and to do this with limited funds. In most situations the bulk of the funds will be used for print materials to support reading activities. Because of staff limitations, the collection may actually serve in lieu of the reading guidance routinely offered in well-supported libraries.

Paradoxically, the rural librarian, who has a greater need to be more selective, often has fewer opportunities to review or examine materials before purchase. Publishers' complimentary copies are generally not available because of the library's limited budget. Even though a trained children's librarian can develop a good collection using printed reviews, local librarians in a cooperative system would benefit from the opportunity to examine titles. Should the school have librarians interested in joint reviewing, costs for examination copies could be shared. Several state library agencies provide examination centers, as do some of the larger cooperative library systems that may be within driving distance. The examination collections offered by some jobbers also represent another opportunity.

Collections in a Cooperative System

Consultants have encountered small libraries accustomed to selecting their materials from current publishers' catalogs or relying on the stock of the nearest department store. It will require considerable tact to break old habits, but the presence of appealing alternatives, plus the standard titles in attractive formats, can become in themselves a persuasive argument for change. If it is easier to purchase the latest title in a long-running series than a replacement copy of *Ramona the Pest,* the process should be reevaluated. Replacement lists can include titles submitted by member libraries and those standard titles the consultant has discovered lacking in many libraries. The number of new titles on buying lists should not be excessive; member libraries should be advised to allocate funds for needed replacement and added copies that are still in print.

Another method of improving the quality of collections in a cooperative system is through the use of small rotating collections selected by the consultant. These are generally assigned for a period of three to six months and then sent on to another library. At the end of the rotation schedule, they may be assigned to a member library or returned to the system collection, available for requests. Useful titles no longer needed in a member library can also be sent to the system's pool collection to be made available to other member libraries or offered to another institution.

Collections in a Consolidated System

Most of the materials in consolidated rural systems are selected cooperatively, processed centrally, and considered the property of the system as a whole. Materials are assigned to a service outlet on a temporary basis, although exceptions are often made for the larger libraries or for units assuming special responsibilities, such as central reference or special populations. Keeping the bulk of the circulating collection fluid is necessary because an avid reader of a particular genre could exhaust the resources of a small community library in a very short time.

A rotation system is often used to change the collections by sending a specified number of titles in various categories to the headquarters pool and receiving a like number in return. A monthly or bimonthly schedule is frequently offered, with local librarians having the option of requesting additional shipments for special needs. Rotation shipments should be selected by or under the supervision of the children's coordinator. Some local librarians may prefer to select their own shipments, but unless they are knowledgeable about children's materials, the coordinator should periodically check the composition of the collection, either by perusing the shelflist or locator file, or the shelves themselves during a branch visit. There should be titles to encourage children into the next level and to interest both the special and potential reader. On the basis of library and community needs, the coordinator may also designate an equitable number of new titles to add to the rotation shipment. The local librarian is usually responsible for selecting the titles to be returned to the pool collection. These usually include titles that are "read out," in need of repair, ready to discard and/or replace, or, in general, having no readership. Although this practice may serve the needs of adults who are more aggressive in the use of the reserve system, children are more susceptible to what Ruth Hill Viguers once called "the dragon Availability."[19] If the guidelines for removing adult materials are followed without exception for children's titles, a local collection could be shorn of *Alice in Wonderland, Tale of Peter Rabbit,* and *Grimm's Fairy Tales.* Even though these titles may not have circulated in the past three months, their constant presence speaks of their importance. Some method should be devised to keep a small core group of a hundred or more titles in all collections serving children. These may be marked with some term, such as basic book, to indicate their permanent status, and to be replaced with a fresh copy when needed.

The reserve and interlibrary loan systems in which any title listed in the system's catalog can be borrowed, also serve to change the composition of collections. Depending on system policy, these titles often remain in the borrowing library until rotated out or requested by another library. This practice may result in a library having a disproportionate number of horse stories, Judy Blume titles, or joke books. One of the difficulties in this situation is to convince the local librarians to return these circulation builders in order to receive different titles in the genre, or to provide space for materials that would interest other kinds of readers.

Bookmobiles may use the pool collection or the circulating collection in a large branch rather than maintaining their own. Whatever the practice, the buying lists prepared under the coordinator's supervision should consider the needs of the users of bookmobiles as expressed by their staffs. A books-by-mail service is sometimes provided in lieu of, or in addition to, bookmobile service. The children's coordinator may serve in an advisory role for the development of the children's collection. Most of the materials will be purchased in a paperback format, with excess copies of older titles transferred to the pool collection.

The children's coordinator should involve as many of the local staffs as possible in the selection process. In a large region this can be done by restricting the number of meetings annually and holding them in different areas of the library district. Working from a consideration file of titles with several reviews attached or summarized, the group can offer opinions on a title's projected usefulness, estimate the number of copies the system needs, and recommend the initial locations. Because the coordinator usually has responsibility for expenditures, the final responsibility for the number of copies must remain with her or him. Although time-consuming, this process provides information on the kinds of materials needed in various parts of the system; for the participants it strengthens a sense of involvement and evokes interest in reading and promoting specific titles to prospective readers. Problem titles for which a decision is difficult may be ordered in single copies and assigned to a member(s) to read and evaluate for the group.

The pool collection should be weeded regularly, and individual branch collections periodically checked for condition during branch visits. Some procedure should be established to alert the children's coordinator when last copies (or a previously agreed upon number) have been discarded. The decision can be made at that time whether the title should be replaced with new copies or a newer title, or permanently withdrawn.

Basic and Progamming Services

The children's consultant or coordinator in a rural library system must constantly remember that the competencies of the local staff are critical in improving services to children and child-serving adults. She or he may work behind the scenes by:

1. Recommending a schedule for updating various reference aids, e.g., encyclopedias, almanacs, atlases, etc.
2. Identifying a number of reader's advisory aids appropriate for the various types of communities—*Bookfinder, Children's Catalog,* etc.
3. Evaluating the request and interlibrary loan procedures for their effectiveness in meeting children's needs
4. Recommending a policy and procedure for responding to teacher's blanket assignments
5. Developing an outline of recommended activities for orientation visits by classes or other children's groups
6. Providing an ongoing series of training sessions to improve competencies in reference services and advice in program planning
7. Recommending, with other system staff, a procedure for dealing with a challenged title.

Reference Services

Although the children's consultant or coordinator generally works through other staff, there are requests which require attention: subject requests and loans to teachers or other child care workers in the community.

Children's Subject Requests. Requests for a specific title and author, or another title by a favorite author, can be delegated to a library assistant, but subject requests are usually handled by the children's consultant or coordinator because of the professional judgment required. These requests also reveal weaknesses in local collections, the content of school curricula, and the current interests of children. Staffs, especially of cooperative systems, should also be encouraged to record unfilled subject requests as a guide to their own collection development.

Teacher or Subject Loans. These are comprised of materials loaned to an individual for use with children. Depending on the policies developed by the system, these loans may include 10–25 titles on one or more subjects, e.g. science for third-graders, arts and crafts for a scouting group, biographies of religious figures for a church school's use. This type of request should be filled by the children's coordinator or consultant or under her or his supervision. Policies concerning the number of titles on a single subject, eligibility and responsibility of the borrower, and procedures for submitting requests need to be carefully outlined. In rural library systems where school library resources may be inadequate, the demands could seriously curtail the system's ability to serve other segments of the community, or weaken the argument for school library development or support.

Programming

In academic communities there is often a social division between "town and gown." The same phenomenon has been observed in some rural communities between "farm and town," with the library seen as a "town" institution. Consequently, farm residents may engage in activities and use information channels that are different from those of the town residents. One rural children's librarian recommended that programming be used to overcome these barriers. A farm resident invited to be a presenter in a program is introduced to the possibilities of library service while contributing to the education of the townspeople. The programs could involve making cheese, exhibiting a farm animal (who could resist a pig named Wilbur?), or demonstrating a craft.[20]

The goal of preparing local librarians to assume total responsibility for their programming will never be completely realized, given the staffing levels of most rural libraries. But the coordinator or consultant can support the local librarians' efforts in a number of ways. The procedures for system-wide programs should be simplified as much as possible, keeping in mind the many demands made on the local librarian's time. Packaged programs that include materials and instructions should be made available upon request. A file of program resources in the area and funding sources outside of the system can prove useful not only to the system staff but also to the public.

Library Resources for Programming. A system can provide an array of materials for programming, such as flannel boards, puppet scripts and portable stages, collections of tellable stories, filmstrips, fingerplays, music and games for storytimes, and suggested formats for program themes. These provide fitting adjuncts to in-service training sessions as well as resources for ongoing assistance. With a committee representing the member libraries, a summer reading club theme can be selected and materials prepared, thus permitting the local staffs to spend their time in assisting the children. The consultant can also alert the local librarians of upcoming media tie-ins that can be promoted to the users.

Resource File of Programmers. Included in this file should be individuals within the system (at all levels), volunteers whose performances have met the library's standards, and paid talent—puppeteers, storytellers, mimes, etc. Other community groups that plan activities for children—PTA, 4-H groups—would find this type of information useful. These contacts from community groups also present opportunties to offer library resources in their planning.

Funding Sources for System-wide Programming. Many good programming ideas for rural libraries are shelved for lack of funding. Because the rural library may provide the best (or only) public space in a community, it has a greater responsibility and opportunity to serve as a cultural center where diverse segments of a community can meet. Federal aid made available through the state library agency has been a source of assistance for all types of libraries in both rural and urban areas. Priorities have been given to those projects and programs serving populations, either rural or urban, with a high concentration of low-income families. Guidelines and application procedures can be obtained from the state library agency.

Another possible funding source is the National Endowment for the Humanities which accepts applications to its state offices (Division of State Programs) and also directly to the national body through its Division of Public Programs. As explained by one of its officials:

> Public programs in rural and urban settings alike should work toward accomplishing one or more of the following objectives: fostering an appreciation of cultural works; illuminating historical ideas, figures, and events; or promoting an understanding of the disciplines of the humanities. Grant proposal should focus on one of these three objectives.[21]

Guidelines for proposals can be requested from the national or state offices. The requesting agency is expected to provide some support for the proposed program.

Time, facilities, services, materials and money donated by participants and non-participants should, at a minimum, be valued in equivalence to the requested grant amount.[22]

Grants have ranged from $100 to $100,000 for special projects, and topics have included telephone interviews with authors, a multi-generational program of reminiscences (which included artifacts from each generation), and training for leading book discussion.[23] NEH does not fund materials except those needed in the program itself.

Rural libraries that serve economically disadvantaged children should investigate the assistance provided by Reading Is Fundamental (RIF). Founded in 1966, the organization's primary purpose was to place books in the hands of children who might otherwise never know the thrill and pleasure of book ownership. Libraries in some communities have served as a sponsoring agency for the distribution of books. Since its founding, RIF has broadened its activities, but reductions in funding in recent years have curtailed its book distribution program. A newsletter keeps volunteers and sponsoring agencies abreast of its various services, publications, and activities that would be useful to libraries and local groups that might be willing to finance a book distribution program.[24]

Private foundations are also a funding source for library programs; however, a considerable amount of time and effort must be invested in grant writing. These efforts are not always successful, but proposals submitted to local and state foundations may receive greater consideration.[25] If the *Foundation Directory*, which provides information on many private foundations, is not available locally, copies of appropriate pages (with those foundations interested in libraries or rural areas) can probably be supplied by the state library.[26] The *Bowker Annual* has occasionally included a listing of foundations that have made grants to libraries.[27]

In-Service Training

All coordinators and consultants in rural systems have a responsibility to provide those learning experiences designed to improve staff performances. These experiences also convey to the staff the standard of service the library has adopted as its goal. Because of the limitations under which rural library systems operate, the system staff must use every avenue available to help staff improve their service competencies. These may include (1) branch visits, (2) workshops, (3) procedure or policy manuals, and (4) newsletters.

Branch Visits

Monthly contact with the local librarian is desirable, whether this involves a visit to the library or a meeting of branch personnel at a central location. Realistically, the frequency of contacts depends on the distances involved and the level of staff resources. In a system with twelve libraries, the children's specialist might be able to visit each of them five or six times during most of the year. Frequent contact not only prevents many problems from arising, but also benefits staff morale.

The branch visitor should prepare a list of topics to discuss, and the local librarian should be encouraged to do the same. One children's coordinator asked member librarians to evaluate the physical environment of their children's area using a prepared outline. The coordinator also marked a copy from her perspective. The two completed outlines provided the basis for discussing what was exemplary and what might be done to improve the facilities. Other topics that may need attention are:

1. Progress made on objectives
2. Collection needs, current and projected
3. Effectiveness of system policies or procedures
4. Problems arising with schools and other community groups
5. Service needs not met
6. Effective use of reading guidance and reference aids
7. Programming and other methods of promoting services
8. Recent children's titles that need promotion.

The topics may be the same in both the cooperative and consolidated systems, but the treatment and approach will differ. For example, the children's coordinator can insist that sex education materials for children be placed on the open shelves in accordance with system policy. The consultant, whose authority does not extend to internal matters, may be limited to offering reasons why these materials should be on the open shelves.

Workshops for Systems Staffs

Bringing staff together is the most efficient means of presenting information that cannot be conveyed effectively through a memo or newsletter. Staff workshops can be used by the system staff to:

1. Improve skills in serving users' library needs
2. Introduce proposed changes in system services, policies, and procedures
3. Develop and maintain collections that meet the needs of local communities
4. Promote library use through effective programming and promotion
5. Increase the rapport among system and local staffs.

Most libraries in rural systems have very small staffs that are responsible for services to all age groups, from preschoolers to the aged. An all-staff workshop usually includes one or more sessions dealing with children's services. The children's specialist and other system staff must work cooperatively to develop a cost-effective workshop that meets the objectives of the system, and addresses the concerns of the local staffs. In addition to problems common to a number of libraries, and those critical areas that need regular reinforcement or refinement, such as intellectual freedom and reference skills, workshop topics should also recognize the needs created by changes in society, e.g. home schoolers, adult and young adult illiteracy, etc. Because rural staffs have few opportunities to attend library-related events of an inspirational nature, a workshop should occasionally include a session of this type: an author or illustrator, a library or book historian from a library school, a noted storyteller or folklorist, etc.

The children's specialist may offer a session on the upcoming summer reading club, with suggestions for promotion, a review of procedures, recommendations for helping children broaden their reading experiences, and a brief introduction of titles or types of materials to promote. Other sessions might spotlight a particular genre, e.g. poetry for children of all ages. Various staff could demonstrate the use of poetry in programming, displays, trivia games, creative dramatics, and films, with a follow-up session on using poetry indexes to locate titles for subject requests of children, teachers, and other caregivers. Sessions that deal with general skills or competencies should be available not only to the system's staff, but also to interested volunteers, personnel of child-serving agencies including schools, trustees, and, as a courtesy, staffs of the unaffiliated libraries in the area.

The length of a workshop depends on how frequently it is offered, distances the participants must travel, available funding for substitutes in one-person libraries, mileage (not inconsequential in western states), and, perhaps, lodging. In systems that extend over large areas, a noon-to-following-noon schedule, with a less demanding evening session, allows for daytime travel and periods of sociability.

Methods of instruction include demonstrations by the system staff or experienced community librarians. Children's specialists often introduce booktalking and picture book presentations using this method. Role-playing or reader's theater has proven to be an effective way of conveying rather complex information, and talent can be found at all levels of staff. Responding to an irate parent's demand to remove a children's title, or handling a problem patron, lend themselves to role-playing. Lectures are the least desirable, although they may be the most efficient way of conveying some types of information, such as procedural or policy changes. To improve their effectiveness, transparencies, slides, and other props should be used.

Group discussions can be highly effective if they are planned with clear objectives in mind. One such discussion included all levels of staff from the director to the bookmobile driver who were assigned to groups of six or seven, after having read a contemporary children's book with a somewhat controversial theme. Because many of the participants had not read a children's book since their own childhood, care was taken to select titles that could not be dismissed as lacking in literary value. In addition to the predicted outcomes, other benefits were observed. For new staff this became the means of interacting and feeling comfortable with the group. Plots were shared across the groups, and subsequent checks of circulation records revealed that these titles enjoyed a high turnover in the member libraries.

Procedural and Policy Manuals

The staff manual serves as a backup resource for information previously given in workshops, branch visits, newsletters, and memos, but which is here organized and indexed for quick reference. Manuals used in a consolidated system may reflect a more obligatory tone than those provided in a cooperative system, but their role in in-service training is the same. The information provided is usually more complete than that furnished a professionally trained staff. Detailed instructions for actually conducting a variety of children's services or programs can be included, such as:

1. Storytimes, with bibliographies and sample formats
2. Orientation visits, grade by grade
3. Instructions on weeding
4. Requests for subject or teacher loans
5. Information requests
6. Service and program reports
7. Use of volunteers.

These instructions can be written so that the objectives of the activity or the underlying philosophy can be conveyed as well. For example, in treating the topic of information requests, the instructions can be stated within the context of the child's right to equal access to the total collection, a concept that should underlie all children's services. In discussing orientation visits, the steps outlined may include ways to reach the family through the child, thereby reinforcing one of the objectives. Manuals in a looseleaf format are, of course, easier to update.

Newsletters

The newsletter contributes to a number of functions, yet assumes total responsibility for none of them: communication, staff morale, procedural information, and in-service education. It may be viewed primarily as a communication link among staff and administration, but it cannot be the only means by which information is sent or received. As a vehicle for staff education, the newsletter can offer a follow-up explanation of service priorities, review a new reference title that will improve response time for requests, or outline the pros and cons of a proposed policy change. The newsletter also provides staff members an opportunity to share their successful service or program activities.

In a rural system the newsletter is not a vehicle for a philosophical discussion of national information policies or a forum to display a consultant's erudition. Library jargon and acronyms need to be held to a minimum. To be successful, a newsletter must first of all be read. If this requires chatty news and recipes, consider it part of the evolution of systems. Interspersed with what some might consider trivia can be nuggets of wisdom, lightly communicated. Quotes from a new book, a human interest story garnered from a branch report, or a review of a new book on parenting are likely to be read. I once made an unscheduled visit to a bookmobile headquarters when copies of the system's newsletter had just been delivered. As no one would talk to me until they had finished reading, I realized the system's newsletter was a success.

School-Public Library Relationships

The proper relationship of these two tax-supported institutions is not easily achieved, as it depends on an understanding and appreciation of each other's role within its institution and community, and the professional standards each supports. If all the words ever penned, typed, or word processed on this topic were laid end to end, they might span a continent; yet, each generation seems to discover the issue anew and to search for a workable pattern within the context of existing technology, available resources, and current philosophy.

School and Public Library Roles

Inevitably, there will be areas of overlap in the roles of school and public libraries, especially in rural areas; but the role of each can be summarized according to the major functions each assumes within its respective jurisdiction.

School Library and Media Center. The school has a responsibility to provide materials that support the curriculum and the educational goals of the school, and to make them available to teachers, students, and staff. The function of a school library is similar to that of a special library, except that acquisition of library and information skills is a student-learning objective. (The special library user is handed the information needed.) The school librarian has knowledge of all facets of the instructional role of the teachers, and considerable time is spent assisting them in planning educational activities. The school library is also responsible for those non-textbook materials required for classroom instruction, e.g. multiple copies of assigned readings. Even though its resources will reflect to a large extent the instructional program, the school's overall educational goals may require a sizable collection of literature which is often considered by some observers as recreational reading. In the school situation these materials may be an integral part of the literature program, or selected to help children develop the reading habit. Their inclusion may prompt some onlookers to conclude that there is unnecessary duplication in the school and public library collections.

The school has a responsibility to promote an awareness and use of other community resources as part of the educational process. Referring children to the public library for additional information, publicizing its programs, and taking classes for orientation visits are some of the ways that this responsibility can be met.

Public Library Children's Services. The public library has a responsibility to serve the general library needs of all age groups in its jurisdiction. Attempts are made to serve the child as an individual, wherever she or he lives and regardless of school or out-of-school interests.

It is difficult to draw hard and fast distinction between the responsibilities of school and public libraries that will serve every community, whether rural or urban. Nevertheless, these institutions must develop guidelines for developing collections and designing services if scarce resources are to be used effectively. Some public libraries attempt to differentiate between the mass assignment (a book or reference on Nigeria for each child in the classroom) and material on Nigeria requested by the child who has selected this subject for a report. In the former instance, the public library responds to the extent possible or practical; in the latter, the resources of the library system are made available on the same basis offered any other user, including access to the reserve and interlibrary system. This distinction can also be applied to other users—for instance, an engineer in a local firm. If job-related technical materials were needed by the engineer, the firm's library would be considered the primary provider, with the public library making available its materials upon request. If the engineer also wanted information on Chinese cooking as a result of a business contact with a Chinese engineer, the public library would consider this within its primary responsibility. Even though the requests of the child and engineer were, in part, job related, they originated from an individual choice, and the materials supplied were those having value for a general public library audience. Textbook materials are seldom, if ever, acquired, but general titles on subjects frequently requested by students are considered legitimate purchases. I've never attended a selection meeting when at least one children's librarian didn't remark, "I need one or two copies of that (trade book) title for school assignments."

The public library has a responsibility to nurture interests and reinforce information skills developed in the school's program by providing relevant services, progams, and exhibits. It also shares a responsibility to acquaint children with other community agencies and individuals who have a contribution to make to their education.

The Public Library's Dilemma

The growth of elementary school libraries in the 1960s and 1970s was impressive. Unfortunately, these gains have not been protected by legislation that requires elementary schools to establish and maintain a school media library. Along with other public institutions that deal with shrinking budgets, school libraries in many areas have declined in quality in the past decade. Even though this is a nationwide problem that strikes urban as well as rural schools, the situation in the latter represents a unique twist. Support for libraries in an urban school can be fairly well assessed by knowing the per student capita expenditure; in a rural area, this figure is less revealing. The expenditure of $25 per student in a rural elementary school of 175 students, in addition to being unlikely, would not be adequate to maintain a collection of library books, reference materials, audiovisual materials, computer software, periodicals, binding, and supplies. There may be no professional staff, either on a part-time or supervisory basis, thus producing a vacuum of leadership and professional expertise that the public library system may be asked to fill. Some school officials, in an attempt to solve this problem, turn instinctively to the public library, with the suggestion that bookmobile service be made available to the children and teachers during the school day, or that a public library branch be placed in the school building or on its grounds. Such requests reveal a lack of understanding of the role of the school library as a basic component of an educational program, as well as the mission of the public library to serve the general information needs of all ages.

A sizable number of children in rural areas live in widely dispersed locations; but, for several hours a day, from September to June, they are in school, brought there by buses traveling long distances. Some form of direct service to schools may be the most efficient or the only method of providing public library service to these children. Regardless of residence, the public library has an obligation to serve the people in its jurisdiction, wherever they live.

The public library's dilemma grows out of its historical involvement with direct services to schools. In many instances these services inadvertently retarded the development and growth of school libraries, while consuming a disproportionate share of their own resources. If public libraries provide direct service to schools whose libraries are totally inadequate, there is a concern that financially strapped school officials may divert funds from library services to another pressing need. Public library resources, always distressingly finite, must be stretched to address many other current needs, e.g. literacy, preschool programs, etc. In committing large resources to the school population, other audiences will be shortchanged.

Until recent times, most of the literature on school-public library relationships discussed the issues in the context of urban libraries, failing to recognize the differences imposed by geography and population density. But, whether regarding rural or urban areas, there is one question common in all situations: Should the school library and public library combine or cooperate? There is no one answer that is correct for every community.

The School and Public Library Combination

There are a few examples of successful to moderately successful school and public library mergers throughout the country. This type of combination requires a legal contract that identifies the governing body for the combined facility, the responsibilities of each institution, and the terms for dissolution. Woolard concluded from a study of combined facilities in 1977 that this type of facility could be successful under certain conditions:

> The optimum environment would be communities with 10,000 residents or less, and which need a school and/or public library facility and/or public library facility and/or professional staff.[28]

In the first phase of a three-part study on school and public libraries, Aaron offered two major conclusions that should be heeded by communities considering this option:

> First, it is unlikely that a community able to support or now supporting separate types of libraries will offer better school and public services through a combined program. This is because the combination of factors required to promote a successful program seldom occurs.
>
> Second, when a community is unable to provide minimum library services through separate facilities and no option for improved services through system membership exists, the combined program presents a possible alternative to limited or non-existent services under certain conditions ... communities with limited resources should not select the combined program unless the implementation of the concept: (1) allows the hiring of professional personnel where none previously were employed; (2) provides a means for strengthening resources; (3) offers an adequately planned program to meet the needs of all community members, and (4) utilizes a systematic evaluation procedure to assess the status of the program and provide future directions.[29]

From the studies that have been done on this topic, there is no evidence that combining libraries results in savings; on the contrary, the reverse is the more likely result if service is maintained at an adequate level for all age groups. When the principal motive for the merger is to save money rather than to improve services, the public may be shocked to learn that more money is needed to bring the resources up to standard. Aaron's final report should be carefully studied in communities contemplating this type of merger.[30] Her recommendation that a community library affiliate with a public library system if one exists, offers fewer problems. Along with this preferable option, however, is the necessity to invest considerable effort in cooperative activities for the benefit of those users who are at a critical stage of their development—the children.

School and Public Library Cooperation

In determining which cooperative activities are the most cost-effective, the children's specialist must cope with several factors that are ever present in this situation.

Illusion of Adequacy. The optimistic belief of the funding agencies that cooperation will solve all problems without more money or an investment of staff time is a myth that must be dispelled over and over again. It would be comforting to believe that adequacy can be achieved with cooperation (or combination), but, in most situations, cooperation can only increase or improve the resources that exist, not produce what is lacking for a quality education. If the resources of both libraries in many rural communities were added together, the school's educational program would still not have the necessary support. One-fourth cup of sugar combined with one-third cup does not, alas, add up to one cup.

Staffing Levels. Cooperation requires a considerable investment of staff time, a commodity often in short supply in rural libraries. During the decade of the sixties, there were several demonstrations of effective ways to achieve cooperation between school and public libraries. One key element to success appeared to be a staff member who was given the mobility to consult with personnel in both institutions, develop lines of communication, and explore ways of mutual assistance.[31] For the vast majority of rural systems, this staff position would be a luxury, considering the staffing levels of most of the member libraries. It would overcome one of the present barriers to communication, however. The working schedules of children's and school librarians seldom mesh; free time of one coincides with the busy time of the other. There is also the problem of the educational credentials of the key staff in each institution. When both staffs at the local, as well as the district or system, level are certified librarians, communication is relatively easy. Because this ideal is seldom realized in a rural area, more time as well as tact may be necessary to forge a working relationship.

Multiplicity of School Districts. A rural consolidated or cooperative system may encompass an area with several school districts, each with its own textbooks, educational goals, and curriculum. The children's coordinator or consultant should become aware of the conditions in as many districts as possible in order to identify the most promising areas for cooperative activities, given the resources available. Whenever these activities involve contributions of money or staff, discussions should involve the administrative bodies of both institutions. All of the difficulties inherent in cooperation identified above do not excuse either institution from working to surmount these problems. Any effort can only improve the existing situation and, more importantly, develop an ongoing relationship that may result in future progress. Resources of two libraries are better than one, and each, no matter how small, undoubtedly has something to share, whether materials, equipment, or expertise.

Some of the following examples of cooperation may be dependent, in some areas, on the willingness and abilities of the local librarians, and, in others, on the consultant or coordinator's available time:

1. Invite the other library's staff to selection meetings and in-service programs
2. Share costs and responsibilities for outside programs, e.g., telephone interviews with authors and illustrators, storytellers, *Book Week* activities, etc.
3. Select expensive materials cooperatively, e.g., professional aids and reference books, and share their use
4. Publicize each other's services and programs
5. Develop guidelines and procedures for mass assignments with students' needs in mind
6. Provide display space for artwork of students
7. Exchange copies of each other's catalog, if in book or microform format, or work for joint access, if online
8. Offer short-term loans of materials and equipment
9. Share responsibility for a book column in the local newspaper
10. Compile and print bibliographies and bookmarks representing the collections of both
11. Explore new technologies capable of improving cooperation, e.g., facsimile transmission.

In speaking to groups of teachers and parents, the public librarian reiterates (diplomatically) the contributions a school library with a qualified staff can offer, especially if available to students and teachers at the optimal learning time. The supplementary role of the public library should always be underscored.

Public Library Services to Rural Schools

When public library systems develop policies for their relationships with schools, they tend to make exceptions for rural schools that draw from sparsely populated areas, and which are located beyond walking distance of a community library. They recognize the difficulties these schools have in providing adequate library resources, as well as their own problems in serving these hard-to-reach children. New schools may also be designated an exception when they are making a concerted effort to build an adequate library program, but need added resources for a few years.

Policies that govern direct services to schools either by bookmobiles, regular classroom visits, or teacher loans need to be understood by both parties. School personnel must understand that what is being provided is public library service to children who happen to be at school. Therefore, policies of access and use which allow children free choice must be accepted as part of the service. In addition, policies should acknowledge that the services provided are intended to supplement the school library, not supplant it or retard its development.

Whenever public and school librarians convene for any purpose, the discussion ultimately centers on the "common enemy": teachers who do not alert librarians of their upcoming assignments. This is not a problem unique to rural areas. Librarians need to move beyond lamentation and make it easier for teachers to make more effective use of the library resources that do exist. Assignment Alert Forms can be completed and mailed or phoned in (or someday soon telefaxed) by the office secretary. School librarians who serve on curriculum committees need to remind teachers of this necessary step. In spite of all the groundwork, success may not be spectacular; repetition is necessary. Compared to the teacher's responsibilities, the librarian's problem may not loom as immediate as a case of suspected child abuse, the fight that occurred on the playground, or the child who lost his lunch. The reasons for advance notification should stress the advantages to the learning process rather than the convenience it affords the librarian.

The public library has to determine if its resources, or those of the system, can support teachers' loans and to what extent. If loans are offered, a procedure should be developed that doesn't bypass the school library. One rural library system required that teachers requesting materials on any topic for classroom use submit the request to the school librarian. This procedure ensured that materials in the school library were called to the attention of the teacher, and it alerted the school librarian of the need to consider this topic when materials were ordered. If there is no school librarian, the public library may wish to provide a periodic report of requests received for the use of the teacher or committee responsible for ordering materials.

The use of technology offers the promise of real progress being made in school and public library cooperation; but, in areas where the telephone, typewriter, and photocopier represent the highest level of technology, progress may be dependent on foundation, state, or federal funds for the start-up costs. In addition, a lack of staff able to institute and use online systems effectively represents another problem.[32] When these barriers can be overcome, access to a wider range of resources will be possible. A couple of decades ago, copies of the public library's microform catalog were placed in the schools served by a rural consolidated library. Supported by a state grant (LSCA), microfiche readers were purchased for those schools serving children in sparsely populated areas. A librarian was hired on a temporary basis to instruct the children and teachers in the use of the machines and in filling out requests for materials. With online catalogs, access to collections can be provided with a computer terminal, modem, and telephone. More immediate reference service from the headquarters library to the branches and school libraries will also be possible as facsimile transmission [FAX] machines follow the developmental pattern of personal computers in size, capability, and cost. Even so, these may not become affordable for all communities without outside funds.* Crucial to such institutional linkages, however, is the necessity to involve the school media library as the conduit to the school population.

Users in rural areas are not indifferent to computer technology; many have personal computers in their homes and could become a ready audience for online catalogs. In one rural library system in Washington State, computer software in the public domain has been one of the most popular circulating items.

Cooperative Agricultural Extension Agency

Although chapters of several state or national organizations may exist in rural areas—Lions, Kiwanis, Veterans of Foreign Wars, Business and Professional Women, etc.—the outside activities of many rural families center around the church and those agencies devoted to the business of agriculture: the Grange, Farm Bureau,

---

*The National Rural Information Clearing House of the National Rural Center maintains a special library for the purpose of meeting requests for sources of technical assistance, financial aid, and research findings.

cooperatives, marketing commissions. The most important agency, in terms of its organizational structure and service program, is the Cooperative Agricultural Extension Agency (CAEA).

Established in 1914 under the general supervision of the Department of Agriculture, the CAEA is frequently cited as a model for federal, state, and local partnership; it has a small administrative group at the national level, a state level staff working with land-grant universities and their research programs, and the bulk of its service personnel located at the county level. Long a vital force in all rural and small community life, it has extended its services to the urban areas since the 1960s. Of the three divisions within this organization, two have special implications for children's services: the offices of the home economists and family living agents and the 4-H youth agents (the county agricultural agent is the third division).

Librarians will find that several of the agency's goals complement those of the library. The mission of the agency is to disseminate useful information based on research in agriculture, home economics, and related subjects, and to help families apply this information to their farm, home, and community lives. The improvement of community and family life is a commitment the public library shares, although there are perceived differences in the roles of their staff:

> The librarian is concerned with matching the customer with the information he wants or needs. The agricultural extension agent is concerned with finding the proper action to eliminate the problem and teaching the customer how to do it.[33]

Called the largest adult education agency in the world, the CAEA uses various methods of instruction often in combination: demonstrations, informational tapes, telephone assistance, bulletins, newsletters, personal visits, and the mass media.[34] Many weekly newspapers in rural areas carry regular columns by the county agricultural agent and home economics agent. The public library could profit from this type of information network and, in turn, serve as one of the dissemination points.

The home economics and family living division is an obvious resource for advice on developing parenting collections and for expertise in planning staff and parent education workshops. The literature-related programs offered by librarians may also be useful to activities planned for this division's clientele. But because recent information on 4-H programs is difficult to find in library literature, this particular division of cooperative extension will be discussed in more detail.

The 4-H program goal is to foster character development and good citizenship through a wide variety of projects that emphasize the "head, heart, hands, and health." It serves the needs and interests of both rural and urban members. The lower age requirement is now set at first grade with the upper age at nineteen. When 4-H members encounter problems with their projects, they should be referred to their leader or other 4-H youth personnel, for the process is an important part of the learning experience. Beyond this caution, however, there are several areas where cooperative action would benefit both agencies. Librarians should make an appointment with their county 4-H youth agent to explore possibilities for cooperation.

Although policies and procedures governing 4-H programs are developed nationally, each state tailors its publications and projects to the interests and needs of its own population. All libraries should obtain from their county 4-H office the free booklet *4-H Projects and Publications: A Guide to Enrollment*. It identifies the various areas under which projects may be chosen, and lists each project's required and optional publications for both members and leaders. Like many of the materials for scouts, some of these free and inexpensive materials could also be used in serving general information needs.

As librarians and 4-H youth agents develop a working relationship, they may encounter several ways that each can support the other's goals. The following represent only a few:

1. Provide a list of recent titles (or program announcement) on a particular project theme for inclusion in a 4-H newsletter
2. Request a roster of 4-H leaders and their project topics to add to a local library's community information file
3. Offer to tailor a library program to the needs of a 4-H audience; topics could include storytelling techniques, preschool literature, or booktalks on a topic of current concern (safety tips for latchkey children, teenage suicide, etc.)
4. Provide subject booklists or bookmarks of library materials on current issues for distribution through the 4-H office
5. Acquire selected 4-H publications for reference use by members and prospective members
6. Provide an audience for members to demonstrate their projects, when suitable to library programming.[35]

In discussing possible areas of cooperation with any community agency, librarians should not assume that their knowledge of the agency is current, or that the agency staff is aware of the full range of library services. If the librarian learns as much as possible about the goals and activities of the agency before the personal contact, the outcome will be more successful.

Conclusion

Much will be demanded of librarians who assume responsibility for children's services in sparsely populated areas because staff with professional credentials are often few in numbers. In general, children's librarians will interact more frequently with local trustees and officials, represent the library to a wider audience, and be expected to assist with library matters outside their specialty. If they operate within a library system, much of their time and energy will be devoted to teaching and demonstrating service competencies and programming skills and to developing resources behind the scenes to support the local staffs in providing public services. Adaptations of library practices will be necessary to accommodate the variety of service outlets represented in the average rural system.

Because the resources to support library service in rural areas are limited, cooperation with other child-caring institutions is not a choice but a necessity. An understanding of the role of the school library media program is necessary in any cooperative planning. The excellent communication channels of the Cooperative Agricultural Extension Agency offers opportunities to reach prospective users while assisting that agency in its goal of improving the quality of rural life. Librarians in rural situations tend to use the resources of their state library for information and assistance more often than those who work in urban libraries. All of these relationships can become both professionally and personally rewarding.

Along with the advantages of a rural lifestyle, librarians must deal with the professional isolation imposed by their environment. They sometimes feel apart from the broader currents of library development because of fewer opportunities to discuss professional issues. At times they may find it difficult to validate the importance of their role, because success of their efforts is largely dependent on improvements in the programs of service carried on in the system's libraries. Children's librarians in urban libraries often find the role of their rural counterpart ah best a paradox and at worst not quite within the acceptable range of library practice. In order to deal successfully with these attitudes, rural children's librarians need a sense of humor, a high level of self-esteem, and the patience to wait for the rewards of their efforts. In the meantime they can derive much satisfaction from the knowledge that children are gaining a more valid concept of the public library as an institution that can enrich their lives, and from the strong citizen support for those who serve the needs of children. Almost without exception, groups and individuals are receptive to requests for assistance, whether the need involves a fresh coat of paint for the children's room or a judge for a poster contest.

CHAPTER 7

Rufus stared at her in silence. The library lady
was eating. Rufus had never seen her do anything
before but play cards, punch books, and carry
great piles of them around. Now she was eating.
Mama said not to stare at anybody while they
were eating. Still Rufus didn't know the library
lady ate, so it was hard for him not to look at
her.—Eleanor Estes, *Rufus M* (New York: Harcourt, 1943), pp.23–24.

The Professional Role and Responsibilities of the Children's Librarian

Children's librarians must assume many roles, both within and outside the library, if they are to fulfill their professional responsibilities. These extend beyond service to the individual user and groups attending library programs. They have responsibilities to the staff, professional colleagues, and administration within the library or system. Outside the library, the children's librarian, both individually and as a member of a professional association, is expected to be (1) a supporter of library development at the local, state, and national levels, and (2) an advocate for children, working with others in advancing legislation and policies that address the overall needs of children at all levels of government. In order to serve effectively in these roles, children's librarians have an obligation for their own continuing education through engaging in (1) opportunities offered through membership in library and allied professional associations, (2) formal courses offered by library schools or other academic departments, and (3) a personal regimen of selected reading within the general librarianship, their own specialty, and other child-serving professions. And finally, if children's librarians are to be effective in their professional roles, they must attend to their own growth and development as individuals with adult interests and concerns. In dealing with the power structure both within and outside of the library, a children's librarian, who is also seen as an adult conversant with the broader societal concerns, is more effective than a narrowly focused individual able to deal only with issues that directly affect her or his specialty.

The Professional Role

The hallmark of professional persons is not only the competencies and skills they have acquired whether through formal education or experience, but also the attitudes and standards of behavior they exhibit for themselves and expect from their staffs and colleagues. Professional schools begin the process of socializing the individual into a profession. It is continued by colleagues in the library who act as role models and mentors, while associations provide opportunities to observe further modeling and to interact with others in dealing with issues that demand a professional response. One hears occasionally of someone described as being a "true professional." This appellation, not limited to those who possess a library degree, often refers to someone who is able to consider issues without becoming personal in argument, focuses on the benefits to the public in decision-making, works to uphold the service standards of the overall library, and considers issues before professional associations from the standpoint of potential benefits to the profession at large, rather than as opportunities to enhance her/his own status.

Philosophical Basis of Children's Librarianship

Like all professionals, librarians have, through their national association, developed a code of ethics that purports to guide librarians in their work. In addition, each library specialty may develop a set of goals or a philosophical statement that serves to describe its particular contribution to society. There is no current statement of goals or philosophy that describes the essence of children's services that has been widely discussed and endorsed at the national level. Children's divisions of several state associations have included such statements in their standards or guidelines. In the "Philosophy of Service" statement that precedes the *Standards for Youth Services in Public Libraries of New York State*, the philosophy of children's services is expressed as follows:

> Providing access to knowledge broadens the minds of young people, stimulates their imaginations, and expands their horizons. These positive and enriching experiences found in the library environs will have an impact on individuals, their society, and their world. Librarians serving young people must be advocates for children and young adults. Their concerns should include an awareness of forces in today's world which affect the quality of life of young people . . .[1]

Children's librarians, perhaps more than other specialists, have not lacked critics ready to identify their shortcomings. The criticisms have ranged from children's librarians' overemphasis on the "library faith," an untested belief that reading good literature improves the reader, to a failure to incorporate scientific management principles into their services.[2] In the past two decades, management competencies have become an important part of a children's librarian's preparation and working experience. These should not become an end in themselves, but rather a more effective means to realizing the higher-level goals articulated above. It is relatively easy to evaluate services by using statistical measures, but their real importance rests on their contribution to the lives of the children. William Summers once observed that children's librarians adhered to the concept of librarianship as an art rather than as a science.[3] Funding officials and library administrators expect children's services to be expressed in management terms; the general public respond more positively when services "as art" are described. The challenge to children's librarians is to describe their services in ways that both funding officials and the general public understand.

Professional Role with Users

Librarians need to take a hard-headed look at the reasons they wish to work as children's librarians. Children are not impressed by academic credentials, but they do respect competence and respond to adults who demonstrate interest in them as individuals. Unfortunately, the three customary tests for fitness undergone by the hero of the traditional folktale do not exist for children's librarians. However, if it were possible to devise such tests, we would ask to measure a candidate's need to (1) be in control or to be an acknowledged authority figure, (2) perform before a less critical audience (at least vocally), and (3) escape what is often perceived as the more exacting standards adults set for service. Assuming that our candidate scored low on the above tests, we would then expect that she or he would achieve a high score on tests that revealed (1) flexibility in implementing policies, (2) respect for the dignity of the individual, whatever the age, (3) the grace to learn from children, and (4) the ability to laugh or sympathize *with* children in their attempt to understand the world.

In maintaining a professional relationship with users of the children's department, the children's librarian is governed by the same standards of behavior that operate in dealing with the adult public. The privacy of all users should be respected and accounts of their amusing blunders or intimate secrets kept within the children's department walls. Neither Mrs. X nor her eleven-year-old daughter Susie X should fear that her request for sex information will be told to other library staff or friends. If Mrs. X wishes to monitor what Susie reads, she may do so at home or accompany her daughter to the library to oversee her use of library resources. There may be times, of course, when intimate secrets or a physical condition provide rather clear evidence of child abuse. Should this occur, the role of the librarian is not unlike that of a teacher, and the library administration must be consulted on the appropriate action to be taken.

If we want children to develop into adults who feel comfortable in the library, we need to recognize that each stage of childhood is characterized by behaviors that can usually be predicted, or at least understood. It is the responsibility of the children's librarian to take the leadership in helping the staff understand these behaviors and to recommend a standard response to them. The exuberance and spontaneity of a four-year-old requires one reaction; the disturbance created by a group of thirteen-year-olds, another.

Children should be allowed a great deal of freedom, but that freedom is more comfortably handled when there is an adult in charge who sets limits. Children of all ages need adult mentors to prepare them for entering the adult world. They have less need for grown-up playmates. Librarians who have little or no difficulty with discipline are generally those who have only a few rules for behavior, but make sure that staff and those users who have reached the age of understanding are aware of them.

They naturally assume that children's behavior will be appropriate until proven otherwise, ignore minor infractions unless they disturb others, and are consistent and fair in dealing with behavioral problems. Sarcasm and irony have no place in a relationship with children; however, a light touch and a sense of humor add the leavening needed in dealing with those who slip beyond the bounds of acceptable behavior. When children must be removed from the library, it should be done as quietly and calmly as possible. The offenders should know that their removal is the result of behavior that disturbs others, when and under what conditions they will be welcomed back, and that the librarian still values them as individuals.

In dealings with all children, it is necessary to look at library situations from their point of view. The four-year-old who stamps into the library, carefully and noisily putting each foot down on the tile floor, probably has acquired new shoes that beg to be noticed. This significant event should be recognized, commented upon, and admired before the noise abatement problem is tackled. Actually, the problem may disappear after such acknowledgment has been made. The group of noisy thirteen-year-olds may be exhibiting an all-too-normal reaction in escaping the restrictive environment of a classroom and need a brief period to settle comfortably into the relaxed atmosphere of the library.

The perception of appropriate library behavior is not universally shared either among the ranks of the library staff or the users. Children who view the library as an extension of school and act accordingly usually win the approbation of the staff or escape their notice, while those who test the limits may find that the boundaries vary among the staff. Children often receive conflicting messages from parents who experienced a quiet-as-a-mouse library in their childhoods and teachers who are comfortable in a busy, bustling library where the public and staff speak in conversational tones. In speaking to children about their inappropriate behavior, the staff should be aware that the blame may rest on the library for failing to inform young users of the standards. Courtesy would require that the staff attempt to discover if this is the case before responding to what may be an innocent transgression. Because consistency and fairness are vital in dealing with children, the public service staff should be involved in developing behavior policies; aware of the agreed-upon standards, and in consideration to staff colleagues and the children, they should be expected to enforce them. When policies defining appropriate library behavior are developed, they should not include one set of rules for children and another for adults. Children who are reprimanded for speaking in extremely loud voices shouldn't have to observe adults who are not admonished for the same behavior. Basic to any policy for behavior are definitions of appropriate and inappropriate behavior, defined here by the Santa Clara County (Calif.) Library policy:

> Appropriate activities include: doing homework, writing reports, researching, browsing for books, thinking, daydreaming, and reading. If games, puzzles, or listening tables are available, they are to be used quietly so as not to disturb others.
>
> Inappropriate activities include: running, throwing, eating, loud or abusive talking, fighting, moving furniture, excessive socializing, or any other activities which disrupt the library. Vandalism will not be tolerated.[4]

Many children in our society suffer from a lack of parental attention and supervision in their lives, and seek to fill the void whenever they encounter a friendly, approachable adult. For some children, this search ends with the children's librarian. Often this child will spend as much time as possible at the library, bending the listening ear of the children's librarian or staff and, if permitted, monopolizing the librarian's attention to the detriment of service to others. One humane response to such children is to assign them some simple tasks to bolster their generally poor self-esteem. Even so, there will be times when it will be necessary to tell the child that other users or duties require attention, and to suggest other library activities.

In any public institution where parents and children gather, an observer is treated to a variety of parenting practices. The children's librarian must be aware that the relationship between parent and child is not only one to be respected, but is also one given considerable leeway by the legal system. Although middle-class librarians may find an adult's parenting skills personally abhorrent, a great deal of tact must be exercised if they expect the family to return. In some instances, interfering with a parent-child relationship could result in more harm to the child than accepting the parameters of behavior set by the parent and to which the child has probably adjusted. The librarian can, of course, attempt to broaden the child's vicarious experience with many patterns of family life through literature, and, if an appropriate opportunity arises, assure the parent that the library expects children to enjoy a considerable amount of freedom in their use of its collections. The restrictive attitudes of some parents result from their being uncomfortable in the library and a belief that their children's behavior is a reflection of their own worth as individuals.

Another situation that frequently arises is one in which the parent leaves a young child under six or seven at the library to do shopping or other errands. Problems may arise if the child, who is too young to be separated from the parent for an extended period of time, becomes anxious or bored and creates a disturbance. The library should not rush to impose rules that inconvenience the majority of users in order to solve a problem that may occur only infrequently. The library system that required children to be accompanied by their parents or an adult in order to use the library was undoubtedly responding to this situation, but using a plank to swat a fly creates a larger problem than the one it solves. The strength of the public library for children is that they are free to use its services as individuals, and as members of a classroom or family. Such a restriction negates these advantages. The parent who habitually uses the library as a babysitting service should be made aware of the child's fears and anxieties, the inability of the staff to ensure the physical safety of the child, and the concern the staff has for the child's future relationship with the library, given such a negative introduction.

The situation with latchkey children discussed in chapter 1 requires a different response depending on their needs and behavior. Children who use the library as a safe haven after school need a sympathetic staff who operate with a clear policy that sets forth the behavior expected. Those who use the library appropriately should be treated like other users. One library system distinguished between children who were able to care for themselves and those who required adult intervention by defining the unattended child as a

> child, under the age of thirteen (13), and unable to care for self left in library unattended for long periods of time on a regular basis or not picked up at closing time. This is considered a form of child neglect.[5]

Professional Role with Staff

Librarians should be involved in the hiring procedures for staff they will supervise. In most, if not all, libraries, there will be basic job descriptions for each level of staff, and departments will be expected to assign responsibilities within the competency guidelines of that level. Not all support staff are interchangeable; some are more effective and comfortable with adult users although, even here, the library should insist that all public service staff be able to interact positively with children of all ages. Staff may be of any age, contrary to the assumption by some that only young employees should be assigned to the children's room. Children's services should not be a haven for pleasant persons whose intellectual abilities are judged lacking for adult services. A high degree of competence as well as flexibility is necessary to serve children of all ages and those adults who have responsibility for their welfare: parents, caregivers, teachers, etc. A competent professional and support staff are extremely important if the least vocal of library users is not to be shortchanged. The response of children to incompetence is usually with their feet. Many children's coordinators have commented on the surge of use by children in a community library when a pleasant, competent librarian follows a pleasant, but incompetent, one.

Although the line between professional and support staffs may not be closely adhered to in every instance, major differences clearly do exist. The professional staff bears the responsibility for the design and planning of a program of services that nurture the imagination and spark the curiosity of children through connections with literature, regardless of format. The support staff is responsible for the routines and procedures that are critical to the execution of any successful service. Because of this, the staff development programs offered to the professional staff are different from those provided the support staff. It is necessary, however, for librarians to understand library procedures and routines in order to evaluate their effectiveness and to evaluate the support staff's performance. New librarians conscious of their status may be disappointed to discover that a certain amount of clerical work may be necessary from time to time. After observing me performing such a task, one of my library directors remarked that "when librarians do nonprofessional tasks, the task is no longer a nonprofessional one." Should it become necessary for librarians to shelve materials during an emergency, for example, they view the task differently than a page does. Librarians observe the condition of the materials, the range of items being used, the gaps where more materials might be needed, etc. If these kinds of duties extend beyond the emergency period, the staffing level needs to be reevaluated and changes made that allow the librarian to meet the responsibilities implied in a professional position.

Supervision. Many children's librarians are thrust into the role of day-to-day supervision of support staff before they have had time to become comfortable with their own role. Such is the nature of the public library that is often understaffed. The librarian-supervisor may be nonplussed to discover that the staff is more knowledgeable than he or she about the internal routines of the department, the overall library, and the community. In establishing a working relationship with staff, it is important to acknowledge these obvious facts and to enlist the staff's cooperation in sharing their knowledge. Some librarians are able to accept gracefully this assistance while contemplating possible changes to be made at an appropriate future time. There are others who feel immediately compelled to assert their authority by instituting ill-advised changes, at the expense of staff respect and public service.

At the other end of the scale are those supervisors who avoid responsibility by touting a we-are-all-equal stance. While staff are equal in their individual worth as persons, the supervisor is paid to take responsibility for leadership in staff development and for supervision, as well as for a host of other professional tasks, such as the design and implementation of services, development of collections, community relations, etc. If authority is not exercised, a vacuum will result that staff may attempt to fill, creating a situation that impairs staff morale. Supervisors should remember that real authority stems from professional knowledge, an understanding of the situation at hand, and a willingness to act. Although staff-supervisor relationships should be two-way, with each party sharing their knowledge and insights for the improvement of services, it is the librarian-supervisor who is delegated the responsibility and authority.

Basic to good supervision is a mutual understanding of the job description for the particular service area. A discussion of the requirements at the time of employment or subsequent assignment should be followed at intervals during the probationary period and whenever performance standards are not met. In addition to the stated requirements of a position, the staff should be advised of activities that are the responsibilities of others. For instance, pages should understand why they should not attempt to answer an information question when approached by a diffident patron, even if they are certain they possess the answer to the question.

It is important to provide constant feedback, both positive and negative, on staff's performances, not only during the probationary period, but at other times as well. Most libraries also require an annual performance rating that is conducted by the supervisor following a standard procedure. This allows for an airing of problems perceived by both parties and offers an opportunity to build a relationship on more solid ground. After an experienced library assistant had been hired to work in the children's room under my supervision, I found her performance puzzling. When other duties took me out of the library, she obviously assumed responsibility and performed admirably. Yet, when we worked together, she deferred to me for even the most trivial of decisions in spite of encouragement. During the annual performance interview, I discovered the reason. Because of a personality conflict she had experienced in another department, she had resigned her previous position, even though the fault did not lie with her performance. She had assumed, erroneously, that her present appointment had been forced upon children's services, and felt uncomfortable when we worked together. The truth of the matter was that we felt extremely fortunate to have her, for she had all the necessary qualities and competencies. Obviously, I had not provided enough positive reinforcement in the early months of her employment or this could have been cleared up much sooner. As it was, we settled into a rewarding and productive relationship.

Situations may arise when it becomes necessary to discuss with the employee reasons for an unsatisfactory performance. Interviews concerning repeated or significant shortcomings are usually documented with an account of the problem(s) and the corrective actions to be taken. Nonproductive employees create morale problems for others and should be terminated if corrective action fails. The procedures are determined by policy and offer the employee opportunities to rectify the documented shortcomings. In all instances, the librarian must strive to act in a professional, even-handed manner, respecting the employee as an individual, but not condoning the poor quality of her/his performance.

Staff Development. Two types of training or staff development activities should be available to each staff member: (1) those that enable employees to acquire skills necessary to perform their assigned duties or that will prepare them for promotional opportunities within the library and (2) those that provide a clearer understanding of the mission of the library and where their contribution fits into the larger pattern. The children's librarian may not be the best trainer for the first type of activity; an experienced, competent page or technician may be more successful in teaching the basic techniques to a new page, for instance. The children's librarian assumes responsibility for helping all staff gain an understanding of the goals of the department and a working knowledge of resources, and for ensuring that standards of performance established by the administration are met.

Children's librarians are responsible for identifying staff development activities for their own staff as well as contributing suggestions for those activities planned across departmental lines. The most effective support staff are those who have opportunities to improve their competencies or to acquire new ones. Many such positions carry a great deal of routine that can deaden curiosity and interest unless their importance to the whole operation is constantly reinforced. Knowledgeable support staff not only serve as interpreters of library services within their own circle of family and friends, but they also have talents and insights to contribute during the various activities involved in planning.

New graduates of a professional library program may experience some internal conflict at the thought of sharing with staff something they have learned at great expense of time and money. They may feel that the line between their positions and those at the nonprofessional level is being blurred or erased. If this were possible, it would be a sad reflection on professional preparation. Library education has as its one common characteristic a vision—not just what is, but what can be. It is not acquired through the transmission of skills. Professional education includes, in addition, the ability to plan and design services for a variety of communities—not just one. Giving an assistant the opportunity to review books for purchase or to conduct preschool story hours will not diminish the role of the children's librarian, and it may provide staff a better opportunity to see how their position contributes to the overall service. It may also provide for the library, expanded or improved services.

Communication. Communication within a library, as in other organizations, is a persistent problem. All librarians who supervise staff have a responsibility to see that the communication links operate effectively. Failures usually result when a key member of the chain asks, "Why should the staff know this?" rather than "Why shouldn't this be shared with the staff?" Staff supervised by one with the former attitude quickly learn that "information is power." Communications from the top downward may offer opportunities for increasing staff awareness of the functions of the overall library, while the route upward ensures that staff contributions and concerns are noted.

Recruitment. The librarian is also in a position to identify, within the ranks of staff, genuine talent and potential for a library career. Such candidates should be encouraged to consider librarianship, whether in children's services or another specialty. Even in periods when there appear to be a sufficient number of librarians, our profession, like others, can never have too many intelligent and able members. We cannot assume that such individuals will automatically discover the varied opportunities that exist and apply for admission to the nearest library school. There may also be those with unrealistic expectations who should be counseled not to enter the field. Excellent performance in a nonprofessional position does not ensure success in a graduate program or in a professional role.

Professional Role with Colleagues and Administration

As previously mentioned, children's librarians must resist being compartmentalized as a rare and different species incapable of comprehending the professional issues of the day. This tendency may be encountered within a library staff, professional association, or a library school faculty. It may require a forceful response at times, a gentle or humorous reminder at others. After a week-long workshop on the use of computers in library operations to prepare staff to work in the library exhibit at Seattle's 1962 World Fair, the instructor apologized to the children's librarians in the group for subjecting them to such a rigorous experience. Carolyn Field of the Philadelphia Free Public Library rose to her feet and said to the instructor, "I am, first of all, a librarian, and secondly, a children's librarian. . . ." Within their libraries, communities, and professional groups, children's librarians may be sought for their knowledge of children's services, materials, or children. But they and their colleagues also share many things in common, including exploring new ways of promoting the use of materials or developing promotional devices to reach new audiences within their user groups. Much can be shared across age-level and type-of-institution lines.

A children's librarian can aid colleagues and administrators in many ways. In addition to the usual reports on children's services, the children's librarian should also share useful information acquired as a member of a professional association or as a representative to a community organization. If individuals in the community have expressed gratitude for specific services of the overall library, these should be shared with the administration. After coping with budgets, staff shortages, and building problems, administrators appreciate knowing that their efforts are valued. Adverse comments should also be noted and placed in the necessary context for discussion. As the representative of the children's librarians in a system, children's coordinators and consultants have an added responsibility to provide information resulting from their meetings and activities within and outside of the library.

If the administration has fostered an atmosphere of trust in which staff can freely discuss conflicting views, coupled with a tolerance for ambiguity, the conditions are right to build a congenial, smoothly operating staff. Good staff morale provides the environment for quality public services. In relationships with colleagues and staff, the children's librarian must be able to consider and discuss issues on a professional level, confine disagreements to the period of discussion, maintain a congenial manner whether one's views have prevailed or not, and refrain from criticizing colleagues publicly. Perhaps the most difficult axiom of all is the requirement to support policies with which one does not agree. A policy of fines for overdue books may strike the children's librarian in a working-class neighborhood branch as unfair. Even though it is unlikely that the policy will be changed, the librarian not only has a right but also an obligation to request that the policy be reconsidered. By receiving no response, the administration assumes that everyone is satisfied with the status quo.

It is not necessary for professional colleagues to be fond of one another in order to create a congenial environment. I was reminded by a director of this fact when I once interviewed candidates for a children's position. "Remember," she cautioned, "you are not going to marry this person; you only have to work together." Librarians need to take opportunities that naturally arise to strengthen interdepartmental relationships. A children's librarian with a major in classics may be the most qualified to weed the adult classics section; the reference librarian with impressive science credentials may be the best evaluator of the controversial children's book on addictive drugs or evolution. These occasional exchanges across departmental lines serve to develop an interest in another's department, build an atmosphere of trust and respect, sharpen little-used skills, or develop new ones.

Some library systems conduct regular staff development programs for all professional staff with each department responsible, in turn, for conducting one of the sessions. Librarians from adjoining libraries may also be invited to attend. Programs may be designed to meet the needs of a particular situation. In one library system, the staffing in the branch libraries was reduced to a level that required adult service librarians to serve children during certain periods of the week. The children's coordinator was asked to provide a workshop for adult service librarians to prepare them for this responsibility. A brief list of representative children's titles to be read was distributed prior to the first session. For some, this was an initial experience with children's literature or the first in several decades. All who completed the assignment expressed amazement that children's literature was so good (enjoyable), and a few asked for more suggestions. As a result of the workshop series, many of the adult service librarians were more comfortable with the reading guidance role and phoned children's librarians on duty in other branches for advice whenever they were not successful on their own. Other possible topics for in-service sessions are bibliographies and indexes that extend the use of children's collections, goals and objectives of parent-toddler programs or booktalks (with demonstrations), and children's nonfiction titles having special interest for adult users.

In a small library, new children's titles of interest or use to adult users could be displayed in the staff room for a few days. Some libraries set aside a portion of their staff meetings to hear reports on conferences and meetings attended by various staff or to highlight materials of value across age levels—indexes, bibliographies, and nonfiction that cover subjects unique to the library. The frustrated thespians who can be found on all staffs may enjoy being drafted for a reader's theater cast or performing as a folk singer at a chidren's program. These experiences provide opportunities for a better understanding of the goals of children's service program.

The children of one's colleagues represent a special service group that should not be overlooked. Providing titles to meet the interests and needs of these children can serve two purposes: the parent, grateful for this attention, is more aware of children's resources, and the children's librarian is more likely to receive an honest appraisal of materials filtered through a parent-librarian who can interpret the child's response in the context of service goals.

Every children's librarian knows that while good children's literature is not wasted on children, it is too good to be restricted only to children. This is particularly true when determining the audience for picture books. Occasionally titles appear that remind one of a colleague's or administrator's interest or acknowledged foibles (*Frog and Toad Are Friends* for the listmakers or *Milton the Early Riser* for those with that affliction). Place the title on the staff member's desk; it may relieve the daily tension or serve as a reminder that reading guidance is one of the important functions of children's services.

Children's librarians, like other specialists, may find it comfortable to confine their personal and professional contacts to colleagues within their field, for they share a common understanding of problems and responsibilities. In so doing, however, an opportunity for professional growth becomes limited, and the specialty may become the center of the universe, making it difficult to view issues facing the institution as a whole in a reasonable manner. Professional and personal relationships with librarians in other fields and types of libraries offer the children's librarian one of the easiest and most effective continuing education opportunities available, not unlike a cross-cultural study where one's own culture can be measured against another's and new approaches borrowed and adapted for use in one's own situation. With the current emphasis on families of young children, a professional or personal relationship with an adult educator, early childhood specialist, and a government documents librarian, for instance, could greatly enhance the ability of the children's librarian to serve this client group, as well as provide stimulation for overall professional growth. With the proliferation of library literature, it is often difficult to keep abreast of articles and titles outside of one's specialty. Children's librarians can serve as information gatekeepers for their colleagues by sharing items of interest encountered in their reading. This opportunity may lead ultimately to a two-way exchange benefiting both parties.

Role and Responsibility to the Community

With an increasing aging population and generational factions emerging in our society, those in our communities who have a vital concern for the welfare of children cannot assume that children will be considered a first priority, in spite of the rhetoric that usually surrounds children's issues. One obvious response is to develop coalitions with professionals from such diverse areas as health, recreation, legal protection, and education who share a concern for the welfare of children and their families. The library's representative is traditionally the highest ranking children's specialist. Where such coalitions need to be organized, the librarian, who considers members of the other professions as clients as well as colleagues, may be in the best position to act in a coordinating role. In addition to the role of a working member of the coalition, these contacts will offer the children's librarian opportunities to interact with the individual groups as a guest speaker, a provider of materials for meetings or workshops, or in other ways.

In order for the library to receive as much benefit as possible from this investment of effort, the children's librarian must act as a representative of the library as a whole, not just children's services. As such, she or he should regularly inform both administration and colleagues of the issues and concerns under discussion. Not only is it important that other librarians learn as much as possible about the community, but they may also have knowledge and resources to contribute.

As a member of a coalition seeking solutions to community problems or improvements in community services, the children's librarian should consider the unique contribution he or she can make to the group: information. It should be culled from a variety of sources and offered in a format that is most usable to the members. The librarian's contribution need not be limited to information, of course, but it is of first importance.

As a speaker for an organization's meetings, the children's specialist may be brought into contact with diverse segments of the community, ranging from family social workers to PTA councils. Although chosen because of their knowledge of children and their literature, children's librarians again are representing the library as a whole and are obligated to promote appropriate services and materials from the library's resources.

Responsibilities to the Profession

Librarians serve their profession through individual efforts in their communities and through professional associations in which collective action is focused on goals beyond the attainment by any individual member. There are many opportunities for individual contributions from informing a state legislator of the need for a library law, to serving on local literacy councils.

As an Individual

In this age of action committees and various types of lobbying groups, it is easy to underestimate the impact that a dedicated individual can have as a change agent. A few years ago, a young children's librarian took her first position in a community that had no elementary school librarians. She made a point to attend school board meetings, which were, of course, open to the public. At one meeting, she spoke when the opportunity arose about the need for school librarians, emphasizing the benefits to children and the contributions that library services to teachers can make in meeting educational goals. Her eloquence so impressed the board that they promised to consider the proposal in the next budget. Several meetings later, when the preliminary budget was presented for comment, the positions were not included. At the appropriate time, the children's librarian tactfully called this omission to the board's attention, in light of their favorable response in the past. Indeed, the board had forgotten. In the discussions that followed, the positions were established, demonstrating that professionally motivated individuals can affect the development of library services.

Individual responsibility is the basis for success in many areas of professional endeavor, including cooperative arrangements among libraries for sharing materials and staff expertise, as well as improving services to a population outside of one's immediate responsibility. Without commitment of individual members, professional associations would not be able to fulfill their role in society.

Professional Associations

Although it may appear that associations relieve the librarian of individual effort, the reverse is probably true. When the Little Red Hen attempted to enlist assistance from her barnyard companions, she had an objective firmly in mind: a loaf of bread to ward off hunger. However, she failed to enlist any assistance. One might conclude from the evidence presented that she lacked the leadership to inspire all those laggards to take up the hoe and scythe to raise wheat for enough loaves for everyone. It would be interesting to contemplate what our industrious fowl might have accomplished had she organized the barnyard into an association. This development would have undoubtedly led to a committee structure to share the work and to a system for recognition of exemplary contribution to common goals, cooperatively established. Working collectively for the promise of bread is more successful when individual accomplishment is rewarded through recognition or higher status. Obviously, the looming specter of hunger was not enough to motivate the barnyard residents.

Professional associations allow members to express ideas with more authority, and to address needs that require strength in numbers backed by resources beyond the scope of an individual or single library. Library associations offer publications and conference programs that feature the practical applications of recent research or demonstration projects in using literature with children, effective service options in dealing with audiences new to children's services, or other aspects of continuing education. Among the several topics that library associations address are: (1) legislation, (2) development of goals, standards, and guidelines, (3) intellectual freedom, (4) continuing education, (5) recruitment, and (6) publishing. National associations are also involved in fostering international relations.[6]

There is certainly no lack of opportunity to join a library or library-related association. A perusal through the *Encyclopedia of Associations* will reveal an impressive number to fit all types of libraries and persuasions of political, religious, or social thought. They exist at the local, state, regional, national, and international levels. The mission of library associations ranges from improving library service to enhancing the librarian's professional role.

In deciding which association to join, the children's librarian will want to consider the opportunities for participating in the work of the association, the support given by the library for attendance at conferences and committee work, and the amount of time that can reasonably be allocated away from library responsibilities. Most, if not all, libraries allocate some funds for this purpose, the amount dependent on budgetary constraints. Administrators generally recognize that staff participation not only results in a more informed and productive work force, but also contributes to the advancement of the profession's goals.

Local Associations. Children's librarians should consider membership in any local or area association that brings them into contact with professionals in other types of libraries in their community. The improvement of library services locally depends on effective use and sharing of community resources. Getting to know the area's librarians and libraries is the foundation on which cooperative ventures can develop. State associations of school library media personnel are often regionalized and librarians in other types of libraries are welcomed as members or associate members.

State and Regional Library Associations. Membership in state library associations should be considered a primary obligation, for it is at this level that issues are addressed that directly affect the local library. Some state associations allow for the formation of chapters or interest groups such as youth services, intellectual freedom, outreach services, etc. These foster the development of support groups that mitigate the isolation that specialists can experience if they are the only one in their library. While participation in these interest groups is beneficial, it should not detract from those functions that benefit the larger library community, such as the legislative program, continuing education, and recruitment, all of which are tailored to the specific needs of the state. A regional association offers opportunities to discover how neighboring states or provinces have dealt with common problems given differences in legal and financial bases or in service philosophy. They also offer a broader base for dealing with such needs as continuing education, regional publishing, and resource sharing.

National Associations. Differences among the various levels of library associations should exist if their resources are to be used effectively. A national association addresses concerns affecting library and information-related issues at that level, expresses the profession's views on federal legislation, and undertakes a publishing program that meets needs not filled by the commercial press. An association should not be criticized for failing to offer or support programs that should be sponsored at another level. A national or regional association should not be expected to effect changes in aid allocation in a particular state, or to publish a title that has relevance only for libraries in one state.

There are librarians who fail to join a national association because, as they explain, they can't attend conferences and hence "don't get anything out of it." It is difficult to respond to such a display of ignorance, when one knows that library associations exist to do things that librarians cannot do as individuals. Inevitably, there will be times when an association will take a position on an issue that one finds ill-advised. Controversy is unavoidable if an association deals with issues of importance. As Peggy Sullivan once noted:

> [there is] a kind of tension which drives individuals or institutions to form cooperative groups. ... Librarians and others have demonstrated it [tension] by their love/hate relationships with associations. . . .[7]

The basis for evaluating an association rests on how well it is advancing the overall goals of the profession, rather than on how it stands on a single issue. Library associations, like other types, do suffer at times from leadership more interested in advancing personal careers than organizational goals. Membership does exact an obligation for intelligent voting.

American Library Association

There are several national library associations in the United States including, among others, the Special Library Association, the American Association of Law Librarians, and the Catholic

Library Association. The oldest is the American Library Association, founded in 1876. Because it addresses many of the issues and needs that children's librarians have, I have chosen to examine it in detail.

Since its inception, the American Library Association has undergone many changes in an attempt to keep pace with professional and societal changes. Divisions have arisen, divided, combined, and sometimes disappeared when their activities were no longer supported; organizational patterns by type of library and by type of activity have each been offered. There has been no lack of creativity in devising either a dues or a governance structure. Like any large organization, it has experienced periods of stress and intense philosophical struggle, and eras of calm and relative inactivity.

In responding to the belief that benefits accrue only through conference attendance, let us discuss the efforts of this association to fulfill its overall mission of promoting and improving library services and librarianship. In support of this mission, members' dues contribute to the following:

1. Programs and publications for members and the public on the freedom to read; national monitoring of censorship attempts; representation at national forums on intellectual freedom issues; support for librarians involved locally in censorship attempts
2. The Legislative Office in Washington, D.C., with a highly competent staff to monitor national legislation affecting federal library support and cooperative efforts among types of libraries; access to government information, etc.
3. Implementation of standards for library education and national recruitment of exceptional candidates for the profession
4. A publication program that fills needs expressed by members and fills the gaps left by the commercial press; it also provides current information for members on association and library developments through the monthly journal *American Libraries*.
5. Monitoring development of goals, standards, and guidelines for various types of libraries and service activities
6. Continuing education through publications and audio and video recordings of conference programs.

After membership in the American Library Association, the first of its divisions that children's librarians usually join is the Association for Library Service to Children. Although this type-of-activity division cannot address institutional problems within the public library, it can offer opportunities to interact with school librarian members through common interests in services to children, evaluation of materials, and societal issues affecting the welfare of children. A quarterly publication, *Journal of Youth Services in Libraries* (formerly *Top of the News*), is included as part of membership. Indicative of its national role, ALSC maintains liaison relationships with a number of organizations having a concern for children. These range from the Boy Scouts of America to the Parents Without Partners, with efforts made to establish a foundation for cooperative efforts that can be built upon at the local level.

While school librarians have their type-of-library issues addressed by the American Association of School Librarians (AASL), public children's librarians, along with other specialists, should look to the Public Library Association (PLA) to consider issues affecting their functions and status within the library. This division carries the responsibility for the development of standards and guidelines for children's services, works to increase support for public libraries, and, like other divisions, offers continuing education opportunities for its members and develops publications relevant to their needs. This division's quarterly publication, *Public Libraries*, often includes articles on children's services. The ALA annual *Handbook of Organization* lists officers, committees and their functions, and liaisons to other organizations for each of the eleven divisions.

In addition to library associations, there is no dearth of child-related organizations in which children's librarians would benefit professionally and personally. These range from the National Association for the Education of Young Children to the Council for Exceptional Children. Some of these would merit a library membership because of the value their publications offer to the general public. A selected listing appears in Appendix D.

Responsibility for Professional Growth

No profession can survive unless its members have opportunities for growth and development. Professional education is but one milestone on a journey that lasts throughout one's career. With the completion of a formal library education program, the responsibility shifts from the library school to the individual who must determine her or his own career plan and identify the continuing education activities necessary to support it.

Those who entered the profession in the 1940s and 1950s, during the period of high demand for librarians, had a wide range of choices available to them in almost every geographic area; it was relatively easy to move from one position or type of institutional setting to another. Although this job mobility served as an effective form of continuing education for the young librarian, it also exacted a high price for the average library faced with constant staff turnover. With the financial constraints imposed in the 1970s, libraries were forced to reduce staff, and a more competitive situation resulted. A better educated and more career-oriented staff was demanded. With career mobility reduced, more emphasis was placed on formal continuing education opportunities.

Continuing Education

Unlike staff development activities that are the obligation of the library to provide, the responsibility for continuing education is shared by the library, professional associations, state library agencies, library schools, and the individual librarian. The librarians may be expected to cover at least part of the expenses when the program is designed to improve overall professional competencies and knowledge, rather than job-related skills. Continuing education should update professional competencies and prepare the librarian to advance to higher levels of responsibility or to serve in other types of library situations.

Children's librarians have been criticized for their rather single-minded devotion to children's literature.[8] Programs devoted to authors and illustrators attract a large attendance, while those on management skills or current research related to children or services are sometimes dropped because of a lack of interest. It has been suggested that the first type of activity be considered inspirational rather than educational, although it could be argued that such offerings often increase the librarian's literary knowledge. In apportioning the resources available for continuing education activities, the contributions to the children's librarians' overall competencies should be weighed. Inspirational activities are certainly not to be avoided for they can add seasoning to a bland diet—but they should not comprise the whole menu. A high priority should be placed on those activities and experiences that further the children's librarian's abilities to help children develop intellectually as well as creatively. Knowledge of child psychology, individual learning styles, and the effects of social changes on children may in some situations be as important as knowledge of the collection.

Children's librarians, either individually or collectively, can influence what is offered by identifying needs that should be addressed in continuing education programs. The provider should be allowed to translate that need into activities that may also be of value to other child care professionals. The opportunity to interact with school librarians, early childhood educators, and child psychologists, for example, provides an educational experience in itself.

A plan for reading professional literature is one of the simplest and most effective methods of continuing education available to librarians. Even with the resources of the information world at their disposal, librarians, like other professionals, place considerable reliance on colleagues or their professional school faculty to identify sources of relevant information for a particular problem. Within a library system, the children's librarians can volunteer to monitor specific journals, identifying articles that relate to their work. One of my young adult colleagues who is remarkably well informed includes in her personal schedule a time to use the resources of a nearby university library in keeping apprised of publications in her specialty, as well as those in related fields: social work, education, psychology, etc. Not everyone has convenient access to a research library, but local resources can be supplemented by interlibrary loans or photocopies from the state library. School librarians would probably be pleased to make available materials from their professional library.

Research on children's responses to literature in various formats and, to a lesser degree, on children's library services is slowly making an impact on children's services and should be included in the children's librarian's reading. Evidence that summer reading programs do make a difference,[9] that the amount of overlap between school and public library children's collections is well within the bounds of necessary duplication,[10] that an increasing proportion of the users of children's services are adults,[11] and that a good predictor of adult library use is library use as a child[12] can now be stated with some certainty, supported as these are with recent research findings. Review articles of contemporary research are often carried in general library periodicals, while some studies are easily accessible as rewritten journal articles. Children's librarians can also take a more active role in encouraging research in their specialty by identifying questions or issues that should be explored, and, whenever possible, agreeing to collect data for an investigator.

Personal Development

In interviews for professional positions at the close of the century, librarians can expect to be asked about their career expectations five or six years hence. There is a growing recognition that personal growth and responsibilities must be weighed in any career plan. During some periods of a professional life, family or community responsibilities will consume considerable time and energy, precluding the acceptance of some professional opportunities. At other times, the individual will be ready and eager for more challenging professional responsibilities. These decisions must be part of a career plan if the individual and the organization are not to be shortchanged.

On the day-to-day level, the demands of the professional role will inevitably compete with personal responsibilities and needs. Priorities in both spheres will have to be set if a healthy balance is to be achieved. How much time beyond the stated work week should be given to professional duties is a common question, and one that each librarian needs to consider. Realistically, there will be meetings to attend and professional reading to be done beyond ordinary working hours. Emergencies will arise that require extra staff conferences or attention. Children's librarians will probably plan or prepare an occasional program on their own time, but this should not become habitual or accepted as standard practice. If it does, the question should be asked whether the library can afford to offer the program. This kind of assessment is necessary if the librarian is not to become a drudge or experience burnout. Librarians who find no pleasure or joy in their work have little of value to offer a public whose attention is fastened on the future.

Conclusion

If the prospect of meeting the obligations inherent in the role of the children's librarian appears formidable, the reader should be aware that most libraries recognize that beginning librarians need a period of time to become comfortable in their new role. The direct supervisor is usually expected to serve as a mentor during this process. As in any profession, the practitioner's understanding grows and changes through work experiences and continuing education. Because of this, the librarian can expect to find continuing challenges and opportunities for professional growth in a position for several years.

As a group, children's librarians are not noted for their assertiveness in insisting that they be considered when supervisory positions are open or salary scales are discussed. Although it is true that many children's librarians continue to find their service area highly rewarding and therefore have no intention of making a change, the opportunity should not be closed to them. When personnel studies are conducted for the purpose of achieving salary equity, children's librarians cannot assume that their administrators are aware of the full range of competencies and skills involved in a successful children's service program. Modesty may be a virtue in a social situation, but it has no currency value in the occupational realm.

Children's librarians as a group are often complimented on their collection knowledge, commitment to their users, and well-planned and successful programs that highlight the library in the community, etc. While pleasant to the ears, these accolades would be more significant translated into tangible forms, such as salary and status. Children's librarians have a responsibility to advance their own specialty, if not for themselves, then for the purpose of making this career option attractive to the best candidates (both men and women) who are considering a library education program. Their client groups deserve no less.

An underlying message in these seven chapters is that management competencies are essential in every facet of children's services; yet, management cannot be divorced from the principles that shape the service. First comes an understanding of children's needs and a commitment to helping children develop to their highest potential as individuals and as responsible citizens. The library's goals and objectives chart the course, and management techniques supply the vehicle. Both of these can be changed or adapted as the need arises. It is, however, the principles on which children's services are based that give meaning to the journey and that are the least subject to change.

APPENDIXES

A. Budgeting Forms
  Line-Item Budget
  Program Budget Form
  Personnel Budget Request
  Programmatic Change Description

B. Programming Forms
  Request for Program Approval
  Program Resources Form
  Program Resource File
  Program Monitor Report for Central Library
  Program Evaluation Form

C. Bibliography of Collection and Service Aids
  Reference and Information
  Reading Guidance
  Programming
  Collection Development
    Finding Guides
    Selective Aids for Retrospective Titles
    Materials for Special Needs
    Reviews for Current Materials
    Annual Lists and Awards
    Miscellany
    Association Catalogs and Lists of Publications
  Library Instructional Activities or Resources

D. Related Professional Associations

Appendix A. Budgeting Forms

Line-Item Budget

Account Number	Classification	Actual Expend. 1987	Actual Expend. 1988	Budgeted Expend. 1989	Budget Request 1990	Recomm. by City Mgr.	Final Budget
	Personnel						
100	*Salaries*						
110	Librarian						
120	Technical						
130	Custodial						
150	Other:						
	Employee						
200	*Benefits*						
210	FICA						
220	Pension						
230	Health Ins.						
240	Group Ins.						
	Materials/						
300	*Supplies*						
310	Books						
320	Periodicals						
330	Video/films						
340	Recordings						
350	Office supplies						
360	Custodial						
370	Other:						
	Contract						
400	*Services*						
410	Postage						
420	Utilities						
430	Bldg. maint.						
440	Printing						
450	Telephone						
460	Training						
470	Travel						
480	Service contracts						
	Lease/						
500	*Purchase*						
	Capital						
600	*Outlay*						
610	Equipment						
620	Land						
630	Improvements						
	Categorical						
700	*Funds*						
710	Peabody Endow.						
720	Friends support (VRC)						

Adapted from a model presented in *Basic Budgeting Practices for Librarians*, by Margo C. Trumpeter and Richard S. Rounds (Chicago: American Library Assn., 1985), p. 65.

Program Budget Form

PROGRAM TITLE: Children's Services   PROGRAM NO.: 8204

GENERAL PROGRAM DESCRIPTION:

The Children's Department is responsible for providing materials and services to children from infancy through grade eight. Major activities include:

1. Coordinating the development and maintenance of children's print materials
2. Providing reading guidance, reference service, and programs for children and interested adults
3. Communicating information on children's literature and children's library service through booklists, booktalks, displays, lectures, and library tours
4. Promoting and coordinating Children's Department activities within the library system
5. Working cooperatively with other community institutions and agencies dedicated to serving the needs of children.

LONG-TERM PROGRAM GOALS:

1. Develop methodology for evaluating effectiveness of children's service activities
2. Continue to establish and maintain guidelines for collection development, program planning, and reference service based on Pierce County Library goals and objectives
3. Develop criteria for periodic evaluation of Children's Department goals and performances
4. Increase awareness of community agencies serving youth to identify resources available in each branch area, and to avoid duplication of service efforts
5. Maintain flexibility in planning Children's Department activities in order to respond to the changing needs of the library system as it builds new facilities and expands services.

SHORT-TERM OBJECTIVES:

1. Participate in development of building plans for new branch facilities and the Processing and Administrative Center
2. Complete collection development plan for new and expanded collections; purchase substantial percentage of bond materials
3. Upgrade existing collections, including day care, with replacement buying; coordinate with purchase of bond materials
4. Evaluate impact of opening new facilities of Children's Services programs and staff; adjust responsibilities of department personnel to meet the new situation.

Source: Pierce County (Wash.) Library

Program Budget Form
Page 2 of 3

PROGRAM TITLE: Children's Services   PROGRAM NO.: 8204

	ACTUAL FY '87	CURRENT FY '88	PRELIMINARY FY '89	FINAL FY '89

INPUT:

Personnel Man Years (FTE)
Personnel Expense
Non-Personnel Expense
TOTAL:

	ACTUAL FY '87	CURRENT FY '88	PRELIMINARY FY '89	FINAL FY '89

OUTPUT:

Selection Activity
  Hardbacks selected (vols)
  Paperbacks selected (vols)
  Bond Materials selected (vols)

Maintenance Activity
  Hardback books discarded

Programming Activity
Programs for Preschool Children
  —Storytime series
  —Daycare storytimes*
  —Toddler storytime series
  —Summer series
  —Library tours
  —Special (films, music)

Programs for School-age Children
  —Summer storytelling
  —Summer reading programs**
  —Puppet shows
  —Special (craft, holiday, contests, etc.)
  —Library tours
  —School/classroom visits

Programs for Community Groups
(cooperative, PTA, festivals, exhibits, etc.)
  —General programs, exhibits
  —Daycare workshops*

---

*LSCA grant program August 1984–December 1985. Regular PCL [Pierce Country Library] funded program beginning January 1986. See next page for further output data.
**Number of participants increased over 100% from 1983 to 1986; 77% from 1986 to 1987. . . .

Program Budget Form
Page 3 of 3

PROGRAM TITLE: Children's Services   PROGRAM NO.: 8204

	ACTUAL FY '87	CURRENT FY '88	PRELIMINARY FY '89	FINAL FY '89

OUTPUT:

READY-TO-READ DAYCARE SERVICE

Book Selection Activity

Programming Activity
—No. of centers served
—No. of preschool programs
—No. of summer booktalk programs
—No. of daycare staff observers

Book Delivery Activity
—No. of centers served
—No. of children receiving books
—No. of adults receiving books
—No. of books circulated
—No. of theme packets circulated
—No. of special request books
—No. of J paperbacks circulated during school year†
—Total number of books circulated

Workshop/Community Meetings Activity
—No. of workshops
—No. of workshop attendees
—No. of community/advisory meetings

Librarians Serving Daycare

†The service of providing school-age paperbacks (beyond Summer Reading Program paperbacks) has been extended to those centers serving large numbers of school-age children all year.

Personnel Budget Request

PROGRAM TITLE: Children's Services   PROGRAM NO.   8204

LOCATION: Service Center   1.   RANGE/STEP

POSITION TITLE: 2.   RANGE/STEP

3. Is this a new position ( ), or does it represent added hours for an existing position ( )? If added hours for an existing position, answer these questions:
   a.   Budget Position Number (available from Business Office)
   b.   Present scheduled hours per week

   For requests for additional hours for existing positions, indicate additional hours only in Section 4.

4. CHECK CATEGORY: INSERT DATA

a.) Full-time permanent (40 hr/wk)   [ ]
b.) Full-time temporary   [ ]   b.2 Duration of appointment
c.) Part-time permanent   [ ]   c.2 Hours per week
d.) Part-time temporary   [ ]   d.2 Duration hours/week
e.) Extra hire   [ ]   e.2 Total extra hire hrs. reqst
f.) Overtime hours   [ ]   f.2 Total overtime hours reqst.

5. What benefits to your program will be derived from the addition of this position or hours?

6. What are the consequences of not adding this position at this time?

7. Identify any additional expenses necessary for the support of this position such as desks, chairs, training, travel, calculator, typewriter, etc. Do not include these additional expenses in other accounts until it is known if this request will be funded.

8.   For business office to complete:
a.   Base salary expense   e. Benefits:
b.   Overtime expense   MA/II
c.   Extra hire expense   FICA
d.   Total salary   Retirement
                                                      Medical
                                                      Dental
                                                  f. Total benefits

Program Priority No.   PCL Priority No.   Approved: Yes   No

Source: Pierce County (Wash.) Library

Programmatic Change Description

DEPARTMENT NAME:	LIBRARY	PROGRAM NAME: PROGRAM CATEGORY: Several	
PROGRAMMATIC CHANGE:	Outreach to children	CPMS CODE 5885,5894 4902	FUND: 10401

PROGRAMMATIC CHANGE:

Children's reading and learning activities would be increased through an aggressive program to parents and children, especially in low-income areas. All parenting groups in the community would be identified and presentations would be made once per year to promote the importance of children's reading. In addition, the three FTE children's librarians hired would actively work with Seattle Housing Authority to identify needs of children in all housing projects and to promote use in those low-use communities. Twelve innovative programs per year would be conducted. School visits with booktalks and promotional presentations, now made only once per year to selected classes in public schools, would be increased to twice per year to all classes in all public and private schools. The "Rainbow" truck would be used at child-oriented locations.

REASON FOR REQUEST:

The high rate of illiteracy among high school graduates, the scholastically poor showing among certain ethnic groups in Seattle schools, and the educational problems found in many low-income families can be helped by stimulating children's interest in reading and learning. A recent report from the U.S. Department of Education shows ". . . the amount of leisure time spent reading is directly related to children's reading comprehension, the size of their vocabularies, and the gains in their reading." The ability to read, and to learn, will help a child reach beyond present circumstances. As he/she grows, more life choices will be available as the result of childhood intellectual and educational development.

CONSEQUENCES IF CHANGE IS NOT APPROVED:

Seattle children, especially those whose parents are uninformed about library service and its benefits to lifelong learning, will not be stimulated to investigate this service. Opportunities for changing their environment in later years may be lost.

ALTERNATIVE:

N/A

REVENUE IMPLICATIONS, IF ANY:

N/A

Source: Seattle Public Library

BUDGET IMPACT:

CFMS

Account	Description/Item*	Amount
51110	[Salaries, full time]	73,350
51310	[FICA—Social Security]	5,244
51320	[Pension]	6,534
51330	[Health care]	6,465
51340	[Industrial insurance]	630
51360	[Dental]	1,404
51370	[Death benefit]	18
51380	[Unemployment insurance]	252
52100	[Office supplies]	300
52290	[Other operating supplies]	750
53520	[Copying]	150
		TOTAL 95,097

*Explanation of budget codes has been added.

****

Author's Note: The figures listed above do not represent the total cost of the program. Because of the planning and preparation time involved in this first year, other categories of the budget were expected to absorb the additional costs. We could expect that subsequent budgets for this program would include expenditures for: equipment (desks, chairs, typewriters, fax machines, vans or cars, etc.) materials (books, videos, realia, periodicals, etc.) publications (for staff training) public relations (printing, promotional materials, etc.).

Appendix B. Programming Forms

Request for Program Approval

January 7, 1989

To: Amanda Nelson, Happy Land Community Librarian

From: Susan Smiley, Children's Librarian

Re: Nonfiction film/book program series for fifth/sixth-grade classes from Happy Land Elementary
      School

    In line with the library system's objectives to increase reference use 5 percent this year, and to increase circulation of materials from 3.4 to 4 per capita, we believe the attached program supports these objectives as well as the library's goal to develop effective community relations.

    We have had difficulty attracting the children from this school. As you may recall, the achievement scores of these students are the lowest in the city. Their teachers are concerned that their transition to junior high will be especially difficult, and they have asked for our cooperation. I believe the attached program can provide the foundation for their continued public library use.

    The brochures, flyers, etc., that the children take home may entice parents and siblings to visit the library also. Further, Pamela Pettigrew, the school librarian, and I believe that the teachers' awareness of public library resources could result in more effective instruction.

    Considering the long-range benefits of the program and the difficulties of reaching this type of audience, the cost per participant ($13.25) is not excessive.

    If this program proposal meets with your approval, we will plan the sessions with Ms. Carlin, and explain the program objectives to the branch staff, for they will need to be prepared to deal with past fines and lost cards. As with all our programs, we hope to make this series an enjoyable one for the children, not merely an extension of classroom activities.

cc: Charlotte Carlin, Children's Coordinator

273

Proposed Program

1. TITLE OF PROGRAM: Nonfiction film and booktalk series (6 sessions)

2. PERIOD OF TIME: March 15 to April 30, 1990.
Fridays: 2:15 to 3:30 p.m.

3. AGE GROUP INVOLVED: Fifth- and sixth-grade classes (62 children) from Happy Land Elementary School. Two teachers.

4. PERSONNEL NEEDED: (a) Children's librarian: 41 hrs. (b) library page: 7 hours; (c) library assistant: 15 hrs. ($760.50)

5. LIBRARY GOALS AND OBJECTIVES THIS PROGRAM SUPPORTS: To increase cooperation with educational agencies.
    a. Public service units . . . to increase use of system-wide reference services by 5% per annum and nonfiction by 4%.

6. GOALS AND OBJECTIVES FOR THIS PROGRAM.
    1. To increase children's awareness of the informational resources
    2. To increase the number of juvenile registrations and circulation
    3. To strengthen relationships and communication with the Happy Land Elem. School faculty and students.

7. PROGRAM DESCRIPTION:
Each program will include film(s), booktalks on related nonfiction materials, and a browsing period.
Ex: *Hardware Wars* (13 min. film) with time to discuss the film (10–12 min.); books: *Secret Life of School Supplies; Secret Life of Hardware; Toolchest; From Hand to Mouth;* etc. (20 min.). Browsing period (20–25 min.).

The second program will instruct the children (and teachers) in the use of the microfiche catalog and introduce the nonfiction library collections. The films and videos will be on high-interest topics (e.g., hand-gliding) or on a class-related topic (e.g., energy). In addition to promoting nonfiction titles, periodicals and vertical file resources will also be featured.

8. MATERIALS: 1. Bibliographies of titles used in each session, with holdings included for both libraries
    2. Bookmarks and flyers on classification system; instruction sheets on how to use the microfiche catalog, brochures on services   ($10.00)
    3. Rental for films not in the system   ($52.75).

9. EVALUATION: 1. Number of renewals or new library cards issued
    2. Circulation increase of nonfiction collection
    3. Increase in reference questions over same period last year
    4. Written comments of teachers and school librarian (using our standard program evaluation form with addition of questions related to student improvement)
    5. Staff comments.

Adapted from a model developed by Arlene Bielefield, in *Reader in Children's Librarianship*, ed. Joan Foster, Readers in Librarianship and Information Science, no. 27 (Englewood, Colo.: Information Handling Services, 1978), p.352.

Program Resources Form

Title: Flights of Fancy   Topic: Paper Airplane

Audience: P E YA A F   Ideal Audience Size: 15–30

Length of Program: 45 min.   Set-up Time: 15 min.

Pre-program time: 15 min.

Submitted by: G. Cole/S. Creighton   Date: 5-6-85

Brief description: A program to encourage use of library materials on airplanes, paper airplanes, aerodynamics, gliders, and kites.

Books/media read or presented:
Floating Free or *Skyscrapers*

Activities:
Discuss various books on display
Show film (optional)
Make paper airplanes.

Supplies needed (per participant):
Plain typing paper, crayons or markers, scissors.

Extra staff needed:
None.

Equipment needed (projector, tables, etc.);
16mm projector; tables.

Step-by-step format: (1) Discuss books on display, (2) show film, (3) show examples of paper airplanes, (4) demonstrate steps in folding, (5) let children decide which one they want to make, and (6) practice flying (you can have contests for which one flies farthest, circles most, etc.).

Comments:
Many will already know how to make different kinds of airplanes, let them help others, or make one of the more complicated ones.

Source: Stockton–San Joaquin County (Calif.) Public Library

Program Resource File

Date:_____

Presenter's Name:_____

Program Title:_____

Address:_____

City_____Zip_____Telephone (work):_____(home):_____

Description of program:

Subject heading under which you would list this program. For example: Legal Advice, Self-Help, Arts & Crafts, etc.

_____

Qualifications of Presenter:

Fees (if any):   Transportation Fee:_____

Program Fee:_____   Materials Fee:_____

Space Needed (or other special requirements):_____

_____

Age Recommendation: Adults only☐   Young Adults only☐   Children only☐   Families☐

Additional Information:_____
(Attach resume, clippings, or related information as appropriate.)

_____

_____

Return completed form to: Suggested by:

_____   _____

Source: King County (Wash.) Library System

Program Monitor Report for Central Library

NAME OF PROGRAM_____

PERSON INTRODUCING PROGRAM:

   Library Staff_____
                (name)

   Non-staff_____
              (name)

> **IMPORTANT**
>
> Staff assigned to monitor special library programs are to fill out this report in triplicate and forward next day as follows:
> - White copy to Deputy Director (Top Copy)
> - Blue copy to PSD
> - Green copy to Librarian Central Library (CEL)

Date of Program_____Time_____Specific Location_____

CHECK ONE:

☐Library Program   ☐Co-sponsored program_____
                                                (name of co-sponsoring group)

TOTAL ATTENDANCE

CHECK AUDIENCE COMPOSITION: (Double check predominant group)

☐Children   ☐Teenagers   ☐Adults   ☐Senior Citizens

LIST MATERIALS USED IN CONJUNCTION WITH PROGRAM

Book Titles	Film Titles	Library Publications	Other

CRITICAL COMMENTS OF AUDIENCE (Pro and Con)

LIBRARY MONITOR'S COMMENTS OR SUGGESTIONS (including judgment of success or failure of the program)

_____
(Program Monitor's Signature)

Source: Queens Borough Public Library

Program Evaluation Form

Branch_____Date_____Time_____Day_____

Name of Group_____

Contact_____Telephone_____

PROGRAM

AGE GROUP: Preschool☐   School Age☐   Young Adult☐   Adult☐

TYPE OF PROGRAM: Story Hour☐   Family Story Hour☐   Group Visit☐   Film☐
Class Visit☐   Library Tour☐   Puppet show☐   Craft☐   Guest speaker☐
Performance by Outside Group☐   OTHER_____

MEDIA MATERIALS: Films☐   Slides☐   Posters or Flips☐   Records☐   Tapes☐
Books☐   Stories☐   Puppets☐   Other_____

_____

_____

PUBLICITY: Posters☐   Flyers☐   Bookmarks☐   Tickets☐   News Release☐
Class Visits☐   Letters to Schools☐   Radio Announcements☐   TV Spots☐

EVALUATION

ATTENDANCE:_____   Librarian_____

Audience Reaction: Enthusiastic☐   Responsive☐   Some Interest☐
Disinterested☐   Inappropriate Reaction or Behavior☐   Other_____

_____

Recommendations for further programs of this sort (cover as separate topics where appropriate
such items as program content, presentation style and aids, audience recruitment, layout, etc.)

_____

_____

_____

Source: Seattle Public Library

Appendix C
Bibliography of Collection and Service Aids

Reference and Information

Best Science Books and AV Materials for Children. Ed. Susan M. O'Connell, Valerie Montenegro, and Kathryn Wolff. Washington, D.C.: American Assn. for the Advancement of Science, 1988.

Supplements *Best Science Films, Filmstrips and Videocassettes for Children 1982*, and *Best Science Books for Children 1983*.

Bishop, Cynthia, and Deborah Crowe, eds. *Science Fair Project Index: 1981–1984*. Metuchen, N.J.: Scarecrow, 1986.

Second supplement to *Science Fair Project Index, 1960–72*. Science and Technology Division, Akron-Summit County Public Library. Metuchen, N.J.: Scarecrow, 1975. First supplement, 1983. Indexes selected books and periodicals. Arranged by subject for grades 5 through 12.

Blackburn, G. Meredith, III, comp. *Index to Poetry for Children and Young People: 1982–1987*. Bronx, N.Y.: Wilson, 1989.

Offers access to titles, subjects, authors, and first lines. Fifth supplement to John E. and Sara W. Brewton, *Index to Children's Poetry* (Wilson, 1944).

Breen, Karen. *Index to Collective Biographies for Young Readers*. 4th ed. New York: Bowker, 1988.

Listed by biographee. Subject index by profession/occupation/nationality.

Children's Magazine Guide. Bowker, Inc. (formerly Madison, Wis.)

Indexes nonfiction as well as stories, poetry, plays, book and movie reviews, etc. Nine issues yearly, cumulated semiannually.

Ireland, Norma Olin. *Index to Fairy Tales, 1949–1972, Including Folklore, Legends, and Myths in Collections*. Westwood, Mass.: Faxon; distributed by Metuchen, N.J.: Scarecrow, 1973.

Continues series by Mary Huse Eastman. 3 vols. 1926–1952.

————. Fourth supplement, 1973–1977. 1979

Junior Books of Authors. 2nd ed. Eds. Stanley J. Kunitz and Howard Haycraft. New York: Wilson, 1951.

Five supplements: 1963, 1972, 1978, 1983, 1989 (various editors).

Learning Economics through Children's Stories. Eds. Robert Henricks, Robert Nappi, George G. Dawson, Mindy M. Mattila. New York: Joint Council on Economics Education, 1986.

There are 273 annotated titles for elementary school students; subject index.

Lima, Carolyn W. *A to Zoo: Subject Access to Children's Picture Books*. 3rd ed. New York: Bowker, 1989.

Also provides author, title, and illustrator indexes.

MacDonald, Margaret Read. *Storyteller's Sourcebook: A Subject, Title, and Motif Index to Folklore Collections for Children*. New York: Neal-Schuman; distributed by Detroit: Gale, 1982.

Indexes 556 collections and 389 picture books.

Richter, Bernice, and Duane Wenzel, comps. *Museum of Science and Industry Basic Lists of Children's Science Books, 1973–1984*. Chicago: American Library Assn., 1985. Annual supplements, 1985–88.

Annotated and evaluative list for preschool through grade 12, plus adult references. Arranged by subject, includes books, children's magazines, review journals.

Sader, Marion, ed. *Reference Books for Young Readers*. Bowker Buying Guide Series, no. 1. New York: Bowker, 1988.

"Presents approximately 200 extensive, descriptive evaluations of encyclopedias (online as well as printed versions), world atlases, dictionaries, and word books, and large-print reference works . . . appropriate for age levels from preschool through high school."—Preface.

Science Books for Children: Selections from Booklist, 1976–1983. Ed. Denise Murcko Wilms. Chicago: American Library Assn., 1985.

Arranged by broad topics, with author-title and subject indexes. Preschool to grade nine.

Siegel, Mary-Ellen. *Her Way; A Guide to Biographies of Women for Young People*. 2nd ed. Chicago: American Library Assn., 1984.

A brief annotated list of acceptable titles follows a short profile of each. Appendixes list biographees by nationality and ethnicity, and by vocation or avocation.

Smith, Dorothy B. Frizzell, and Eva L. Andrews, comps. *Subject Index to Poetry for Children and Young People, 1957–1975*. Chicago: American Library Assn., 1977.

Supplements *Subject Index to Poetry for Children and Young People*. Comps. Violet Sell, Dorothy B. Frizzell Smith, Ardis Sarff O'Hoyt, and Mildred Bakke. 1957.

Something about the Author: Facts and Pictures about Authors and Illustrators of Books for Young People. Ed. Anne Commire. (Vol. 57 published in 1989.) Detroit: Gale, 1971– .

Trefny, Beverly Robin, and Eileen C. Palmer. *Index to Children's Plays in Collections 1975–1984*. Metuchen, N.J.: Scarecrow, 1986.

Supplements *Index to Children's Plays in Collections*, 2nd ed., ed. Barbara A. Kreider. 1977. Single listing of authors, titles, and subjects. Also includes skits, monologs, puppetry, etc.

Wynar, Christine Gehrt. *Guide to Reference Books for School Media Centers*. 3rd ed. Littleton, Colo.: Libraries Unlimited, 1986.

Annotated list arranged under broad topics. Index provides access by subject, authors and editors, titles, and formats (e.g., computer software, audiovisual, periodicals, review journals, etc.).

Reading Guidance

Adventuring with Books: A Booklist for Pre-K–Grade 6. Eds. Mary Jett-Simpson and the Committee on the Elementary Booklist of the National Council for Teachers of English. 9th ed. Urbana, Ill.: National Council of Teachers of English, 1989.

Selective, annotated lists of approximately 1,800 titles, published 1984–88, arranged by reader interest categories, e.g., prehistoric times, science fiction, sports, and games.

Azarnoff, Pat. *Health, Illness and Disability: A Guide to Books for Children and Young Adults.* New York: Bowker, 1983.
Annotated bibliography of some 1,000 fiction and nonfiction titles, 1960–83. Subject and title access.

Baskin, Barbara Holland, and Karen H. Harris. *More Notes from a Different Drummer, a Guide to Juvenile Fiction Portraying the Handicapped.* New York: Bowker, 1984.
Includes titles published 1976–81 and supplements *Notes from a Different Drummer,* 1980. Each title is given extensive plot coverage and an analysis of the treatment of the disability. Title and subject indexes.

Bernstein, Joanne E., and Masha K. Rudman. *Books to Help Children Cope with Separation and Loss.* vol. 3. New York: Bowker, 1989.
Covers publications for 1983–88. Fiction and nonfiction titles for ages 3 to 16. Part II is an annotated bibliography arranged by theme: going to a new school, desertion, AIDS, foster care, etc. Author, subject, title indexes.

BookBrain 4–6. Rev. ed. Phoenix: Oryx Press, 1988.
A searchable database of fiction for grades 4 through 6. There are 756 annotated titles; over 1,300 additional titles linked as other titles to enjoy are keyed to a series of questions asked of the user.

Carroll, Frances Laverne, and Mary Meacham. *Exciting, Funny, Scary, Short, Different, and Sad Books Kids Like about Animals, Science, Sports, Families, Songs, and Other Things.* Chicago: American Library Assn., 1984.
Short, descriptive annotations for titles proven popular with children. Arranged by subject: baseball, families, a book "like Judy Blume's," etc.

Children's Books, 1911–1986: Favorite Children's Books from the Branch Collections of the New York Public Library. New York: Office of Children's Services, New York Public Library, 1986.
Annotated listing by decade, and grouped by genre.

Choices, a Core Collection for Young Reluctant Readers. Eds. Carolyn Sherwood Flemming and Donna Schott. Evanston, Ill.: John Gordon Burke Pubs., 1983– .
Annotated list of over 350 highly selective titles for readers, second-through sixth-grade. Arranged by subject, with entries for interest and reading levels (readability scores).

———. Eds. Julie and Blair Cummins. Vol. 2. Evanston, Ill.: John Gordon Burke Pubs., 1990– .

Dreyer, Sharon Spredemann. *Bookfinder, a Guide to Children's Literature about the Needs and Problems of Youth, Ages 2 to 15.* 4 vols. Circle Pines, Minn.: American Guidance Service, 1977–89.
Arranged by author with full annotations, keyed to a subject index with many access points.

Field, Carolyn W., and Jaqueline Schachter Weiss. *Values in Selected Children's Books of Fiction and Fantasy.* Hamden, Conn.: Library Professional Publications, 1987.
Annotated list of over 700 titles, 1930–84, arranged by values like courage and ingenuity, under broad age groupings.

Friedberg, Joan Brest, June B. Mullano, and Adelaide Weir Sukunneh. *Accept Me As I Am: Best Books of Juvenile Non-fiction on Impairments and Disabilities.* New York: Bowker, 1985.
Descriptive evaluation of plots, with analyses of the treatment of the impairment. Grouped by broad category of disability, e.g., hearing, emotional disturbances, etc.

Hauser, Paula, and Gail A. Nelson. *Books for the Gifted Child.* vol. 2. New York: Bowker, 1988.
Supplements a title published in 1980. Includes titles published 1981–87 for ages 3–12. Indexed by ability levels, titles, and subjects.

Kimmel, Margaret Mary, and Elizabeth Segel. *For Reading Out Loud! a Guide to Sharing Books with Children.* Rev. ed. New York: Delacorte, 1988.
Over 300 child-tested titles of quality. Annotated titles are grouped by subject and length.

Lynn, Ruth Nadelman. *Fantasy for Children: An Annotated Bibliography.* 3rd ed. New York: Bowker, 1989.
Covers period 1900–88. Titles are arranged under broad subjects, e.g., animal fantasy, ghost fantasy, time travel. Author/illustrator, title, and subject indexes.

Mahoney, Ellen, and Leah Wilcox. *Ready, Set, Read: Best Books to Prepare Preschoolers.* Metuchen, N.J.: Scarecrow, 1985.
Text discusses books and their use with children from infancy through age five, with bibliographies for each age group. Author, title, subject indexes.

Oppenheim, Joanne F., Barbara Brenner, and Betty D. Boegehold. *Choosing Books for Kids: How to Choose the Right Book for the Right Child at the Right Time.* A Bank Street Book. New York: Ballantine, 1986.
Grouped by interest/age levels from infancy through grade 12. Aimed at parents, but of value to librarians. Author, subject, title indexes.

Pilla, Marianne Laino. *Resources for Middle Grade Reluctant Readers, a Guide for Librarians.* Littleton, Colo.: Libraries Unlimited, 1987.
Annotated lists of books, software, and software reviewing sources. Also includes program ideas and guidelines for assessing readability of materials.

Polette, Nancy, and Marjorie Hamlin. *Exploring Books with Gifted Children.* Littleton, Colo.: Libraries Unlimited, 1980.
Activities and discussion guides that can be adapted to a number of situations.

Popular Reading for Children II; a Collection of the Booklist Columns. Introduction by Barbara Elleman. Chicago: American Library Assn., 1986.

Supplements *Popular Reading for Children,* 1981. Focuses on grades 4–7. Titles are briefly annotated and arranged under subjects like humor, mysteries, "after Beverly Cleary," etc.

RIF Guide to Encouraging Young Readers: A Fun-filled Sourcebook of over 200 Favorite Reading Activities for Kids and Parents. New York: Doubleday, 1987.
Annotated listing of titles proven popular with children in the Reading Is Fundamental program, plus activities and techniques to promote interest in reading.

Roman, Susan. *Sequences: An Annotated Guide to Children's Fiction in Series.* Chicago: American Library Assn., 1985.
"[for] the average and special reader from grade three through young adult."—Preface. Selective list, arranged by author with brief description of series, followed by annotated titles. Title, main character, and series indexes.

Sutherland, Zena, comp. *Best in Children's Books: The University of Chicago Guide to Children's Literature, 1979–1984.* Chicago: Univ. of Chicago Pr., 1986.
Supplements earlier volumes covering 1966–72 and 1973–78. Reviews selected from the *Bulletin of the Center for Children's Books,* alphabetically arranged by author, with indexes for title, subject, type of literature, reading level, curricular use, and developmental values.

Trelease, Jim. *The New Read-Aloud Handbook.* New York: Penquin, 1989.
Trelease's third annotated bibliography. Arranged by genre: wordless, picture book, novel, etc. Provides techniques and programming suggestions.

Wilson, George, and Joyce Moss. *Books for Children to Read Alone: A Guide for Parents and Librarians.* New York: Bowker, 1988.
There are 350 titles published from the early 1950s to 1985, grouped by half-grades for children from pre-Kindergarten through third grade. Indexes by subject, author, title, and readability level.

Your Reading: A Booklist for Junior and Middle School Students. James E. Davis and Hazel K. Davis, eds. Committee on the Junior High and Middle School Booklist of the National Council of Teachers of English. Urbana, Ill.: National Council for Teachers of English, 1988.
Annotated listing of nearly 2,000 books, arranged in reader interest categories like sports, supernatural, and trivia. Title and author indexes.

Programming

Baker, Augusta, and Ellin Greene. *Storytelling: Art and Technique.* 2nd ed. New York: Bowker, 1987.
Practical guide to sources, program planning, lists of stories for various audiences.

Bauer, Caroline Feller. *Handbook for Storytellers.* Chicago: American Library Assn., 1977.

Bibliographies for various age groups and themes; aids for auxiliary activities (e.g., puppetry, music, poetry, magic); guidelines for program planning; sample program formats.

———. *This Way to Books.* New York: Wilson, 1982.

Ideas for booktalks, programs, games, crafts, and exhibits. Bibliographies.

———. *Presenting Reader's Theatre: Plays and Poems to Read Aloud.* New York: Wilson, 1987.

Scripts of folktales, episodes from books, poems, etc.; suggestions for staging, programming.

Bodart, Joni. *Booktalk! 3: Booktalking for All Ages and Audiences.* New York: Wilson, 1988.

Third volume of sample booktalks. Includes instructions for preparation and presentation. Bibliographies by age level, theme, and genre. Recommended films for use in programming.

Burroughs, Lea. *Introducing Children to the Arts: A Practical Guide for Children's Librarians and Educators.* Boston: G. K. Hall, 1988.

Suggestions for children's workshops for the arts, ranging from architecture to theater. Bibliographies, discographies, and filmographies for each. Activities for individual and group participation.

Champlin, Connie, and Nancy Renfro. *Storytelling with Puppets.* Chicago: American Library Assn., 1985.

Ways to enhance storytimes, primarily for the one-person puppeteer.

First Steps to Literacy: Library Programs for Teachers, and Caregivers. Association for Library Services to Children. Preschool Services and Parent Education Committee. Chicago: American Library Assn., 1989.

Instructions for planning, advertising, and conducting seven programs for adult audiences, including expectant parents, parents of preschoolers, relatives who buy books for children, etc.

Foster, Joanna, comp. *How to Conduct Effective Picture Book Programs: A Handbook.* Westchester, N.Y.: Westchester Library System, 1967.

Written to accompany the 16mm. film *The Pleasure Is Mutual.* Recommended for training library assistants to program for three- to five-year-olds.

Gaffrey, Maureen. *What to Do When the Lights Go On: A Comprehensive Guide to 16mm Films and Related Activities for Children.* New York: Oryx Press, 1981.

Suggestions for relating films to follow-up activities, such as crafts, art, etc.

Greeson, Janet and Karen Taha. *Name That Book! Questions and Answers on Outstanding Children's Books.* Metuchen, N.J.: Scarecrow, 1986.

Focuses primarily on post-1970 titles in all genres for elementary through junior high school. Also includes programming ideas, games, ideas for bulletin boards, etc.

Hawkins, Melba. *Programming for School-Age Child Care: A Children's Literature Based Guide.* Littleton, Colo.: Libraries Unlimited, 1987.

For child caregivers of five- to eight-year-olds. Literature is linked to art, drama, music, cooking, and special days. Bibliographies.

Hunt, Mary Alice. *A Multimedia Approach to Children's Literature*. 3rd ed. Chicago: American Library Assn., 1983.

Selective list of films, videocassettes, filmstrips, and recordings based on children's books. Title, format, and subject indexes.

Kobrin, Beverly. *Eyeopeners! How to Choose and Use Children's Books about Real People, Places, and Things*. New York: Viking, 1988.

Over 500 nonfiction annotated titles are arranged by subject. Suggestions of activities are included.

MacDonald, Margaret Read. *Booksharing: 101 Programs to Use with Preschoolers*. Hamden, Conn.: Library Professional Pubs., 1988.

Program themes include seasons, holidays, ethnicity, science, art, music. Bibliographies of books and films.

Missouri Library Association. Children's Service Round Table. *Drop-in Delights, Activities for the Leisurely Patron*. Columbia: Missouri Library Assn., 1986.

Ideas for creative writing, quizzes and contests, arts and crafts, etc., for latchkey children. Excellent bibliographies. (Publications list available from MLA Executive Office, Parkade Plaza, Suite 9, Columbia, MO 65203.)

Nichols, Judy. *Storytimes for Two-Year-Olds*. Chicago: American Library Assn., 1987.

Program rationale, planning, and program suggestions.

Paulin, Mary Ann. *Creative Uses of Children's Literature*. Hamden, Conn.: Library Professional Pubs., 1986.

Hundreds of ideas for promoting literature. Also includes puppets, riddles, jokes, and multimedia. Title and subject indexes.

Programming for Very Young Children. ALSC Support Publications 1. Association for Library Services to Children. Chicago: American Library Assn., 1980.

First in a series of leaflets designed to assist children's librarians in providing programs and services for various audiences. Topics include children with special needs, book discussion clubs, using media, multicultural awareness, summer activities, interpretive activities, and more.

Sierra, Judy. *Flannel Board Storytelling Book*. Bronx, N.Y.: Wilson, 1987.

Directions for making and using flannel boards. Patterns for figures and follow-up suggestions for creative dramatics are provided for each story, rhyme, or song. Ages 3–5.

Sitarz, Paula Gaj. *Picture Book Storyhours: From Birthdays to Bears*. Littleton, Colo.: Libraries Unlimited, 1987.

Formats for 22 programs with activities, books, AV, fingerplays, etc., for each. Resources and programming techniques included.

Spirt, Diana L. *Introducing Bookplots 3: A Book Talk Guide for Use with Readers Ages 8–12*. New York: Bowker, 1988.

Follows *Introducing More Books: A Guide for the Middle Grades*, 1978. Grouped by theme, each of the 81 titles featured is given an extensive plot summary, a theme analysis, recommended episodes for telling, related book titles, recordings, films, etc., to use in programming. Subject, author, and title indexes.

Tashjian, Virginia. *Juba This and Juba That: Story Hour Stretches for Large and Small Groups.* Boston: Little, 1969.
Stories, chants, riddles, etc., that invite audience participation.
————. *With a Deep Sea Smile.* Boston: Little, 1974.
For older audiences.
Thomas, Rebecca L. *Primary Plots: A Book Talk Guide for Use with Readers, Ages 4–8.* New York: Bowker, 1989.
Brings together related titles and offers activities for each featured title.

Collection Development

Finding Guides

Bowker's Forthcoming Children's Books, Pre-K through Grade 12. Vol. 1. 1987– . Six issues yearly.
Author, subject, title, illustrator listings. Also includes paperbacks, imports, revised editions, and reprints. Taken from *Forthcoming Books.*
Children's Books in Print; an Author, Title and Illustrator Index to Children's Books. New York: Bowker, 1969– . Annual.
Includes titles in trade, library, and paper editions with estimated grade levels. Latest editions also include current and retrospective winners of major children's book awards in the United States and in several English-speaking countries.
Children's Media Market Place. Ed. Delores Blythe Jones. 3d ed. New York: Neal-Schuman, 1988.
A directory to children's media sources: books, periodicals, AV, and computer software; producers and publishers by subject areas; review sources; bookstores; etc.
Horning, Kathleen T. *Alternative Press Publishers of Children's Books: A Directory.* 3rd ed. Madison, Wis.: Friends of the Cooperative Children's Book Center, 1988.
Describes 139 independent publishers that have published children's titles. Appendixes for bilingual, geographical, distributors, and subjects.
NICEM Indexes. National Information Center for Educational Media. Albuquerque, N.M.: Access Innovations.
Indexes for film and video, audiotapes, filmstrips, overhead transparencies, etc. Comparable to *Books in Print.*
Publishers Weekly. New York: Bowker. Fall and spring announcement issues of children's books.
Lists trade book titles with brief annotations, arranged by publisher. Also lists titles in paperback editions.
Software for Schools. New York: R. R. Bowker, 1987– .
Indexes software by computer family, grade, professional software, title, and publisher. Includes directory of periodicals on the subject.
Subject Guide to Children's Books in Print. New York: Bowker, 1970– . Annual.
Subject entries for both fiction and nonfiction titles.

Selective Aids for Retrospective Titles

Best Books for Children, Preschool through the Middle Years. Eds. John Thomas Gillespie and Corrine J. Naden. 4th ed. New York: Bowker, 1990.
Entries listed under reader interest and curricular topics, with title, author, and subject indexes.

Children's Catalog. Eds. Richard H. Isaacson, Ferne E. Hillegas, and Juliette Yaakov. 16th ed. New York: Wilson, 1986.
Published at five-year intervals with annual supplements. Author, title, subject, and analytic indexes are also useful in providing reference assistance.

Elementary School Library Collections: A Guide to Books and Other Media. 17th ed. Williamsport, Pa.: Brodart, 1990.
Includes audiovisual materials (except 16mm films but including videocassettes), magazines, reference works, and professional titles for educators. Indexes for titles, subjects, and authors. Biannual.

Junior High Catalog. Ed. Juliette Yaakov. 6th ed. New York: Wilson, 1990.
Published at five-year intervals with annual supplements.

Katz, William A., and Linda Sternberg Katz. *Magazines for Libraries: For Elementary, Junior High School and High School Libraries.* New York: Bowker, 1987.
Entries and taken from author's *Magazines for Libraries,* 5th ed. New York: Bowker, 1986.

Notable Children's Books, 1976–1980. Notable Children's Books, 1976–1980 Reevaluation Committee. Association for Library Services to Children. Chicago: American Library Assn., 1986.
Second supplement to *Notable Children's Books, 1940–1970.* (First supplement, 1971–1975.) Compilation of annual lists of Notable Children's Books (with deletions and additions) arranged by author with brief annotations. Followed by a broad age-level guide and title index.

Parents' Choice Guide to Videocassettes for Children. Ed. Diana Huss Green and others. Mt. Vernon, N.Y.: Consumers Union, 1989.
Arranged by subjects—cartoon classics, fantasy/science fiction, sports, etc. Annotations provide age range, running time, release date, producer. Appendix of sources; title and age indexes.

Parents' Guide to Highly Rated Educational Software. Water Mill, N.Y.: Educational Products Information Exchange Institute, 1988.
Over 200 programs arranged under 15 subjects—including aviation, early learning/preschool, reading, social studies, mathematics, etc.—for preschool through high school.

Richardson, Selma K. *Magazines for Children: A Guide for Parents, Teachers, and Librarians.* 2nd ed. Chicago: American Library Assn., 1991.
Selected list with descriptive critical evaluations. Subject index.

Materials for Special Needs*

Austin, Mary C., and Esther Jenkins. *Promoting World Understanding through Literature, K–8.* Littleton, Colo.: Libraries Unlimited, 1983.
Selective, annotated titles about African Americans, Mexican Americans, and native North Americans. Provides overviews of the characteristics of the literature of each group.

Bibliography of Nonsexist Supplementary Books K–12. Northwest Regional Education Laboratory Center for Sex Equity. Phoenix: Oryx Press, 1984.
Arranged by readability scores, 1.1 to 12.9. Annotations, subject entries, and number of careers mentioned are provided for each title. Author, title, subject indexes.

Jenkins, Esther C., and Mary C. Austin. *Literature for Children about Asians and Asian Americans, Analysis and Annotated Bibliography, with Additional Reading for Adults.* New York: Greenwood, 1987.
Selective lists for Chinese and Chinese Americans, Japanese and Japanese Americans, Koreans and Korean Americans, and Southeast Asian Americans. Subject, title, author indexes.

Kruse, Ginny Moore, and Kathleen T. Horning. *Multicultural Children's and Young Adult Literature.* Madison, Wis.: Cooperative Children's Book Center, 1989.
Distributed by Friends of CCBC, Inc. Lists 250 recommended titles written by or about people of color, and published between 1980 and 1988.

Pearl, Patricia. *Children's Religious Books: An Annotated Bibliography.* New York: Garland, 1988.
Critical annotations for over 1,000 titles from religious and trade book publishers. Includes titles on Judaism, various Christian denominations, Bahaism, Buddhism, Hinduism, Islam, Native Americans, American cults, etc. Preschool through sixth grade.

Rollock, Barbara. *Black Experience in Children's Books.* New York: New York Public Library, 1989.
There are 450 titles arranged by country and by genre with brief, descriptive annotations. Author-title index. Lists Correta Scott King Award titles from 1970 to 1989.

Schoen, Isabel. *Basic Collection of Children's Books in Spanish.* Metuchen, N.J.: Scarecrow, 1986.
There are 500 recommended titles, preschool through sixth grade. Fiction, picture books, reference, nonfiction, professional titles. Appendix lists dealers.

———. *Books in Spanish for Children and Young Adults; an Annotated Guide.* Metuchen, N.J.: Scarecrow, 1987.
Updates three previous volumes since 1984. Annotated list of titles from 12 Spanish-speaking areas. Each is rated as either outstanding, marginal, or not recommended. Includes list of reliable dealers.

*These titles also useful for reading guidance.

————. *A Hispanic Heritage, Series III: A Guide to Juvenile Books about Hispanic People and Cultures*. Metuchen, N.J.: Scarecrow, 1988. "Most in-print books in English" published in United States since 1984.

Reviews for Current Materials

Appraisal: Science Books for Young People. Children's Science Book Review Committee, Boston, Mass.: 1967– . Quarterly.
Two reviews with ratings are provided for each title: one by a librarian, the other by a specialist.

Booklist, Including Reference Books Bulletin. Chicago: American Library Assn. 1905– . Semimonthly; monthly in August.
Titles reviewed are generally recommended for purchase. In-house reviewers for various age levels: children, young adults, adults, and audiovisual and computer software for all ages. Includes occasional bibliographies on special topics, e.g., science fiction, children's books in Hebrew, notable lists, etc.

Bulletin of the Center for Children's Books. Chicago: Univ. of Chicago Pr., 1950– . Monthly, except August.
Reviews by the editors and advisory committee. Includes a brief bibliography of articles and references for librarians, teachers, and parents.

The Horn Book Magazine. Boston, Mass.: 1924– . Bimonthly.
Reviews of recommended titles by an in-house committee. Focus is primarily on literary qualities rather than institutional use. Arranged under broad age groups. Paperback editions for titles previously reviewed are announced. Announces recent award winners.

Jim Kobak's Kirkus Reviews. New York: Kirkus Service, 1985– . Semimonthly.
Continues *Kirkus Reviews*. Includes a children and young people's supplement. In-house reviewers.

Publishers Weekly. New York: Bowker, 1893– . Weekly.
Twenty-five to 30 children's titles are reviewed under "PW Forecasts."

School Library Journal. New York: Bowker, 1961– . Monthly.
Continues *Junior Libraries*. "The Magazine of Children's, Young Adults, and School Librarians." Reviews of books, audiovisual materials, computer software, and professional titles are by practicing librarians, editors, or specialists. Reviews are also available on 3- × -5 cards. Occasional bibliographies on timely topics; current award winners announced.

Science Books and Films. Washington, D.C.: American Assn. for the Advancement of Science, 1985– . Five issues yearly.
Continues *AAAS Science Books*. "Reviews trade books, textbooks, 16mm films, filmstrips and videos in all areas of science and mathematics . . . [for all ages]."—masthead.

VOYA, Voice of Youth Advocates. Metuchen, N.J.: Scarecrow, 1978– . Bimonthly.

Reviews titles for middle school through young adult audiences. Book, audiovisual, professional titles, and mass-market series are reviewed by practicing librarians. Provides sources for ephemera, and occasional bibliographies on topics of current interest.

Annual Lists and Awards

ALSC Notable Films/Videos, Filmstrips, and Recordings. Association for Library Services to Children.

"Best Books." Editors, *School Library Journal.* December issue.

A list of 50–60 outstanding titles for children and young adults.

Books for Children. Comp. Margaret N. Coughlan. Children's Literature Center. Washington, D.C.: Library of Congress, 1985– . Annual.

There are 60 to 75 briefly annotated titles for ages from infancy through elementary grades.

Children's Books: Awards and Prizes, Including Prizes and Awards for Young Adult Books. New York: Children's Book Council, 1986– .

Published irregularly. Also includes selected foreign awards, state and regional popularity awards.

Children's Books: One Hundred Titles for Reading and Sharing. Office of Children's Services. New York Public Library.

Several large library systems provide annual lists of this kind.

Children's Choices. In October issue of *Reading Teacher.*

A joint project of the International Reading Association and the Children's Book Council, Inc., conducted in representative school districts over the country. Reprint available from International Reading Association. Send SSAE, postage for four oz.

"Fanfare." Outstanding titles selected by the Book Review Committee, *The Horn Book Magazine.* April or June issue.

Notable Children's Books. Association for Library Services to Children.

These annotated lists are published annually in a spring issue of *Booklist,* or may be obtained from ALSC, American Library Association, 50 E. Huron St., Chicago, IL 60611, for 50¢ each.

Notable Children's Trade Books in the Field of Social Studies. National Council for the Social Studies-Children's Book Council Joint Committee.

Appears in April issue of *Social Education.* Reprint available from Children's Book Council, Inc. Send SSAE, postage for three oz.

Only the Best 1990: The Annual Guide to Highest Rated Educational Software, Preschool to Grade 12. New York: Bowker, 1989.

Describes 185 new software programs, plus 158 programs listed in the previous edition. Includes grade levels, program objective, hardware needed, review sources.

Outstanding Science Trade Books for Children. National Science Teachers Association-Children's Book Council Joint Committee.

Appears in March issue of *Science and Children.* Reprint available from Children's Book Council, Inc. Send SSAE, postage for three oz.

Miscellany

CBC Features. New York: Children's Book Council, 1984– . Semiannual. Continues *Calendar.* Lists free and inexpensive promotional items from publishers; Book Week materials; upcoming special days and weeks of significance for book promotion; etc. One-time charge for inclusion on mailing list.

"Culturgram Series." David M. Kennedy Center for International Studies. Publication Services, 280 HRCB, Brigham Young University, Provo, UT 84602.

Four-page cultural orientation covering customs, manners, lifestyles, socioeconomic statistics, maps, and addresses of embassies and national tourist offices for nearly 100 countries. Publication list available.

Educator's Guide to Free Films. Randolph, Wis.: Educators Progress Service. Annual.

Although intended for classroom use, many items have value for public libraries. Postage charges for loan of AV materials. Other guides in the series cover filmstrips; health, physical education, and recreational materials; science; social studies; computer materials; etc. K-12.

"List of Lists." Information Center on Children's Cultures, U.S. Committee for UNICEF, 331 E. 38th St., New York, NY 10016.

List of bibliographies available on countries, mostly third world, and on topics of international interest. Send SSAE.

Vertical File Index: Guide to Pamphlets and References to Current Topics. New York: Wilson, 1955– . Monthly, except August.

Continues *Vertical File Service Catalog.* A source for current and inexpensive pamphlets, charts, posters, maps, etc., for general audiences.

Association Catalogs and Lists of Publications

Action for Children's Television (ACT), 20 University Road, Cambridge, MA 02138.

Boy Scouts of America, 1325 Walnut Hill Lane, Irving, TX 75038.

Camp Fire, Inc. (formerly Camp Fire Girls), 4601 Madison Avenue, Kansas City, MO 64223.

Center for Early Adolescence, Carr Mill Mall, Suite 211, University of North Carolina at Chapel Hill, Carrboro, NC 27510.

Children's Defense Fund, 122 C St., N.W., Washington, DC 20001.

Church and Synagogue Library Association, P.O. Box 19257, Portland, OR 97219.

Girl Scouts of the U.S.A., 830 Third Ave. and 51st St., New York, 10022.

Media Center for Children, Three W. 29th St., New York, NY 10001.

Reading Is Fundamental (RIF), 600 Maryland Ave., S.W., Suite 500, Washington, DC 20560. *RIF Newsletter* (quarterly).

Library Instructional Activities or Resources

Participatory Activities for Grades 3–6

1. Dewey Decimal Game: bookmark with selected subjects in all classes.

   In developing the bookmark, give attention to popular subjects: sports, riddles, dinosaurs, cooking, secret codes, monsters, etc.

   Select nonfiction materials on the group's reading and interest levels. The game has the librarian giving children the classification number, and the children responding with the subject from the bookmark. The librarian shows cover of book to verify the answer and gives a 30-second booktalk on the title. Children are encouraged to use the bookmark during the browsing period and during subsequent visits.

   This exercise may satisfy the request for a how-to-use-the-library lesson from the teacher or adult leader. It can be done within the time limitation set for most library visits, and provides a foundation for future instruction in catalog use.

2. Shelving and Finding Materials:

   a. Use large cardboard squares with call numbers for nonfiction. Give each child a square and divide group into teams of 6 to 8. Ask the teams to arrange themselves in order, after explaining that "nothing (629) comes before something (629.13)."

   b. Ask the children in the teams to assume they have each written a fiction title, and to arrange themselves into the sequence their books would be found on the shelves.

Instruction in Using the Library's Catalog

If the school library is staffed, insist that children have instruction in using the school library's catalog before coming for instruction in using the public library's catalog.

1. Computer-produced catalogs: book, microfiche, or microfilm.

   The use of these catalogs is easier to teach than the dictionary card catalog. The librarian should demonstrate with examples appropriate to the probable interests of the group. The only stumbling block may be confusion between title and author volumes or sequences, if divided. If the title is known and the author's name is needed, children are apt to look in the author volume or sequence. (Rule: look first under what you know—the title.)

2. Online catalogs:
   The lack of typing and spelling skills may be the only barriers to efficient use. A list of popular subjects could be placed at the terminal(s) children use.
3. Card catalog use:
   For instruction provided by the children's librarian, tailored to the needs of each group, see references below.

   Although intended for school situations, many suggestions can be adapted to public libraries.

   If a media format is desired, libraries should consider making their own production, specific to their own library. A slide-tape production requires fewer resources and can be transferred to a video format, if preferred.

Selected Resources for Library Instruction

Beck, Margaret V., and Vera M. Carney. *A Guidebook for Teaching Library Skills,* Book One. Minneapolis, Minn.: T. S. Denison & Co., 1982.
   Provides activities to enhance card catalog skills. Grades 3–5.
"Enlarged Wilson Catalog Cards." Sturgis Library Products, Sturgis, Mich.
Getting to Know the Library. Scholastic Skills Books. Teacher's edition. New York: Scholastic Book Service.
   A series of three booklets (paper) for grades 2–6, done in an informal cartoon style.
Hardendorff, Jeanne B. *Libraries and How to Use Them.* New York: Watts, 1979.
   Trade book for children. Historical review of libraries, how to use the card catalog, etc.
Hart, Thomas L. *Instruction in School Library Media Center Use (K–12).* 2nd ed. Chicago: American Library Assn., 1985.
   Includes sources for kits, games, activities, filmstrips, charts, and more.
Kuhlthou, Carol Collier. *School Librarian's Grade-by-Grade Activities Program, a Complete Sequential Skills Plan for Grades K–8.* West Nyack, N.Y.: Center for Applied Research in Education, 1981.
Let's Learn About the Library. Troll Association, 1986, 1987.
   Three computer disks, guide. Apple II family. Grades 3–5. Reviewed in *School Library Journal,* Sept. 1988: "Offers practice with media skills related to the card catalog, fiction, nonfiction, and biography . . . offers short lessons to review classroom instruction. . . ."
Snoddon, Ruth V. *Ready to Use Library Skills, Games, Reproducible Activities for Building Location and Literature Skills.* West Nyack, N.Y.: Center for Applied Research in Education, 1987.
   Bingo with Dewey numbers; games using titles, characters', authors' names; library trivia; etc.

Appendix D
Related Professional Associations

American Film and Video Association (formerly Educational Film Library Association), 920 S. Barksdale Rd., LaGrange Park, IL 66525.
Focuses on various aspects of AV education.
Publications: *AFVA Quarterly; Evaluations* (twice yearly); *Sightlines* (quarterly). Also books and pamphlets.

Association for Childhood Education, International, 11141 Georgia Avenue, Suite 200, Wheaton, MD 20902.
"Promotes good educational practices for children from infancy through early adolescence."—*Encyclopedia of Associations*.
Publications: Professional books, children's books, bibliographies. *ACEI Exchange* (monthly); *Childhood Education* (five times annually); *Journal of Research in Childhood Education* (biennial).

Children's Literature Association, 210 Education, Purdue Univ., West Lafayette, IN 47901.
Encourages serious scholarship and research in the area of children's literature. Annual award for outstanding published criticism of children's literature.
Publications: *Children's Literature Association Quarterly* and *Children's Literature* (annual).

Council for Exceptional Children, 1920 Association Dr., Reston, VA 22091.
Advocates rights to full educational and employment opportunities for handicapped and gifted. Operates ERIC Clearinghouse for this audience; provides Exceptional Child Education Resources, a reference online database, and a library.
Publications: Books, audio- and videocassettes, films, and microfilms. *Exceptional Children; Teaching Exceptional Children; Exceptional Child Educational Resources*.

International Reading Association, P.O. Box 8139, 800 Barksdale Rd., Newark, DE 19714.
Promotes the improvement of reading instruction at all levels and the development of the reading habit.
Publications: Books, pamphlets, etc. Publications list available. *Reading Teacher* (elementary division); *Reading Today* (newspaper) with a parents' newsletter. Issues "Children's Choices" annually in cooperation with Children's Book Council, Inc.

National Association for the Education of Young Children, 1834 Connecticut Ave., N.W., Washington, DC 20009.
Concerned with the needs and rights of young children, with its primary focus on the provision of educational services and resources. Sponsors "Week of the Young Child."
Publications: *Young Children; Early Childhood Research Quarterly*. Publications list available.

National Council of Teachers of English, 1111 Kenyon Rd., Urbana, IL 61801.
Promotes improvements in the teaching of the English language and literature at all levels.

Publications: Books, pamphlets, literary maps. *Language Arts* (elementary section). Publications list available.

National Council for the Social Studies, 3501 Newark St., N.W., Washington, DC 20016.

Concerned with improvement in the teaching of social studies. Emphasizes creative classroom activities, research, and teaching theories.

Publications: Bulletins and bibliographies, including "Notable Trade Books in the Social Studies" (annual), in cooperation with the Children's Book Council, Inc.; *Social Education; Social Studies and the Young Learner* (K–6 emphasis).

National Science Teachers Association, 1742 Connecticut Ave., N.W., Washington, DC 20009.

Seeks to foster excellence in the whole of science teaching from learning styles of students to facilities needed.

Publications: "Outstanding Trade Books in Science" (annual) in cooperation with Children's Book Council, Inc.; *Science and Children* (elementary division). Publications list available.

Notes

Chapter 1. Audiences to Be Served

1. Faith H. Hektoen, "Connecticut Research Documentation Project," *School Library Journal* 26:24 (April 1980).

2. *Planning and Role Setting for Public Libraries,* prepared for the Public Library Development Project by Charles R. McClure and others (Chicago: American Library Assn., 1987).

3. *Planning and Role Setting,* pp.17–18.

4. Public Library Association, Committee on Standards, Subcommittee on Standards for Children's Services, *Standards for Children's Services in Public Libraries* (Chicago: American Library Assn., 1964), p.15.

5. New York Library Association, Youth Services Section. *Standards for Youth Services in Public Libraries of New York State.* Approved by the Council, July 1984, p.5.

6. Robert J. Havighurst, *Developmental Tasks and Education,* 3rd ed. (New York: McKay, 1972), pp.9–18.

7. Nancy E. Curry and Sara H. Arnaud, "Play in Developmental Preschool Settings," in *Child's Play: Development and Applied Education,* eds. Thomas D. Yawkey and Anthony D. Pellegrini (Hillsdale, N.J.: L. Erlbaum Associates, 1984), p.276.

8. Zena Sutherland, Dianne L. Monson, and May Hill Arbuthnot, *Children and Books,* 6th ed. (Glenview, Ill.: Scott, Foresman, 1981), p.29.

9. Linda Lucas and Marilyn H. Karrenbrock, *The Disabled Child in the Library: Moving into the Mainstream* (Littleton, Colo.: Libraries Unlimited, 1983), p.108.

10. Curry and Arnaud, *Play in Developmental Preschool Settings,* p.276.

11. *Ibid.,* p.282.

12. For a detailed description of characteristics and literature needs of children from birth to 36 months, consult Ann D. Carlson, *Early Childhood Literature Sharing Programs in Libraries* (Hamden, Conn.: Library Professional Pubs., 1985).

13. Havighurst, *Developmental Tasks,* p.19.

14. U.S. Congress, House, Select Committee on Children, Youth and Families, *U.S. Children and Their Families: Current Conditions and Trends,* 1987. 100th Congress, 1st sess., 1987, p.19.

15. Havighurst, *Developmental Tasks,* p.34.

16. Adele M. Fasick and Claire England, *Children Using Media; Reading and Viewing Preferences among the Users and Nonusers of the Regina Public Library* (Regina, Saskatchewan, Canada: Regina Public Library, 1977), p.23.

17. Lucas and Karrenbrock, *The Disabled Child in the Library,* p.108.

18. Fasick and England, *Children Using Media,* p.23.

19. Margaret Harding, " 'Where Have All the Children Gone?'—the Seventh-Grader as Public Library Dropout," *Public Libraries* 22:92–93 (Fall 1983).

20. Faith H. Hektoen, "The Children's Librarian as Viewed by Adults Served by Children's Services," in *Children's Services of Public Libraries,* ed. Selma K. Richardson. Allerton Park Institute, no. 23 (Urbana-Champaign: Univ. of Illinois, Grad. School of Library Science, 1978), p.64.

21. Marcia J. Bates, "Library and Information Services for Women, Homemakers, and Parents," in *Library and Information Service Needs of the Nation: Proceedings of a Conference on the Needs of Occupational, Ethnic, and other Groups in the United States* (Washington, D.C.: Govt. Print. Off., 1973), p.133.

22. Marguerite Baechtold and Eleanor Ruth McKinney, *Library Service for Families* (Hamden, Conn.: Library Professional Pubs., 1983) p.14.

23. Association of School Librarians and Association for Educational Communications and Technology, *Information Power, Guidelines for School Library Media Programs* (Chicago: American Library Assn., and Washington, D.C.: Assn. for Educational Communications and Technology, 1988), p.26.

24. *America's Children and Their Families: Key Facts* (Washington, D.C.: Children's Defense Fund, 1982), p.2, 13.

25. U.S. Congress, House, Select Committee on Children, Youth and Families, *U.S. Children and Their Families,* p.19.

26. *America's Children and Their Families,* pp.2–3.

27. U.S. Congress, House, Select Committee on Children, Youth and Families, *U.S. Children and Their Families,* p.28.

28. Susan W. Denniston, *Library Child Care Link: Linking Libraries with the Child Care Community* (Santa Clara, Calif.: South Bay Cooperative Library System, [1985]).

29. James Garbarino, "Latchkey Children: Getting the Short End of the Stick?" *Vital Issues* 30:[2] (Nov. 1980).

30. Mick Coleman, Bobbie H. Rowland, and Bryan E. Robinson, "School-Age Child Care: The Community Leadership Role of Educators," *Childhood Education* 66:79 (Winter 1989).

31. *Ibid.,* p.78.

32. *Ibid.,* p.79.

33. *Latchkey Children in the Public Library, a Position Paper,* prepared by the Services to Children Committee, Public Library Associa-

tion, in collaboration with the Library Service to Children with Special Needs Committee, Association for Library Service to Children (Chicago: American Library Assn., 1988), p.12.

34. *Ibid.*

35. Edward N. Howard, *Local Power and the Community Library,* Public Library Reporter, no. 18 (Chicago: American Library Assn., 1978), p.4.

36. *Ibid.,* pp.5–10.

37. For an example of this type of directory in printed form, *see* Child Advocacy Advisory Committee to the Dallas [Texas] City Council, *Directory of Services for Young Children,* ed. Ann Karkmas (Dallas: Dallas Public Library, 1974).

38. *Special Collections in Children's Literature,* ed. Carolyn W. Field, National Planning for Special Collections Committee, Association for Library Services to Children, American Library Association (Chicago: American Library Assn., 1982).

Chapter 2. Children's Librarian as Manager

1. Diana Norton and Laurel Goodgion, "Documenting Information Requests," *School Library Journal* 26:27 (April 1980).

2. Gene W. Dalton, Paul H. Thompson, and Raymond L. Price, "Four Stages of Professional Careers—A New Look at Performance by Professionals," *Organizational Dynamics* 6:19–42 (Summer 1977).

3. Margaret Mary Kimmel, "Baltimore County Public Library: A Generalist Approach," *Top of the News* 37:297–301 (Spring 1981).

4. Public Library Association, Committee on Standards, Sub-Committee on Standards for Children's Services, *Standards for Children's Services in Public Libraries* (Chicago: American Library Assn., 1964).

5. American Library Association, Public Libraries Division, Coordinating Committee on Revision of Public Library Standards, *Public Library Service: A Guide of Evaluation, with Minimum Standards* (Chicago: American Library Assn., 1956).

6. Public Library Association Standards Committee, *Minimum Standards for Public Library Systems, 1966* (Chicago: American Library Assn., 1967).

7. Public Library Association, Goals, Guidelines, and Standards Committee, *The Public Library Mission Statement and Its Imperatives for Services* (Chicago: American Library Assn., 1979).

8. "Community Library Service—Working Papers on Goals and Guidelines," *School Library Journal* 20:27 (Sept. 15, 1973).

9. Vernon E. Palmour, Marcia C. Bellassai, and Nancy V. DeWath, *A Planning Process for Public Libraries,* prepared for the Public Library Association, American Library Association (Chicago: American Library Assn., 1980), pp.98–101.

10. *Planning and Role Setting for Public Libraries: A Manual of Options and Procedures,* prepared for the Public Library Development

Project by Charles R. McClure and others (Chicago: American Library Assn., 1987).

11. Illinois Library Association, Children's Librarians' Section, *Foundations of Quality: Guidelines for Children's Services to Children in Illinois* (Chicago: Illinois Library Assn., 1981).

12. Selma K. Richardson, *An Analytical Survey of Illinois Public Services to Children in Illinois* (Springfield: Illinois State Library, 1978).

13. Douglas Zweizig and Eleanor Jo Rodger, *Output Measures for Public Libraries: A Manual of Standardized Procedures,* Goals, Guidelines and Standards Committee, Public Library Association (Chicago: American Library Assn., 1982).

14. *Output Measures for Public Libraries: A Manual of Standardized Procedures,* 2nd ed., prepared for the Public Library Development Project by Nancy A. Van House and others (Chicago: American Library Assn., 1987).

15. Douglas Zweizig, Joan A. Braune, and Gloria A. Waity, *Output Measures for Children's Services in Wisconsin Public Libraries: A Pilot Project, 1984–1985* (Madison, Wis.: Dept. of Public Instruction, Division for Library Services, 1985).

16. *Planning and Role Setting for Public Libraries,* p.28.

17. Ronald A. Dubberly, "Why You Must Know Your Library's Mission," *Public Libraries* 22:89–90 (Fall 1983).

18. Elizabeth Gross Kirkpatrick, "Do We Need New Directions?" *Top of the News* 24:399 (June 1968).

19. *Planning and Role Setting for Public Libraries,* p.43.

20. *Ibid.,* p.57.

21. Pierce County Library District, "1989 Budget Procedures," Tacoma, Washington, [1988], p.3.

22. Margo C. Trumpeter and Richard S. Rounds, *Basic Budgeting Practices for Librarians* (Chicago: American Library Assn., 1985), pp.42–43.

23. *Ibid.,* p.20.

24. Adapted from information provided by Arlene Bielefield in "Time-and-Money Management Plan," in *Reader in Children's Librarianship,* ed. Joan Foster, Readers in Librarianship and Information Science, no 27 (Englewood, Colo.: Information Handling Service, 1978), pp.342–352.

25. Trumpter and Rounds, *Basic Budgeting Practices for Librarians,* p.136.

26. Callie Israel, *Budgeting for Children's Services,* Library Services to Children, no. 2 (Ottawa: Canadian Library Assn., 1987), p.7.

Chapter 3. Selection and Design of Services

1. American Association of School Librarians and Association for Educational Communications and Technology, *Information Power,* (Chicago: American Library Assn.; Washington, D.C.: Assn. for Educational Communication and Technology, 1988), p.16.

2. Conversation with Brenda Dervin, School of Communication, University of Washington, Seattle, 1985.

3. Samuel Rothstein, "Reference Service: The New Dimension in Librarianship," *College and Research Libraries* 22:12–13 (Jan. 1961).

4. Vincent J. Aceto, "Children's Librarians: Passive Provider or Active Agent for Change?" *RQ* 7:74–75 (Winter 1967).

5. Kathleen M. Heim, "Stimulation," in *The Service Imperative for Libraries, Essays in Honor of Margaret E. Monroe,* ed. Gail A. Schlachter (Littleton, Colo.: Libraries Unlimited, 1982), pp.148–149.

6. *Intellectual Freedom Manual,* comp. Office of Intellectual Freedom of the American Library Association, 3rd ed. (Chicago: American Library Assn., 1989), pp.18–20.

7. *Ibid.,* pp.55–57.

8. *Ibid.,* p.66.

9. "Access for Children and Young People to Videotapes and Other Nonprint Formats; An Interpretation of the Library Bill of Rights," *Newsletter on Intellectual Freedom* 37:156 (Sept. 1989).

10. Toronto Public Libraries, "Goals, Objectives and Priorities," Boys and Girls Services Task Force Report, p.35–36. (Jan. 1976).

11. *Ibid.,* p.35.

12. Robert S. Taylor, "Question-Negotiation and Information-Seeking in Libraries," *College and Research Libraries* 29:183 (May 1968).

13. Faith H. Hektoen, *Connecticut Research Documentation Project in Children's Services: A Monograph,* 2 vols. (Hartford: Connecticut State Lib., 1981), 1:19–21.

14. Lillian M. Wehmeyer, "School Media Center as a Specialized Collection," in *Reader in Children's Librarianship,* Reader in Librarianship and Information Science, no. 27, ed. Joan Foster (Englewood, Colo.: Information Handling Services, 1978), p.223.

15. Charlotte S. Huck, "Books for Ages and Stages," *Children's Literature in the Elementary School,* 4th ed. (New York: Holt, 1987), pp.64–72.

16. Lois Lowry, *Anastasia Again* (Boston: Houghton, 1981).

17. Hektoen, *op. cit.,* 1:11–12.

18. H. Thomas Walker and Paula Kay Montgomery, *Teaching Media Skills: An Instructional Program for Elementary and Middle School Students,* 2nd ed. (Littleton, Colo.: Libraries Unlimited, 1983), p.13.

19. Walter H. Kaiser, "Self-Shelving by Children," *School Library Journal,* 11:21 (May 1964).

20. Thomas Simpson, "The Marketing Challenge in Public Libraries," in *Marketing for Libraries and Information Agencies,* ed. Darlene E. Weingand (Norwood, N.J.: Ablex Publishing Corp., 1984), p.23.

21. Adele M. Fasick and Claire England, *Children Using Media: Reading and Viewing Preferences among the Users and Non-Users of the Regina Public Library* (Regina, Saskatchewan: Regina Public Lib., 1977), p.4.

22. Marcia Posner, "P.P. and P.R., Two Keys to Circulation Success," in *Reader in Children's Librarianship,* ed. Joan Foster, p.242.

23. Conversation with Carol Gill, Kitsap Regional Library, Bremerton, Wash., April 1987.

24. For detailed information on the characteristics and needs of children ages 15 to 36 months, *see* Ann D. Carlson, *Early Childhood Literature Sharing Programs in Libraries* (Hamden, Conn.: Library Professional Pubs., 1985).

25. Frances A. Smardo and John F. Curry, *What Research Tells Us about Storyhours and Receptive Language* (Dallas, Tex.: Dallas Public Lib.; Denton: North Texas State Univ., 1982), p.49.

26. Barbara Heyns, *Summer Learning and the Effects of Schooling* (New York: Academic, 1978), pp.169–171.

27. Agnes Greer, "Sins of Omission and Commission in Library Work with Children," in Pacific Northwest Library Association, *Proceedings of Fourth Annual Conference* (Tacoma, Wash., June 12–14, 1913), p.46.

Chapter 4. Children's Collection

1. Information is taken from *Bowker Annuals,* 1978 to 1988. The publisher's definition of a juvenile title is accepted in these statistics and may include titles considered young adult by librarians.

2. Joseph Turow, *Getting Books to Children: An Exploration of Publisher-Market Relations* (Chicago: American Library Assn., 1978), pp.48–52.

3. U.S. Library of Congress, Rare Book Division, *Children's Books in the Rare Book Division of the Library of Congress* (Totowa, N.J.: Rowman and Littlefield, 1975), Vol. 2.

4. Vernon E. Palmour, Marcia C. Bellassai, and Nancy V. DeWath, *A Planning Process for Public Libraries,* prepared for the Public Library Association, American Library Association (Chicago: American Library Assn., 1980), pp.245–247.

5. Elizabeth Nesbitt, "Book Selection for Children, Its Perplexities and Pleasures," in *Contents of the Basket, and Other Papers on Children's Books and Reading,* ed. Frances Lander Spain (New York: New York Public Library, 1960), pp.80–81.

6. *Newsletter on Intellectual Freedom* 39:39–40 (March 1990).

7. Connie C. Epstein, "Looking Harder at the Backlist," *Publisher's Weekly* 232:121 (July 24, 1987).

8. Connie C. Epstein, "A Publisher's Perspective," *Horn Book* 64: 246–248 (March/April 1988).

9. "Community Library Service—Working Papers on Goals and Guidelines," *School Library Journal* 98:27 (Sept. 1973).

10. Carol A. Doll, "A Study of Overlap and Duplication among Children's Collections in Selected Public and Elementary School Libraries," *Library Quarterly* 54:288 (Fall 1984).

11. *Intellectual Freedom Manual,* pp.49–50.

12. *Ibid.,* pp.71–72.

13. *Ibid.,* p.32.

14. *Newsletter on Intellectual Freedom* 39: 40 (March 1990).

15. Lester E. Asheim, "Selection Not Censorship," *Wilson Library Bulletin* 28:63–67 (Sep. 1953).

16. Diane G. Farrell, "Library and Information Needs of Young Children," in *Library and Information Service Needs of the Nation: Proceedings of a Conference on the Needs of Occupational, Ethnic, and Other Groups in the United States* (Washington, D.C.: Govt. Print. Off., 1973), p.144.

17. *Alternative Press Publishers of Children's Books: A Directory,* ed. Kathleen Horning, 3rd ed. (Madison, Wis.: Friends of the Cooperative Children's Book Center, 1988.)

18. "What Makes a Good Review? Ten Experts Speak," *Top of the News* 35:146–152 (Fall 1978).

19. Diane P. Shugert, "About Rationales," *Connecticut English Journal* 15:1–4, 136 (Fall 1983).

20. A number of certified binders and rebinders are listed in *Literary Marketplace: The Directory of the American Book Publishing Industry* (New York: Bowker, annual).

Chapter 5. Planning Facilities

1. *Children's Environment Quarterly* (New York: City Univ. Center for Human Development, 1984–).

2. Robert H. Rohlf, "Why a Building Program," in *Library Buildings: Innovations for Changing Needs,* ed. Alphonse E. Trezza. Proceedings of the Library Buildings Institute conducted at San Francisco, June 22–24, 1967, (Chicago: American Library Assn., 1972), p.143.

3. Ellsworth Mason, *Mason on Library Buildings* (Metuchen, N.J.: Scarecrow, 1980), p.15.

4. Norma L. Rogers, "Getting Involved: Where Do You Fit In?" *Illinois Libraries* 60:855 (Dec. 1978).

5. Robert H. Rohlf, "The Consultant's Role in Library Buildings," in *Library Buildings: Innovations for Changing Needs,* p.169.

6. Aaron Cohen and Elaine Cohen, *Designing and Space Planning for Libraries: A Behavorial Guide* (New York: Bowker, 1979), pp.48–51.

7. Mason, *Mason on Library Buildings,* p.19.

8. Margaret Bush, "Library Facilities for Children, or the Candy-Colored Polyurethane 10-Speed Learning Environment," in *Children's Services of Public Libraries,* ed. Selma K. Richardson. (Urbana-Champaign: Univ. of Illinois Grad. School of Library Science, 1977), pp.109–110.

9. Ruth I. Griffen, "Doing Your Homework," *Illinois Libraries* 60:862–863 (Dec. 1978).

10. Mason, *Mason on Library Buildings,* p.19.

11. Interview with Kathryn Crosby and Diane Thompson, Pierce County Library District, Tacoma, Wash., Feb. 15, 1989.

12. *American National Standard for Buildings and Facilities—Providing Accessibility and Usability for Physically Handicapped People* (New York: National Standards Institute, 1986).

13. Linda Lucas and Marilyn H. Karrenbrock, *The Disabled Child in the Library: Moving into the Mainstream* (Littleton, Colo.: Libraries Unlimited, 1983), pp. 231–232.

14. *Ibid.*, pp. 224–225.

15. Elizabeth Huntoon, "Their Turn—Kids Speak Out on Library Facilities," *Illinois Libraries* 60:877–878 (Dec. 1978).

16. Nolan Lushington and Willis N. Mills, Jr., *Libraries Designed for Users: A Planning Handbook* (Syracuse, N.Y.: Gaylord Professional Pubs., 1979), p.164.

17. Cohen and Cohen, *Designing and Space Planning,* p.vii.

18. Leslie Edmonds, "Sorry About Safety," *Illinois Libraries* 60:869–870 (Dec. 1978).

19. *Planning and Role Setting for Public Libraries,* prepared for the Public Library Development Project by Charles R. McClure and others (Chicago: American Library Assn., 1987), p.32.

20. *Ibid.*, p.36.

21. Suzanne H. Crowhurst Lennard, "A Child's Conception of Built Space: An Exploratory Study," *Education* 99:158 (Winter 1978), citing Paul Shephard, "Play and Human Development," address to the Symposium on Children, Nature and the Urban Environment (Washington, D.C., March 1975).

22. *Ibid.*

23. George Rand, "Children's Images of Houses: A Prolegomena to the Study of Why People Still Want Pitched Roofs," in *Meaning and Behaviour in the Built Environment,* eds. Geoffrey Broadbent, Richard Bunt, and Tomas Llorens (New York: Wiley, 1985), p.278.

24. *Ibid.*, p.275.

25. Stuart Miller and Judith K. Schlitt, *Interior Space: Design Concepts for Personal Needs* (New York: Praeger, 1980), p.21.

26. Leanne G. Rivlin and Maxine Wolfe, *Institutional Settings in Children's Lives,* Wiley Series on Personality Processes (New York: Wiley, 1985), p.103.

27. Marian H. Bass and Malcolm S. Weinstein, "Early Development in Interpersonal Distance in Children," *Canadian Journal of Behavorial Science* 3:368 (Oct. 1971).

28. *Ibid.*

29. Sherry Ahrentzen and Gary W. Evans, "Distraction, Privacy, and Classroom Design," *Environment and Behavior* 16:439 (July 1984), citing Patricia J. Krantz and Todd R. Risley, *The Organization of Group Care Environments: Behavioral Ecology in the Classroom,* paper presented at the Annual Convention of the American Psychological Association at Honolulu, Hawaii, Sept. 2–8, 1972 (Lawrence: Kansas Univ., 1972). ERIC document ED 078 915.

30. Sylvia Shapiro, "Pre-School Ecology: A Study of Three Environmental Variables," *Reading Improvement* 12:239 (Winter 1975).

31. John R. Aiello, Donna E. Thompson, and Andrew Baum, "Children, Crowding and Control: Effects of Environmental Stress on Social Behaviors," in *Habitats for Children: The Impacts of Density,* eds. Joachim F. Wohlwill and Willem van Vliet (Hillsdale, N.J.: Lawrence Erlbaum Assoc., 1985), p.108.

32. Maxine Wolfe, "Childhood and Privacy," in *Children and the Environment,* eds. Irwin Altman and Joachim F. Wohlwill. Human

Behavior and Environment: Advances in Theory and Research, Vol. 3 (New York: Plenum, 1978), p.196.

33. Rivlin and Wolfe, *Institutional Settings in Children's Lives*, p.191.

34. Albert Mehrabian, *Public Places and Private Spaces, the Psychology of Work, Playing and Living Environments* (New York: Basic Books, 1976), p.155.

35. Irene Sever, "Children and Territory in a Library Setting," *Library and Information Science Research* 9:95–103 (April 1987).

36. Mehrabian, *Public Places and Private Spaces*, p.156.

37. Lennard, "A Child's Conception of Built Space," p.159.

38. Julie Cummins, "Table Legs and Chair Arms: The Anatomy of Children's Furniture in Libraries," *Illinois Libraries* 60:888 (Dec. 1978).

39. Anders Dahlgren gives a method for projecting growth of the collection for a 20-year period in *Public Library Space Needs, a Planning Outline* (Madison, Wis.: Dept. of Education, 1988), p.7. The rate of growth of each category is determined by subtracting the withdrawals from the additions. The average rate of growth may be taken from the average of the past four to five years. Multiply this figure by 20 and add to the current collection size.

40. Ruth A. Fraley and Carol Lee Anderson, *Library Space Planning* (New York: Neal-Schuman, 1985), p.27.

41. Lushington and Mills, *Libraries Designed for Users*, p.169.

42. Interview with Crosby and Thompson.

43. Edwin P. Beckerman, "Planning and Construction of Buildings," in *Local Public Library Administration*, ed. Ellen Altman, 2nd ed. (Chicago: American Library Assn., 1980), p.220; Dahlgren, *Public Library Space Needs*, p.12.

44. Faber Birren, *Light, Color and Environment* (New York: Van Nostrand Reinhold, 1969), p.85.

45. Faber Birren, *Color and Human Response* (New York: Van Nostrand Reinhold, 1978), p.118.

46. "Blue Is Beautiful," *Time* Sep. 17, 1973, p.66, cited in Birren, *Color and Human Response*, p.51.

47. Birren, *Color and Human Response*, p.103.

48. Birren, *Light, Color and Environment*, p.31.

49. *Ibid.*, p.84.

50. Albert O. Halse, *Use of Color in Interiors*, 2nd ed. (New York: McGraw-Hill, 1978), p.37.

51. Tae Ho Byum, "Environment, Color and Light," master's thesis, University of Washington, 1987, p.19.

52. Nancy D. Ryan and Sharon Orienter, "Signage for Monroe County Library System (New York)," *Unabashed Librarian* 49:7 (1983).

53. Blaise Cronin, *A National Graphic Resource Centre for Libraries in the United Kingdom* (London: ASLIB, 1981), p.1.

54. Ryan and Orienter, "Signage for Monroe County Library System," p.9.

55. *Ibid.*, p.8.

Chapter 6. Children's Services in Rural Areas

1. Bernard Vavrek, "Rural Librarianship in the United States," *Encyclopedia of Library and Information Science* 43:193 (New York: Dekker, 1988).

2. Gretchen Schenk, *County and Regional Library Development* (Chicago: American Library Assn., 1954), pp.154–162.

3. Carleton B. Joeckel, *Library Service*, prepared for the (United States) Advisory Committee on Education, Staff Study no. 11, (Washington D.C.: Govt. Print. Off., 1938), p.59.

4. *American Library Laws*, ed. Alex Ladenson, 5th ed. (Chicago: American Library Assn., 1984), p.72, citing U.S. Code Annotated 1982, Title 20, sec. 352.

5. David Shavit, *Federal Aid and State Library Agencies, Federal Policy Implementation*, Contributions in Librarianship and Information Science, no. 52 (Westport, Conn.: Greenwood, 1985), p.131, citing *Congressional Record*, March 29, 1984, p.S3427.

6. Effie L. Power, *Work with Children in Public Libraries* (Chicago: American Library Assn., 1943), p.155.

7. Frances Sullivan, "Children's Library Services through State Library Agencies," *Top of the News* 14:48 (Dec. 1957).

8. F. William Summers, "The State Consultant on Services to Children," *Top of the News* 29:312–313 (June 1973).

9. Elizabeth Burr, "ASL Policy Statement: The Role of the State Library Consultant on Public Library Service to Children," *Top of the News* 29:317 (June 1973).

10. *Ibid.*, pp.317–318.

11. John A. McCrossan, "Public Library Systems," in *Encyclopedia of Library and Information Science*, vol. 36, supp. 1., ed. Allen Kent (New York: Dekker, 1983), p.472.

12. Walter H. Kaiser, "Libraries in Non-Consolidated Systems," *Library Trends* 14:441 (April 1966).

13. Ruth W. Gregory and Lester L. Stoffel, *Public Libraries in Cooperative Systems: Administrative Patterns for Service* (Chicago: American Library Assn., 1971), p.6.

14. Daniel Barron and Charles Curran, "Assessing the Information Needs of Rural People: The Development of an Action Strategy for Rural Librarians," *Library Trends* 28:522 (Spring 1980).

15. Susan Raftery, "Rural Society in America: The 1980s and Beyond," *Rural Libraries* 6:8 (No. 1, 1986).

16. Dorothy M. Broderick, "The Roles of a Consultant in a Cooperative System Headquarters," *Library Trends* 13:351 (Jan. 1965).

17. Gregory and Stoffel, *Public Libraries in Cooperative Systems.*, p.201.

18. *Ibid.*, p.22.

19. Ruth Hill Viguers, "On Reviewing Books," *The Horn Book Magazine* 41:23 (Feb. 1965).

20. John M. Houlahan, "Midwest Library Conference Raises Rural Awareness," *Public Libraries* 24:65 (Summer 1985).

21. Thomas Phelps, "The Future of NEH Programming," *Rural Libraries* 4:30 (No. 1, 1984).

22. Margaret Coval and Paul G. McKanna, "Flagler Humanities Programs: Success in a Tiny Library," *Rural Libraries* 6:9 (No. 2, 1985).

23. Richard Cheski, "Current Trends in Humanities Programming," *Rural Libraries* 4:46 (No. 1, 1984).

24. All correspondence should be addressed to Reading Is Fundamental, Inc., 600 Maryland Avenue, S.W., Suite 500, Washington, DC 20560.

25. Advice on preparing grant proposals is provided in Marguerite Baechtold and Eleanor Ruth McKenney, *Library Service for Families* (Hamden, Conn.: Library Professional Pubs., 1983), Appendix C, pp.225–228.

26. *Foundation Directory* (New York: Foundation Center, distributed by Columbia University Press, Annual).

27. *Bowker Annual of Library and Trade Book Information* (New York: Bowker).

28. Shirley L. Aaron, "School/Public Library Cooperation," *Catholic Library World* 52:283 (Feb. 1981), citing Wilma Lee Broughton Woolard, "The Combined School Public Library Concept: Will It Work?" (masters thesis, Illinois State University, 1977), p.100.

29. Aaron, "School/Public Library Cooperation," p.283.

30. Shirley L. Aaron, *A Study of Combined School/Public Libraries*, School Media Centers: Focus on Trends and Issues, no. 6 (Chicago: American Association of School Librarians, American Library Assn., 1980).

31. Laurence G. Hill and Dorothy Goldberg, "Public Library-School Library Cooperation: LSCA-ESEA, 1964–1966," *Bookmark* 26:111–112 (Jan. 1967).

32. John W. Head, "The National Rural Library Reference Survey," *RQ* 23:321 (Spring 1984).

33. Sue Wanchock Lithgo, "Public Libraries/Agricultural Extension Agencies: Potential for Cooperation," *Rural Libraries* 7:34 (No. 1, 1987).

34. *Encyclopedia Americana*, Int. ed. 1988, s.v. "Cooperative Agriculture Extension," by J. Paul Leagons.

35. Sandy Potter, 4-H Agent, Snohomish County, Wash., interview held June 15, 1989.

Chapter 7. Professional Role and Responsibilities

1. New York Library Association, Youth Services Section, *Standards for Youth Services in Public Libraries of New York State*, approved by the Council, July 1984.

2. F. William Summers, "'Take This Coal and Go Make a Hell of Your Own'—Children's Services and Library Administrators," in *Changing Role in Children's Work in Public Libraries: Issues and Answers*, a Post Conference Report on a [American Library Association]

Pre-Conference Workshop, June 16, 1977 (Detroit: Detroit Public Library, 1977), pp. 14–17.

3. *Ibid.*, p.15.

4. *Latchkey Children in the Public Library, a Position Paper*, prepared by the Services to Children Committee, Public Library Association, in collaboration with the Library Services to Children with Special Needs Committee, Association for Library Services to Children (Chicago: American Library Assn., 1988), p.22.

5. *Ibid.*, p.21.

6. Peggy Sullivan, "Library Associations," *Library Trends* 25:143 (July 1976).

7. *Ibid.*, p.136.

8. Pauline Wilson, "Children's Services in a Time of Change," *School Library Journal* 25:24 (Feb. 1979).

9. Barbara Heyns, *Summer Learning and the Effects of Schooling* (New York: Academic Press, 1978), p.161.

10. Carol A. Doll, "A Study of Overlap and Duplication among Children's Collections in Selected Public and Elementary School Libraries," *Library Quarterly* 54:288 (July 1984).

11. Faith H. Hektoen, "Connecticut Research Documentation Project," *School Library Journal* 26:24 (April 1980).

12. Ronald R. Powell, Margaret T. Taylor, and David L. McMillen. "Childhood Socialization: Its Effect on Adult Library Use and Adult Reading," *Library Quarterly* 54:260 (July 1984).

Bibliography

Aaron, Shirley L. "School/Public Library Cooperation." *Catholic Library World* 52:280–285 (Feb. 1981).

———. *A Study of Combined School/Public Libraries*. School Media Centers: Focus on Trends and Issues, no. 6. Chicago: American Association of School Librarians, American Library Assn., 1980.

"Access for Children and Young People to Videotapes and Other Nonprint Formats: An Interpretation of the Library Bill of Rights." *Newsletter on Intellectual Freedom* 37:156 (Sept. 1989).

Aceto, Vincent J. "Children's Librarians: Passive Provider or Active Agent for Change?" *RQ* 7:74–78 (Winter 1967).

Ahlers, Eleanor. "Weeding the School Library Media Center." School of Librarianship, Univ. of Washington, 1973. (Mimeographed.)

Ahrentzen, Sherry, and Gary Evans. "Distraction, Privacy, and Classroom Design." *Environment and Behavior* 16:437–454 (July 1984).

Alternative Press Publishers of Children's Books: A Directory. Ed. Kathleen Horning. 3d ed. Madison, Wis.: Friends of the Cooperative Children's Book Center, 1988.

Altman, Ellen, ed. *Public Library Administration*. 2nd ed. Chicago: American Library Assn., 1980.

American Association of School Librarians and Association for Educational Communications and Technology. *Information Power*. Chicago: American Library Assn.; Washington D.C.: Assn. for Educational Communications and Technology, 1988.

American Library Association. Public Library Division. Coordinating Committee on Revision of Public Library Standards. *Public Library Service: A Guide of Evaluation, with Minimum Standards*. Chicago: American Library Assn., 1956.

American Library Laws. Ed. Alex Ladenson. 5th ed. Chicago: American Library Assn., 1984.

American National Standard for Buildings and Facilities—Providing Accessibility and Usability for Physically Handicapped People. New York: American National Standards Institute, Inc., 1986.

America's Children and Their Families: Key Facts. Washington, D.C.:
Children's Defense Fund, 1982.

Asheim, Lester E. "Selection Not Censorship." *Wilson Library Bulletin*
28:63–67 (Sept. 1953).

Association for Library Services to Children. Pre-School Services and
Parent Education Committee. *Opening Doors for Pre-School Children
and Their Parents.* Chicago: American Library Assn., 1981.

———. Program Support Publications Committee. *Programming for Very
Young Children.* ALSC Program Support Publications, no. 1. Chicago:
American Library Assn., 1980.

———. *Programming for Children with Special Needs.* ALSC Program
Support Publications, no. 4. Chicago: American Library Assn., 1981.

Baechtold, Marguerite, and Eleanor Ruth McKinney. *Library Service for
Families.* Hamden, Conn.: Library Professional Pubs., 1983.

Barron, Daniel, and Charles Curran. "Assessing the Information Needs
of Rural People: The Development of an Action Strategy for Rural
Librarians." *Library Trends* 28:619–631 (Spring 1980).

Bass, Marian H., and Malcolm S. Weinstein. "Early Development of
Interpersonal Distance in Children." *Canadian Journal of Behavioral
Science.* 3:368–376 (Oct. 1971).

Bates, Marcia J. "Library and Information Services for Women, Homemakers, and Parents." In *Library and Information Services Needs of
the Nation: Proceedings of a Conference on the Needs of Occupational,
Ethnic, and Other Groups in the United States*, pp.129–141. Washington, D.C.: Govt. Print. Off., 1973.

Benne, Mae. *The Central Children's Library in Metropolitan Public
Libraries.* Seattle: Univ. of Washington, School of Librarianship,
1977.

Bevington, Christine Benglea. Review of *Children's Spaces—50 Architects and Designers Create Environments for the Young*, by Molly and
Norman McGrath. *Architectural Record* (Oct. 1980), pp.41, 43, 45.

Bielefield, Arlene. "Time-and-Money Management Plan." In *Reader in
Children's Librarianship*, pp.341–352. Ed. Joan Foster. Readers in
Librarianship and Information Science, no. 27. Englewood, Colo.:
Information Handling Services, 1978.

Birren, Faber. *Color and Human Response.* New York: Van Nostrand
Reinold, 1978.

———. *Light, Color, and Environment.* New York: Van Nostrand Reinhold, 1969.

"Blue Is Beautiful." *Time* 17 September 1973, p.66.

Brink, Mary L. "Role of the Children's Consultant in a Cooperative
Library System." *Bookmark* 39:25–28 (Fall 1980).

Broderick, Dorothy M. *Library Work with Children.* New York: Wilson,
1977.

———. "The Roles of a Consultant in a Cooperative System Headquarters," *Library Trends* 13:342–352 (Jan. 1965).

Burr, Elizabeth. "ASL Policy Statement: The Role of the State Consultant on Public Library Service to Children." *Top of the News*
29:315–318 (June 1973).

Byum, Tae Ho. "Environment, Color and Light." Master's thesis, University of Washington, 1987.

Carlson, Ann D. *Early Childhood Literature Sharing Programs in Libraries*. Hamden, Conn.: Library Professional Pubs., 1985.

"Challenged Materials." *Newsletter on Intellectual Freedom*. 39:40 (March 1990).

Changing Role in Children's Work in Public Libraries: Issues and Answers. A Post Conference Report on a [American Library Association] Pre-Conference Workshop, June 16, 1977 (Detroit: Detroit Public Library, 1977, pp.14–19.

Cheski, Richard. "Current Trends in Humanities Programming." *Rural Libraries* 4:37–47 (No. 1, 1984).

Child Advocacy Advisory Committee to the Dallas [Texas] City Council. *Directory of Services for Young Children*. Ed. by Ann Karkmas. Dallas, Tex.: Dallas Public Library, 1974.

Children and the Environment. Ed. Erwin Altman and Joachim F. Wohlwill. Human Behavior and Environment: Advances in Theory and Research, Vol. 3. New York: Plenum, 1978.

Children's Environment Quarterly. Center for Human Development. New York: City University, 1984–.

Children's Services of Public Libraries. Ed. Selma K. Richardson. Allerton Park Institute no. 23. Urbana-Champaign: Univ. of Illinois Grad. School of Library Science, 1977.

Children's Services Round Table. Missouri Library Association. *Drop-in Delights, Activities for the Leisurely Patron*. Columbia: Missouri Library Assn., 1986.

———. *Showing Off: Display and Exhibit Ideas for Children's Library Services*. Columbia: Missouri Library Assn., 1984.

Cohen, Aaron, and Elaine Cohen. *Designing and Space Planning for Libraries, a Behavioral Guide*. New York: Bowker, 1979.

Coleman, Mick, Bobbie H. Rowland, and Bryan E. Robinson. "School-Age Child Care: The Community Leadership Role of Educators." *Childhood Education* 66:78–82 (Winter 1989).

"Community Library Services—Working Papers on Goals and Guidelines." *School Library Journal* 20:21–27 (Sept. 15, 1973).

"Competencies for Librarians Serving Children in Public Libraries." *Journal of Youth Services in Libraries* 2:219–223 (Spring 1989).

Connecticut Library Association, Children's Section. Environments for Children Committee. *Considerations Before Writing a Public Library Building Program in Children's Services*. Hartford: Connecticut Library Assn., 1976. ERIC Document 208 854.

Connor, Jane Gardner. *Children's Services Handbook*. Phoenix: Oryx Press, 1990.

Coval, Margaret, and Paul G. McKenna. "Flagler Humanities Programs: Success in a Tiny Library." *Rural Libraries* 6:7–15 (No. 2, 1985).

Creekmore, W. N. "Keeping Classroom Walls from Distracting Learners," *Education Digest* 53:44–46 (Oct. 1987).

Cronin, Blaise. *A National Graphic Resource Centre for Libraries in the United Kingdom*. ASLIB Occasional Pub. no. 26. London: ASLIB, 1981.

Crosby, Kathryn, and Diane Thompson. Pierce County Library District, Tacoma, Washington. Interview, Feb. 15, 1989.

Cummins, Julie. "Table Legs and Chair Arms: The Anatomy of Children's Furniture in Libraries." *Illinois Libraries* 60:887–891 (Dec. 1978).

Curry, Nancy E., and Sara H. Arnaud. "Play in Developmental Preschool Settings." In *Child's Play: Developmental and Applied Education*, pp. 273–290. Eds. Thomas D. Yawkey and Anthony D. Pellegrini. Hillsdale, N.J.: L. Erlbaum Associates, 1984.

Dahlgren, Anders. *Planning the Small Public Library Building*. Small Libraries Publication no. 11. Chicago: American Library Assn., Library Administration and Management Assn., 1985.

———. *Public Library Space Needs, a Planning Outline*. Madison, Wis.: Dept. of Public Instruction, 1988.

Dalton, Gene W., Paul H. Thompson, and Raymond L. Price. "Four Stages of Professional Careers—a New Look at Performance by Professionals." *Organizational Dynamics* 6:19–42 (Summer 1977).

Denniston, Susan W. *Library Child Care Link: Linking Libraries with the Child Care Community*. Santa Clara, Calif.: South Bay Cooperative Library System, [1985].

Dervin, Brenda. School of Communication. University of Washington, Seattle, 1985. Personal conversation.

"Diversity in Collection Development." *Newsletter on Intellectual Freedom*. 39:39–40 (March 1990).

Doll, Carol A. "A Study of Overlap and Duplication Among Children's Collections in Selected Public and Elementary School Libraries." *Library Quarterly* 54:277–289 (Fall 1984).

Donelson, Kenneth. "Enemies Within: Teachers and Librarians As Censors." *Top of the News* 53:233–236 (Spring 1979).

Dreseng, Eliza T. "There Are No Other Children: Special Children in Library Media Centers." In *Reader in Children's Librarianship*, pp.307–317. Ed. Joan Foster. Englewood, Colo.: Information Handling Services, 1978.

Dubberley, Ronald A. "Why You Must Know Your Library's Mission." *Public Libraries* 22:89–90 (Fall 1983).

Eastman, Ann Heidbreder, and Roger H. Parent, eds. *Great Library Promotion Ideas*. Chicago: American Library Assn., 1984.

Edmonds, Leslie. "Sorry about Safety." *Illinois Libraries* 60:868–874 (Dec. 1978).

Elleman, Barbara. "Evaluating the 'Good Read.'" *Booklist* 75:300–301 (Oct. 1, 1978).

Encyclopedia Americana, Int. ed. 1988. S.v. "Cooperative Agriculture Extension," by J. Paul Leagons.

England, Claire, and Adele M. Fasick. *ChildView: Evaluating and Reviewing Materials for Children*. Littleton, Colo.: Libraries Unlimited, 1987.

Epstein, Connie C. "Looking Harder at the Backlist." *Publisher's Weekly* 232:119–121 (July 24, 1987).

———. "A Publisher's Perspective." *The Horn Book Magazine* 64:246–250 (March/April 1988).

Evaluation Strategies and Techniques for Public Library Children's Services: A Sourcebook. Ed. by Jane Robbins, Holly Willett, Mary Jane Wiseman, and Douglas L. Zweizig. Madison: Univ. of Wisconsin School of Library and Information Studies, 1990.

Farrell, Diane G. "Library and Information Needs of Young Children." In *Library and Information Service Needs of the Nation: Proceedings of a Conference on the Needs of Occupational, Ethnic, and Other Groups in the United States*, pp.142–170. Washington, D.C.: Govt. Print. Off., 1973.

Fasick, Adele M., and Claire England. *Children Using Media: Reading and Viewing Preferences Among Users and Non-Users of the Regina Public Library*. Regina, Saskatchewan, Canada: Regina Public Library, 1977.

Fast, Elizabeth T. "Media: The Language of the Young." In *Reader in Children's Librarianship*, pp. 104–119. Ed. Joan Foster. Englewood, Colo.: Information Handling Services, 1978.

Fox, Beth Wheeler. *The Dynamic Community Library: Creative, Practical, and Inexpensive Ideas for the Director*. Chicago: American Library Association, 1988.

Fraley, Ruth A., and Carol Lee Anderson. *Library Space Planning*. New York: Neal-Schuman, 1985.

Frank, Robyn, and Patricia John. "The Rural Information Center." *Wilson Library Bulletin* 63:40–43 (May 1989).

Freiser, Leonard. "Students and Spoonfeeding." *School Library Journal* 10:15–17 (Sept. 1963).

Futas, Elizabeth. *Library Acquisitions Policies and Procedures*. 2nd ed. New York: Oryx, 1984.

Garbarino, James. "Latchkey Children: Getting the Short End of the Stick?" *Vital Issues* 30:[1–4] (Nov. 1980).

Gill, Carol. Kitsap Regional Library, Bremerton, Washington, April 1987. Conversation.

Greer, Agnes. "Sins of Omission and Commission in Library Work with Children," In Pacific Northwest Library Association. *Proceedings of Fourth Annual Conference*, pp. 45–48. Tacoma, Wash., June 12–14, 1913.

Gregory, Ruth L., and Lester L. Stoffel. *Public Libraries in Cooperative Systems: Administrative Patterns for Service*. Chicago: American Library Assn., 1971.

Griffin, Ruth L. "Doing Your Homework." *Illinois Libraries* 60:860–863 (Dec. 1978).

Habitats for Children: The Impacts of Density. Eds. Joachim F. Wohlwill and Willem Van Vliet. Hillsdale, N.J.: Lawrence Erlbaum Assoc., 1985.

Halse, Albert O. *The Use of Color in Interiors*, 2nd ed. New York: McGraw-Hill, 1978.

Hamilton, Ruth H., Peter Hiatt, Preston LeBreton, and Douglas L. Zweizig. *Staff Development Study: Seattle Public Library*. Seattle: Univ. of Washington School of Librarianship, 1976.

Harding, Margaret. " 'Where Have All the Children Gone?'—The Seventh-Grader as Public Library Dropout." *Public Libraries* 22:92–96 (Fall 1983).

Hart, Roger. *Children's Experience of Place*. New York: Irvington Pub., distributed by Halstead Pr., 1979.

Havighurst, Robert J. *Developmental Tasks and Education*. 3rd. ed. New York: McKay, 1972.

Haviland, Virginia. "Building the Foundation: The Book Collection." *Library Trends* 12:14–23 (July 1963).

Head, John W. "The National Rural Library Reference Survey." *RQ* 23:316–321 (Spring 1984).

Heasley, Daryl K. "What Selected Research and Literature Tells Us About Rural People." *Rural Libraries* 1:1–15 (No. 1, 1980).

Heim, Kathleen M. "Stimulation." In *The Service Imperative for Libraries: Essays in Honor of Margaret E. Monroe*, pp.120–154. Ed. Gail A. Schlachter. Littleton, Colo.: Libraries Unlimited, 1982.

Hektoen, Faith H. "The Children's Librarian as Viewed by Adults Served by Children's Services." In *Children's Services of Public Libraries*, pp.63–67. Ed. Selma K. Richardson. Allerton Park Institute, no. 23. Urbana-Champaign: Univ. of Illinois, Grad. School of Library Science, 1978.

———. "Connecticut Research Documentation Project." *School Library Journal* 26:22–24 (April 1980).

———. *Connecticut Research Documentation Project in Children's Services: A Monograph*. 2 vols. Hartford: Connecticut State Library, 1981.

———. Formerly Consultant Services, Connecticut State Library, letter, July 30, 1989.

Henderson, Bruce B. "The Social Context of Exploratory Play." In *Child's Play: Development and Applied Education*, pp.171–201. Eds. Thomas D. Yawkey and Anthony D. Pellegrini. Hillsdale, N.J.: L. Erlbaum Associates, 1984.

Heyns, Barbara. *Summer Learning and the Effects of Schooling*. New York: Academic, 1978.

Hill, Laurence G., and Dorothy Goldberg. "Public Library-School Cooperation, LSCA-ESEA, 1964–1966." *Bookmark* 26:111–112 (Jan. 1967).

Hines, Theodore C. "Children's Access to Materials." In *Children and Books*, pp.624–627. By Zena Sutherland and May Hill Arbuthnot. 5th ed. Chicago: Scott, Foresman, 1977.

Houlahan, John M. "Midwest Library Conference Raises Rural Awareness." *Public Libraries* 24:65–66 (Summer 1985).

"How Color Affects Children's Lives: An Interview with Elaine Ryan." *Academic Therapy* 23:47–53 (Sept. 1987).

Howard, Edward N. *Local Power and the Community Library*. Public Library Reporter, no. 18. Chicago: American Library Assn., 1978.

Howes, Mary. "Evaluation of the Effects of a Public Library Summer Reading Program on Children's Reading Scores between First and Second Grade." *Illinois Libraries* 68:444–447 (Sept. 1986).

Huck, Charlotte S. *Children's Literature in the Elementary School.* 4th ed. New York: Holt, 1987.

Huntoon, Elizabeth. "Effective School Visits." *School Library Journal* 25:33 (April 1979).

———. "Their Turn—Kids Speak Out on Library Facilities." *Illinois Libraries* 60:877–878 (Dec. 1978).

Iffland, Carol. "Partnership in Service: Working in Cooperation with Children's Organizations." *Illinois Libraries* 62:916–922 (Dec. 1980).

Illinois Library Association. Children's Librarians' Section. *Foundations of Quality: Guidelines for Children's Services.* Chicago: Illinois Library Assn., 1981.

Imholte, Rod. "Planning a Children's Area." *Wisconsin Library Bulletin* 74:61–64 (March/April 1978).

Intellectual Freedom Manual. Compiled by the Office of Intellectual Freedom of the American Library Association. 3rd ed. Chicago: American Library Assn., 1989.

Israel, Callie. *Budgeting for Children's Services.* Library Services to Children, no. 2. Ottawa: Canadian Library Assn., 1987.

Izard, Anne R. "Children's Books: Comparative Binding Survey." *Unabashed Librarian* 12:19–27 (Summer 1974).

Jean, Jill. Letter on the Seattle Public Library's After School Happenings (S.P.L.A.S.H.) July 22, 1989.

Joeckel, Carleton. *Library Service.* Prepared for the (United States) Advisory Committee on Education. Staff Study no. 11. Washington, D.C.: Govt. Print. Off., 1938.

Kaiser, Walter H. "Libraries in Non-Consolidated Systems." *Library Trends* 14:440–450 (April 1966).

———. "Self-shelving by Children," *School Library Journal* 11:21 (May 1964).

Katz, Bill, and Ruth A. Fraley. *Reference Services for Children and Young Adults.* Reference Librarian Series, no. 7–8. New York: Haworth, 1983.

Kimmel, Margaret Mary. "Baltimore County Public Library: A Generalist Approach." *Top of the News* 37:297–301 (Spring 1981).

Kirkpatrick, Elizabeth Gross. "Do We Need New Directions?" *Top of the News* 24:399–406 (June 1968).

Klein, Stephan Marc, and Jamie Horowitz. "Helping Children Grow." *Residential Interiors* 5:82–83 (July/August 1980).

Krantz, Patricia J., and Todd R. Risley, "The Organization of Group Care Environments: Behavioral Ecology in the Classroom." Paper presented at American Psychological Association, Sept. 2–8, 1972, at Honolulu, Hawaii. Lawrence: Kansas University, 1972. ERIC Document ED 078 915.

"Latchkey Children in the Public Library." *Public Libraries* 29:196–198 (Winter 1988).

Latchkey Children in the Public Library, a Position Paper. Prepared by the Services to Children Committee, Public Library Association, in collaboration with the Library Service to Children with Special Needs Committee, Association for Library Service to Children. Chicago: American Library Assn., 1988.

Lennard, Suzanne H. Crowhurst. "A Child's Conception of Built Space: An Exploratory Study." *Education* 99:157–162 (Winter 1978).

Library Administration Division, American Library Association. *Weeding the Small Library Collection.* Small Libraries Project, no. 5, sup. A. Chicago: American Library Assn., 1962.

Library and Information Service Needs of the Nation: Proceedings of a Conference on the Needs of Occupations, Ethnic, and Other Groups in the United States. University of Denver, May 24–25, 1973. Eds. Carlos A. Cuadra and Marcia J. Bates. Washington, D.C.: Govt. Print. Off., 1974.

Library Buildings: Innovation for Changing Needs. Proceedings of the Library Buildings Institute, conducted at San Francisco, Calif., June 22–24, 1967. Ed. Alphonse F. Trezza. Chicago: American Library Assn., 1972.

Literary Marketplace: The Directory of the American Book Publishing Industry, 1989. New York: Bowker, 1989.

Lithgo, Sue Wanchock. "Public Libraries/Agricultural Extension Agencies: Potential for Cooperation." *Rural Libraries* 7:7–36 (No. 1, 1987).

Long, Marie Ann. *The State Library Consultant at Work.* Illinois State Library Research Series, no. 6. Springfield: Illinois State Library, 1965.

Lowry, Lois, *Anastasia Again.* Boston: Houghton, 1981.

Lucas, Linda, and Marilyn H. Karrenbrock. *The Disabled Child in the Library: Moving into the Mainstream.* Littleton, Colo.: Libraries Unlimited, 1983.

Lushington, Nolan, and Willis N. Mills, Jr. *Libraries Designed for Users: A Planning Handbook.* Syracuse, N.Y.: Gaylord Professional Pubs., 1979.

Mahnke, Frank H., and Rudolf H. Mahnke. *Color and Light in Man-Made Environment.* New York: Van Nostrand Reinhold, 1987.

Mason, Ellsworth. *Mason on Library Buildings.* Metuchen, N.J.: Scarecrow Press, 1980.

McClendon, Charles B., and Mick Blackistone. *Signage: Graphic Communication in the Built World.* New York: McGraw-Hill, 1982.

McCrossan, John A. "Public Library Systems," pp.469–484. In *Encyclopedia of Library and Information Science.* vol. 36, sup. 1. Ed. Allen Kent. New York.: Dekker, 1983.

McMillan, Mary Amos. "No Eleventh Book." *Horn Book* 60:251–254 (June 1964).

Meaning and Behavior in the Built Environment. Eds. Geoffrey Broadbent, Richard Bunt, and Thomas Llorens. New York: Wiley, 1980.

Mehrabian, Albert. *Public Places and Private Spaces: The Psychology of Work, Play, and Living Environments.* New York: Basic Books, 1976.

Miller, Marilyn L. "Children's Access to Materials." *Library Quarterly* 51:38–53 (Jan. 1981).

Miller, Stuart, and Judith K. Schlitt. *Interior Space: Design Concepts for Personal Needs.* New York: Praeger, 1985.

Mind Child Architecture. Eds. John C. Baird and Anthony D. Lutkus. Hanover, N.H.: Published for Dartmouth College by Univ. Pr. of New England. 1982.

Myers, Shirley. "Interior Design Can Improve Performance—Or Inside the Learning Box." *Thrust* 16:35–36 (Oct. 1986).

Nesbitt, Elizabeth. "Book Selection for Children, Its Perplexities and Pleasures." In *Contents of the Basket, and Other Papers on Children's Books and Reading*, pp.75–83. Ed. Frances Lander Spain. New York: New York Public Library, 1960.

New York Library Association. Youth Services Section. *Standards for Youth Services in Public Libraries of New York State.* Approved by the Council, July 1984.

Norton, Donna E. *Through the Eyes of a Child: An Introduction to Children's Literature.* 2d ed. Columbus, Ohio: Merrill Pub. Co., 1987.

Output Measures for Public Libraries: A Manual of Standardized Procedures. 2nd ed. Prepared for the Public Library Development Project by Nancy A. Van House and others. Chicago: American Library Assn., 1987.

Palmour, Vernon E., Marcia C. Bellassai, and Nancy V. DeWath. *A Planning Process for Public Libraries.* Prepared for the Public Library Association, American Library Association. Chicago: American Library Assn., 1980.

Paulin, Mary Ann. *Creative Uses of Children's Literature.* Hamden, Conn.: Library Professional Publications, 1982.

Peterson, Carol Sue. "Sharing Literature with Children." In *Start Early for an Early Start: You and the Young Child*, pp.100–104. Preschool Services and Parent Education Committee, Children's Services Division. Ed. Ferne Johnson. Chicago: American Library Assn., 1976.

Phelps, Thomas. "The Future of NEH Programming." *Rural Libraries* 4:23–36 (No. 1, 1984).

Piaget, Jean, and Barbel Inhelder. *Psychology of the Child.* Trans. Helen Weaver. New York: Basic Books, 1969.

Pierce County Library District. "1989 Budget Procedures." Tacoma, Washington, [1988].

Pierce, William S. *Furnishing the Library Interior.* New York: Dekker, 1980.

Planning and Role Setting for Public Libraries. Prepared for the Public Library Development Project by Charles R. McClure and others. Chicago: American Library Assn., 1987.

Posner, Marcia. "P.P. and P.R., Two Keys to Circulation Success." In *Reader in Children's Librarianship*, pp.237–246. Ed. Joan Foster. Reader in Librarianship and Information Science, no. 27. Englewood, Colo.: Information Handling Services, 1978.

Potter, Sandy. 4-H Program Assistant. Snohomish County, Wash. Interview, June 15, 1989.

Powell, Ronald R., Margaret T. Taylor, and David L. McMillen. "Childhood Socialization: Its Effect on Adult Library Use and Adult Reading." *Library Quarterly.* 54:245–264 (July 1984).

Power, Ellie L. *Work with Children in Public Libraries.* Chicago: American Library Assn., 1943.

Public Library Association. Committee on Standards. Sub-Committee on Standards for Children's Services. *Standards for Children's Services in Public Libraries.* Chicago: American Library Assn., 1964.

———. Goals, Guidelines, and Standards Committee. *The Public Library Mission Statement and Its Imperatives for Service.* Chicago: American Library Assn., 1979.

———. Standards Committee. *Minimum Standards for Public Library Systems, 1966.* Chicago: American Library Assn., 1967.

Raftery, Susan. "Rural Society in America: The 1980s and Beyond." *Rural Libraries* 6:1–18 (No. 1, 1986).

Revlin, Leanne G., and Maxine Wolfe. *Institutional Settings in Children's Lives.* New York: Wiley, 1985.

RIF Guide to Encouraging Young Readers. Ed. Ruth Graves. Garden City, N.J.: Doubleday, 1987.

Roberts, Anne F., and Susan Griswold Blandy. *Public Relations for Librarians.* Englewood, Colo.: Libraries Unlimited, 1989.

Rogers, Norma L. "Getting Involved: Where Do You Fit In?" *Illinois Libraries* 60:854–860 (Dec. 1978).

"Role of the State Library Consultant." (Supplement.) *Top of the News* 29:311–330 (June 1973).

Rollock, Barbara. *Public Library Services for Children.* Hamden, Conn.: Library Professional Publications, 1988.

Rothstein, Samuel. "Reference Service: The New Dimension in Librarianship." *College and Research Libraries* 22:11–18 (Jan. 1961).

Rummel, Kathleen Kelly, and Esther Perica. *Persuasive Public Relations for Libraries.* Chicago: American Library Assn., 1983.

Ryan, Nancy D., and Sharon Orienter. "Signage System for the Monroe County Library System (New York)." *Unabashed Librarian* 49:7–10 (1983).

Schenk, Gretchen. *County and Regional Library Development.* Chicago: American Library Assn., 1954.

Scherer, Marge. "Loneliness of the Latchkey Child." *Instructor* 91:38–41 (May 1982).

Segal, Joseph. *Evaluating and Weeding Collections in Small and Medium-sized Public Libraries: The CREW Method.* Chicago: American Library Assn., 1980.

Sever, Irene. "Children and Territory in a Library Setting." *Library and Information Science Research* 9:95–103 (April 1987).

Shapiro, Sylvia. "Pre-School Ecology: A Study of Three Environmental Variables." *Reading Improvement* 12:236–247 (Winter 1975).

Shavit, David. *Federal Aid and State Library Agencies, Federal Policy Implementation.* Contributions in Librarianship and Information Science, no. 52. Westport, Conn.: Greenwood, 1985.

Shephard, Paul. "Play and Human Development." Address to the Symposium on Children, Nature and the Urban Environment, Washington, D.C., March 1975.

Sherman, Steve. *ABC's of Library Promotion*. 2nd ed. Metuchen, N.J.: Scarecrow, 1980.

Shugert, Diane P. "About Rationales." *Connecticut English Journal* 15:1–4, 136 (Fall 1983).

Sign Systems for Libraries. Eds. Dorothy Pollet and Peter C. Haskell. New York: Bowker, 1979.

Silver, Linda R. "Standards and Free Access." *School Library Journal* 26:26–28 (Feb. 1980).

Simpson, Thomas. "The Marketing Challenge in Public Libraries." In *Marketing for Libraries and Information Agencies*, pp.21–28. Ed. Darlene E. Weingand. Norwood, N.J.: Ablex Publishing, 1984.

Smardo, Frances A., and John F. Curry. *What Research Tells Us About Storyhours and Receptive Language*. Dallas, Tex.: Dallas Public Library; Denton: North Texas State Univ., 1982.

Spaces for Children, the Built Environment and Child Development. Ed. Carol Simmon Weinstein and David G. Thomas. New York: Plenum, 1987.

Special Collections in Children's Literature. Ed. Carolyn Field. National Planning for Special Collections Committee. Association for Library Services to Children. American Library Association. Chicago: American Library Assn., 1982.

Sullivan, Frances. "Children's Services Through State Agencies." *Top of the News* 14:48–49 (Dec. 1957).

Sullivan, Peggy. "Library Associations." *Library Trends* 25:135–152 (July 1976).

Summers, F. William. "The State Consultant on Services to Children." *Top of the News* 29:311–315 (June 1973).

Sutherland, Zena, Dianne L. Monson, and May Hill Arbuthnot. *Children and Books*. 6th. ed. Glenview, Ill.: Scott, Foresman, 1981.

Taylor, Robert S. "Question-Negotiation and Information-Seeking in Libraries." *College and Research Libraries* 29:178–94 (May 1968).

Toronto Public Libraries. "Goals, Objectives and Priorities." Boys and Girls Services Task Force Report, Jan. 1976.

Trumpeter, Margo C., and Richard S. Rounds. *Basic Budgeting Practices for Librarians*. Chicago: American Library Assn., 1985.

Turow, Joseph. *Getting Books to Children: An Exploration of Publisher-Market Relations*. Chicago: American Library Assn., 1978.

U.S. Congress. House. Select Committee on Children, Youth and Families. *U.S. Children and Their Families: Current Conditions and Trends, 1987*. 100th Congress. 1st sess., 1987.

U.S. Library of Congress. Rare Book Division. *Children's Books in the Rare Book Division of the Library of Congress*. Totowa, N.J.: Rowman and Littlefield, 1975. 2 vols.

Vavrek, Bernard. "Rural Librarianship in the United States," pp.191–202. In *Encyclopedia of Library and Information Science*. vol. 43, sup. 8. Ed. Allen Kent. New York.: Dekker, 1988.

Viguers, Ruth Hill. "On Reviewing Children's Books." *The Horn Book Magazine* 41:23 (Feb. 1965).

Walker, H. Thomas, and Paula Kay Montgomery. *Teaching Media Skills: An Instructional Program for Elementary and Middle School Students*. 2nd ed. Littleton, Colo.: Libraries Unlimited, 1983.

Warner, Alice Sizer. *Volunteers in Libraries II*. LJ Special Report, no. 24. New York: Library Journal, 1983.

Wehmeyer, Lillian M. "School Media Center as a Specialized Collection." In *Reader in Children's Librarianship*, pp. 220–231. Ed. Joan Foster. Readers in Librarianship and Information Science, no. 27. Englewood, Colo.: Information Handling Services, 1978.

"What Makes a Good Review? Ten Experts Speak." *Top of the News* 35:146–152 (Fall 1978).

Wilson, Pauline. "Children's Services in a Time of Change." *School Library Journal* 25:23–26 (Feb. 1979).

Woolard, Wilma Lee Broughton. "The Combined School Public Library Concept: Will It Work?" Master's thesis, Illinois State University, 1977.

Young, Diana. "Reading for the Fun of It: Summer Reading Programs." *Public Libraries* 18:39–42 (Summer 1979).

———. "Library Service to Rural Children: A Look at Iowa." *Public Libraries* 26:24–26 (Spring 1987).

Zweizig, Douglas, Joan A. Braune, and Gloria A. Waity. *Output Measures for Children's Services in Wisconsin Public Libraries: A Pilot Project, 1984–1985*. Madison, Wis.: Dept. of Public Instruction, Div. for Library Services, June 30, 1985.

———, and Eleanor Jo Rodger. *Output Measures for Public Libraries: A Manual of Standardized Procedures*. Prepared for the Goals, Guidelines and Standards Committee, Public Library Association. Chicago: American Library Assn., 1982.

Index

Aaron, Shirley L., 230
Access for Children and Young People to Video Tapes and Other Non-Print Materials (Intellectual Freedom Committee), 76
Accessibility, 100
  barriers to, 16, 157–158, 160–161
  policies of, 46, 74–77, 150, 233
  see also Children's collections, bibliographic access to
Aceto, Vincent J., 73
Activities, as support for objectives, 55–56, 92
Administration, relationships with, 31–48 *passim*, 250–251
Administrative organization. *see* Organization of libraries
Adolescents, 13, 15
Adult collections, 114–115, 164
Adult services, 73–74, 114–115
Adult users
  facilities for, in children's areas, 158, 175
  information needs of, 13–14, 26–27
  responsibilities for, 2, 3, 45
  see also Child care providers; Community organizations; Parents; Teachers
Advocacy role of children's librarians,

for children's services, 2, 28, 31–32, 34, 38, 200
  in building program, 191–192
  in legislation, 240
  in policy development, 38, 46, 144
ALA Handbook of Organization, 259
Alternative press titles, 136–137
Amenities for children, 176
American Association of School Librarians (AASL), 259
American Libraries, 136, 258
American Library Association (ALA), 7, 75–76, 129
  activities of, 257–258
American National Standard for Buildings and Facilities— Providing Accessibility for Physically Handicapped People, 157
Anastasia Again (Lowry), 87
Andersen, Hans Christian ("The Swineherd"), 93
Animals in libraries, 190
Annotated Card Service, Library of Congress, 78
Annual lists of titles, 135, 289–290 (Appendix C)
Architect, role of, 154–155, 160–161
Archives, children's literature, 148–149

Association for Library Service to Children (ALSC), 7, 23, 25, 129, 258–259
see also Children's Services Division
Association of Children's Librarians of the Bay Area (Calif.), 140
Association of State Libraries (ASL), 198
Associations, library, 129
functions of, 48, 196, 200, 255–256
types of, 256–257
see also American Library Association
Associations, related professional, 240, 259
bibliography of, 294–295 (Appendix D)
publications catalogs of, 291 (Appendix C)
Attitudes toward children, 47, 74, 79–80
see also Children's librarians, relationship with users
Audiovisual materials, 12, 115, 131–139 passim, 145, 147, 149
see also Videotapes
Audiovisual services, facilities for, 161, 164, 165, 178–179
Awards, 135–136

Baechtold, Marguerite, 16
Bait books, 84, 136
Balanced collections, 126–127
Barriers to use. see Accessibility
Basic collection in rural libraries, 218
Basic selection aids, 126, 137, 146, 147
Basic services, 112
defined, 67
functions of, 73–91
Behavior in libraries, 243–246
Best Books for Children, 26, 137
Bevington, Christine Bengles, 151
Bibliography for Libraries, Teachers, and Parents

(Bulletin of the Center for Children's Books), 136
Birren, Faber, 186
Bonham, Frank, 1
Book bindings, 141–143
Book publishing. see Publishers
Bookdrops for children, 175
Booklist, 136
Bookmobiles, 103, 218, 229
Books-by-mail service, 103, 218
Books-per-shelf measurements, 177
Bookstores, 115, 116, 216
Booktalk programs in schools
design of, 107–109
evaluation of, 109
goals and objectives of, 106
Booktalks as reading guidance, 85, 87
Bowker Annual, 222
Branch librarian as supervisor, 32, 37 42–43
Broderick, Dorothy M., 209
Budget
for materials, 59, 60, 130–133
models, 60–64
process, 46, 58–60, 130
request forms, 266–272 (Appendix A)
responsibilities of children's librarians, 46, 57–58, 60, 133–134
Buffalo and Erie County Library (N.Y.), 189
Building consultant, role of, 154
Building program
defined, 153
factors affecting, 159–167
information for, 156–158, 176–183, 191–192
role of children's librarians in, 152–153, 155–156, 191
Built environment, children's response to, 152, 167–176, 184–186, 189–190
Bulletin of the Center for Children's Books, 136
Bush, Margaret, 155–156

California State Library, 20
Career planning, 259, 260,
    261–262
Carlson, Ann D., 296 *n*12
Carrels, 175
Cat and Mrs. Cary (Gates), 193
Cataloging-in-publication (CIP),
    90, 144
Catalogs for children's use, 75,
    85, 88, 144–145, 175–176,
    234
Celery Stalks at Midnight (Howe),
    94
Censorship. *see* Intellectual
    freedom
Center for the Study of Rural
    Librarianship, 194
Central children's library, 36, 37,
    125, 126, 132
Charlotte's Web (White), 29
Checklist (*School Library
    Journal*), 136
Chicago Public Library, 158
Child care providers
    collection support for, 101
    services for, 19–20
    see also Latchkey children.
Child-caring adults. *see* Child
        care providers; Community
        organizations; Parents;
        Teachers
Child development
    adolescents, 13
    elementary school children,
        10–13
    pre-school children, 7–10
Children of staff, 252
Children's Book Council, 136
Children's Catalog (H. W.
    Wilson), 137
Children's collection specialist,
    35, 125
Children's collections
    arrangement of, 77–78, 85, 145,
        179
    bibliographic access to, 17, 78,
        85–86, 144–145, 279–283
        (Appendix C)
    budget allocations for, 133–134

compared to adult collections,
    114, 115
facilities for, 176–179
growth predictions of, 176–177,
    304 *n*39
range of materials in, 131
see also Collection development
Children's consultant
    as a staff position, 32, 33,
        207–208
    see also Rural children's
        specialist
Children's coordinator
    as a staff position, 31–45
        passim, 203, 207
    collection responsibilities of,
        116–117, 124–125
    see also Rural children's
        specialist
Children's librarians
    collection knowledge of, 3, 86,
        138
    community responsibilities of,
        253–254
    continuing education for, 41,
        140, 260–261
    personal growth of, 240,
        261–262
    professional relationships of,
        250–253
    relationship with users,
        242–246
    responsibilities to the
        profession, 240, 254–259,
        263
    role in planning facilities,
        155–159
    selection and evaluation of,
        40
    service and program
        competencies of, 28, 64–65,
        68, 79–82, 86, 87, 89–90,
        111, 241–242
    see also Management
        responsibilities
Children's services
    age range of children for, 7
    attitudes of staff toward, 47–48,
        68–69

bibliography of aids for,
   279–283, 288–289, 292–293
early development of, 30–31,
   196, 208
facilities for, 180–182
philosophy of, 241–242
see also Basic services
Children's Services Division, 49
see also Association for Library
   Service to Children
Circulation services, space for,
   161, 163, 175
Circulation statistics, 132
see also Output measures
Class visits to the library
   evaluation of, 111
   goals and objectives of, 70, 109
   programs for, 70–71, 109–110
Classics, 118–119, 120, 148
Classroom Reading Teacher
   (*Reading Teacher*), 136
Coleman, Mick, 22
Collection development
   activities, 125–126
   approaches, 117–121
   bibliographies of aids for,
      286–291 (Appendix C)
   evaluation in, 52, 141, 145–149,
      217, 219
   impact of social change on, 120
   in rural libraries, 215–219
   policies, 122, 124–130, 133,
      148–149, 150
   responsibilities for, 124–125,
      150
   selection process in, 138–141,
      218–219
   sensitive materials in, 128
   use of goals and objectives in,
      117–119
   use of network and system
      resources in, 121–123, 149
   see also Children's collections;
      Reviews
Collection materials specialist. *see*
   Children's collection
   specialist
Color in children's facilities,
   185–186, 189

Comfort, Alex (*Joy of Sex*), 76
Communication in libraries, 41,
   42–45, 129, 249–250, 251,
   254, 273–274 (Appendix B)
Community Activities Center, as
   a role, 164
Community information, 4–6, 68
Community Information and
   Activities Center, as a role,
   54
Community organizations, 191
   defined, 24
   goals of, 48, 56–57
   in rural areas, 221, 234–237
   relationships with, 15, 16,
      21–22, 41, 105, 253–254
   resources in, 121–123
   services to, 25–26
   types of, 24–25
Complaints, 129–130
Computers, 161, 179, 180, 234
*Connecticut Documentation
   Study,* 84
Connecticut State Library, 201
Consultant. *see* Children's
   consultant; State children's
   consultant; State library
   consultant
Continuing education, 41, 240,
   253, 260–261
Controversial materials, 128–130,
   140–141
Conveniences, user. *see* Amenities
   for children
Cooperative Agricultural
   Extension Agency, 234–237
Cooperative Children's Book
   Center (Madison, Wis.), 140
Copy machines, 176
Core collections in rural libraries,
   218
Costs, program. *see* Budget;
   Programming, cost
   effectiveness of
Council for Exceptional Children,
   259, 294 (Appendix D)
County agricultural agent, 235
County and regional libraries,
   196, 197

Dallas City Council, Child Advocacy Committee, 299 *n*37
Daycare centers. *see* Child care providers
"Deacon's Masterpiece" (Holmes), 141
Dealing with Concerns About Library Resources (Intellectual Freedom Committee), 129
Decorations in children's libraries, 189–190
Demand, 115, 127–128
Demographics, 18–19, 20, 132, 159–160
Department of Agriculture, 235
Departments, library. *see* Interdepartmental relationships
Directory of Services for Young Children (Dallas City Council Child Advocacy Committee), 299 *n*37
Disabled adults, building standards for, 157
Disabled children
collections for, 118, 121
facilities for, 157–158, 167–168
programming for, 93, 103
Displays, 90, 181–182
Diversity in Collection Development (Intellectual Freedom Committee), 120

Early Childhood Literature Sharing Programs in Libraries (Carlson), 296 *n*12
Editors, children's book, 115, 116
Electronic publication, 123
Elementary school children, library needs of, 10–13
Elementary School Library Collection (Brodart), 137
Elleman, Barbara (*Popular Reading for Children*), 137
Encyclopedia of Associations, 256
Equipment, space for, 179

Equitable services, 214–215
Estes, Eleanor, 239
Ethics, professional, 240–241, 251
Evaluating Library Collections (Intellectual Freedom Committee), 129
Evaluation, 51
of collections, 52, 141, 145–149, 217–218
of programs, 71–72, 101–102, 105–106, 109, 111
of services, 83, 88, 91, 242
Examination centers for materials, 139, 140, 216
Expurgation of Library Materials (Intellectual Freedom Committee), 129

Facilities in children's areas
for adult users, 158, 175
for collections and equipment, 176–179
for services and programs, 94, 180–82
for staff and equipment, 182–183
Family daycare. *see* Child care providers
Family structures, changes in, 18–19
Farrell, Diane G., 133
FAX machines, 234
Features (Children's Book Council), 136
Federal aid to libraries, 132, 196–198, 221
Field, Carolyn W., 250
Field consultant. *see* State library consultant
Formal Education Support Center, as a role, 54, 164–165
Forthcoming Children's Books (Bowker), 135
Foundation Directory, 222
Foundations of Quality: Guidelines for Public Library Services to Children (Illinois Library Association), 50
4-H programs and services, 236

*4-H Projects and Publications:
A Guide to Enrollment,*
236
4-H youth agent, 235
*Free Access to Libraries for
Minors* (Intellectual Freedom
Committee), 76
Fry readability graph, 86
Funding, alternate sources for,
134, 221–222, 234*n*
Furnishings for children's areas,
165, 166–167, 173–176

Gates, Doris, 193
Generalists, 45, 195, 198, 200
Goals and objectives
defined, 55
examples of, 55–56, 69, 117–118
use of, in collection
development, 117–119, 126,
135, 149
use of, in designing services,
68, 69, 70
use of, in planning facilities,
164, 167, 180, 191
use of, in programming, 91–92
Guidelines. *see* Standards,
library

Handicapped children. *see*
Disabled children
Havighurst, Robert J., 10–11
Head Start program, 7, 14, 16
Hektoen, Faith, 14
Hippocrates, 184*n*
Holmes, Oliver Wendell
("Deacon's Masterpiece")
141
Home economist–family living
agent, 235
The Horn Book, 136
Howard, Edward N., 24
Howe, James (*Celery Stalks at
Midnight*), 94
Hudson, Virginia Cary, 113
Hunt Breakfast (*The Horn Book*),
136
Huntoon, Elizabeth, 158
Hyacinths, 184*n*

Illinois Library Association, 50
In-service training. *see* Staff in-
service training
Independent Learning Center, as
a role, 54
Information gatekeeper, 253
*Information Power: Guidelines for
School Library Media
Programs,* 18
Information services, 38, 39, 73,
122–123
bibliographies of aids for,
279–280 (Appendix C)
collections for, 77–79
competencies for, 79–83
evaluation of, 83
in rural libraries, 219–220, 233
policies for, 74–77, 220,
227–228
Institutional-oriented standards,
49
Instruction in library use
activities for, 88–90, 291–292
(Appendix C)
bibliography of aids for, 293
(Appendix C)
evaluation of, 91
responsibilities for, 75, 88–89
Intellectual freedom, 75–76, 124,
129–130, 150
Intellectual Freedom Committee
(ALA), policies statements of,
75–76, 120, 129
Interdepartmental relationships,
38–39, 71, 144, 251
Interior designer, role of, 155, 184
Interlibrary loan. *see*
Reserve–interlibrary loan
services
International Reading
Association, 136, 294
(Appendix D)
Israeli school library, 172

Jobbers, 138, 142, 143
*Journal of Youth Services in
Libraries,* 259
Joy of Sex (Comfort), 76

Juster, Norton (*Phantom Tollbooth*), 93–94

King Award, Coretta Scott, 136
King County Library System (Wash.), 16, 276 (Appendix B)
King, Martin Luther, Jr., 111

Last copy collections, 148–149
Latchkey children, 20–24, 132, 245–246
Latchkey Children in the Public Library (ALSC/PLA), 23
Lewis, C. S. (*The Lion, the Witch, and the Wardrobe*), 146
Librarians' mistakes, 148
Library Bill of Rights, 76
Library Binding Institute, 142–143
"Library faith," 241
Library-Initiated Programs as a Resource (Intellectual Freedom Committee) 76
Library media skills (schools), 88–89, 227
see also Instruction in library use
Library network, 201
Library of Congress, 117
Library Research Center, University of Illinois, 194
Library schools, 199, 200, 250, 259
Library Services Act, 1956 (LSA), 197, 198
Library Services and Construction Act, 1964 (LSCA), 20, 197
Library Services for Families (Baechtold and McKinney), 16
Lighting, 186–187
Line-item budget, 60–61, 266 (Appendix A)
Line relationship, 32, 33, 34, 35, 42
The Lion, the Witch, and the Wardrobe (Lewis), 146
The Little Red Hen, 255

Local staffs. *see* Rural library systems
Lowry, Lois (*Anastasia Again*), 87

McKinney, Eleanor Ruth, 16
MacLachlan, Patricia (*Sarah, Plain and Tall*), 122
Management responsibilities of children's librarians, 2, 3, 31, 64–65
for budgeting, 57–58
for communication, 42–45
for planning, 68–70
for supervision and development of staff, 40, 46–47, 246–250
in determining library's role and mission, 52–53
in evaluating services, 50–52
in policy development, 38, 46
in setting goals and objectives, 48
Manuals. *see* Policy and procedural manuals
Manufacturers and vendors, 155
Marketplace (*Wilson Library Bulletin*), 136
Mason, Ellsworth, 153, 157
Mass market titles, 115–117
Measurement. *see* Evaluation
Mending, 147
Mentor relationship, 43, 262
Minorities, 117, 127, 128, 136
bibliography of materials about, 288–289 (Appendix C)
Mission statement. *see* Role and mission statements
Missouri State Library, 140, 201
Monroe, Margaret E., 73–74
Moore, Anne Carroll, 3
Murals, 189–190
Mystery of the Fat Cat (Bonham), 1

National Association for the Education of Young Children, 259, 294 (Appendix D)
National Building Code, 160

National Council of Teachers of English, 136, 294 (Appendix D)

National Endowment for the Humanities, 221–222

National Rural Center, 234*n*

National Rural Information Clearing House, 234*n*

National Youth Administration, 197

Nesbitt, Elizabeth, 119

Networks, library, 123
  see also Systems, library

New titles
  review sources for, 134–137, 288–289 (Appendix C)
  selection process for, 139–141

New York Library Association (NYLA), 7, 241

Newsletters, 225, 226

Nonfiction collections, integrated, 77–78, 159, 165

North Carolina State Library, 201

Notable children's titles. *see* Annual lists of titles

O Ye Jigs and Juleps (Hudson), 113

Office of Intellectual Freedom, (ALA), 129

Online catalogs, 88, 122, 144
  see also Catalogs for children's use

Organization of libraries, 31–37, 65

Orientation tours. *see* Class visits to the library

Orlando Public Library (Fla.), 16

Out-of-print titles, 120

Output measures
  compatibility of, with children's services, 51, 52, 65
  use of, in collection development, 52
  use of, in programming, 71–72, 101, 105–106, 109, 111
  use of, in services, 83, 88, 91

Output Measures for Public Libraries: A Manual of Standardized Procedures (Zweizig and Rodger), 50–51

Pack-o-Fun, 145

Paperbound editions, 120, 142, 143

Parents
  facilities for, 158, 175
  informational needs of, 14–15
  resources for, 15, 16, 131
  services and programs for, 15–17, 99, 100

Parents' Magazine, 139

Performance ratings, 40, 41, 248

Periodicals, 145, 149

Personal space, 170

Personnel. *see* Staff

Personnel directors, 40

Pets, 190

Phantom Tollbooth (Juster), 93–94

Piaget, Jean, 8, 10

Planning
  steps, 70–73
  timetables for, 70
  use of goals and objectives in, 68, 69

Planning and Role Setting for Public Libraries (PLA) 4, 5, 50, 55

Planning Process for Public Libraries (ALA), 50

Planning process, public library, 5, 52–56

Planning-programming-budgeting systems (PPBS), 61-63

Plants, 190

Poe Award, Edgar Allan, 136

Policies
  development of, 38
  revision of, 46, 251
  types of, 46
  see also Accessibility; Collection development; Information services

Policy and procedural manuals
  for class visits to library, 110
  for staff orientation, 46–47
  in rural libraries, 225–226
Pool collection, 217, 218, 219
Popular books, 84
Popular Materials Library, as a
  role, 165–167
Popular Reading for Children
  (Elleman), 137
Power, Effie L., 198
Prebound editions, 142–143
Preschool children,
  library needs of, 7–10, 132
  projected population of, 10
  story hours for, 7, 9–10, 93, 94,
    95, 99, 100, 101
Priorities, service, 46, 64, 68, 133
Privacy
  children's concept of, 170–171,
    172
  staff responsibilities for,
    242–243
Profession, responsibilities to,
  240, 254–255, 263
Professional conduct, 64–65,
  240–241, 242, 263
Program of services, 67–68, 112,
  149
Program specialist, children's,
  35
Programming
  bibliography of aids for,
    283–286 (Appendix C)
  cost effectiveness of, 72–73,
    100–101, 105, 108–109, 111
  defined, 67
  design factors in, 93–95
  facilities, 94, 164, 180–181
  forms, 275–278 (Appendix B)
  in rural libraries, 220–222, 236
  objectives, 91
  planning for, 68, 69, 70–73
  resources, 101, 131, 220–221
  staff support in, 68–69, 71
  see also Evaluation; Promotion
Promotion, 187
  of programs, 71, 72, 95–96, 105
  of services, 82–83, 87–88, 90

Psychology Today, 139
Public Libraries, 259
Public Library Association, 23,
  49–51, 65, 259
Public library role, 227–228
Public relations, 95, 97
Publishers
  backlist, 120
  catalogs, 135, 142, 216
  library editions, 142, 143
  trade books, 115, 116, 141, 142,
    143
Publishers Weekly, 135
Puget Sound Council for
  Reviewing Children's Books
  (Wash.), 140

Quality in collections, 119, 135,
  216

Ranger Rick, 145
Rationales for controversial titles,
  141
Readability formula, 86
Reader's advisory service. *see*
  Reading guidance services
*Reader's Guide to Periodical
  Literature,* 89, 149
Reading clubs
  design of, 102–103
  evaluation of, 105–106
  goals and objectives of, 102
  issues in, 103–104, 105
Reading guidance services, 75,
  114–115, 128
  bibliography of aids for,
    280–283 (Appendix C)
  collections for, 84–86, 118–119
  competencies for, 86–87
  defined, 83–84
  evaluation of, 88
Reading incentives, 104
Reading Is Fundamental (RIF),
  222
Reading Teacher, 136, 294
  (Appendix D)
Realia, 131, 138, 145, 190
Rebound editions, 142–143, 147

Recruitment for the profession, 250

Reevaluation. *see* Evaluation

Reference collections, children's, 78–79, 131

Reference interview, 80–82

Reference services. *see* Information services; Instruction in library use; Reading guidance services

Religious materials, 122, 137

Remodeling of facilities, 160, 191

Replacement titles, 133, 141, 216–217

Reports, children's services, 41, 43–45
  see also Communication in libraries

Research
  on built environments, 152, 168–173, 185–186
  on combined school-public libraries, 230
  on users and libraries, 3, 11–12, 13, 73, 84, 261
  related to reading clubs, 104, 106, 261
  responsibilities for, 205, 261

Researchers and scholars, services to, 26–27

Reserve–interlibrary loan services, 46, 128, 218, 228, 233–234

Resource sharing, 18, 121–123, 231–232

Restricted Access to Library Materials (Intellectual Freedom Committee), 76

Restrooms for children, 176

Retrospective titles, 137–138, 287 (Appendix C)

Reviews
  criteria for, 140–141
  for new titles, 134–136
  for problem areas, 136–137
  for retrospective titles, 137–138
  in-house, 139
  sources for, 286–287 (Appendix C)

Reviews-on-cards (*School Library Journal*), 140

Robinson, Bryan E., 22

Rodger, Eleanor Jo (*Output Measures for Public Libraries*), 50

Rohlf, Robert H., 153

Role and mission statements
  defined, 53
  development of, 52–55
  examples of, 54, 165, 166
  in designing facilities, 164–167, 180
  in planning services, 69

Rotation of collections, 217–218

Rothstein, Samuel, 73

Rowland, Bobbie H., 22

Rufus M. (Estes), 239

Rural areas
  defined, 194–195
  population in, 205

Rural children's specialist
  competencies of, 211–213
  in-service activities of, 222–226
  role and responsibilities of, 203, 204, 207–211, 213–222
  passim, 237

Rural library systems
  development of, 195–198, 208
  political environment of, 213–214
  problems of, 194–195, 205, 228–229
  professional environment in, 206–207, 237
  relationships with member staffs, 209, 210, 211
  relationships with schools, 196, 229–234
  types of, 202–204
  see also Collection development; Information services; Programming

Safety hazards in facilities, 160–161, 174

Safety of children, 21, 22, 163, 185

Santa Clara County Library (Calif.), 244
Sarah, Plain and Tall (MacLachlan), 122
School assignments, 74–75, 122, 227–228, 233
School librarian, role of, 17
School libraries, 132–133
  problems of, in rural areas, 228–229
  program defined in, 67
  resources in, 121–122
  response to facilities in, 171–172, 185–186
  role of, 56, 227
School Library Journal, 136, 140, 142
School-public library combination, 230–231
School-public library cooperation, 18, 121, 122–123, 139–140, 216, 231–232
School visiting. *see* Booktalk programs in schools
Schools, public library services to, 18, 89, 99, 107, 196, 220, 229, 232–233
Seating options for children, 174, 175
Selection of materials. *see* Collection development
Series books, mass market, 116
Service counters for children, 175–176
Services. *see* Children's services
Shelving. *see* Children's collections, facilities for
Signage, 90, 187–189
Simpson, Thomas, 95
Smith, Betty, 66
Social interaction, children's need for, 171–173
The Source (*American Libraries*), 136
South Bay Cooperative Library System (Calif.), 20
Special libraries, 227
Staff
  exchanges, 47–48
  facilities for, 182–183
  in-service training, 46–48, 195, 209–210, 222–226, 248–249
  relationships in rural libraries, 211, 212–213, 220
  supervision of, 246–248
  see also Children's librarians
Staff relationship (as an administrative concept), 32–33, 34, 36, 42
Standard (book) titles, 119–120
Standards for Children's Services in Public Libraries, 1964 (PLA), 7, 49
Standards for Youth Services in Public Libraries of New York State (NYLA), 7, 241
Standards, library, 48–50, 146
State aid to libraries, 196, 203
State children's consultant, 192, 198–200
State library agencies, 195–196, 197–203 *passim*
State library associations. *see* Associations, library
State library consultant, 195–196, 200–201
Statement on Labeling (Intellectual Freedom Committee), 129
State school specialist, 198
Stimulation, as a service component, 73–74
Story hour programs
  collection support for, 101
  design of, 96–100
  evaluation of, 101–102
  goals and objectives of, 97–98
Strategies. *see* Activities, as support for objectives
Subject Guide to Children's Books in Print (Bowker), 137, 147, 286 (Appendix C)
Subject Guide to Children's Magazines, 149
Subject Index to Poetry for Children and Young People, 137, 280 (Appendix C)
Sullivan, Peggy, 257

Summers, F. William, 242
Supervisors of children's services,
    31–45 passim
"The Swineherd" (Andersen), 93
Systems, library, 201–202
    consolidated, 202–203, 205–206
    cooperative, 203–204
    equitable services in, 214–215
    federated, 204

Tables for children's use, 175
Task Force on Children's Services
    (CSD/PLA), 49
Taylor, Robert S., 80
Teachers
    informational needs of, 17–18
    loans to, 219–220, 233–234
    relationships with librarians,
        18, 20, 233
Technology, 97, 161, 234
Telefacsimile service. see FAX
    machines
Textbooks, 122, 228
Toddler story hours, 7, 99
Top of the News, 259
    see also Journal of Youth
        Services in Libraries
Toys, 15, 18, 133, 138
Trade books. see Publishers
Training. see Staff in-service
    training
A Tree Grows in Brooklyn
    (Smith), 66
Trustees, library, 45, 195,
    202–203

U.S. Bureau of the Census, 194
User involvement
    in building program, 158–159,
        188
    in collection development, 132,
        139

in the planning process, 28, 53
in programming, 13, 98
User-oriented standards, 49

Vandalism, 173
Vanity press books, 139
Vendors, 155
Vertical file, 137, 149
Videotapes, 15–16, 100, 108–109,
    111, 119, 138
Viguers, Ruth Hill, 218
Volunteers, 25, 92, 101, 102, 105,
    111, 221, 238

Weeding, 145–149, 217, 219
What's So Great about Books
    (Orlando Public Library,
    Fla.), 16
White, E. B., 29
White, James Terry, 184n
Wilson Library Bulletin, 136
Woolard, Wilma Lee Broughton,
    230
Work with Children in Public
    Libraries (Power), 198
"Working Paper on Goals and
    Guidelines" (CSD/PLA), 49
Works Progress Administration
    (WPA), 197
Workshops
    for child-care providers, 20
    for parents, 15, 21
    for staff, 47, 223–225

Young Adult Division (ALA), 7
Young adult services, 13, 164

Zero-based budgeting, 63–64
Zweizig, Douglas L. (Output
    Measures for Public
    Libraries), 50

Mae Benne, professor emerita, Graduate School of Library and Information Science at the University of Washington, Seattle, holds a bachelor of science in education/history as well as an MLS. She has been active in numerous professional associations and has published articles in several journals including *School Library Journal, Wilson Library Bulletin,* and *PNLA Quarterly.* In 1988, she was honored with the President's Award from the Washington Library Association in recognition of distinguished and dedicated service to libraries in the state.